Democracy and th

One of the key issues in the analysis of t
democracy. To what extent can a capitalist s...
democratic institutions intervene in the management and control of capitalism? Has
the emergence of democracy changed the composition of the state? These questions
lead inevitably to the basic issue of the interconnections between economics and
politics, economy and polity, with which this volume is concerned.

The aim of the book is to build a useful framework for the analysis of the state, and to
indicate how its democratic potentialities can be realised. Consisting mostly of hitherto
unpublished essays, it contains general analytic contributions discussing ways of
theorising the state; studies of classical or grand conceptions of the state, such as
republicanism, liberalism, and the theories of Marx, Mill, Weber, Habermas, and the
Fabians; and concrete analyses of particular issues concerning the state, including state
workers, state sponsorship and ownership, political organisation and economic policy,
corporatism and industrial democracy. It ends with a defence of the welfare state.

This wide-ranging and eclectic collection, combining theoretical and empirical
material, and containing contributions from several leading authorities on the modern
state, will be of value for teachers and students of political science, sociology, and
political economy, as well as appealing to historians and philosophers interested in the
nature of the state.

Democracy and the Capitalist State

EDITED BY

GRAEME DUNCAN

Department of Government, University of Queensland

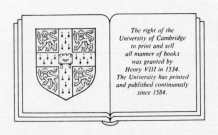

The right of the
University of Cambridge
to print and sell
all manner of books
was granted by
Henry VIII in 1534.
The University has printed
and published continuously
since 1584.

CAMBRIDGE UNIVERSITY PRESS

Cambridge

New York   New Rochelle   Melbourne   Sydney

Published by the Press Syndicate of the University of Cambridge
The Pitt Building, Trumpington Street, Cambridge, CB2 1RP
32 East 57th Street, New York, NY 10022, USA
10 Stamford Road, Oakleigh, Melbourne 3166, Australia

First published 1989

Printed in Great Britain by
Redwood Burn Limited, Trowbridge, Wiltshire

British Library cataloguing in publication data
Democracy and the capitalist state.
1. State. Theories
I. Duncan, Graeme
320.1'01

Library of Congress cataloguing in publication data
Democracy and the capitalist state / edited by Graeme Duncan.
p.   cm.
Includes index.
ISBN 0 521 23599 5. ISBN 0 521 28062 1
1. Democracy.   2. State, The.   3. Capitalism.   I. Duncan, Graeme
Campbell.
JC423.D4398 1988   88–11895 CIP
321.8—dc 19

ISBN 0 521 23599 5 hard covers
ISBN 0 521 28062 1 paperback

CONTENTS

v

NOTES ON CONTRIBUTORS

PAUL BOREHAM is a Senior Lecturer in Government at the University of Queensland, Brisbane, where he is Director of the Labour and Industry Research Unit. He is a co-author with Stewart Clegg and Geoff Dow of *Class, Politics and the Economy* (1986) and co-editor of *The State, Class and the Recession* (1983) and *Work and Inequality*, volumes 1 and 2 (1980). His interests are in comparative studies of class structure, economic and industry policy and labour-movement strategies in the OECD countries.

TOM BOTTOMORE is Professor Emeritus of Sociology at the University of Sussex. He has taught at the London School of Economics and at the Simon Fraser University, Vancouver. He was president of the British Sociological Association from 1969 to 1971 and president of the International Sociological Association from 1974 to 1978. His main publications are *Elites and Society* (1964), *Sociology: A Guide to Problems and Literature* (3rd edn, 1987), *Political Sociology* (1979), *A Dictionary of Marxist Thought* (ed.) (1983), *The Frankfurt School* (1984) and *Theories of Modern Capitalism* (1985). He is a contributor to *Encyclopaedia Britannica*, the *New York Review of Books* and *The Times Literary Supplement*.

JOHN CALLAGHAN is Lecturer in Politics at the Polytechnic, Wolverhampton. He is the author of *British Trotskyism* (1984) and *The Far Left in British Politics* (1987). He is currently working on a book on the Labour Party and the Soviet Union.

APRIL CARTER studied politics at the London School of Economics, lectured in politics at Lancaster University from 1966 to 1969 and taught part-time for the Open University from 1971 to 1976. She was Fellow and Tutor in Politics at Somerville College, Oxford from 1976 to 1984 and is now a freelance writer. Her books include *Direct Action and Liberal Democracy* and *Democratic Reform in Yugoslavia*.

ALAN CAWSON is Reader in Politics in the School of Social Sciences at the University of Sussex. He is the author of *Corporatism and Welfare* (1982) and *Corporatism and Political Theory* (1986), as well as a number of articles on aspects of corporatism, state theory and democracy.

STEWART CLEGG is Professor of Sociology and Head of Department at the University of New England, Armidale, Australia. He holds a doctorate from Bradford University and a first degree from Aston University. He has produced seven books, the most recent of which are the co-authored *Class, Politics and the Economy* (1986) and the co-edited *Organisation and Management in East Asia* (1986). His interests range over class theory, the state and the sociology of power.

BERNARD CRICK is Professor Emeritus of Politics at Birkbeck College, University of London, and Honorary Fellow of the University of Edinburgh. He studied at University College, London, the London School of Economics and Harvard University, and has taught at the London School of Economics, Sheffield University and Birkbeck College. His publications include *The American Science of Politics, The Reform of Parliament, In Defence of Politics, The Elementary Types of Government, Political Theory and Practice, George Orwell: A Life* and *Socialism*. He took early retirement in 1984 to work on a short book on representative government and a trilogy on the relations of the nations of the British Isles.

GEOFF DOW teaches interdisciplinary social science at Griffith University, Brisbane. He trained as an economist and sociologist at the University of Queensland and has lectured in Sweden, Denmark, the UK and throughout Australia. He is joint editor of *Work and Inequality* (1980) and *The State, Class and the Recession* (1983) and is joint author of *Class, Politics and the Economy* (1986). He is currently researching political responses to economic crisis and comparative economic policy (especially since 1974) in OECD countries.

GRAEME DUNCAN teaches politics at the University of Queensland. He has also taught at Monash University and the University of Adelaide in Australia, and at the University of East Anglia. He is the author of *Marx and Mill* (1974), and the editor of *Democratic Theory and Practice* (1983) and *Critical Essays in Australian Politics* (1978). He has also published a number of articles. His main academic interests are democratic and Marxist theory, and theories of human nature.

PETER FAIRBROTHER lectures in political sociology and labour studies at the University of Warwick. For a number of years he has also been a tutor in trade-union education. He has held visiting fellowships at the University of Melbourne and Monash University, Australia. He is author of *All Those in Favour: The Politics of Union Democracy* (1984). His research interests are broadly concerned with studies of trade unionism, changes in employment organisation and practice, and state policies. Currently he is engaged in research on the patterns of employment and trade unionism in the West Midlands.

PHILIP K. LAWRENCE is Senior Lecturer in Politics at the Polytechnic, Wolverhampton. Previously he taught sociology at the University of East Anglia. He is the author of several articles and *Democracy and the Liberal State* (1987) and *Preparing for Armageddon* (1988).

The late C. B. MACPHERSON taught at the University of Toronto, Department of Political Science, from 1935 to his retirement in 1977, receiving the title of University Professor in 1975. During his lifetime he held visiting professorships in many parts of the world and received numerous honorary degrees. In 1976 he was appointed officer of the Order of Canada. His books include: *Democracy in Alberta: Social Credit and the Party System*; *The Political Theory of Possessive Individualism: Hobbes to Locke*; *The Real World of Democracy*; *Democratic Theory: Essays in Retrieval*; *The Life and Times of Liberal Democracy*; *Burke*, in the Past Masters series; *The Rise and Fall of Economic Justice and Other Essays*; *Thomas Hobbes' Leviathan* (ed.); *Property, Mainstream and Critical Positions* (ed.); and *John Locke's Second Treatise of Government* (ed.).

RALPH MILIBAND is Professor of Political Science at York University, Toronto. He taught for many years at the London School of Economics and was Professor of Politics at Leeds University from 1972 to 1977. He then taught on a part-time basis at Brandeis University, Massachusetts, until 1985. His publications include *The State in Capitalist Society*, *Marxism and Politics* and *Class Power and State Power*. He has been co-editor of *The Socialist Register* since 1964.

STEVE SMITH is Senior Lecturer in International Relations at the University of East Anglia. He has also taught at Huddersfield Polytechnic and the State University of New York (Albany). His publications include *Foreign Policy Adaptation* (1981), *Politics and Human Nature* (ed. with Ian Forbes) (1983), *International Relations: British and American Perspectives* (ed.) (1985), (edited with Mike Clark) *Foreign Policy Implementation* (1985) and (edited with Richard Crockatt) *The Cold War Past and Present* (1987). He is currently working on a book on foreign-policy theory.

JOHN STREET is Lecturer in Politics at the University of East Anglia. He is the author of *Rebel Rock: The Politics of Popular Music* and of several articles on work, technology and democracy. He is currently writing a book on the links between politics and technology.

1

Introduction

GRAEME DUNCAN

The title of this collection is *Democracy and the Capitalist State*. That title makes the capitalist rather than the democratic character of the state central. There is both an historical and an analytic warrant for placing the capitalist character of the state at the centre. After all, political democracy came after capitalist industrialisation, and one basic question is whether it constitutes icing on the cake or whether it has changed the composition of the cake.

What are the possible relations between economy, society and polity in a capitalist world? To what extent can a capitalist state be democratised? Where and how do democratic institutions intervene in the management and control of capitalism? What are the relations between a democratic economy, a democratic society and a democratic polity? Has democracy ever been achieved anywhere? Is the state in capitalist society necessarily a capitalist state? Even advocates of liberal democracy concede that the unequal and coercive arrangements associated with free-market organisation of production and distribution pose problems for the democratic ideal. What then do market freedoms impede? What do they achieve? How, precisely, do we evaluate the costs and benefits of capitalist forms of political and economic development? To what extent do and can reformist or collectivist interventions change the relations between economy, society and polity?

The fundamental issue underlying these questions is the interconnection(s) between economics and politics, economy and polity. How, in the different theories considered in this collection, are economy and polity, *and* the relations between them, conceived? Is politics seen as a separate realm? If interconnected, what are its actual and possible effects upon capitalism? Or does economics always and inevitably have the last word, however weak that word may be? There is no reason to think that answers to these questions should be timeless or universal. It may be the case, for example, that before the advent of industrial capitalism the state and the state bureaucracy were substantially autonomous, and that the relative power of the economy grew with the burgeoning capitalist system, which was associated with a minimal state. Again, the economy may be somewhat weaker now, following the democratisation and growth of the state and the ageing of capitalism. The critiques of both Habermas and the free marketeers are relevant here. But even this moderate form of grand theorising, suggesting temporal changes from pre-industrial capitalism through the heyday of capitalism to something identified roughly as post-capitalism needs close scrutiny against the details of development in different societies. No neat master-theory can capture even the significant variations.

On a long perspective of capitalist development, then, it appears that we cannot assume a constant relationship between politics and markets. As that relationship changes, so does that between capitalism and democracy. As capitalism matures as a mode of production, its early political and cultural bed-mates – liberal democracy and individualism – may become less appropriate, and pressures for institutional intervention will mount. This may lead to an extension of democracy. If politics displaces markets as the major area of economic decision-making, this may mean only that parliamentary democracy – sharply limited in scope and levels of participation – is giving way to, or being supplemented by, a form of democracy with more-embracing places of participation and a wider range of issues being discussed. Capitalism is still a young economic system: as a fully liberal-democratic system it is even younger. It is not yet clear how far it can accommodate democratic pressures, or how far and in what ways it can continue to promote individualism.

In order to build a useful analytic framework for analysis of the capitalist state, including a role for social and political theory, a significant body of empirical and judgmental literature must be confronted. Assaults on the contemporary welfare state are both budgetary and ideological: its basic programmes, rights and benefits are seen as neither permanent nor legitimate. Part of the background for this collection is, then, the considerable and generally bad press, academic and popular, that modern governments or the modern state, in the sense of a complex of institutions, an institutional ensemble, or the political apparatus, receives: ideologically, if not in fact, the state appears to be in bad shape. There is a good deal of pessimism or suspicion, stemming from different perspectives, about the capacity of the governments of advanced societies to do much, or much of value, especially from those who don't bother to examine the comparative evidence. In the Introduction and in several of the essays in this volume, an attempt is made to identify key elements of the capitalist state, to discuss the range of critiques of its operations from both Right and Left, and to indicate a rigorous and even strategically useful way of reformulating these investigative and political projects. However, the circumstances in which the modern (advanced) state finds itself are paradoxical, in that they do not all point the same way, and appear capable of development in different directions, implying different strategies or actions.

This complexity underlies doubts about the possibility of constructing general theories of the state, whether the more precise stimulus is pessimism, cynicism, relativism, empiricism or anti-scientism. The world has rarely fallen in with theoretical anticipations, whether in sociology, political science or political economy. Amidst the polemical noise, we find a marked insistence on the specificity of all institutional developments in the public realm, and a commensurate hostility to attempts to unify overmuch the diverse range of state phenomena.

THE MODERN STATE

The most notable fact about the modern state is its growth. Not only the size of the state, but the range of institutions, interventions and policy spheres has expanded dramatically in the post-war era. By the 1980s public sector spending on OECD countries accounted for 45 per cent of all economic activity, ranging from 31.7 per cent (Switzerland) to 67 per cent (the Netherlands) (OECD, 1986, Table R8, p. 163). Governments have taken on more functions, through more institutions, in response to a greater array of perceived societal problems, than seemed imaginable even at the high point of interventionist fervour in the immediate post-war period. The causes and consequences of this development have yet to be appreciated theoretically. Neither neo-liberal assertions of the destructive effects of this expansion nor neo-Marxian claims about its functionally supportive role for capitalism have grasped it convincingly. From the contemporary denunciations of excessive democracy to ascriptions of the essentially anti-democratic character of state intervention, the relations between states and democracy, between state and society, and between different forms, or stages, of democracy in capitalistic society, remain underformulated. Even the object of inquiry may be uncertain. When we hear criticisms of the state, is it the welfare state, the regulatory state, the authoritarian state or the permissive state which the detractors have in mind?

The modern welfare state has, then, undoubtedly grown steadily and become increasingly complex. As indicated above, one clear trend in most developed countries during the past century has been the expansion of the weight, cost and range of the state. The growth of the public sector, penetrating society in a far-reaching way, is revealed not only in the high proportion of national income of which the state disposes, but also by the increasing proportion of public employees in the total work force, and the variety of enterprises and activities in which the state is engaged. There are general problems of measurement: of data (what is included?), of interpretation (how big is big?), and of comparison (are the bigs strictly comparable?). Against this information, the emergence of small government movements in Australia and the United States may be greeted with amazement, given their standing in the big government league tables. Is it a result of hallucination, or of borrowing images and arguments from somewhere else? Or is it less a serious theory than a tactical ploy in relation to immediate political issues?

It is worth underlining again how much fog, rhetoric and ideology there is in argument over that grand abstraction, the modern state. There is firm evidence about such matters as changing levels of governmental expenditure and number of public employees – though 'privatisation' and rival methods of calculation create uncertainties even here. The extent of challenges to the welfare state – is it in fact declining? – remains hard to assess. Rhetoric intervenes again, as when Mrs Thatcher says that welfare services are not being reduced while also claiming that the frontiers of the state are being rolled back. The figures for the level of public expenditure or of the Public Sector Borrowing Requirement do not suggest at all a significant retreat, although the large figures need to be broken down, as they may hide a shift of resources, which pursuit of a free economy/strong state regime is sure to involve. It may also be the case, furthermore, that the figures commonly cited in polemical contexts provide inaccurate assessments of the long-term trends in public-sector expansion. Keynes, after all, advocated an expansion of public-sector involvement in the private economy during times of crisis and a retreat from this involvement in the recovery phase, when socialised investment or public-sector-generated fiscal expansionism would be less necessary. The post-Keynesian critiques of this position have concentrated not only on the need for differential interventions in the economy according to stages of the cycle, but also on the long-term politicisation of the social relations of capitalism. In so far as this has become, as in Sweden, a long-term strategy for democratisation of decision-making, it might not be the role of the state but the role of collective decision-makers (both employer associations and employee associations) which is expanded. In so far as public sector debt expands as a consequence of borrowing to finance counter-cyclical demand stimulations, no long-term or permanent structural deficit appears and what has become known as the Public Sector Borrowing Requirement disappears.

Difficulties and differences multiply when it comes to diagnosing the condition of the state and defining the route to good health. The state's bad press *may* be bad press only, as polemics often miss the point. The sources of rhetoric and polemic are not necessarily the particular political reality out there, which is the supposed object of assessment and attack. The polemicist may be fighting other battles altogether. Hence rhetorical claims that government is impotent, wasteful, unable to meet genuine needs and so on, cannot be taken at face value. The traditional liberal may reveal a general concern for both abstract and concrete (market) freedoms, but the resurgence of empirical work by sociologists, political economists and political scientists provides a substantial literature on the actual impact of state intervention on macro-economic performance. The conclusions from these studies are sharply at odds with the normal presumptions of economic liberalism, and they throw considerable light on the extent of the state's power to influence or effect outcomes.

Any perusal of OECD countries' unemployment statistics, for example, shows no support for the argument that large state sectors are an impediment to good economic performance; there is similarly no empirical warrant for the claim that big government causes inflation. Sometimes high levels of unemployment and inflation are associated with above-average levels of public-sector activity (and taxation), sometimes not. Sometimes low levels of unemployment and inflation are achieved when government is small, sometimes not. These findings cast doubt on both the liberal's insistence that minimalist government achieves the greatest good for the greatest number and the Marxist theories which try to equate all state activity with the needs of the economy or the requirements of accumulation.

Given the diversity of economic outcomes associated with similar types and levels of state activity, it is simply not possible to maintain that state intervention necessarily aids capital or that it necessarily impedes economic performance. Further investigation of actual institutions and of the actual content of the policies attempted or implemented by the state is demanded. Given the evidence, assertions of the necessary fit between democracy and capitalist economic imperatives are weakened also. Once a full range of forms or stages of democracy – political democracy, social democracy, industrial democracy and economic democracy – is allowed, simple equations between democracy and market freedom cannot be sustained. The most extensive form of democracy, the right of collectives to influence the content of economic activity and the arrangements under which it is conducted, certainly implies a significant reduction of economic individualism. Further, the development of capitalism itself may be undermining the individualism with which it is, supposedly, tightly linked. Marx certainly imagined that eventually the bourgeois freedoms ushered in by the bourgeois revolutions of the eighteenth century would become impediments to the ability of capitalism to develop or to deliver its promises of material prosperity. Capitalism itself may foster collectivist rather than individualistic relations (Abercrombie, Hill and Turner, 1986), though that collectivism would be different in character to that espoused and valued by foes of capitalism.

Contemporary government remains enormously powerful by any reckoning. Even if it is notoriously unable to guarantee macro-economic policy outcomes such as full employment or price stability or high standards of living, its efficiency or appropriateness is certainly no less than that of private organisations in relevant areas, and its condition is probably no worse. It is misleading to speak of the state or government alone in crisis, as if it exists in some kind of isolation: corporations, banks, unions, indeed the whole system of institutions may be in crisis, though that term needs further exploration. And, although contemporary critiques of the extensive web of government often assert the bluntness and wastefulness of government instrumentalities, their destructive effects upon human capacities, or the lack of resources and arrangements to meet adequately and effectively the proper claims made upon them, the demand for better government is compatible with demands for less, as much, or even more government. In other words, as will be argued later in this collection, extensive if more flexible government remains necessary to satisfy legitimate needs.

There are, in relation to the state as to many other things, overlaps in the critiques emanating from what we loosely call Left and Right. In the end, of course, explanations of and answers to the difficulties of the state differ significantly. For example, Hayek and Habermas may appear to have reached the same point, in recognising the incapacity of modern governments to meet the varied and extensive demands made upon them and in seeing the contemporary crisis as systemic weakness, but their routes to that destination are very different, and they move off in opposed directions. Hayek arrives via a protracted attack on the aggrandisement of politics over the past century and a half, and seeks salvation through the freeing of (spontaneous) economic forces. Habermas reaches the central problem of the state through an account of the developing expectations of democratic citizens, which cannot be met by a system suffering from a crisis of accumulation. The overwhelming need in this account is for a new binding morality – and new social institutions – which represent a reassertion of the claims of the public or the political. Both Hayek and Habermas tend to grandiose generalisation, keeping the actual world at some distance.

DEFINITION AND EVALUATION

It is clear, then, that argument over the state, as well as argument over its class character, is highly complex. It occurs at different levels, different definitions are used (what the state is and the range of phenomena it encompasses) and evaluations penetrate both definitions and (rival) theories. Rigorous definitions may facilitate discussion, but they are connected so integrally with theoretical perspectives that they generally occupy or map the ground arbitrarily. At best they constitute an early stage on the journey. Even given an agreed definition of what the state or political apparatus is, which is unlikely given conflicting traditions and their evaluative contents, the crucial question of the relationship of the state to other elements is not settled. A formal definition in terms of legal sovereignty is not much help, as it indicates only what counts as a state in international law. Pejorative definitions, for example, that the state is a badge of lost innocence, or the executive committee of the ruling class, run into the immediate difficulty that they arise within particular and controversial traditions of political thought. Even the apparently neat definitions familiar in the British liberal and socialist traditions – that the state is the political machinery of government in a community, or that state theory is a theory of the governmental act – don't take us far. While some adopt a narrow definition of politics and of the state, which is conceived simply as the formal political apparatus, others broaden the notion to include everything that affects its functioning, or helps determine its role. The theory of the state becomes a theory of society. Not that the mind need boggle unduly at this: one could define the state narrowly while seeing it as 'socially determined' (or with its social basis remaining to be decided), or define it broadly by incorporating whatever makes it what it is, and discussion could still take place. Still, a narrow definition of the state is likely to be associated with theories giving it a reasonable amount of autonomy.

This general introductory point is both familiar and fair. Disagreement does not begin with an agreed definition and move logically from there, but arises within different and perhaps incompatible perspectives, theoretical structures and traditions of thought. The journey may begin with an apparently neutral definition, but the different routes have been mapped out carefully and often it seems simply a question of using one of the available sets of maps with the goal of marginally increasing its accuracy. Yet while substantive disagreements and their deeper sources are real and unavoidable, they can be identified with reasonable clarity.

While drawing boundaries between the political, the economic and the social is difficult, and easily becomes abstract and misleading, *some* idea of the nature of the inquiry is needed. In broad terms, what does argument over the state encompass? Theories of the state generally contain both empirical and normative elements, although these should be separated only provisionally at this stage. A sociology of the state is inevitably also a theory of society, that is, a theory of the relationship between political institutions and arrangements *and* economic and social forces and structures. Even if we begin with some segregated or very formal notion of the political, as machinery of government or the body of rules, practices and institutions which defines the area within which group conflicts occur, we will be forced back finally to the intimate connections between state and society. Hence the early-nineteenth-century assumption of the crucial importance of establishing the relationship between the economic–social and the political worlds or, more narrowly, between production and the state, needs to be taken seriously (as does the relationship between cultural values and the state). But to accept an organic connection complicates the question of causal hierarchies. Different assumptions about the weight of economic or material factors and the possible extent of interactionism inevitably give a very different significance and character to state institutions, defining the range of features and powers a state may have, for example, whether it can be neutral, independent, free-floating or decisive, or whether it is inescapably partisan, subordinate or epiphenomenal. While general assumptions of this sort may leave some scope for interpretation or variation in detailed analysis, and even for concessions to radically different perspectives, they do set broad limits within which answers will be sought and, more often than not, found.

SOME MODERN PERSPECTIVES ON THE STATE

Theories of the state have emerged, not simply to comprehend, but to contain and, in some cases, to exacerbate current difficulties and conflicts, through demonstrating the inability of the state, as presently constituted, to deal with them. The choice of terminology is itself deeply loaded politically: whether we refer to the modern state, or to the industrial state, or to the capitalist or to the corporatist state, stems from particular world-views, of which the most relevant ones are pluralist, managerial, and Marxist or class.

The liberals and the pluralists tend to postulate a neutral and independent state, at least potentially: governments rule, and they can do so rationally. The problem is that of confining the state within its proper area. 'Consensus' and legitimate social diversities, rather than class conflict, are valued, in that the neutral and independent state serves the public interest, supported by the increasingly informed public's agreement on what that is.

Pluralist theory emphasises the differentiation and diversity of societies. Power is seen as fragmented, and competition and interaction between its possessors is valued. Group competition is seen as a viable form of democratic participation: the democratic state mediates and represents a multiplicity of cross-cutting groups. While it may not be independent in any strong sense, it can at least act as an arbiter or umpire in measuring or recording relevant strengths.

Liberal and pluralist theories have been the subject of sustained critique. Put broadly, it is suggested that the shadow of capitalism is not allowed to fall. Hence there is a systematic mismatch between theory and reality. State and economy are falsely described and weighted, or falsely separated. In pluralist theory, the capacity of groups to enter the competitive process is disguised or not closely examined, as the rules of the game or formal openness do not guarantee access to relatively weak groups. In addition, governments and political cultures may be biassed in regard to the groups which are legitimated. There are more faces to power than the typical pluralist is ever able to admit.

Recent discussions of the 'power' of the state have been marked increasingly by the recognition that other, collective actors are at work too. In economic policy, for example, parliamentary institutions may be less effective than extra-parliamentary institutions and forums. This is the central issue raised by those who see a development towards corporatism. In so far as parliaments are bypassed, the new tendencies may be lamented as undemocratic. In so far as issues are opened up for public debate and decision-making (for example, questions of investment and income distribution), new institutions might expand democracy even when employers or trade unions rather than political parties provide the key personnel. The content as well as the form of decision-making must be considered. Acceptance of this argument may lead to an understanding of the state not as an actor, but as merely the terrain or the arena upon which familiar class conflicts are played out. If old conflicts appear on a new terrain, the balance of power may well shift, and theoretical understandings will need revision.

Analysts of corporatism exhibit several mutually exclusive views of the compatibility of democracy and the state. On the one hand are those theories of interest representation which see the *ad hoc*, unrepresentative bodies established under state auspices as inherently contradictory. The operations of such bodies are said to be constrained by the ability of the state to establish the agenda for political intervention and the boundaries of legitimate action, thus leading to a strengthening of bourgeois domination. Democracy is thereby negated. On the other hand, certain corporatist developments may be seen as heralding a resurgence of class politics and even as increasing representativeness. The institutional representation of the labour movement then replaces the familiar atomised competitive interest-group politics. This conception could sustain an optimistic view of the potential for an anti-capitalist strategy, challenging the hegemony of private accumulation.

The common Marxist assumption is the dependence of the state upon something else, something deeper or more significant. Political and cultural institutions and issues are *ultimately* dependent upon economic relationships. In Marx's original formulation, the modern state arose in tandem with the modern bourgeois epoch in order to facilitate new activities. This view of the emergent capitalist state has been exaggerated into a Marxist theory of the state according to which all state activity is capitalist and therefore oppressive. Even democratic gains are denounced as supportive of social peace. Yet Marx recognised the significance of some reforms, which might challenge capitalist power itself, and it is compatible with his general enterprise to see capitalist state activity as historically progressive *just because* its rationale is political, in contrast with *laissez-faire*.

All Marxist theories of the state emphasise class struggle. They differ in the extent to which classes are conceived unambiguously, and in the extent to which support for accumulation is regarded as good or bad. One significant

Marxist instrumentalist view sees the state as an arena of only capitalist interests, which may be divided between themselves. This can require a state which transcends the divisions and conflicts of capital, representing its common interest. The second major perspective is structuralist and anti-conspiratorial, and treats the primary function of the state as guaranteeing accumulation. Historical and political variants, and the expressed interests of governments and classes, are essentially irrelevant to this primary function. In relation to state-sponsored or initiated production, it is clear that the capitalist state is interested not merely in direct profitability, but in the general service of state activities to the long-range interests and survival of the capitalist mode of production. The capitalist state may have to subsidise new technology in order to keep national capital internationally competitive. In any case, the state 'representing' national capitalist interests comes to be identified – in true hegemonic manner – with the national interest. The weaknesses of both approaches concern the difficulty in recognising the autonomy of the political and of the particular. The first can become a vulgar, conspiratorial Marxism, and the second a fudged or elastic structuralism which gobbles up independent phenomena without adequately acknowledging them. Marxists clearly differ about the ability to change the capitalist state by democratic arrangements, about the degree to which trade unions and working-class parties can embed democratic responsive policies within the basic structure of the state. Thus, while we may accept the ambiguous formulation that 'in the last analysis' a state in a capitalist society must function in such a way as to protect the continued possibility of capitalist accumulation in the hands of capitalists, there are many forms and structures through which that end is achieved. But capitalist society is torn apart by contradictory requirements which make it impossible for the state to perform that function adequately.[1] Dilemmas arise, for example, how can one know whether a particular state action is in the interests of the system, of particular capitalists, of the working class, or of no one in particular, because it is a result of confusion, stalemate and ignorance? The claim that structuralist Marxism needs empirical and historical criteria to establish the consequences and biasses of state action is not a request for the confirmation of revealed truth: it is an acknowledgment that structuralist generalisations and the political impotence which commonly flows from them are likely to be undermined by flexible empirical analysis.

Students and activists, observers and chroniclers, theorists and ideologues, might well be asking: where do we go from here? Has the work of the past two decades, along with more traditional work, given us an adequate understanding of the state? What are the likely futures of capitalism and democracy? It is now possible to identify an emergent 'post-Marxist' perspective on the disputed relations of state and society. The core elements of this more flexible political analysis of the state have been summarised in the following propositions (Pierson, 1986). First, the state is seen as the institutional expression of a complex pattern of social relationships which include the historical outcomes of class struggle and at the same time mould the terrain of future class and popular struggles. Second, and consequentially, is a denial that the state is an institution that can be occupied or that state power can be 'seized' or radically transformed. Third, the state therefore cannot be viewed instrumentally, as necessarily acting in the interests of a capitalist class or as the expression of the divided interests of different fractions of capital. Fourth, the state cannot be conceived as the mechanistic outcome of economic forces (the mode of production) even in its weakened, but still economic, relative autonomy form. Fifth, class struggles in no way exhaust the struggles arising in the state/civil society matrix. New social movements engage in emancipatory politics within popular democratic struggles. Sixth, the state remains an essential institutional structure of modern society. It cannot be 'smashed', nor can it 'wither away'. Finally, there can be no general model of *the* state in capitalist societies. Theoretical analyses of the state must be placed within the history and contemporary forms of struggle both within and between national states in the world system of capitalism.

The state's role as an organised claimant to power is significantly reduced in the 'post-Marxist' perspective, which itself contains a number of contestable, if potentially fruitful claims. Further normative and empirical work must go hand in hand. Contemporary defenders of 'the state' – though not necessarily of any particular state – will have to examine empirical studies as well as take a position in relation to the established perspectives on the state. To the Marxist, part of the response may be that the state is not simply a capitalist state, and to the neo-liberals that it is not just a marauding bureaucratic monster. To both it will be urged that the state can be both more amenable to people's purposes and needs and more flexible, though these two are likely to go together. This requires a rejection of the Fabian emphasis upon order, efficiency and expertise rather than representation, equality and participation, and of the related illusion that their disinterested professionals can successfully challenge the values of capitalism and the market place. Rejection of the paternalist Fabian state does not lead inevitably to acceptance of a rolled-back or a laid-back state. My own goal, and that of most contributors to this book, is a state which is expansive, flexible and democratic, without an arbitrary and destructive separation of democracy in the state from democracy in a wide variety of particular arenas, including the economy and the work place. This involves a rejection of one Fabian image – that of bureaucratic collectivism – in favour of its other emphasis upon voluntary groups and associations and on the responsible character of ordinary social institutions. Put another way, the state is to be filled out – sustained and examined continuously – by the diverse structures and arrangements of civil society, which is the only means whereby

its capitalist character might be threatened while its democratic potentialities
are realised.

NOTES

My thanks to Bob Alford, once engaged on this project, for his critical remarks, and to Paul
Boreham and Geoff Dow, for criticism of and suggestions for the Introduction.
1. Historical evidence may make it hard to accept an argument that the state always preserves the
   long-term interests of capital accumulation. The industrial wastelands and high unemployment – perhaps never to be overcome – of contemporary Britain are a case in point. A
   weakened and disconsolate labour movement can scarcely take comfort from the spectacle of
   capital accumulation there grinding painfully to a halt. If class conflict were to produce a
   stronger labour movement, accumulation – under changed auspices, naturally – might be
   regenerated.

REFERENCES

Abercrombie, N., S. Hill, and B. Turner, 1986. *Sovereign Individuals of Capitalism*. London, Allen
    and Unwin
OECD, 1986. *Economic Outlook*, 40 (December)
Pierson, C., 1986. *Marxist Theory and Democratic Politics*. Oxford, Polity Press

THEORISING THE STATE

Macpherson's well-known article explores the question of the need for a contemporary grand theory of the state. In their traditional form, such grand theories are both normative and explanatory, relating the state to human needs, purposes, potentialities and capacities. Macpherson is critical of much recent empirical theory, which fails to confront the state adequately, because its assumptions are time-bound and because it rests upon a morally repugnant view of human nature, with 'maximising market man' as the norm. He also finds its descriptive basis deficient in that it offers a pluralist account of society at the very time when its plural character is diminishing, with the relative growth of corporate-managed and state-managed sectors as against the competitive market sector. The new and relatively autonomous state pluralises capital rather than responding to genuinely plural forces within the society. It has taken on significantly new functions which are necessary to support (the accumulation process of) capital in general, though the interests of particular capitals may be opposed.

Macpherson seeks to correct and enlarge liberal democratic and Marxist conceptions of the state through drawing together the valuable features of each. Marxist political economy provides a probing account of the nature of the bourgeois society in which the state operates. Progressive liberal democracy has a humanist and developmental side, though its appealing values cannot be realised in bourgeois society. He discusses and appeals to a new awareness in capitalist societies, in which human purposes are placed above those of capital, but his optimism about the emergence of new participatory groups, including militant unions and his (cautious) utopianism about a change of consciousness away from market values seem somewhat faded with the successes of neo-liberal politics in America and the United Kingdom. Over the past decade, since Macpherson wrote the article, capitalist and market values have been reaffirmed sharply in many areas of life, including the universities.

The question raised in Smith's clear and straightforward piece concerns the place of the state in International Relations literature. It is part of his claim that contemporary theories of the state must acknowledge new and highly potent forms of international organisation and influence, drawing national states into complex, limiting networks and arrangements. Many economic and political changes since the mid 1970s have apparently challenged the state as primary actor: increasing economic interdependence, the growing power of multinational corporations, the impending exhaustion of many minerals, the oil crisis, and the rise of Third World demands for the redistribution of world resources. All of these are linked with a decline of US world economic hegemony, which proceeds despite occasional imperialistic adventures.

It is no longer possible, then – if it was ever justifiable – to treat the rest of the world as a backdrop against which national states play out their own particular dramas. The state in international relations and international political economy may seem less and less an entity, a closed unit for analysing political behaviour, and more and more penetrated by the influence of other states and their connections and by non-state actors also. If the important thing is the role of each particular state within the international system, then whether or not the state is democratic or capitalist will not be central. Accounts of politics which take the state as an autonomous unit of analysis or a boundary within which politics operates will be far more likely to stress the differences between states (whether the focus is on the capitalist or the democratic aspect of the state), whereas if one starts with the role of the state internationally one will be far more likely to see its internal differences as less important than its size, wealth, militancy, capacity and other 'external' features. The international system, as a set of institutionalised relations, diminishes sharply the autonomy of the state. In these accounts, what it can do and what it does depend less on its ideology, its political complexion, its domestic policy, its leaders, than on its place in the world as a whole.

Smith's chapter indicates clearly both the limitations of focussing upon 'the kind of state' in international politics and the weaknesses in a state-centric view of international politics. There are questions on the other side which are worth pursuing. What are the effects of the world system and of the new international actors upon the organisation and the policies of states which may regard their own structure and values as central? Are they forced to adapt to external demands, despite themselves, so that different kinds of state are made more alike, and further from their own self-images?

2

Do we need a theory of the state?

C. B. MACPHERSON

My question is not whether we need a theoretical understanding of the political process in modern states, but whether we need a theory of the state in the grand manner of the acknowledged 'great' theories, ranging in modern times from, say, Bodin and Hobbes to Hegel and the nineteenth-century juristic theories of sovereignty, and on to the lesser (but, in intention, equally grand) theories of Green and Bosanquet and such twentieth-century thinkers as Barker and Lindsay and MacIver.

It is clear that in order to understand the operation of contemporary states we need theories of the political process in our own liberal-democratic states (and, if we are to be comprehensively informed, in Communist and Third World states as well). There is no lack of such process theory, especially of the liberal-democratic state: that is where the bulk of the work of political scientists has been done for the last few decades, and it has given us a new understanding of the role of parties, pressure groups, and bureaucracies, the determinants of voting behaviour, and so on. The general theory that has come to prevail – which may be described as a pluralist-elitist-equilibrium theory – may be thought not entirely adequate even as a descriptive and explanatory theory – it has come under considerable fire from a number of radical liberal-democratic theorists,[1] and W. J. M. Mackenzie (1975) has recently pointed out its failure to take account of political violence. However, my concern here is not with an appraisal of that empirical theory, except in so far as the rise of such a theory may throw light on the reasons for the decline of grand theories of the state.

My concern is whether we now need something more than theories of the political process. Do we need a theory of the state in the grand tradition? The hallmark of the grand theories is that they all tied the state back to supposedly essential human purposes and capacities, to a supposedly essential nature of man. In doing so they were of course both descriptive and prescriptive or justificatory. They sought both to explain what the actual state was, and to show either that it was justified or necessary or that it ought to be, and could be, replaced by something else. But what deserves emphasising is that they did relate the state normatively to supposed essentially human purposes.

Do we again need such a theory of the state? To raise this question is, of course, to assume that we do not have an adequate one now. An answer to this question depends obviously on who 'we' are. I take 'us' to be those living in late-twentieth-century liberal-democratic societies, especially those of us whose vocation is the study of politics. Do we, then, need a new theory of the state? I shall argue that some of us do and some of us do not.

We may divide this whole constituency into three distinctively different parts.[2] In the first category (I) I put those who, on the whole, accept and uphold the existing liberal-democratic society and state, with no more than marginal reservations or hopes that they can be made somewhat better (within the same framework, by for instance more informed citizen participation, or less or more welfare-state activity). This category includes the bulk of the contemporary empirical theorists and, at a different level, some normative theorists who may be called philosophic liberals.

The second category (II) is made up of those who accept, and would promote, the normative values that were read into the liberal-democratic society and state by J. S. Mill and the nineteenth- and twentieth-century idealist theorists, but who reject the present liberal-democratic society and state as having failed to live up to those values, or as being incapable of realising them. This includes the bulk of contemporary social democrats and those socialists who do not accept the whole of the Marxian theory.

The third category (III) contains those who reject both the idealist normative theory and the present liberal-democratic society and state, and would replace both of them totally by Marxian theory and practice.

NEGATIVE AND POSITIVE NEEDS FOR A THEORY

I shall now argue that those in the first category do *not* need a grand theory of the state, and that those in the second and third categories *do* need one.

(I) The first category, as noted, includes both most of the current empirical theorists and some normative liberal theorists. Their needs may be considered separately.

(a) The empirical theorists generally claim to have abstained from any value judgment about the processes they are analysing. But their theories usually have strong commendatory overtones. If they had really avoided all value judgment, not only would they not need a grand theory of the state, they would be incapable of one. For such a theory is always normative as well as explanatory. But since a value judgment is at least implicit in their theories, it might be argued that they do need a theory of the state after all; that they need to make explicit and to develop the values that underlie their theorising (which would enlarge their empirical theory to the dimensions of a theory of the state).

But they cannot afford to do this. Having rejected the 'classical' liberal-democratic model of John Stuart Mill and Green, and their twentieth-century followers, with its humanistic striving – rejected it as unrealistic (that is, as beyond the capacities of the average twentieth-century citizen) – the empirical theorists cannot afford a theory which would tie the state back to some supposedly essential nature of man. For to do so would be to reveal that they have reverted to a Benthamist or even Hobbesian model of man as possessive individualist. They have, it is true, come some distance from the Hobbes–Bentham model of society as a series of freely competitive market relations. They have been able to adjust their model of society to some of the realities of managed capitalism. But even managed capitalism presupposes maximising market man, and they have accepted – even while they have refined – that concept of man. That concept of man has become, increasingly, morally unacceptable in the late twentieth century. Thus for the empirical theorists to go on to a theory of the state would be to expose the inadequacy of their basic assumptions. It would endanger their position as the spokesmen for liberal democracy, given that their model of man and society is becoming morally repugnant to increasing numbers of people within the liberal democracies and in the world at large. I conclude that the empirical theorists do not need – in the sense that they cannot afford – a theory of the state.

(b) What of the contemporary normative theorists, the philosophers who have concerned themselves with the political, of whom the most influential and widely discussed at present are Rawls (1971) and Nozick (1974)? They also are working with a market model of man and society. There is of course a sharp difference between them: Rawls is happy with the welfare state encroachments on unalloyed capitalism and can even contemplate their extension. On the other hand, Nozick argues for a return to the minimal state. But they both endorse the fundamental relations of capitalist market society and its property institutions. And since they assume maximising market man as the norm, they need not go behind that to inquire into the nature or potential of man and to relate that to the state. They need not be concerned with any necessary or historical relation of the state to society or to supposedly essential human purposes or capacities. They do not need a theory of the state, but only a theory of distributive justice, that is, of the just distribution of 'primary goods' (Rawls) or of 'holdings' (Nozick), or a theory of liberty (i.e., of the allowable or morally desirable amount and kind of individual liberty). The state can be treated as simply an agent which does, or should, subserve the principles of justice or liberty which the theorist argues for.

It thus appears that the philosophic liberals, like the empirical theorists, do not need a theory of the state. It may even be suggested that contemporary

philosophic liberals cannot afford to attempt one. The philosophic liberals of
fifty or ninety years ago (MacIver, Barker, Lindsay, Green) could afford to,
because while they accepted capitalist society in its main outlines, they were
far from accepting the market model of man. Having a broader vision of the
nature of man, they could and did try to relate the state to it. But not much can
be done – beyond what was done by Hobbes and Bentham – to relate the state
to market man. An attempt to do so in any depth would reveal the time-bound
quality of the basic assumptions about man.

Rawls, indeed, in the last part of his book, does go on to a different vision of
the nature of man, as a creature who wants to maximise his 'primary goods'
only as a means to realise a plan of life or concept of the good, or to develop his
capacities to the fullest. But Rawls does not explain how this is consistent with
the market model of man on which his whole theory of justice is based. He is
thus unable to go beyond a theory of distributive justice to a theory of the state.

Turning to my second category (II) – those who accept the humanistic
values read into liberal democracy by Mill and the idealists but who reject
present liberal democracy as having failed to realise those values – it can
readily be seen that they *do* need a theory of the state. Believing as they do that
the state should embody certain moral values, which they find *not* being
realised by liberal democratic states, they are committed to a theory which is
both normative and explanatory – that is, to a theory in the grand tradition
which relates the state to human needs, capacities, and potentialities. It
follows that they need a new theory of the state to the degree that the theory
they have inherited from humanist liberals and idealists (ranging from Mill
and Green to Barker, Lindsay, MacIver, etc.) is inadequate.

That the inherited theory is seriously inadequate is sufficiently evident from
the ease with which it was eclipsed in the mid twentieth century by the
empiricists' theories. Its eclipse was due chiefly to the fact that the explanatory, or descriptive, side of the twentieth-century traditional theories was
demonstrably inaccurate. Citizens of the Western democracies did not behave
like the rational, informed, and public-spirited citizens postulated by the
traditional theory.

The traditional theorists might have defended their position by pointing out
that they were not trying to describe and reduce to operative principles the
political process in those contemporary states commonly called democracies,
but were trying to deduce the essential requirements of democracy from their
vision of human needs and capacities. This gave them the concept of democracy as a kind of society and political system which would provide the equal
possibility of self-development by all. To complete that defence it would only
be necessary to argue – as they did – that people are capable of a degree of
rational and moral self-development which would enable them to live in a fully
democratic society and to participate actively in a fully democratic state.

But such a two-fold defence could not save their position. For while they were indeed seeking to show 'the essentials of democracy' rather than merely to describe existing democratic institutions, they did present the existing liberal democracies as having met the essential requirements to a substantial degree. They did so, it may be surmised, because they were all more or less explicitly concerned to build a case for existing democracies versus existing or threatened dictatorships. So they had to argue that the existing Western democracies had the root of the matter in them. To do this they had to examine the existing system of parties, pressure groups, and public opinion formation, and argue that it did, however roughly, come up to the essential requirements. So they had to argue not merely that people were capable of the required degree of rational and moral self-development but that they had already reached it or nearly reached it.

They thus came up with a pluralist theory of society and of the democratic state. The democratic state was an arrangement by which rational, well-intentioned citizens, who indeed had a wide variety of different interests but had also a sense of common interest or even a 'general will' (MacIver, 1926, p. 342), could and did adjust their differences in an active, rational, give-and-take of parties and interest groups and the free press. The empirical theorists were able to show that most citizens of liberal-democratic states were far from being such active rational participants, and were thus able virtually to demolish the traditional theory.

Perhaps the fundamental weakness of the traditional theorists was that they had unconsciously adopted the notion of the democratic process as a competitive market. They did not make the market analogy explicitly, as the empirical theorists were to do. That analogy implies a society made up of narrowly self-interested maximising individuals, and this was incompatible with the traditional theorists' image of man as a moral being whose essence was to be realised only in the self-development of all his human capacities. But their model of a plural society was a market model.

This in itself could not have led to their eclipse by the empirical theories, for the latter were openly based on the market analogy. But it has meant that late twentieth-century liberal attempts to revive the traditional theory have run aground. For they have adhered to the pluralist model, while the society for which they are prescribing has become increasingly less plural. As I shall argue, late capitalist society still exhibits some measure of pluralism, but its amount has shrunk and its character has changed as the corporate-managed sector and the state-operated sector of the economy have encroached on and diminished the competitive market sector. I conclude that contemporary theorists in my second category *do* need a new theory of the state.

Turning finally to those in my third category (III), I think it is clear that these people also need to develop a theory of the state. Marx's theory was certainly

normative as well as analytical. The role of the state was crucial to his whole
theory, yet he did not provide more than fragments of a theory of the state.
Lenin did rather more, but however appropriate his conclusions were when he
wrote, they are not adequate for the late twentieth century. It follows that
contemporary Marxists *do* need a new or more developed theory of the state
than they have inherited. And Marxist scholars in the West have in the last
decade become very much aware of this and have plunged vigorously into the
effort to provide it. There is already a substantial body of work, to mention
only the almost simultaneous books by Poulantzas (*Pouvoir politique et classes
sociales*, 1968) and Miliband (*The State in Capitalist Society*, 1969), the subsequent extended debate between them, and independent discussions in
Europe and America, which have taken the matter further and in different
directions, as in the Genoa conference sponsored by the Council for
European Studies in 1973 (Lindberg *et al.*, 1975), in the papers in the journal
Kapitalstate (1973–) produced by a joint editorial group now mainly in the US
but drawing on many West European writers; and in seminal books by Jurgen
Habermas, *Legitimation Crisis* (1976), and James O'Connor, *The Fiscal Crisis
of the State* (1973). This work, still continuing, is in the tradition of grand
theory.

A grand theory of the state, I have said, has to tie the state back to the
supposed nature, purpose and capacities of man. At the same time it has to
take account of the underlying nature of the society in which that state
operates. The contemporary Marxist theorists do both, though with varying
emphasis on the two aspects. Indeed much of the dispute amongst them may
be reduced to that difference of emphasis – some of them building on Marx
the humanist and some on Marx the analyst of capitalist society. The two can
be, and to a limited extent have been, drawn together by the recognition
(growing since the publication of Marx's *Grundrisse*) that there is no dichotomy between Marx the humanist and Marx the analyst of capitalism. But there
are still deep divisions on how, or whether, Marx's own position on the role of
the state in capitalist society (which he never fully spelled out) can be applied
to the relation between state and capital in 'late' or 'advanced' capitalism (see,
for example, the controversy between Miliband and Poulantzas, 1972).

It is worth asking about the relevance of this sort of work to those who are in
my second category. What, if anything, can be learned from it by those who do
not accept (or do not fully accept) the classical Marxian position, and yet do
not accept the existing liberal-democratic society and state as morally adequate? I find the question worth asking because I place myself in category (II),
and because I believe that some contemporary liberal theorists are inclined to
move from category (I) to (II). In the rest of this paper I shall preach to them. A
preacher must have a message. My message is, learn from those in category
(III).

CONTEMPORARY MARXIST LESSONS FOR LIBERAL-DEMOCRATIC THEORY

I think there is a lot to learn from the Marxists who see more clearly than most others that what has to be examined is the relation of the state to *bourgeois* society. And they are examining it in depth. In this they are repairing a great defect of twentieth-century traditional liberal theory which accepted bourgeois society but did not examine the implications of that acceptance.

One characteristic of the grand tradition – if we take it from the seventeenth to the early twentieth century – is its move from a materialist to an idealist view of man and society. One cannot say that this move is the measure, or the cause, of the twentieth-century eclipse of the grand tradition. (Hegel's theory of the state is, after all, rather more penetrating than Locke's or Bentham's, for Hegel knew that he was talking about the state in bourgeois society.) But one can say that the later idealists increasingly departed from that insight. They played down, or virtually dismissed (or at any rate could not cope with), the fact that it was the bourgeois state, or the state in bourgeois society, that had to be dealt with. They sought to rise above that specific society, not by examining any inherent momentum in it which might be transforming it or leading to its supersession, but by reaching for an archetype of all human society.

So they were led to what I have called a 'bow-and-arrow theory' (Macpherson, 1970). This is rather like the economic theory which, seeking a similar level of generality, defines 'capital' so broadly as to cover both modern capital and the primitive hunter's bow and arrow. Such a concept of capital is formally intelligible: the bow and arrow and the capital of a modern corporation are both the outcome of their owner's abstinence from immediate consumption of some of what they produce or collect. They are both, if you like, the product of their owner's investment decisions. But such a broad concept misses the difference between the two, a difference not just in degree but in kind, and so obscures some essentials of modern capital.

Here, as in theories of the state, the judgment of what are the essentials – the judgment whether the common features are more important or less important than the specific features – is a value judgment (though the theorists often fail to see that it is). On this choice depends the extent to which the resulting theory will implicitly justify or criticise the specific modern phenomena. The bow and arrow gives you abstinence as the source of capital and so makes modern capital a wholly admirable thing. Similarly with the state: the common feature may be seen as provision for a human desire for the good life or the full life, or for community. In that case the state – any state – is a wholly admirable thing. Or the common feature may be seen as the need for an authority able to hold in check the contentious nature of man: in that case, the state, any state, is still an admirable thing.

It is true that twentieth-century traditional theorists, for the most part, offered a theory of the liberal-democratic state rather than a theory of the state as such. But they are still caught up in bow-and-arrow thinking in so far as their argument moves from 'the good state' to the liberal-democratic state, justifying the latter as the best or the nearest possible approach to the former.

In any case the twentieth-century traditional theorists have not given much attention to the specific nature of the state in capitalist society. It was easy for them to abstract from the capitalist nature of their society, since the one theory which made that central – that is, Marxist theory – was, through most of the twentieth century, unsatisfactory in several ways. It was associated with dictatorships. It was frequently doctrinaire. And it took so little account of twentieth-century changes in the nature of capitalism that it could readily be dismissed as less realistic than a refined pluralism which talked of 'post-industrial society', countervailing powers, and so on. This refined pluralism is not entirely wrong. But it does distract attention from the fact that the motor of our system is still capital accumulation. And the presumption must surely be that this is bound to have a lot to do with the nature of the state.

The new generation of Marxist scholars in the West has largely overcome the defects just mentioned. Their work is not doctrinaire and it is mainly concerned with the changed, and changing, nature of capitalism in the late twentieth century. They are, that is to say, examining the necessary and possible relationship of the liberal-democratic state to contemporary capitalist society, which has changed in significant ways since Marx and since Lenin.

That relationship is crucially important to those of us who want to preserve some liberal-democratic values. And I do not see anyone other than the contemporary Marxist scholars examining it in any depth. That is reason enough for us to try to learn from them. Let me draw attention to some of their main theses, and suggest some implications for liberal democracy.

(1) They assume, with Marx, (a) that the human essence is to be fully realised only in free, conscious, creative activity; (b) that human beings have a greater capacity for this than has ever hitherto been allowed to develop; and (c) that a capitalist society denies this essential humanity to most of its inhabitants, in that it reduces human capacities to a commodity which, even when it fetches its exchange value in a free competitive market, receives less than it adds to the value of the product, thus increasing the mass of capital, and capital's ability to dominate those whose labour it buys.

This is the philosophic underpinning of Marx's whole enterprise. It is difficult for a liberal to fault (a) and (b), the assumptions about the nature and capacities of man: virtually the same position was taken by, for instance, Mill and Green. And it is short-sighted for the liberal not to give serious consideration to the validity of (c) – the postulate of the necessarily dehumanising nature of capitalism – for that does not depend on the ability of Marx's labour theory of value to explain market prices (which has been the main complaint about his economic theory) but only on his path-breaking argument that the value produced by human labour-power (i.e. by its capacity of working productively) exceeds the cost of producing that labour-power, the excess going to the increase of capital. This position is more difficult to fault than is the adequacy of his price theory.

The present Marxist theories of the state start from Marx's ontological and ethical position, and go on to consider where the state fits with this depiction of capitalism. And, given that, what are the prospects that late capitalism (which is supported, but also encroached upon, by the state) may be transcended, as Marx believed capitalism would be? In pursuing this inquiry they are naturally preoccupied with the analysis of late capitalism, taking as given the ethical dimension of the problem. Because of that concern, their work may not appear to be in the grand tradition of theories of the state. It may appear, that is to say, not to be relating the state to a concept of essentially human needs and capacities. But this is an appearance only. Their work, no less than Marx's, is designed to serve the realisation of the supposed essential nature of the human species. So if, in my ensuing description of some of their leading arguments, I appear to move out of the realm of philosophy and political theory into that of political economy this must not be taken to derogate from their role in the grand tradition.

(2) It is assumed that an indispensable job of the state in capitalist society is to maintain the conditions for capitalist enterprise and capital accumulation. This, however, does not imply that the state is the lackey or the junior partner of the capitalists. Indeed, for reasons that will be mentioned, the state is seen to have been moving away from being a mere superstructure and to have attained a significant degree of autonomy. The point is rather that, given a state's commitment to capitalist enterprise as the mainspring of the economy, the holders of state office must in their own interest maintain and support the accumulation process because the state's revenue – hence the power of the state's officers – depends on it. Therefore, in a democratic capitalist society, although the electorate determines who shall hold office as the government, governments are not free to make what use they like of their constitutional power. The government must stay within the limits imposed by the requirements of the accumulation process, limitations generally imposed on social-democratic governments through the mediation of the permanent bureaucracy and sometimes of the military.

(3) The need to promote accumulation has, with the maturation of late capitalism, required the state to take on a new range of functions, the performance of which has raised new problems. The change has been from the minimal support provided by the classical liberal state (law and order, contract definition and enforcement, and some material infrastructure – roads, canals, ports, etc.), to what might be called maximal support. Five areas of new or greatly increased support may be identified, all

apparently necessary: (i) the whole apparatus of the welfare state, which, in providing cushions against unemployment and against the costs of sickness, old age, and reproduction of the labour force, takes some of the burden that otherwise would have to be met by capital, or if not so met, would endanger public order; (ii) the Keynesian monetary and fiscal management of the economy, designed to prevent wide swings and to maintain a high level of employment; (iii) greatly increased infrastructure support, for example, in technical and higher education, urban transportation systems, urban and regional development schemes, public housing, energy plants, and direct and indirect state engagement in technological research and development; (iv) measures to prevent or reduce the damaging material side-effects of particular capitals' search for profits, for example, measures against pollution and destruction of natural resources (these, like the welfare-state measures – which are designed to prevent or reduce the damaging human side-effects of particular capitals' operations – are increasingly required in the interests of capital in general, but do limit the profits of some particular capitals); (v) a large new apparatus of state-imposed marketing boards, price-support schemes, wage arbitration procedures, etc., designed to stabilise markets in commodities and labour and capital.

It is held that while all those new supports are required, they also, in some measure, undermine what they are intended to support. The extent to which, and the way in which, each does so is different.

The first does not directly undermine it, but since it has to be financed out of the profits of capital, it reduces accumulation (or at least appears to particular capitals to reduce it, though it does so only in comparison with a wage–capital relation that is now insupportable). And it may be said to reduce it by preventing capital driving such a hard wage bargain as it could otherwise do. The second appears to reduce it by limiting the very swings on which capital had relied to redress, in the downswings, the gains made by labour in the upswings. This reduction, like the first or even more so, is partly illusory: it leaves out of the calculation the loss of accumulation in prolonged periods of depression. The third, like the first, is very costly, and the cost must be met out of the profits of capital. This is not all loss to capital, since some of these state activities – notably technical education and research and development – do increase the productivity of private capitals. But the balance-sheet is hard to draw. The fourth is a clear interference with the freedom of particular capitals. The fifth is perhaps the most serious, in that it replaces freely made market decisions by political decisions. Particular capitals (and particular segments of organised labour) are compelled to accommodate their conflicting private interests to public decisions. This erodes the ability of capital to make the most of itself, and reduces its accumulative freedom.

All five of these state activities, then, while they are necessary supports to capital in general (i.e., to the continuance and stability of a capitalist economy) appear to be opposed to the interests of particular capitals. And between them these activities may undermine the accumulation of capital in general. By enlarging the public sector, they take an increasing proportion of the labour force and the capital flow out of the operation of the market, and so may reduce the scope of capital accumulation. But this need not amount to a net reduction in private accumulation. It will not do so in so far as the state is thereby taking over unprofitable but necessary operations and/or is absorbing the cost of looking after the part of the labour-force which technological change has made redundant.

(4) The late capitalist economy is seen as consisting of three sectors: (a) the corporate oligopolistic sector, the firms which are largely able to set their own prices and thus can both invest heavily in technological advances and afford high wages, so that the labour force in this sector is relatively advantaged; (b) the remaining competitive private sector of smaller firms, unable to afford either, so that they can neither accumulate through technological investment nor provide secure wages (which leaves its labour force relatively disadvantaged); and (c) the public sector, the labour force (blue and white collar, and managerial) which has its compensation set by political rather than market bargaining, and which is consequently relatively advantaged: if 40 per cent of the whole labour force is employed in the public sector, so is roughly 40 per cent of the whole electorate.

(5) The combined effect of the increase in the role of the state, and the fragmentation of labour and capital into the three sectors, has been a considerable alteration in the classic capitalist relations of production and the relation of capital to state. The economy has become politicised, reverting in this respect to the pre-capitalist pattern. Yet the state now relies, for its own power, on maintaining capitalist accumulation. And since the state is now democratic it faces two new difficulties: it must reconcile the requirements of accumulation with the demands of the electorate, and it must extract an increasing revenue from capital to finance its support of capital and its response to the electorate.

Consideration of these difficulties has led outstanding contemporary Marxist scholars to develop theories of crisis. Habermas (1976) writes of the need for the accumulation-supporting state to legitimate itself to the electorate: this is the 'legitimation crisis'. O'Connor (1973) finds a contradiction between the state's need for expanded revenues and the maintenance of capital accumulation: this is 'the fiscal crisis of the state'.

'Crisis' suggests either the impending breakdown of capitalism or, if capitalism is to survive, the breakdown of democracy. Either of these is evidently now possible but, I shall suggest, not necessary. Certainly the late-capitalist state has a legitimation problem which the earlier-capitalist state did not have.

Earlier, when the market not the state was, and was seen to be, responsible for the economy and all the recurrently damaging effects of depressions, and when the market allocation of rewards was thought to be either fair or inevitable, the state had no great difficulty about legitimating its existence and the performance of its minimal functions. But now that the state takes, and is seen to take, heavy responsibility for the economy and its side-effects, the state has a serious legitimation problem. And as the state takes on more (and increasingly expensive) support functions, it runs into a series of fiscal crises which could lead to the breakdown either of democracy or of capitalism. The outcome of the legitimation and fiscal crises is indeterminate, since it depends not on objective forces alone but also on conscious political action.

I have touched on only some of the main points in the contemporary Marxist analyses of the state. But it is already evident that there are suggestive lines that should be followed up. The prospect of any measure of liberal-democratic values surviving, and the question of the possible means of assisting such survival, are more complex than indicated so far. In the following section I want to suggest some amendments and extensions of the Marxist analyses sketched above which may carry us a little way towards a more adequate view of the liberal-democratic problem.

WAYS AHEAD?

I wish now to argue, first, that as a result of the changes set out in paragraphs (3) and (4) above, the nature of the legitimation problem has already been altered; second, that the same changes have set up a new kind of pluralism, a pluralism in reverse; third, that the possibility of saving any liberal democracy depends on a change of consciousness, which depends on a public awareness of the real nature of the new pluralism; and, fourth, that this sets an agenda for a useful theory of the state in the late twentieth century.

First, the legitimation problem has changed. For the advanced capitalist state can, quite easily, legitimate itself to three very large sections of the public.

(i) The whole personnel of the public sector who owe their relative job security and relatively higher wages to the state. It is true that increasing numbers of public employees, both blue and white collar, have recently unionised (and some have become quite militant) (see Fairbrother's chapter in this volume) in order to protect their position against government retrenchment policies, from which they would otherwise be among the first to suffer. But they are still more secure and better paid than employees in the competitive private sector.

(ii) The recipients of welfare-state benefits. These also (especially those most in need) are beginning to organise – into welfare rights groups, tenants' organisations, and community coalitions of various sorts – to secure the benefits that are theirs on paper, or to demand further benefits. This makes them seem adversaries of the state. But they are still clients, and the more they win the more dependent they are.

This is not to say that they are inert dependents of the state. No one would doubt that the rise of the elaborate welfare state in all the Western democracies was due to the political strength of organised labour, whether expressed in trade-union pressure on established parties or in the rise to power of social-democratic and labour parties. But to say that it was their power which created the welfare state, and which requires its continuance, is not to deny that they, as well as the unorganised and redundant labour force, all of whom are its beneficiaries, are now dependent on the state for the continuance of their benefits. The relation is reciprocal: they created the welfare state, but now they are its creatures.

They still indeed have the potential of turning out a government which fails to give them what they have come to count on. But since the failure will have been due to the fiscal crisis of the state, this electoral action will not improve their position as long as they accept the need for private capital accumulation. So to the extent that they are kept by the state, they will keep the state.

(iii) The strongly organised part of the labour force in the private sector. They can see quite well that they owe their relatively advantaged position to the state's support and subsidising of their employers' operations. Consequently they can readily accept the legitimacy of the state which serves them.

Against this it may be argued that they, along with the employees of the public sector, are the first to bear the brunt of the now apparently endemic wage and price controls and that they have shown by their strenuous opposition to such devices no great affection for the state which imposes them. It must be granted that, to the extent that such controls are permanent, the state will have more difficulty in legitimating itself to them. But realistic trade unionists in the advantaged sectors can see that in spite of this, their gain from the continuing state support and subsidising of their employers outweighs their loss from what they hope will be temporary wage controls.

These three categories together make up a substantial majority of the electorate. As long as the state can find the money, it will have no great difficulty in legitimating itself to them.

But what about (iv), the holders and operators of capital? Is not the real crisis of legitimation, now, whether the state can legitimate itself to them, rather than to the electorate? To speak of this as a problem of legitimation is to stretch the concept of legitimation considerably beyond its original and its current Marxist usage. There, it has been a matter of the state, or of a virtual merger of state and corporate capital (which merger is seen as parasitic on the body politic), having to legitimate itself to the body politic by mystifying its true nature.

I do not mean to deny the reality of this position. To have seen the problem of legitimation in this way was a substantial step forward. But I suggest that the problem I have posed is also a problem of legitimation. For the state, whether or not it is seen as jointly parasitic with capital, is still sufficiently different from corporate capital to have to justify its activities to the latter. If the state cannot do so, capital can go on strike: it can make impossible, or severely reduce, the state's operation of all the mechanisms which now legitimate the state to (i), (ii) and (iii), and can thus accentuate the legitimation problem. This seems to me to be the central problem of the advanced capitalist state. But I think it not insoluble.

The state may be able to legitimate itself to (iv) in either or both of two ways: (a) by persuading particular capitals that the state's support of the interests of capital in general is more to their long-term benefit than would be the state's leaving particular capitals to their own devices. This persuasion is not impossible. It has succeeded at least once within recent memory: after sustained opposition to Roosevelt's New Deal, particular capitals finally admitted their benefit from it. A similar persuasion, at the higher level that would now be required, might succeed again.

(b) By making each of the particular capitals (and the particular segments of organised labour) conscious, if they are not already sufficiently conscious, that each of them, separately (not firm by firm, but industry by industry) owes whatever prosperity it has to the state's continuing subsidies and regulation. In all those industries in which the state has become an indispensable source of subsidies (which includes virtually the whole of the big corporate sector), the state has considerable leverage. It can hold them separately to ransom by threatening to reduce or withdraw its support. Pig producers, wheat producers, steel producers, motor car and tank producers, textile producers, armaments producers (and their unionised labour forces), and so across the whole of the organised private sector – all of them may be more or less *bought* by guaranteed prices, guaranteed purchases, tariff protection, government contracts, tax concessions, or other preferential treatment.

Second, this treating of particular capitals separately is the heart of the new pluralism of the late twentieth century. The new pluralism both is narrower than the received pluralist model, and embodies a reverse pluralism. Its difference from the presently received pluralist model is evident. It is not the give-and-take between the government and a myriad of voluntary associations and interest groups, which was supposed to give every alert citizen, ranged in one or more of those associations, a fair share of influence on government decisions. The received model was, indeed, never entirely realistic. For, while treating the democratic political process as something like a market (which it was), it abstracted too far from the capitalist nature of the society. It did not recognise that the requirements of capital accumulation set limits to, and set the direction of, the state's response to the plural pressures. And it was inclined to treat all pressures as eliciting from a neutral state responses proportional to their size. But at least the received pluralist theory was, for the era of full market competition, fairly accurate in one respect: the state acted upon pressures, but did not itself do much to interfere with those pressures.

This, I suggest, is what is now changing. The pressures which now operate effectively on the state are those of particular organised capitals (and particular segments of the organised labour force) each of which depends upon the state for the security and preferential treatment it enjoys. This is what has given the state such relative autonomy from capital in general as it now has. Pluralism, in this respect, has gone into reverse: the state now pluralises capital, by its ability to reduce or withhold favours to separate particular capitals.

There is indeed some measure also of what might be called reverse-reverse pluralism. Multinational corporations can play off particular nation states against each other for favours, because of their ability to move their capitals. And in federal nation-states, capitals can play off different levels of the state: that is of governments and bureaucracies. But the nation-state's ability to pluralise capital is still significant.

It is true that the whole range of interest groups celebrated by the received pluralist theories is still alive, and that it comprises not only corporate producers' interest groups and various levels and segments of organised labour, but also many others – professional groups, women, ethnic minorities, scientists, banks, universities, the performing arts, even publishers, not to mention all the ethical groups concerned with such issues as abortion, capital punishment, marijuana, and privacy. They all engage in lobbying. Their voices are heard. But are they heeded? It is a reasonable presumption that all of the demands of these other interest groups which would cost money will get increasingly short shrift as the fiscal difficulties of the state increase. The interest groups that will remain at all effective will be those organisations of particular capitals (and the parallel labour groups) who can show that the state's continuing support of them is essential to the maintenance of the capitalist economy. And these are the ones that the state can separately hold to ransom. The undoubted fact of increasing concentration of capitals in particular industries does not affect this: the greater the concentration in any one industry – steel, textiles, wheat, oil, cement, communications – the stronger their lobbies become, but the more they are dependent on the state's favours, and the more they can be held in line.

The new pluralism, then, is a two-way affair: the new element is the ability of the state to pluralise capital. The pressure groups that will continue to be effective are those corporate and labour groups over which the state has a stranglehold, if it wishes (or is financially compelled) to use it. And it is likely to have to do so increasingly.

There is a historical parallel to this state pluralisation of capital. The capitalist state from the beginning expropriated the communal life of earlier society, atomised it, absorbed the powers people had exercised together, and used those powers to rule the people in the interests of capital in general (cf. Wolfe, 1974, pp. 145ff.). In much the same way, in advanced capitalism, the state has to add a parallel operation: it absorbs from particular capitals some of their powers (i.e., some of their revenues, and hence of their ability to accumulate) and uses that power, still in the interests of capital in general, to make particular capitals dependent on the state.

It is probable that this reverse pluralism, and the relative autonomy of the state, will increase as the state gets more deeply involved in the management of the economy, the stabilisation of markets, and the subsidisation of production and prices. And the relative autonomy of the state from capital will also be aided as the public sector expands and moves more of the whole labour force and capital force from market determination to political determination.

There are, however, clear limits to any such increase in relative autonomy, *as long as the electorate continues to support, that is, not to reject, capitalism*. So long as capitalism is thus maintained, the state is still dependent on the accumulation of private capital. Even with the enlarged public sector, the state must still operate within the limits of maintaining capital accumulation in general, however skilful it may be in manoeuvring between particular capitals. The state in a capitalist society cannot be a neutral uncle: it must serve the interests of capital.

Third, what becomes of the relative autonomy? How it will be used depends, now, on whether, or how rapidly, the public becomes conscious of the real nature of advanced capitalism and is moved to political action to alter it. The relative autonomy of the state, or the reverse pluralism, will not be the spark of any such new consciousness. The spark can only be an awareness of the incompetence of advanced capitalism, and of the state which supports and tries to manage it. The relative autonomy of the state is merely the conduit in which the spark may ignite.

There are already some indications of such a new awareness emerging. There is a growing disbelief in technology as the cure-all, in view of the damaging uses to which managed capitalism puts it (e.g., pollution and ecological destruction). There is a growing restiveness within the labour force over its subordination to organisation and technology (wildcat strikes and shop-steward militancy). And, as the state runs into deepening fiscal difficulties, there is likely to be increasing restiveness among some of those sections of the public who were said earlier to be fairly easily persuaded of the legitimacy of the state as long as the money held out, that is, (i) workers in the public sector (as expenditures on hospitals, schools, etc., are cut back, so reducing or cancelling their relative job security), and (ii) some of the recipients of welfare-state benefits (e.g., the unemployed) as budgeting provision for them is reduced.

Such disenchantments with the capitalist state are important, for the maintenance of capitalism requires not only all the legal and material supports which the state now supplies, but also a general acceptance of the rightness of the system, or at least a belief that there is no acceptable alternative. In the earlier days of capitalism, *competition* was presented as 'the natural system of liberty', beneficial to all. In advanced capitalism, *organisation* takes the place of competition as the universal benefactor: the 'post-industrial', technological, managed society is presented as the solution to all problems and contradictions (Mandel, 1975, p. 501). In the measure that this belief in organisation crumbles, there opens up a possibility that political action can put human purposes above capital purposes.

This is indeed no more than a possibility. The belief, reinforced as it is by the ubiquitous presence of the corporate sector in our channels of political socialisation, may not crumble. And the inherent tendency of the Western party system to obfuscate basic issues (cf. Macpherson, 1977, pp. 64–9) works to prevent a public consciousness of the real nature of the political economy of capitalism. But there is at least the possibility that reality will break through.

Fourth, it is here that a realistic and normative theory of the state can contribute, by delineating first the necessary, and necessarily changing, relation of the state to capitalist society and second, the limits of the possible relation of the capitalist society and state to essential human needs and capacities. The contemporary Marxist theorists are doing a good job on the first of these, but in most cases to the relative neglect of the second. To reinstate the tradition of grand theories of the state, further work on the second is now needed.

The theory of the state does have to come back effectively in the measure that it has probed political economy. It also needs more empirical and theoretical work on human needs, wants and capacities (cf. Fitzgerald, 1977) and a full reassessment of the behaviouralists' findings about the present processes of political socialisation from childhood through adulthood (Wolfe, 1977).

A euphoric vision is that all this can be done co-operatively, or in friendly rivalry, by the adherents of my categories (ii) and (iii). This is not impossible, for some of the contemporary Marxist scholars whom I have placed in category (ii) have been led by their analyses to doubt the present relevance of the classical Marxian revolutionary prescription, adherence to which was the main thing that separated category (iii) from (ii). A still more euphoric, even utopian, vision is the coinciding of a merger of (ii) and (iii) with a significant shift of theorists from (i) to (ii). If that were to happen, the political-theory profession could be said to have entered the late twentieth century.

NOTES

This chapter is reprinted with the permission of *Archives européennes de sociologie*, 18 (1977), 223–44.

1. E.g., general contributors to three collections: McCoy and Playford (1971); Connolly (1969); Kariel (1970).
2. I would not claim that this classification is exhaustive. One might, for instance, make a separate category of those who take a philosophical anarchist position, who need at least a theory of the negative relation of the state to essential human purposes: they need a theory of the state in order to abolish the theory of the state. Nor would I claim that the lines between the three classes are entirely clear and sharp, but I think the classification makes some sense in the context of my subject.

REFERENCES

Connolly, W., 1969. *The Bias of Pluralism*. New York, Atherton Press

Fitzgerald, R., ed., 1977. *Human Needs and Politics*. New York, Pergamon

Habermas, J., 1976. *Legitimation Crisis*. Boston, Beacon

Kariel, H., ed., 1970. *Frontiers of Democratic Theory*. New York, Random Associates

Lindberg, L. N. *et al.*, eds., 1975. *Stress and Contradiction in Modern Capitalism: Public Policy and the Theory of the State*. Lexington, Mass., Lexington Books

McCoy, C. and J. Playford, 1971. *Apolitical Politics*. New York, Crowell

MacIver, R. M., 1926. *The Modern State*. London, Oxford University Press

MacKenzie, W. J. M., 1975. *Power, Violence and Decision*, London, Peregrine Books

Macpherson, C. B., 1970. 'Bow and arrow power', *The Nation*, 19 January
    1977. *The Life and Times of Liberal Democracy*. Oxford, Oxford University Press

Mandel, E., 1975. *Late Capitalism*. London, New Left Books

Miliband, R., 1969. *The State in Capitalist Society*. London, Weidenfeld and Nicolson

Nozick, R., 1974. *Anarchy, State and Utopia*. New York, Basic Books

O'Connor, J., 1973. *The Fiscal Crisis of the State*. New York, St Martin's Press

Poulantzas, N., 1968. *Pouvoir politique et classes sociales*. Paris, Masp.

Rawls, J., 1971. *A Theory of Justice*. Cambridge, Mass., Belknap Press, Harvard University Press

Wolfe, A., 1974. 'New directions in the Marxist theory of politics', *Politics and Society*, 4, no. 2,
    Winter 1974: 131–59
    1977. *The Limits of Legitimacy*. Boston, Beacon

3

The fall and rise of the state
in international politics

STEVE SMITH

The other chapters in this book are concerned with the nature of the capitalist state in its internal setting: this chapter has a rather different concern, as its focus is on the character of the capitalist state in its external setting.[1] Two major differences result from this shift of focus: first a concern with the external face of the state introduces an awareness of the theoretical limitations of any approach that treats states as closed units; and, secondly, it calls into question the utility of treating capitalist states as a class of phenomena with regard to international behaviour. Although at first sight this aim may seem somewhat heretical in a collection of essays on the topic of the capitalist state, the claim underlying this chapter is that there is one arena, the international one, in which treating capitalist states as primarily *capitalist* may distort and colour our analysis. My point is that we are unable to explain major areas of the behaviour of capitalist states if we attempt such explanations on the basis that their being capitalist is of central theoretical importance. This chapter will argue that in significant areas of their international behaviour capitalist states behave as do all states; that the causes of their behaviour, whilst evidently including some features that are derived from their capitalist nature, are predominantly to be found in the structure and processes of international and not domestic society. In short, the very existence of the structure of international society poses significant problems for any approach based on the differences between types of state.

Before turning to elucidate that claim, I want to be quite clear as to what is not being advanced here. It is neither being argued that there exists a neat division between the internal and the external settings of state, nor that there is an uncomplicated division between economics and politics; indeed both of these positions will be attacked in the analysis that follows. I do not wish to accept the claim of many international relations theorists with regards to the potency of a billiard-ball model, one in which the state operates to allow economic policy to be formed internally whereas foreign policy is formed externally. This position is clearly inadequate since much internal economic policy is crucially affected by external events and many decisions over whether to go to war are equally importantly affected by internal economic and political factors. What I do wish to claim, though, is that the focal point of the majority of contributions to this volume sees the state as an analytical ceiling, and, accordingly, is preoccupied with the types of states that exist and with the ways in which these different types of states affect human potentiality and development. But, just as a focus brings certain features more clearly into view so does it make other factors rather fuzzy, and my concern is with the limitations of a focus on the state as an analytical ceiling and with the aspects of state behaviour made more explicable by a focus on the state as an analytical floor. In this way, states are units of a society, and it is the fact that they are units that matters more than their internal structures. Now, as will become clear, the range of behaviour covered by this analytical focus is nowhere near as extensive as implied by the billiard-ball theorists, but it is more significant than economic determinist theories would suggest. In this way, this chapter is premised on the notion that the discussion of capitalist states' external behaviour indicates the fundamental deficiencies of both billiard-ball realist international theory and economic determinist political theory and the analysis that follows will hopefully be equally heretical to both. I will now turn to say a few words about the theoretical implication of an analytical focus on the state as a ceiling, then turn to outline the ways in which international theory has discussed the state as an analytical floor, focussing on the challenges to the predominant view of the state as the central unit in international society.

Virtually all discussions of the capitalist state, or indeed of any other type of state, tend to construct theories by treating (analytically at least) the state as *an* entity, that is, they make assumptions as to the importance of sovereignty for the ability of states effectively to allocate resources and control populations within their territory. If a state is unable to meet these requirements we talk of it being in a situation of civil war. The point is that the kinds of assumptions that are commonly made, whether for empirical/institutional, normative, or explanatory analysis, treat the state as an essentially closed unit. Despite Marxists' concerns over the possibility of socialism in one country, or liberals' propositions as to the need for the universalisation of democracy, most discussions of the state treat influences from the outside as exogenous. Of course, the existence of an environment external to the state is recognised, but this is secondary to a focus on the state in its domestic setting. After all, it is the highest body that political action in a given territory can alter; naturally, therefore, it appears to be *the unit* for analysing political behaviour. This is reinforced by the characteristics of law-making (in which the phenomenon of sovereignty is crucial), and the rival claims of institutions and groups within societies. Finally, the state is the focus of political activity within a country. It has, historically, been able to claim the loyalty and allegiance of the vast majority of the population; it is the target of political activity; and politicians in power both justify their actions in terms of the state and see it as the highest political structure relevant to their society. The state is sovereign, and thus most discussions of it concern the proper demarcation of that sovereignty with regard to other structures and groups in society. Despite the fact, then, that precisely what the state consists of is essentially controversial – a major issue in this volume – most political analysis treats it as the fundamental unit of political life.

Yet, just as sovereignty provides good reason for treating the state as the unit of political life and a rationale for analysing political behaviour within the state, so does the concept illustrate very clearly the second, external, face of the state. Sovereignty may well mean that the state has ultimate authority over a given territory and population, but it also means that it is the state that represents this territory and population externally. In fact, in terms of international law, it means that only the state can legitimately act on behalf of the domestic society. Again, although precisely what the state is in international law constitutes a major area of debate, it is nevertheless clear that the fact that states, of whatever political and economic complexion, exist in some kind of system or international society offers a potentially very important alternative (and limiting?) perspective on any analysis of the state from within or below. On the one hand, the external environments of states will, in many ways, influence political behaviour within the states as a result of military, political and economic interactions. Although it has ramifications for any notion of the state, this is essentially an empirical issue. On the other hand, and in my view far more challenging, is the theoretical implication that whereas an analysis of politics that operates within national boundaries will tend towards portraying states as different (according to level of economic development, political structure, ideology, racial or religious factors etc.), much of the discussion of the role of the state internationally treats states as essentially similar and deems internal factors to be essentially unimportant in determining external behaviour. The point is that it is the very features that are deemed central to much normative or institutional political analysis that are deemed secondary to international political analysis. For these two reasons, the empirical and the theoretical, the international face of the state constitutes the setting within which any discussion of the capitalist state must take place and it is to the nature of that discussion to which we now turn.

The history of international relations theory has been marked by many debates over methodology, focus of study, the role of economic factors, and so on, but one feature of the subject has remained constant – the central role of the state. For over three centuries, from the foundation of the states-system after the Treaty of Westphalia in 1648, there was little dispute in the literature of the subject that the key unit of international society was the state. Just as political theory concentrated on the relationship between individuals and the state, so international theory concerned the linkage between states and the states-system. Indeed, the domestic analogy became a very powerful one in the analysis of international relations: states were like individuals in the state of nature. As Hedley Bull has noted, there were three main versions of this argument: 'the Hobbesian or realist tradition, which views international politics as a state of war; the Kantian or universalist tradition, which sees at work in international politics a potential community of mankind; and the Grotian or internationalist tradition, which views international politics as taking place within an international society' (Bull, 1977, p. 24). Broadly speaking, these three versions of the domestic analogy dominated discussion about international relations for three centuries (for more recent writings from this school of thought see Butterfield and Wight (1966), Donelan (1978), Linklater (1982) and Mayall (1982)). The major area of debate concerned the distinction between an international (usually Hobbesian) system and an international society, with the former being marked by the continual threat of war, and the latter stressing the role of law, agreements, understandings and rules in determining international relations. To a significant extent, then, this discourse became intertwined with political theory, given the central role of the domestic analogy and the dispute over the importance of societal factors (see Bull, 1977, pp. 53–7).

Once international relations became established as a separate discipline following the First World War, the dominant mode of explaining world politics moved towards an explicitly normative basis, known by its opponents as idealism. The most common perception of the causes of the First World War was that it had occurred largely by accident and therefore the task of studying international relations was to prevent such wars from occurring again. For a twenty-year period, this view of the subject was predominant; it stressed the role of international law, the importance of mediation, and, critically, the peace-enhancing characteristics of democracy. Certain kinds of states, therefore, were inherently peace-enhancing, since in democracies it was possible for public opinion to prevent governments going to war either for the self-interest of certain powerful groups in society or because of misunderstandings. The role of international mediation and international law was twofold: to give governments time to assess accurately the motives of others, and to appeal to public opinion directly, over the heads of government. Underlying this view of international relations was a liberal ethic, that war was the result of either misunderstanding or self-interested 'sinister' interest groups. However, this view of world politics suffered during the 1930s when the activities of Japan in Manchuria, Italy in Abyssinia and, above all, Nazi Germany, refocused attention on the essentially Hobbesian notion of the role of the system in determining the likelihood of war. Idealism came under considerable attack, most notably in E. H. Carr's *The Twenty Years' Crisis*

(Carr, 1939). The mode of thinking reverted to a more systems-based perspective, one most clearly expressed in the work of Hans Morgenthau (1948), and known as realism.

For the realists the key to understanding international relations was to accept that human beings were essentially and irredeemably selfish. This selfishness was innate, and explained both the nature of international relations, as power politics, and the possible ways of preventing war, the balance of power. According to this view, understanding international relations meant understanding how human nature resulted in the formation of states, and how this translated, in the absence of world government, into an international system in which states acted according to national interests defined in terms of power (see Smith, 1983, for a discussion of this viewpoint). States were back on centre stage, and were caught up in an immutable set of power relations. In this set of relations, it was less important to know the political complexion of the states concerned than to assess their national interest, and this could only be ascertained by comprehending the specific nature of international power politics. Hence, if the balance-of-power mechanism were to operate, it was essential for states, whatever their ideology or political structure, to be willing to shift alliances: the capitalist state was essentially a state, like any other, and its foreign policy was affected less by its ideology, although this would serve as a legitimising or justificatory device, than by a rational assessment of its national interests. Of course ideology would be important in determining these national interests, but for Morgenthau such a factor was at best secondary to system constraints, and at worst a possible impediment to the smooth working of the balance-of-power system.

Such a representation of the realists' position is an oversimplification: clearly Morgenthau did not believe that everything was predetermined, as the breakdown of the balance-of-power mechanism in 1939 illustrated, but in essence realism pointed to the impact of international structure as being of critical importance. To ignore the requirements of the balance-of-power system for reasons of ideology was to court disaster. This is because there are two main features of the international system that no state can alter, and which fundamentally affect the international behaviour of states: these are the anarchical structure of international society and its polar configuration. International anarchy refers to the absence of certain features that accompany domestic society, namely government and enforceable law – states have to be judges in their own cause, and there is no body above the state to prevent them from acting as they wish. The only restraint on their actions is the reaction of other states, the other constituent units of international society (although this is precisely the point of departure in discussions of the role of morality, rules and agreements). States are sovereign units. Polarity refers to the number of great powers in the international system. Although there is obvious room for debate over precisely what constitutes a great power, it is evident that in the military dimension the number of such powers will affect both the level and type of war, and the patterns of behaviour in the international system. The most clear-cut distinction is between a multipolar system, where there are five or more great powers, and a bipolar system, in which two states are dominant. In the former, there is regular great-power war precisely to preserve the balance of power; in the latter there is very little *direct* superpower conflict, with the rest of the states in the international system being drawn into competing blocs. No state in the system can alter these factors, and states are the only units that possess the key characteristic of sovereignty. Anarchy imposes the security dilemma on all states, so that each state has, in the final analysis, to ensure its own security, thereby possibly increasing the insecurity of other states. Polarity imposes certain behavioural norms on states, so that whereas, for example, in a multipolar system the mechanism that keeps the system stable, the balance of power, requires regular shifts in alliance structures, in bipolarity the legitimising function of ideology prevents such shifts and 'peace' is kept by the presence of constant tension (see Kaplan, 1957; Waltz, 1964 and Waltz, 1979).

The consequence of seeing states as more homogeneous in their international behaviour than would be implied by discussions about the internal political or economic structures of states is that we are concerned with their role as states and not as certain kinds of states. Whilst the strict determinism inherent in systems models does face serious epistemological and ontological problems, this second face of the state, as a constituent unit in international society, does have to be taken into account in explaining the behaviour of any type of state. By focussing on one feature of a state, its domestic economic/political composition, we may ignore the crucial impact of its existence as a state in a wider structural setting. It must be remembered, however, that this conclusion results primarily from treating one characteristic of international relations as both dominant and defining, namely the phenomenon of war. For three centuries theories about international politics focussed on war as the major difference between domestic and international society, and the view of the importance of states *as states* resulted from this focus. This viewpoint was challenged by what we may call economic reductionism, which argued that it was misleading to focus on war as the defining and central feature of international relations. Economic factors were both central and at the root of most wars, and to understand war therefore required a discussion not of the international system but of the domestic economic structure. The problem with this viewpoint was that whilst economic factors were clearly involved in foreign policy they were somewhat removed from the mainstream of state practices. This may well be because of the specific nature of the state at that time (and this argument was at its height in the late nineteenth and early twentieth centuries), but it did appear insufficient as an explanation at a time when ideology, religion and history all seemed to offer alternative reasons for why wars occurred. This viewpoint was most explicitly expressed in the writings of Marx, Engels and especially Lenin, on imperialism, and here, of course, is a very obvious link with the notion of capitalist states behaving in a certain way. For Marx, Engels and Lenin war was to be explained by the economic structure of states. Yet imperialist theories suffered from two main weaknesses. The first was that economic factors were only one cause of war. Imperialism might well cause some wars, but it could not explain all wars, and certainly not those of pre-capitalist times. Although it can be argued that wars have economic roots, this does seem insufficient to explain the occurrence of war as a phenomenon throughout history. A far more powerful explanation comes from the realisation that anarchy and polarity induce processes that will lead to war in a world divided into separate states; some will be economic, but others will be for religious, or other reasons, and many will be fought precisely because of the impact of the security dilemma and the need to maintain the balance of power. The second weakness arose out of Marx's prescription for international peace, which was the abolition of capitalism. As Berki (1971) and Waltz (1959) have argued, simply altering the domestic structure of states does not transcend the states-system. Even if communism could occur as a world-wide transformation, the units of international society would still be states and would still face a world of finite resources. Indeed, given Marx's materialism, there are very good reasons to expect even a world of communist states to find themselves at war, since each would define the requirements of their economy and society according to their stage of economic development. If the answer to this is that abolishing capitalism would lead to the abolition of the state then there is the problem of how to preserve peace until such time as the state can be altered so as not to be an oppressive and coercive entity; the only way out of this dilemma would be to institute some form of world government, yet this would succeed in abolishing war in name only, if we mean by war organised violence between political units. In fact the way in which capitalism has been transcended reinforces this problem, in that different regimes will have different definitions of communism and thus we are left with communist *states*, which behave in their international relationships much like any other. Indeed the evidence suggests that no one type of state is any more 'peacelike' than any other; this suggests that war is to be explained not by what happens within states but by what happens between them as members of an international states-system. Recent events have indicated that the division of the world into states leads to one characteristic, nationalism, that seems to transcend particular ideologies. Just as the First World War surprised many socialists, as individuals soon became swept up in a tide of nationalism, so did the Falklands/Malvinas conflict remind us of how potent, and usually underestimated, a force nationalism is. And, of course, nationalism arises out of the division of the world into states. In short, war will not be transcended until the structure of international society is changed, and merely making all states of one type will not achieve this. This is a fundamental challenge to those who seek to explain the international behaviour of capitalist states in terms of their being capitalist. Indeed, it remains the case that there is no serious class *theory* of international politics; there are a number of very important works on international political economy, and these are of considerable use in explaining the economic dimensions of state behaviour, but they have been rather unsuccessful in moving to an explanation of military behaviour. Again, this is not to fall into the simplistic notion that economic and political issues are separate and unrelated; rather, it is to argue that class theories have been poor at explaining military features of international relations, especially war involvement and alliance formation.

For these reasons, the view of international relations as primarily an international states-system with war being explicable in terms of the structures and processes inherent in that system, dominated the study of the subject for about three centuries. The most developed form of this argument, realism, dominated the discipline for twenty years after the Second World War, and was a view that had much in common with the prevailing views of statesmen and stateswomen after the events of 1939. Just as idealism sought to prevent a recurrence of the First World War, so did realism address itself to preventing the occurrence of another war like the Second World War, and for this to be successful the structural requirements of the balance of power could not be subordinated to demands of ideology or morality. In turn, however, realism came under attack following the widespread adoption of social-science or behaviouralist methods into the study of politics. The main thrust of this attack was that realism relied for its theoretical power on an unobservable, and contentious, view of human nature, the view that individuals were selfish. If this was removed then the edifice of realism fell with it. Furthermore the three key terms of the realist view, power, national interest and the balance of power, were themselves open to major questions of definition. Accordingly, a new wave of behavioural analysis began to dominate the discipline. Despite the fact that this dispute led to acrimonious debates within the subject-area of international relations, debates that are still in progress, what is striking is that certain key assumptions were nevertheless shared by behaviouralists and realists alike, and these assumptions are of critical importance for any discussion of the role of the state. As John Vasquez has argued, despite the considerable superficial differences between the traditional analysis of international relations represented by realism, and the quantitative analysis of the behaviouralists, three assumptions were shared (Vasquez, 1979, p. 211). These were: (a) that nation-states are the dominant actors in international relations; (b) that there is a sharp distinction between domestic politics and international politics; and (c) that international relations is above all a struggle for power and peace, research on other topics is trivial (see also Vasquez, 1983).

Together these three assumptions constituted what can be termed the state-centric paradigm of international relations, a paradigm that encompassed all the major debates in the discipline, be they between Grotians and Hobbesians, between idealists and realists, or between realists and behaviouralists. The first assumption implies that states are central, and that other organisations, such as multinational companies, are of little importance. The second assumption implies that domestic political activities have very little impact on the international behaviour of states; the domestic face is far less important than its international location in an inflexible set of power-relations. Thus, whatever the political or economic structures, these play little role in determining foreign policy in the central areas of the prevention of or involvement in war. Foreign policy, according to this assumption, is made in fairly similar ways by a small group of people divorced from the domestic political scene in all types of societies. Whatever the decoration, the reality is elite dominance and an essentially bipartisan foreign policy. Despite the seeming impact of electoral politics and public opinion in liberal-democratic states, this assumption implies that of much greater importance are the structural givens of anarchy and polarity, which make nationalism such a potent, and manageable, force. The fact that states are in this sense separate units means that critical issues of war and peace can be presented in a manner that represents the interests of those within a society as being common interests. The third assumption means that there is a hierarchy of interests for any state, such that, in this anthropomorphic sense, we can talk of central and peripheral interests, and of a distinction between 'high' (military/political) and 'low' (economic/social) politics.

What this does is to concentrate attention on the military dimension of international relations, thereby focussing on military cleavages in international society such as the East–West split. The three assumptions together imply that any discussion of the capitalist state will miss the wood for the trees if it concentrates upon the fact that it is a capitalist state in explaining its international behaviour; it is far more fruitful to concentrate on the fact that it is a state, that its foreign policy will be little affected by domestic factors, and that the key issues are those of the struggle for power and possible involvement in war. For fairly obvious reasons this became known as the 'billiard-ball' view of international relations: states were essentially black-boxes, and hence to understand their behaviour did not require one to examine what happened within them.

That this perspective suffers from considerable problems is less important than the fact that it dominated the understanding of international relations for three centuries. Its limitations were only really exposed in the 1970s despite two earlier challenges to it in the 1950s and 1960s. The first challenge to this state-centric view of international relations resulted from the development of nuclear weapons, and was most clearly expressed by John Herz (1976a). In an article entitled 'The rise and demise of the territorial state', he argued that four trends were at work that together would lead to the demise of the state as the key unit of international society, as they would remove the 'strongest guarantee of its independent co-existence . . . its hard shell – that is, its defensibility in case of war' (1976a, p. 114). These were the possibility of economic blockade, ideological political penetration by psychological warfare, air warfare, and nuclear warfare. Of these he considered the last to be most important. The territorial state was by the mid 1950s open to economic blockade precisely because its economic development made it dependent on trade; its population was susceptible to the influence of views from other states following the rise of communications technology; it could no longer protect its citizens from direct assault by aircraft; and, crucially, nuclear weapons could not be prevented from reaching their targets. The only solution to this situation, he argued, was world government, and even this was impractical. The nation-state was obsolete, yet its very existence prevented the development of attitudes and perspectives that could lead to a way out of the dilemma. The period when the state was obsolete yet still existed was fraught with dangers, as each superpower attempted to ensure their security by seeking to eliminate the other. This pronouncement of the end of the state was very soon proven to be premature, although it was a view shared by many who were concerned at the effects of the discovery of nuclear fission and nuclear fusion. A few years later, in 1968, Herz reviewed his predictions (1976b) and accepted that the trend was not so much towards the decline of the state but towards its renewal. As empires had been dissolved, as nationalism was being renewed as a potent force in international relations, and as nuclear weapons became weapons not of war-fighting but of war-deterrence, then the state was still going to be the dominant unit in international society. In short, Herz, and others, failed to appreciate that nuclear weapons could serve the function of preventing war, and in this regard these weapons solidified the role of the nation-state by enhancing its ability to defend its territory and population.

If nuclear weapons provided a very popular military challenge to the survival of the nation-state, economic factors were cited by many authors as representing or entailing the decline of the state in another way; this was by the process of integration. During the 1950s the development of the European Coal and Steel Community, Euratom, and the European Economic Community led many writers to forecast the decline of the state as the result of the creation of supranational organisations above the state. Although this had long been forecast in the writings of federalists and functionalists (see Lieber, 1972, pp. 39–42; Mitrany, 1943), developments in Europe gave rise to a new school of thought, neo-functionalism (Haas, 1958; Haas, 1964; Lindberg 1963; Lindberg and Scheingold, 1971), which argued that there was a process at work that would ensure that economic integration would 'spill over' into political integration. Whereas the functionalists had seen the state being transcended by the gradual technicalisation of political tasks through universal international organisations, and this would require states not to notice or not to object as their sovereignty was diminished, neo-functionalism argued that the success of economic integration in one sphere would lead politicians to want further economic integration until such time as all the various economic institutions required a political organisation to co-ordinate their activities. There was an inexorable logic to this process, so that the end result would be the transcendence of the nation-state, and events in Europe in the 1950s seemed to support this argument. Accordingly, it was very common to hear talk of the eventual disappearance of the state, as economic integration led to political integration in region after region. What, of course, had been underestimated was the importance of sovereignty, as was so clearly witnessed by the French walk-out from the European communities in 1965 as a protest against the proposed abolition of the veto in the Council of Ministers. Although the founding treaties had called for a movement towards both majority voting and supranational power vested in the Commission, this was strongly resisted by the French, and, after their accession, by the British. In summary, the integration view of the decline of the nation-state reflected an optimism in the 1950s that was dashed in the 1960s and 1970s. Rather than being ways of transcending the nation-state, the European communities have become ways of enhancing its sovereignty.

At the end of the 1960s the subject of international relations was one in which, despite all the debates and disputes, the state was seen as the key actor. It, and only it, possessed sovereignty; it, and only it, could command the loyalty of its population; and it, and only it, was involved in the key concern of international relations, war. Accordingly, economic issues were peripheral to national interest, and the central dispute after the Second World War was the East–West conflict. Furthermore, in explaining the processes of Cold War or international crises, the structure of the international political system was far more important than domestic political factors. The theoretical challenges to the dominance of the state all failed, because they both underestimated the impact of sovereignty and nationalism and could not explain major aspects of international relations. This theoretical consensus involved an ethnocentric view of the world, one which very evidently represented certain values as to what were the key issues, but it was a view that fitted well with the preoccupations of decision-makers and politicians alike. In this way, capitalist states were first and foremost states, whose behaviour in the important areas of world politics was to be explained by the age-old methods of power politics.

The irony is that this was just at the time when ideology seemed to be more important than ever before, in that the Cold War was said to be about the clash of two ideologies. In fact many of those who wrote on international relations portrayed world politics in just this way, but the underlying logic of their position was in reality one that started from the bipolar split in the world and then explained how ideology was used to justify that split. This is, of course, rather a paradox but it has to be noted that the Cold War was most powerfully explained by those who saw it as one example of what happens in *a* bipolar world, whatever the ideologies of the states concerned. Much popular writing did see it as an ideological split, but the most insightful analyses of it saw it as one more historical example of a general phenomenon (see Kaplan, 1957; Waltz, 1979). In this light, the Cold War was not something new, an ideological struggle, but was one type of international system, to be explained by the same theories that had explained other types of international system from the formation of the states-system. Thus, had the world in 1945 seen another set of two bipolar powers (for example, Britain and the United States or China and the Soviet Union) then, whereas ideological theories would have had severe problems in explaining any ensuing Cold War, systems theories would have expected precisely the same processes to occur as did occur from 1945 onwards (albeit couched in different ideological terms). To those who see international politics determined by ideology this seems counter-intuitive; to those who see international politics determined by the structure of the system this is to be expected. To reiterate a point made earlier, it must be remembered that ideology was seen as being unimportant for explaining international relations for almost three centuries; the balance-of-power system required governments to be willing to switch alliances so as to prevent any one power or group of powers dominating the system, and history is littered with examples of them doing just this in contrast to what would be expected if one took ideology as a determinant.

However, in the 1970s a series of events occurred that fundamentally challenged this view of the behaviour of states in international society. Whilst challenges before had come and gone, in the 1970s something seemed to have changed in a very important way. This change was such as to lead many writers to talk of the end of the state as a dominant unit in world society, and, in fact, many today argue that this has taken place. The change was the increasing role of economic factors in the practice of international relations. For about a ten-year period the traditional focus of international relations, military issues, was shifted to the background as decision-makers and publics alike became concerned with international economic issues. Even those military issues that did arise seemed to indicate that states were no longer dominant in this issue-area. On the economic front there were six main elements of the increased potency of that issue-area. The first was represented most explicitly by the oil crisis of 1973, when the fourfold increase in the price of oil imposed by OPEC states made it clear that economic power could be used politically; it also highlighted the dependence of certain Western economies on oil as an energy source. Whilst it is true to say that oil had been used in a similar way in the past, what was different this time was that the focus of power had altered so that the suppliers were in the more powerful position. The second was the decline of the US-led boom in the international economy in the 1970s, a decline which resulted in considerable changes in the international finance and trading systems. As recession deepened during the 1970s one result was for governments to become increasingly preoccupied with protectionist measures. Again, although recession was not a new phenomenon, the very interdependence in the world economy created in the post Second World War period made its effects more sharply felt, and the institutional structures built to manage growth and trade proved incapable of dealing as effectively with recession. A third element was the increasing role of multinational companies (MNCs) which seemed to have more power than many states in the system (see Vernon, 1971; Barnett and Muller, 1974). The rise of MNCs was clearly linked to the post Second World War boom in the international economy and, as empires disintegrated, they were seen as the new form of imperialism. Not only this but the fact that the major MNCs were US-based led to the very obvious use of them for political purposes, most controversially in Allende's Chile. A fourth factor was the global eco-crisis, reflected in the widespread concern over the possible exhaustion of many minerals and the complications of this for life on earth (see Falk, 1971). This was associated with a rising public concern over the environment and the effects of pollution on the quality of life. Fifth, and underlying and reinforcing the above, were the effects of economic interdependence. As the post Second World War boom led to increasing contact between economies in the form of percentage of gross national product (GNP) represented by foreign trade, the economy of one industrialised country became dependent on economic activity in other countries to a greater extent than ever before. This meant that governments could no longer ignore economic issues or leave them to the market, since citizens' demands for welfare and standard of living provisions involved decisions over economic issues taken in other countries or in international forums. As noted previously, recession exacerbated this trend and governments, which were seen as responsible for the level of economic prosperity in a country, increasingly had to become involved in foreign economic policy. Not only this, but foreign economic policy became politicised and was therefore involved in internal political debate to a greater extent than ever before. Finally, there was the growth of a Third World demand for a New International Economic Order (NIEO) as many newly emergent states called for a radical redistribution of world resources. Attention thus focussed increasingly not on the East–West split but on the North–South split.

Yet these economic factors were not sufficient on their own to alter the traditional agenda of international politics. A set of political changes was also taking place. The most important of these was the blossoming of *détente*; to many writing in the early to mid 1970s it looked as if the process of *détente* represented a once-and-for-all transformation in the nature of US–Soviet relations from a relationship of competition to one of co-operation. The most widely accepted reason for this was the effect of the development of parity in their nuclear arsenals in the late 1960s and early 1970s. With ballistic missile defence limited under the 1972 Anti-Ballistic Missile Treaty to almost a token role, the horrendous effects of nuclear weapons seemed to imply that these weapons could not be used: the two superpowers were now impotent giants. *Détente* was the result of the US and the Soviet Union having to live together and the implication of this, for many theorists, was that the military cleavage in international politics was in decline. In fact, with the benefit of hindsight it seems that the combination of this and the shocks represented by the decline of US international economic hegemony was precisely what led so many (especially US) scholars to forecast the decline of the state as a key unit in international society. Two other political events are worth noting: the first was that those political conflicts that occurred during the 1970s (Vietnam, the Middle East, Angola, Rhodesia/Zimbabwe) could not be understood simply by looking at state behaviour, since in each case at least one of the main parties to the dispute was not a state. The second was that the state seemed to be under attack internally as ethnic groups or sub-national groups demanded independence. Although, of course, each wanted to create their own state, the impression was that the state was no longer as legitimate as had conventionally been assumed. Taken together, these factors indicated that the state was under attack from above and below.

By the mid 1970s it was common to read analyses of international politics that spoke of the demise of the state as the result of these economic and political developments (see Brown, 1974). The old agenda of international politics had altered in that economic factors were now of more importance than hitherto, states did not seem to be the dominant actors in many, if not most, political and economic issue-areas, and *détente* seemed to have reduced the impact of the main military cleavage in the international system. Of the resulting attempts to explain this new role of the state, a role which, of course, has massive implications for capitalist states in view of the potency of economic issues, three are specially important. The most popular was that known as transnationalism, a view that argued that states were simply one unit in international society and over many issues they would not be the dominant one. This was first expressed in the book edited by Keohane and Nye in 1972, *Transnational Relations and World Politics*, in which they forcefully argued that transnational organisations, especially MNCs and revolutionary groups, could fundamentally reduce the ability of states to exercise their sovereignty;

the behavioural attribute of autonomy should therefore replace the legal attribute of sovereignty in defining the main actors in international relations. One empirical study went so far as to claim that states only accounted for some 44 per cent of international behaviour (Mansbach, Ferguson and Lampert, 1976). For proponents of transnationalism, the state-centric view was outmoded, and the most useful way of understanding international relations was to focus on issues and then see which actors were dominant (see Mansbach and Vasquez, 1981; Maghroori and Ramberg, 1982).

The second theoretical response came in the literature on interdependence (see Keohane and Nye, 1977; Cooper, 1968; Scott, 1982; Reynolds, 1979; Reynolds and McKinlay, 1979). It was argued that the rise in interdependence between national economies essentially transformed international relations because states were now both sensitive and vulnerable to events in other economies. This created problems that states could not control and states had, therefore, to spend increasing amounts of time managing interdependence; foreign policy was far more than ever before economic in character. Although some argued that interdependence was actually lower than it had been before the First World War (Waltz, 1970; Waltz, 1979, pp. 129–60), the consensus was that this was a very recent (post-1965) phenomenon, one which *was* a once-and-for-all change and one that affected the content and the context of foreign policy. As Keohane and Nye argued in the most influential of these studies (Keohane and Nye, 1977) the result of these changes was a world composed of 'complex regimes', in which governments had to coexist with non-state actors, and which represented a mix of authority structures and a range of geographical and functional variations (see also Krasner, 1982). This has obvious implications for capitalist as opposed to other types of states.

The third response was in the work of modernisation (see Morse, 1970, 1972, 1976). According to this view the process of modernisation, especially industrial development, undermines the stability upon which international politics previously relied. As Morse comments, modernisation challenges the traditional view which

assumes that the dynamics of international politics have been relatively fixed since the inception of the modern state system. Accordingly, a theory . . . applicable to Europe in the seventeenth century would be appropriate for understanding global politics today. Different actors may have appeared . . . new issues may have become the central concerns of diplomacy, but . . . a set of basic 'rules of the game' has been imposed upon international politics and can be derived from the prevailing conditions of the international system. (1976, p. xv)

Modernisation, he argues, has transformed world politics so much that this traditional view is obsolete. Foreign policy in a modernised world focusses on what was traditionally regarded as 'low politics' and increasingly concentrates

on managing, often by the use of crises, the effects of economic interdependence. This breaks down the distinction between international and
domestic politics, and reduces the importance of military factors in the
international hierarchy of values.

These three theoretical challenges to the traditional view of international
relations, taken together, offer a very different view of the role of the capitalist
state. As foreign policy becomes more economic in content, as the domestic
polity merges with the international polity, and as non-state actors become
dominant in certain issue-areas, the capitalist state is no longer just a state. Its
involvement in the world capitalist economy, and its role of protecting and
promoting certain domestic economic interests make its behaviour explicable
in ways that are very different to those applying to other types of states.
Further, the assumption of homogeneity, central to the state-centric view,
collapses as different capitalist states have to behave in different ways according to domestic economic requirements. And, because the increased importance of economic factors has significant effects on Third World countries,
the reasons for the ways in which capitalist states behave towards them
becomes intrinsically related to economic requirements. This is a very different world to that portrayed by traditional writers, and to the extent that the
North–South cleavage replaces the East–West one the fact that a state is a
certain kind of capitalist state becomes crucial to understanding its foreign
policy. What was before treated as essentially irrelevant to an explanation of
international relations now becomes of primary concern.

However, this challenge to the orthodoxy did not go unopposed. There was
a very strong counter-attack to it in the 1970s, centred, interestingly, in Britain
(see Northedge, 1976; Bull, 1977; Bull, 1979; Northedge, 1979; Hanrieder,
1978). Northedge pointed out that these alternative views of international
politics reflected the very special experience of the US during the 1970s; it
was, therefore, a globalisation of the reaction of the US to the impact of
economic factors. In fact, he argued, the state was not declining, it was gaining
in importance throughout the world. As he noted: 'If an American professor
. . . were to lecture on the demise of the nation-state in most of the countries
in Africa or Asia today, he would in all likelihood be promptly locked up, if not
sent before a firing squad!' (Northedge, 1976, p. 26). As Hanrieder argues,
one of the effects of the rise of interdependence has been to increase reliance
on the nation-state precisely because it, and only it, can try to manage the
effects of interdependence. The result is 'not a new type of international
politics which is "dissolving" the traditional nation-state but a new nation-
state which is "dissolving" traditional international politics' (Hanrieder, 1978,
p. 135). In the most sophisticated counter-attack, Bull (1979) argues that the
state, far from declining, is actually expanding, both geographically and
functionally. Not only this, but states do have a monopoly of the legitimate use

of force, they do set the rules within which other actors have to operate, and they have been remarkably successful over the years in fending off challenges to their dominance. One must not mistake the fact that actors other than states are more active than before for the conclusion that their actions are important. Thus, for example, in the study cited earlier on the quantitative involvement of states and non-states (Mansbach, Ferguson and Lampert, 1976) no account was taken of what the actions involved; it is quite probable that the actions of states were more significant international acts than were those of non-state actors.

Despite these counter-attacks, the transnationalist approach dominated the study of international relations through the 1970s. What really caused its reassessment was a series of events at the end of the decade. The Soviet intervention in Afghanistan in 1979, the election of President Reagan in 1980 and the rearmament policy of that administration, heralded what Halliday (1983) has called the Second Cold War. Just as the demise of the state was being accepted, the re-emergence of major military cleavages in the international system rekindled interest in the state as actor. Once again, the state seemed central to international relations as the public protest in Europe over the deployment of Cruise and Pershing II missiles showed. International relations in the 1980s seem to have more in common with those of the 1950s or 1960s than with those of the 1970s. There are, however, three differences: first, the politicisation of defence issues; second, the massively increased role of economic factors; and third, the very severe problems for governments in managing and co-ordinating security and economic policies in an interdependent world. Whilst, therefore, on the surface the 1970s may look like an aberration, the events that occurred during that decade did change the complexion of international relations so that the traditional models, which applied across time, were no longer adequate to explain events in the 1980s. What has happened is that the three key assumptions of the state-centric view no longer hold: the state is not the dominant unit in *certain* issue-areas; the international–domestic politics distinction has been significantly eroded by both the politicisation of defence and the effects of interdependence; and the notions of military power as the central feature of international relations and the primacy of security issues is untenable, given the obvious impact of economic factors. This has led to much work trying to integrate the importance of economic factors with the traditional state concern with security issues (see, for example, Wallerstein, 1979; Hollist and Rosenau, 1981) and a rise in an approach known as international political economy (Spero, 1981; Blake and Walters, 1983). In the mid 1980s we are confronted with an international political system that is far more complex than was assumed either by the traditionalists or by the transnationalists. Governments are at the same time faced with critical economic issues and major security concerns. As

e former are concerned the fact that a state has a certain type of
economic and political structure is central; as far as the latter are
d these factors are not central in explaining the security behaviour of

hapter began by arguing that political theory and international theory
have been concerned with two rather different notions of the state: for the
political theorist it constitutes an analytical ceiling to analysis, to the international theorist it is an analytical floor. Of course these are paradigmatic
examples, since neither would claim that the state was such a closed unit, but,
at an analytical level, these conceptions of the nature of the state underpin
inquiry. What this chapter has been concerned with is showing how, on the
one hand, the utility of focussing on the state in terms of the type of state has
considerable limitations when it comes to explaining aspects of international
politics; on the other, the chapter has traced the development of the theory of
international relations and has shown that the assumptions of billiard-ball
theorists render their theories incapable of explaining parsimoniously many
dominant issues in contemporary world politics.

The main claim of this chapter, then, relates to the analytical focus of the
other chapters: the epistemological notion involved in this focus is that it is the
type of state (capitalist) that results in certain forms of political behaviour and
organisation. Yet this chapter argues that this theoretical linkage is insufficient
to explain major aspects of international relations: an analytical focus on the
capitalist state as the independent variable will not allow us to explain a whole
range of salient features of international society. To be quite specific, it will *not*
provide much of an explanation of war-involvement (although it may well be
central to explaining specific wars), nor will it be able to explain the changes in
the types of behaviour seen in international society before and after the
Second World War. In short, the fact that the US is capitalist and the USSR is
'communist' (or whichever label seems appropriate) is not the starting point
for an explanation of international relations since 1945. It looks like one,
especially since much of the rhetoric of politicians is couched in these terms,
but it is really only a description or a justification of events, and not an
explanation of them. Such an explanation has to focus on the fact that each is a
superpower in a bipolar world, with the associated assumption that were the
two bipolar powers different types of states then that would not significantly
alter behaviour. Explanations of events such as the Cold War, or of the
differences between the pre-1939 and the post-1945 worlds, must start with
the fact that the structure of the international political system altered from
multipolarity to bipolarity, and it was this change that led to the rather
different processes of international politics. The nature of world politics
changed after the Second World War, with ideology seeming to be of more
importance than hitherto and with very different types of alliances and peace-

keeping mechanisms. The problem with focussing on the type of state involved can now be put very starkly: if ideology was so important after 1945,
why was it so unimportant before? The inter-war international system was one
in which the multipolar structure led to the stabilising factor of the balance-of-
power mechanism, and this meant that ideology could not be a determinant of
alliance-formation or of changes in alliance membership. States did form
alliances in a desire to preserve the balance of power, and it was the very fact
that the operation of this required states fighting short wars to prevent one
state or a group of states dominating the system. After 1945, with the very
different structure of bipolarity, the whole character of world politics changed,
especially with regard to how peace was maintained. The argument advanced
in this chapter is that a focus on the type of states involved in world politics
omits this crucial dimension of the structural pressures on the units of a
system.

But if that indicates a limitation of a focus on the type of state, the other
main argument of this chapter is that events during the 1970s have brought to
light a serious limitation of the state-centric view of international politics. This
state-centric perspective has dominated the subject's history, and it was only
in the 1970s that it came under serious challenge. The dominant issues of the
1970s were economic ones, and these involved rather different types of actors
than had been the focal point of study. Transnationalism and interdependence painted a picture of a world that did not accord with the state-centric
view. According to these theories the fact that a state is a capitalist state is
indeed central to explaining its international behaviour; this is because in the
1970s it was assumed that the major issues were economic and not military.
The state was seen as more involved in international economic relations than
before. But, of course, the rise of economic issues to prominence did not just
'happen'; there were causes, and these related to very specific interactions
between economic and political issues. What did occur, though, was that
during the 1970s politicians paid much more attention to international economic relations than hitherto, and academics struggled to fit this into existing
theories. The world seemed to be becoming one in which economic issues
were more important than before, and new theories were developed to try and
explain this. The problem is that in the 1980s both the simple billiard-ball
view and the transnationalist/interdependence perspective are unable to explain a world in which military and economic issues are central in international
politics. International relations has a problem, then, because it has no way of
coping with this complexity, precisely because military and economic issues
are best explained by theories that have very different notions of the state. This
difference is illustrated in how each answers two questions: first, how much
influence on state behaviour comes from domestic factors and how much from
international structure; second, how do we understand the linkages between

economic, political and military issue-areas? The ways in which we can explain international economic behaviour focus on essentially reductionist analysis; the ways we explain military behaviour focus on structural determinants. To an extent these are mutually exclusive. This, however, is a problem that applies to other areas of state activity, but international politics seems to show it in its starkest relief.

In many respects this problem for international relations relates to the rather misleading distinction that has traditionally been drawn between economics and politics; such a distinction is understandable, but what the last decade or so indicates is that the subject can no longer proceed as if economic issues can be explained by factors internal to the state, and military issues by international factors. In discussions of political behaviour within the state the linkage between politics and economics has received much attention and there are powerful theories that relate the political to the economic; my argument is that the structure of the international system means that such a linkage between the economic and the political is not able to explain major areas of world politics. In explaining international relations the more significant distinction is that between the features of the system and the characteristics of the units that comprise the system. And, in this regard, although the characteristics of the units are important in explaining certain aspects of state behaviour they are not as important as the features of the system in explaining others. If we focussed on *capitalist* states and sought to explain their behaviour in terms of their being capitalist, we would be unable to explain very significant areas of international relations.

The contemporary paradox is that as the state is being called on to satisfy more and more demands, and as the international economy impacts more directly on the domestic economy, states are less able than ever to satisfy these demands and mediate these influences. Clearly the capitalist state, especially as recessions become more serious, will satisfy some of these demands rather than others, and may thereby reveal its true internal character. But we are still left to explain the process that poses the greatest danger to human kind, that of nuclear war, and economic reductionist theories are unable to provide powerful explanations. To understand the processes of international military alliance structures and arms races requires not economic reductionism but an appreciation of the impact of structure on the behaviour of the constituent units. This applies whether we are talking about Athens and Sparta, the US and the Soviet Union, or a bipolar world dominated by Britain and the US, or China and the Soviet Union. This is not meant to imply that there are no differences between these types of state, but it does imply that these are less important than the similarities.

In conclusion, then, this chapter has argued that a focus on a type of state is inappropriate for an explanation of major areas of international relations; it has also indicated, though, that the opposite position has been taken too far by traditional international relations theory, for which the state was a closed billiard-ball, the behaviour of which was explicable only in terms of its setting in the structure of the international system. The inadequacies of this position were illustrated in the 1970s, when state-centric theory was unable to explain the dominant issues, and the fact that a state was capitalist was salient to explaining its behaviour. But the type of state (i.e. capitalist) does not seem relevant to the determination of that state's military relations. Economic reductionist theories do not provide strong accounts of military behaviour. This is evident in the writings of Marx, Engels and Lenin and has remained a major stumbling block to Marxist theories of international relations. As Berki has noted: 'the very existence of international relations poses a serious, and perhaps intractable, *problem* for Marxism . . . since international relations presuppose the horizontal division of mankind into nations or states' (1971, p. 80). This division of the system into states results in the two main structural features of international society, anarchy and polarity, and it is the impact of these that makes economic reductionist theories of very limited utility. The state indeed has two faces and its external face involves it in a different society, one which sets the context for its domestic actions and imposes constraints and requirements on its international behaviour. It is precisely this setting that tends to be ignored in discussions of the internal workings of capitalist states, and it is a setting that applies to states of whatever political or economic complexion.

NOTE

1. I would like to thank Bob Alford, Graeme Duncan, Phil Lawrence and Steve Gill for their helpful comments on an earlier draft of this chapter and trust that they still fundamentally disagree with it.

BIBLIOGRAPHY

Barnett, R. J. and R. E. Muller, 1974. *Global Reach: The Power of Multinational Corporations*. New York, Simon and Schuster
Berki, R. N., 1971. 'On Marxian thought and the problem of international relations', *World Politics*, 24 (1): 80–105
Blake, D. H. and R. S. Walters, 1983. *The Politics of Global Economic Relations*, 2nd edn. Englewood Cliffs, N. J., Prentice-Hall
Brown, S., 1974. *New Forces in World Politics*. Washington, DC, Brookings Institute.
Bull, H., 1977. *The Anarchical Society*. London, Macmillan
   1979. 'The state's positive role in world affairs', *Daedalus*, 108 (4): 111–23
Butterfield, H. and M. Wight, eds., 1966. *Diplomatic Investigations*. London, Allen and Unwin
Carr, E. H., 1939. *The Twenty Years' Crisis*. London, Macmillan
Cooper, R. N., 1968. *The Economics of Interdependence*. New York, McGraw-Hill
Donelan, M., ed., 1978. *The Reason of States*. London, Allen and Unwin
Falk, R. A., 1971. *This Endangered Planet*. New York, Random House

Haas, E., 1958. *The Uniting of Europe*. Stanford, CA, Stanford University Press
1964. *Beyond the Nation-State*. Stanford, CA, Stanford University Press
Halliday, F., 1983. *The Making of the Second Cold War*. London, Verso
Hanrieder, W. F., 1978. 'Dissolving international politics: reflections on the nation-state', reprinted in M. Smith, R. Little and M. Shackleton, eds., *Perspectives on World Politics*. London, Croom Helm, pp. 132–45
Herz, J. H., 1976a. 'The rise and demise of the territorial state', in J. H. Herz, ed., *The Nation-State and the Crisis of World Politics*. New York, McKay, pp. 99–123, originally published in 1956
1976b. 'The territorial state revisited – reflections on the future of the nation-state', in J. H. Herz, ed., *The Nation-State and the Crisis of World Politics*. New York, McKay, pp. 226–52
Hollist, W. L. and J. N. Rosenau, eds., 1981. *World System Structure*. Beverly Hills, CA, Sage
Kaplan, M. A., 1957. *System and Process in International Politics*. New York, John Wiley
Keohane, R. O. and J. S. Nye, eds., 1972. *Transnational Relations and World Politics*. Cambridge, Mass., Harvard University Press
Keohane, R. O. and J. S. Nye, 1977. *Power and Interdependence*. Boston, Mass., Little Brown
Krasner, S., ed., 1982. *International Regimes*. Special edition of *International Organization*, vol. XXXVI (2)
Lieber, R. J., 1972. *Theory and World Politics*. Cambridge, Mass., Winthrop
Lindberg, L. N., 1963. *The Political Dynamics of European Economic Integration*. Stanford, CA, Stanford University Press
Lindberg, L. N. and S. A. Scheingold, eds., 1971. *Regional Integration: Theory and Research*. Cambridge, Mass., Harvard University Press
Linklater, A., 1982. *Men and Citizens in the Theory of International Relations*. London, Macmillan
Maghroori, R. and B. Ramberg, eds., 1982. *Globalism Versus Realism*. Boulder, CO, Westview
Mansbach, R. W., Y. H. Ferguson and D. E. Lampert, 1976. *The Web of World Politics*. Englewood Cliffs, NJ, Prentice-Hall
Mansbach, R. W. and J. A. Vasquez, 1981. *In Search of Theory*. New York, Columbia University Press
Mayall, J., ed., 1982. *The Community of States*. London, Allen and Unwin
Mitrany, D., 1943. *A Working Peace System*. London, Oxford University Press
Morgenthau, H., 1948. *Politics Among Nations*. New York, Knopf
Morse, E. L., 1970. 'The transformation of foreign policies', *World Politics*, 22 (3): 371–92
1972. 'Crisis diplomacy, interdependence, and the politics of international economic relations', in R. Tanter and R. H. Ullman, eds., *Theory and Policy in International Relations*. Princeton, NJ, Princeton University Press, pp. 123–50
1976. *Modernization and the Transformation of International Relations*. New York. Free Press
Northedge, F. S., 1976. 'Transnationalism: the American illusion', *Millennium*, 5 (1), 21–7
1979. 'The nation-state and the coordination of foreign policies', in W. Link and W. J. Feld, eds., *The New Nationalism*. New York, Pergamon, pp. 25–44
Reynolds, P. A., 1979. 'Non-state actors and international outcomes', *British Journal of International Studies*, 5 (2): 91–111
Reynolds, P. A. and R. D. McKinlay, 1979. 'The concept of interdependence: its uses and misuses', in K. Goldmann, and G. Sjostedt, eds. *Power, Capabilities, Interdependence*. Beverly Hills, CA, Sage, pp. 141–66
Scott, A. M., 1982. *The Dynamics of Interdependence*. Chapel Hill, NC, University of North Carolina Press
Smith, S. M., 1983. 'War and human nature', in I. Forbes, and S. M. Smith, eds. *Politics and Human Nature*. London, Frances Pinter, pp. 164–79
Spero, J. E., 1981. *The Politics of International Economic Relations*. 2nd edn. New York, St. Martin's

Vasquez, J. A., 1979. 'Colouring it Morgenthau: new evidence for an old thesis on quantitative international politics', *British Journal of International Studies*, 5 (3): 210–28

    1983. *The Power of Power Politics*. London, Frances Pinter

Vernon, R., 1971. *Sovereignty at Bay*. New York, Basic Books

Wallerstein, I. M., 1979. *The Capitalist World-Economy*. Cambridge, Cambridge University Press

Waltz, K. N., 1959. *Man, the State and War*. New York, Columbia University Press

    1964. 'The stability of a bipolar world', *Daedalus*, 93 (3): 892–907

    1970. 'The Myth of National Interdependence', in C. P. Kindleberger, ed., *The International Corporation*. Cambridge, Mass., MIT Press, pp. 205–23

    1979. *Theory of International Politics*. Reading, Mass., Addison-Wesley

CLASSICS AND GRAND THEORIES

The theorists and theories examined in these chapters bear, with varying degrees of directness and adequacy, upon the relations between society, democracy and (capitalist) state. How far can the state act independently and instrumentally? Is it hindered by the existence of propertied and powerful minorities, or by the basic structure of capitalism? What weight can be attached to plural institutions, actually and ideally, in ensuring the democratic and reducing the capitalist character of the state? Or are other values and goals, such as efficiency or national achievement, more important, requiring that democracy be limited? Is there a parliamentary route to socialism? Questions of the actual and desirable relationships between economy, society and state have come to the fore again, so that much of the earlier discussion strikes contemporary chords. Privatisation and its socialist variant, which we might call communalisation, emerge in the older arguments. Fortunately the thinkers considered here and their interpreters do not agree with each other, nor are they absolutely decided on the right answer(s).

Crick's defence of republicanism is in large part a defence of parliamentarianism and its politics. Republicanism, which at the very least allows institutionally expressed public diversity of interests and values, is linked closely with parliamentarianism: republican government is a regime of government through parliament. In its turn, the theory of parliamentarianism combines classical republican and pluralist feudal ideas. Crick separates the liberal and the republican traditions. Liberal institutions are not simply results of the rise of the capitalist market economy, as they have independent force, and tend to break through class restraints. But the two have close associations, and the *laissez faire* conception of freedom is different from and narrower than that of classical republicanism, which values 'the free acts of citizens'.

Despite both opposition to and the corruption of parliamentary institutions, they are the most important of democratic and republican institutions, serving as communication systems which scrutinise and criticise governments. They are pre-eminently instruments of politics, by which Crick understands experimental and empirical attitudes resting upon an acceptance of diverse interests and values. Impressed by the relative autonomy of the state, he sees parliamentary socialism as both possible and desirable. Parliament is not the possession of the capitalist state, and it could be the means of creating a socialist society. Stripped of its contingent capitalist connections, pure republican parliamentarianism could be at once the expression of the natural diversity of society and a source of social transformation. In a word, parliamentary democracy can defeat the undemocratic tendencies of capitalism.

Miliband seeks to clarify Marx's account of the state and to separate it from that of official Marxism. The Hegelian imprint is marked in the early Marx, who steadily broke with the notion of the reconciliation of civil society and state in the rational state itself, which was a mystification, hiding the subordination of the state to private property. In the early 1840s Marx emphasised the basic distinction between political and human emancipation, which to Miliband began his continuing acceptance of the relative importance of the political realm.

Miliband distinguishes the primary Marxist conception of the state as class instrument from the secondary view of the state as the dominant social force, independent from and superior to all social classes. Marx examined societies based on the Asiatic mode of production, where there was no private ownership of land and when the state clearly appeared to be both a dominant force and 'above society'. In capitalist societies the state became most independent in Bonapartism, where bureaucratic power developed remarkably, although it always remained, to Miliband's Marx, the protector of an economically and socially dominant class. Miliband concludes with a discussion of Marx's serious concern in the late 1860s and the early 1870s with the problems of bureaucracy and political power in post-capitalist societies, and presents a libertarian view of the dictatorship of the proletarian as a free and egalitarian regime. On this account, Marx stood for liberty and autonomy, which required the destruction of capitalism and the dismantling of state power. Crick also sees Marx as attached to the classical ideal of free citizenship. But the true democracy espoused by Marx can only be achieved in very novel conditions.

The difficulties in Marx's vision of the transcendence of the state and the end to structural determination are taken up in the chapter on Mill and Marx. The contrast between their views of the state rests upon the supposed relationship between economy and polity and – arising from the ways in which these are conceived – the capacity of the state to be neutral and independent. Their different accounts of the state are related to differences in theories of social causation, in views of human nature, and in the characterisation and evaluation of contemporary societies. To Mill, rating politics and ideas highly, good states were possible, even in class and capitalist societies, though their worst features needed checking. What was needed was economical rather than overbearing and intrusive state power and good leaders – disinterested and rational thinkers pursuing the public good. The likelihood of impartial and classless leaders – who, incidentally, come predominantly from the middle ranks of society – is doubted strongly. The common voluntarist assumption underlying Mill's conceptions of state neutrality and state independence is rejected. The account of Marx is not significantly different from that of Miliband. Marx's insistence on the dependence of the state upon civil society distinguished his views sharply from Mill's, though Marx's claim (made occasionally and early) of simple dependence was modified severely in the more detailed studies. The state is sometimes a clear-cut class instrument, though its form and its class connections may vary between different capitalist societies, and of course between capitalist and other kinds of society. It also has relative autonomy and separating bureaucratic tendencies. But in the last resort it is a structural theory, assuming the common function of capitalist states – that of maintaining the process of capitalist accumulation.

Weber's theory of the modern state is presented as a theory of the capitalist nation-state in the age of imperialism. Bottomore's examination of Weber's conceptions of democracy, bureaucracy and the nation-state brings out strongly how confined he was by Germany's problems in the early twentieth century, and how his authoritarian prescriptions were to strengthen Germany's place in the world. Neither full democracy nor the dictatorship of the official could do the necessary job. What was needed, in Weber's view, was 'a great general staff' for Germany, meaning strong, effective, real political leadership by outstanding individuals. The emergence of charismatic leaders would both limit the inroads of democracy and challenge bureaucratic domination, which could also be reduced by a strengthening of private capitalism. Such a leader democracy could arouse nationalist fervour and retain control. Thus democracy had no place in Weber's thought, which was permeated by the authoritarian climate of German politics at the time. On the other hand, the capitalist state was to be strengthened. Unlike Mill, who advocated leaders from the middle class but stripped of bourgeois interest, Weber sought consciously to make bourgeois rule effective and traditional bourgeois values dominant.

The basic question facing the Habermas of *Legitimation Crisis* is whether, at the same time, the capitalist state can manage and co-ordinate an economy still based on the logic of private accumulation *and* maintain political legitimacy. That difficulty did not arise seriously under liberal-capitalism, when state and economy were separate and the market was the steering mechanism of society – and when, incidentally, classical Marxian analysis was appropriate. However, under advanced capitalism the state has become the dominant steering mechanism of society and the main distributor of life chances. The attempt to side-step economic crisis has led to an expanded public realm, to a displacement of market crisis on to the state, and to the politicisation of productive relations. The new role and character of the state, and in particular its attempt to contain class conflict, renders it liable to legitimation crisis, as changing values generate expectations which the (capitalist) state cannot satisfy. It may fail to meet demands because it lacks the material resources, or it may face demands which cannot be met by material rewards at all. The focus on culture, on values and on collective social identity, leaves Habermas's Marxism suspect. On Lawrence's account, he seems closer to Kant than to Hegel or Marx.

Against the background of neo-conservatism, Lawrence criticises Habermas because of the state's ability to manipulate needs, and because bourgeois ideologies have not died, even if they do not fit reality. The apparently changing role of the state at once makes it less vulnerable to social-welfare claims from civil society and freer to control it by means of direct coercion. The state denies its responsibility while it actually grows, and hence a deep gap between belief systems and actual practices develops. But Lawrence does not see Habermas as a critical sociologist whose claims can be measured against social developments. He is, rather, a political philosopher producing idealised and systematic theories of a formal character, who may increase our theoretical and moral sense of current dilemmas.

Recent criticisms of the Labour Party for its allegedly statist and paternalist aspect were foreshadowed in arguments early this century between members of the Fabian Society. The winners, including the Webbs, emphasised efficiency, order and expertise, and had visions of a selfless intellectual elite of state bureaucrats doing the national housekeeping, unhindered by democratic encroachment on their authority. The real problem of capitalism often seemed to be waste rather than inhumanity or injustice. The underlying values are probably described better as statist and collectivist rather than socialist.

The subjects of Callaghan's essay are Cole, Tawney and Laski, who challenged the dominant Fabian trend. They argued much of the time that socialism was impossible without the destruction of the dictatorial rule of the capitalists (or the propertied minority), that the emancipation of the labourers must be their own work, that industrial democracy was as vital as political democracy, and that various new forms of democratic participation should be introduced. Cole wanted acknowledgment of functional associations and a combination of workers' control of industry and nationalisation carried through by parliamentary socialists. He was optimistic about the effects of participation, and also about the development of a new service ethic, opposed to the profit motive, amongst professional and technical workers. Tawney envisaged a socialist transformation arising out of a radical change of values generated by the workers themselves, and also urged the extension of democracy into industry. He was deeply conscious of the contradictions within the liberal-democratic state, and particularly of how industrial and social oligarchy destroy democracy. He thought a parliamentary transition to socialism possible. Laski recommended pluralist and participatory democracy, including industrial democracy, against Fabian and liberal paternalism and the rampant state. But ultimately his solution to the problematic relations between capitalism and democracy became a combination of parliamentary control over the boards of nationalised industries and the activities of functional associations, especially trade unions. Aware of, and partly convinced by Marxist theories of the capitalist state, he none the less made a case for British exceptionalism, amongst other reasons because the British people were deeply constitutional and because the professions were civilising. Even more in Laski than his fellows, the difficulty of combining a radical or Marxist critique of capitalism with a convincing theory of democratic change is manifest.

4

Republicanism, liberalism and capitalism: a defence of parliamentarianism

BERNARD CRICK

My minor thesis is simply that 'the State' has an earlier origin than the time of the capitalist market economy, and will probably survive it; and my major thesis is that republican ideas (both as ideals and as theoretical analyses of the conditions in which republics are possible) also preceded the capitalist market economy. So republican ideas are both logically and historically prior to those of liberal democracy and could well survive them. 'Democracy' is, indeed, both a necessary dimension of modern government but also a highly ambiguous and relative term, though not infinitely so – as C. B. Macpherson has shown (Macpherson, 1966).

THE REPUBLICAN TRADITION

The republican tradition (as I now prefer to call what I once simply called 'the political'),[1] is both a theory and an operative ideal. As a theory it simply states that advanced or complex human communities always exhibit some variety both of values and of interests; and as an operative ideal or doctrine it simply asserts that it is normally best to govern by allowing representation of these diverse ideals and interests. 'Normally' usually means until or unless the safety or survival of the state is threatened, though notions of what constitute such threats are highly relative. Also it does not imply that all significant differences are represented or even tolerated, only that some are; and neither does it imply that all the inhabitants are citizens, but only that a large number are; large enough to necessitate the typical techniques of republican government: assemblies, competitive elections and publicity, et cetera, rather than the typical devices of tyranny or autocracy. A citizen body itself can, of course, form an autocracy relative to a majority of the unenfranchised inhabitants, and it can constitute an exploitative class. But the culture and the political institutions of even a minority citizen class are different to those of a traditional autocracy or aristocracy: their practices and principles are capable of extension without proving self-defeating. So to point correctly to the dependence of the citizen culture of classical republics upon the coercive exploitation of labour, even in some circumstances upon slavery (Finley, 1966; Anderson, 1974) is not to deny its uniqueness, still less the lasting effect of even 'the myth' of free republican institutions, whatever the shabby reality.

This classical tradition still shapes the very language and constitutes the uniqueness of characteristically Western political institutions. It has its origins, like Western science, in a particular culture, or constellation of cultures. This Western origin should not discredit the theory or the ideal, only put us on our guard against idealisation, against holding anything but a minimalist, yet essential position: some institutionally expressed public diversity of interests and values. Holding such a minimalist republican, rather than a maximalist liberal position, we need not be in the least surprised or discomforted that the diffusion of such Western ideas will, like the diffusion of science, leave them much changed, having shed most of the specific cultural accretions of their long European history. Sometimes we are surprised and discomforted, so critical analysis must always stress the general dangers of ethnocentricism and the specific facts of the use of historical republican systems for class domination and exploitation; but sometimes there is need to warn against throwing out the baby with the bathwater.

It is at least necessary to remind ourselves how difficult it is to prevent the public example of liberties being exercised and enjoyed among the few exciting the emulation of the many. Example or mimesis is, after all, a basic social mechanism. Broadly speaking, the idea of free citizenship, indeed of political freedom, has its origins in highly elitist cultures; but sources do not always contaminate the products. Certainly it long precedes the capitalist era. My contention is that the classical ideal of free citizenship is not so much superseded by Marx's critique of capitalism, as it is assumed by him, and forms part of his own preconceptions in his important but fragmentary account of how alienated man could be emancipated from social conditions that work against a fully developed human personality. It is hard to make sense of what he says otherwise. Certainly he was closer to the classical tradition than most of his immediate intellectual followers. Much of what I argue could be recast in terms of the contemporary Marxist debate about 'the relative autonomy' of the political, even of the state.[2]

It is simply historically wrong, however, to identify most of the characteristic institutions of what is generally called modern liberal democracy with the rise of the capitalist market economy – as do both Hayek and C. B. Macpherson. Capitalism certainly accelerated the spread of such institutions and their instrumental use both to liberate new productive forces and to impose them as controls on the working class. Even so, it could be argued (as did Marx himself in his writings on French politics) that the concessions involved in establishing a façade of 'free institutions' ultimately threatened any simple class control of the system. The skilled working man demanded by the new technologies was a very different human animal from the peasant of the agricultural mode of production in the autocracies: for one thing, he had to be literate, and for another, he became dangerously concentrated in cities, even in capital cities. He added great power to the state but he was also a constant threat, and difficult to stop from organising, even in restraint of trade. His new masters had to educate him and, indeed, sought to control that education; but on the scale demanded, educators were hard to control completely, were not merely open to new ideas but created new ideas, and even the old educational ideas of autocracy were heavily contaminated with the classical myth of free citizenship. Some, like J. S. Mill, argued that the masses, even the native inhabitants of India, should come into their own, but only when fully educated – which they could be, in time; while others sought to impose a carefully controlled class-structure on education itself to postpone, perhaps indefinitely, the dawning of any full democracy. But the changing technological demands of the capitalist market made all such deliberate gradualism hard to control.

If systems are never quite as systematic as some (both Marxists and behaviourists) have thought, certainly the capitalist created a *more* systematic relationship between rulers and ruled than ever before. In the pre-modern world there could be an extraordinary lack both of congruence and of effects between the culture of ruling classes and of inhabitants. Often they did not speak the same language, and in extreme cases one set of alien rulers could replace another with little change to the life of the common people. But the demands of a market economy were far more systematic, especially when Malthusian workers became Keynesian consumers. Capitalism could maintain its legitimacy and hence support either through claiming to increase *per capita* income (whether in wages or welfare payments), hence gaining a more-or-less pacified managed consent (in the Western European and American manner); or by claims to increase the gross national product, in the *national* interest amid greatly increased coercion (as in pre-war Japan, contemporary South America and in the 'State capitalism' of the Soviet block).

Even so, to identify 'liberalism' wholly with capitalism is either a very crude and unhistorical economic determinism or is strict Hayekian liberalism. Hayek is quite explicit in arguing that liberty is not merely the greatest human value but a specific product of capitalism and wholly dependent upon the maintenance of the competitive, market price system (Hayek, 1960). He is, as it were, Marx turned upside down. Hannah Arendt argued in her *Human Condition* that classical *laissez-faire* economics and Marxism had some striking conceptual similarities amid their more obvious differences. They had one fatal specific point of agreement: that the economy both dominates and explains everything else. Further, she argued that they both underestimated and demeaned specifically political action: they saw it as an irrational intervener in the economic system, rather than a conscious shaper, at the least a

rational response to economic contradictions and inequalities. More fundamentally, they both saw man purely as a creature of necessity, not as also a
maker; and both made 'a religion of labour' demeaning creative action for the
sake of repetitive consumption – her famous distinction between 'labour' and
'work' (Arendt, 1958).

Perhaps Arendt exaggerates. Not all Marxists and not all liberals mean
'necessary relations' even when they say so. The appeal to 'necessity' is often
pure rhetoric and most 'iron laws' turn out, in the fine print of the theory, to be
conditional or to be malleable in practice. It all depends on precisely what one
means by 'in the last analysis the economic factors always predominate'. This
proposition is at best a very general truth, so long as its high level of abstraction
is appreciated: the relationship between theory and practice is neither simple
nor direct. Causal language in sociology can always be better stated in terms of
conditioning factors. (To dare to come between Popper and Marx, man is
always conditioned by physical, material and economic necessity, but never
determined – as Engels said, and, oddly, so did Hayek.)

To establish that the concept or ideology of 'possessive individualism' is one
of the preconditions of a capitalist market, it is necessary for Macpherson *et al.*
to pre-date the emergence of that market and to lapse into an ahistorical
teleology. And, in any case, does 'possessive individualism' wholly subsume
the classical, republican tradition of free citizenship (Macpherson, 1962)? I
think not. It was only one of its possible modulations. What John Pocock has
called 'classical republicanism' or 'the civic tradition' was firmly established,
he has clearly shown (Pocock, 1975), long before that capitalist market and
laissez-faire ideology which Hayek claims is the only guarantee of human
liberty. My contention is that before *laissez-faire* liberalism arose, with its
essentially negative concept of *liberty*, being free from the state, the revival of
classical republicanism had established a significantly different concept of
freedom as the free acts of citizens. *Laissez-faire* liberalism says that we should
take part in politics only to defend the private against the intrusion of the
public, and to defend property against state intervention; but classical republicanism sees political action by free men as the highest and most effective
form of collective human activity. It either denies any rigid distinction between
'the private' and 'the public', stressing the social, that is, interdependencies
rather than independencies, or it says that while there are autonomous
spheres of private and public, of rights and of public interest, men must
constantly and habitually move between the two (Crick, 1973a).

Republicanism, rather than liberalism, then both pre-dates and could
post-date forms of capitalist economy (for, of course, they are many, not one).
It is neither to be confused with liberalism nor discredited by inference from
liberalism's undoubted association with capitalism. The republican tradition
itself takes many forms. French Jacobinism, English chartism, American

Jacksonianism, Mazzini's nationalism, for instance, all very different phenomena and doctrines, were plainly in the republican tradition more than the liberal. Strictly speaking, it is indeed an impossible business to blend the doctrine of *liberalism* with socialism, as Hayek argues, or else very difficult and desperately contingent on economic growth and a consensus about both means and ends, as in (in the modern British usage) social democracy. But I see no necessary incompatibility between *republicanism* and a socialist mode of production, still less with mixed economies.

Let me argue this on more concrete ground by taking the most specific of republican institutions, often denounced as a mere façade of a capitalist state, assemblies or parliaments. I would vindicate the possibility and desirability of 'parliamentary socialism'.[3]

PARLIAMENTS AND STATE FORMATION

Parliaments, usually as 'Estates' representative of the dominant social orders of a realm, were typical of European medieval polity: they preceded the modern state and were mostly swept away with other feudal institutions which appeared to hinder central government and the imposition of law and order; but there were some highly important exceptions. 'The state', certainly as it corresponds to Max Weber's famous definition – the monopolist of the legitimate means of violence – strictly speaking is a unique form of government unknown in Europe before the late fifteenth and early sixteenth centuries. As the concept developed, so did its attendant ideology, the doctrine of sovereignty; and as the reality of the new form developed, so did its characteristic form of society, the nation-state. From a world that had known such varying and sometimes co-existing forms of government as would-be universal empires, city states, the great hybrid system of Rome, despotism and feudalism, there eventually emerged, from the period of European global imperialism, a world entirely composed of nation-states all claiming sovereignty. But remember that when Thomas Hobbes argued in the great masterpiece of the theory of sovereignty, his *Leviathan*, that law is nothing but the command of someone with power to enforce it, he admitted (or made the politic hedge) that this necessary superior can be 'either one man or many', king or parliament, depending on who better could enforce law and thus minimise the chances of individuals dying violently.

It is important to grasp that parliaments were feudal in their origins, and were a typical not an exceptional device of medieval government, arising from the essential plurality of power, both territorial and social, among governing elites.[4] After their general decline or suppression in the sixteenth and seventeenth centuries, they were revived or re-created in the nineteenth century and became an almost universal aspiration, even where they did not exist. The origins of the modern state are bound up with that age of absolutism which, almost everywhere but in England, found the need to destroy parliaments or to reduce drastically their powers; but the continuance of the modern state in the capitalist era, ever more centralised, orderly and bureaucratic, seemed to need, after and through the French Revolution and the industrial revolution, that broader base of power, that capacity to mobilise consent as well as to represent interests, to which parliaments could be adapted.

One old tale can serve as a theoretical paradigm about the special history of the English state and parliament. In England, as in the French, Scottish, Spanish and Habsburg dominions, the royal advisers had been tempted, like Henry VIII himself, to suppress parliament and to assert the maxim of the Roman law over the common law and its custodian, parliament: '*quod principi placuit leges habet vigorem*' (what pleases the prince has the force of law). A former Chancellor of England, the wily Stephen Gardiner, is defending from prison his conduct in the reign of the former king:

The Lord Cromwell had once put into the King our late sovereign lord's head to have his will and pleasure regarded as a law: for that, he said, was to be a very king. And thereupon I was called for at Hampton Court . . . 'Answer the king here', quoth he, 'but speak plainly and directly and shrink not, man! Is not that that pleaseth the king, a law? Have you not there in the Civil Law', quoth he, '"*quod principi placuit*" and so forth, I have somewhat forgotten it now.' I stood still and wondered in my mind to what conclusion this should tend. The King saw me musing and with earnest gentleness said, 'Answer him, whether it be so or no.' I . . . told him that I had read indeed of kings that had their will always received for a law, but, I told him, by the form of his reign, to make the laws his will was more sure and quiet. 'And by thy form of government you are established', quoth I, 'and it is agreeable with the nature of your people. If you begin a new matter of policy, how it will frame, no man can tell; and how this frameth, ye can tell; and I would never advise your Grace to leave a certain for an uncertain.' The King turned his back and left the matter after. (Quoted in McIlwain, 1947, p. 103)

The pseudo-Machiavellian is outmatched by the real Machiavellian. But it is not his pragmatic manner that is the point, rather what was in fact the institutional context of such advice: better to govern through parliament, both more safe and more strong to use parliament. The common lawyers themselves said that the king's power was 'never so great as when he sat in Parliament'. England, in other words, was able to blend the autocratic and the parliamentary traditions. Parliament was a necessary instrument of this compromise. Am I being simple-minded or setting out true basic theory to say that this proves that parliament is not a unique and necessary instrumentality of the capitalist state? It has been, possibly still is in many respects; but not uniquely so, and it could be the instrument of a socialist society – at least of any socialist society whose values are republican rather than themselves autocratic. Yet this anticipates.

The revival of parliaments in continental Europe as a typical form of government was a product of the French Revolution and the Napoleonic Wars. The new parliaments were, however, unlike their feudal precursors, almost everywhere the instrument of bourgeois power against the ancient regime and aristocratic government. The French themselves brought assemblies to Switzerland, the Netherlands and to parts of Italy – a short-lived or premature experience of republican government. But soon, as part of the popular national sentiments that the French example aroused all over Europe, even if largely in opposition to Napoleonic and French national ambitions, demands arose for national parliaments. If a nation wished to be governed as a nation, rather than as a possession of a multinational dynasty, what institution would replace dynastic monarchy? National monarchy, was the answer of the dynasts; but very often this was insufficient either to stem national unrest or to achieve and harness a national military mobilisation against the French. So parliaments were conceded or granted in several of the smaller German states and in Sweden. When the Kingdom of the Netherlands was established in 1815, it was as a parliamentary constitutional monarchy. In 1830 a far more bourgeois parliamentary system was established in France than the aristocratic compromise of the Bourbon restoration. In France even the Bourbon restoration had not dared to govern absolutely without any popular assemblies, as could still happen in Prussia, Austria and Russia.

The risings of 1848, however, accelerated the growth of belief in parliamentary government. Cries for national self-government against autocracy seemed the same thing as demands for limited government; and a constitution implied a parliament. Parliament became seen as the national institution and the court or the palace stood condemned as the dynastic or even cosmopolitan institution. The first wave of struggles for national independence of the 1848 kind all aimed at establishing parliaments and constitutions, unlike the post Second World War wave of struggles for national independence, all of which thought in terms of party government. The events of 1848 moved many monarchies into hastily granting constitutions and summoning national assemblies of one kind or another. In unified Italy the parliament was, right from the beginning, for all its weaknesses and internal divergencies, the most important national institution.

The German *Reichstag*, established in 1871, was formally highly democratic in its electoral base and its procedures, but it lacked real power and much public opinion looked to the Emperor and his advisers, not the *Reichstag*, as the effective unifying factor of the new nation. The granting of a constitution in 1867 for the dual-monarchy of Austria–Hungary also looked better on paper than in practice. But at least national parliaments, however weak, were constitutionally established by the outbreak of the First World War in every major European power. So it was that parliaments inherited government themselves in 1918 after the breakdown of the old Hohenzollern and Habsburg monarchies, albeit in the worst possible circumstances. And when the Japanese decided to Westernise and sent their famous imperial missions to Europe in the 1880s, it was a German-style parliament they recommended. They were impressed that the German parliament challenged imperial authority less than the British – even strengthened it by the appearance of democratic legitimacy.

Only Russia was untouched by these developments in the Western world. Not until 1905 was Czar Nicholas II forced to allow a national assembly or Duma to be called. But the institution was never allowed to develop even a limited independence in a way that, in 1917 and 1918, had Russia been Germany, could have ensured the continuity of national life even amid the change of regime. Events in South America and Spain in the nineteenth century defy summary, but hardly a country in the Hispanic world did not establish an assembly or parliament, even if some of them quickly became fairly nominal bodies, coerced or ignored by dictators and military leaders.

Thus parliaments during the time of high capitalism were almost everywhere the instruments of nationalism. But that there was no necessary connection between parliamentary government and nationalism can be seen by the experience of the large number of new states formed after 1945, from the breakdown or retreat of the European colonial empires. Right from the beginning they had either had no real parliament, or simply an occasional one-party assembly convened to praise and to be instructed. The main instrument of post-colonial nation-building has been the *political party*, indeed the single party, the continuation into the time of liberation of the ethos of unity and struggle engendered in the campaign for liberation.

There were some important and interesting exceptions, however. India, despite grave crises and divisions of language, culture and religion so great as to threaten that things would fall apart or need dictatorial power to hold them together, has remained a parliamentary regime. Israel, created by war, surviving and winning two other desperate wars, in constant threat and crisis, in other words a state that by every criterion of political sociology should be expected to be an autocracy, if only for the duration of the emergency, also remains republican and parliamentary – despite its massive and unjust oppression of the Arab population. And Israel is an example of a state founded by exiles with no national experience or tradition of citizenship. It is a parliamentary republic because its inhabitants passionately believe in citizenship, in the classic sense, because they see it as the very antithesis of their former condition of being mere subjects in oppressive regimes. So much the worse for them that they seek to limit effective citizenship to an ethnically defined group; but this does not (except on idealist criteria) invalidate the description of the regime as actually parliamentary, even if in the long run such discrimination contradicts republican principles.

THE DECLINE OF PARLIAMENTS

Certainly the era of high capitalism saw the greatest articulation of the ideology of parliamentary government. Few people doubted, still fewer denied, that civilisation and progress were somehow bound up with representative institutions and parliaments. Marx had pointed out that parliaments were a bourgeois institution, which were not to be condemned out of hand but accepted as a stage in historical development. What he thought would follow was unclear, perhaps some different form of representative institution, federations or communes? But what is in a name? The essential thing was that there would be popularly elected institutions. In Marx's own thinking the idea that the party, the Communist Party in particular, would supersede parliaments, was hardly developed. For the vast majority of thinkers, educational and industrial progress were somehow bound up with the existence of parliamentary institutions. He probably assumed a revolutionary assembly rather than no assembly.

Some of these beliefs in, as it were, the inevitability of parliamentarianism were shattered simply by the terror and irrationality of the First World War. The Russian defeat destroyed the Czarist regime, but it also destroyed much chance of the Duma surviving: it was both too discredited and too weak to cope with so extraordinary a revolutionary crisis. The German defeat destroyed the monarchy, and opened the door for parliamentary government, an experienced if hitherto fairly powerless parliament being already in existence; but it did so amid circumstances that made the parliamentary regime, indeed the Weimar Republic itself, the scapegoat of nearly every nationalist grievance of economic depression and of defeat. Even amid nominal victory, the Italian parliamentary regime was discredited by the war itself, the conduct of the war, working-class unemployment and fear of communism among the middle classes, so that it fell astonishingly easily, considering the proud and militant republican tradition of the previous century, to the ambiguous, but plainly anti-parliamentary, fascism of Mussolini. Both fascists and communists associated parliamentary government with weakness and failure, and theorists, as usual, followed and exaggerated political rhetoric and found sophisticated rationalisations.

In Germany and Italy, soon in Spain and Eastern Europe, an anti-parliamentary ideology began to emerge. Parliaments, the ideology said, compromised instead of decided; they were 'talking shops' and 'cattle markets'; they were simply channels of self-advancement for self-seeking bourgeois; they were pacific, when the times called for military strength and virtues; they were dominated by socialists and soft to communists, so that they were simultaneously a threat to private property of the small man and the dupes of cosmopolitan monopoly capitalism; and they enshrined liberal virtues of tolerance and compromise at a time when history demanded violent and heroic actions. The anti-parliamentarians were not all Nazis and fascists, though they played into their hands: many conservatives and 'respectable nationalists' in Germany, for instance, played the same tune. *Unpolitische* could turn into *antipolitische* all too easily. And certainly none of the parliamentary regimes of the Western world seemed able to contain unemployment in the 1920s. The German republic was twice hit by inflation of a virulent kind: first it staggered, then it fell.

Many serious writers in the United States and Great Britain did not believe that parliamentary government could cope with unemployment. Many of the absurd fears of Roosevelt and his mild 'New Deal' by American businessmen came from their own belief that unemployment, on the scale of 1931 and 1932, could only be solved (if solved at all) by dictatorial means. Many liberals and social-democrats in England feared that the National Government, the coalition of 1931, would lead to one-party government and a withering away of any real parliamentary restraints. Most observers in England, the United States and France looked at Germany, Russia and Italy in the 1930s and believed what those regimes were saying about their own decisiveness and efficiency; and so such observers talked about 'the price' in terms of efficiency that parliamentary regimes would have to pay to preserve their liberties. The rhetoric of Hitler and Mussolini established a great myth of the superior efficiency of – following Mussolini's boasting concept – the 'totalitarian regimes'. The economic history of the Second World War exposed much of this talk of efficiency, total control and total planning as empty rhetoric. Nazi leader fought Nazi leader for scarce resources for war production: the leader could give instant decisions, but he rarely did, and hardly anyone else dared to. For a German general to win a battle against Hitler's orders was as dangerous as to lose under orders. The totalitarian Nazis could not bring themselves for ideological reasons to conscript women until 1944, when their backs were to the wall; parliamentary Britain had conscripted women since 1941.

Great Britain was, in fact, able to turn a parliamentary system into an extremely effective wartime autocracy largely because leaders would act as a team, had a habit of doing so, and would take decisions on their own, knowing that the penalty for failure would not be death or imprisonment, but being kicked upstairs to the House of Lords or sent to be Governor-General of a small island. Certainly some parliamentary regimes of the inner-war period proved grievously ineffective. The swift collapse of France to the German offensive in 1940 was as much a political as a military matter: the French conscripts had lost faith in their politicians long before they, once again, lost faith in their generals. But in the actual experience of the Second World War, parliamentary regimes proved at least as capable as the one-party states, probably more so, in mobilising their populations for extraordinary efforts and sacrifices.

Since the Second World War some parliaments have never revived, in any but the most formal sense, simply because of conquest and intimidation – as in Eastern Europe. Most of the new African states began with parliamentary regimes, but they have now turned either into one-party regimes, pure autocracies, or military governments, some of which maintain a parliament, in a shadowy East European way, while others have dispensed with the formality. The social conditions of 'developing economies' were said to favour one-party rule: the need to concentrate effort and human resources in the struggle to get rapid economic development. The argument is a difficult one and evidence is both vast and vague. Sometimes this may be true – although a lot depends on what is meant by 'rapid' and why rapid, in the long term, is always assumed to be best. Controlled economic growth, so that ancillary social processes can be adjusted, can well be a better solution. But often the alleged necessity of one-party rule is but an excuse for power-hunger and sheer intolerance. It could be argued that autocracies of any kind find it harder to plan effectively, not easier: planning seems to work best where there is freedom of discussion, where the penalties for mistakes or failures are not drastic, and where part of the plan is the ability to change it easily if it does not work, an experimental, empirical attitude, rather than when attaining the goals of 'The Plan' becomes a matter of the prestige of the party and its beloved leader.

Parliamentary regimes do have some long-term advantages in the business of economic development as well as of personal liberties. The men of 1789 and 1848 did not attack the *ancien régime* simply in the name of civil liberties, but also because autocracy seemed to them economically restrictive, inefficient and usually slow and contradictory, rather than swift and decisive (the fascist myth); and they objected to its spasmodic arbitrariness as much as its regular oppressiveness. But efficiency does not necessarily mean a capitalist market system – Hayek no more than Hegel can pronounce the end of history; capitalism is simply *more* efficient than mercantilism.

The post-war history of parliaments in South America is very mixed, in Africa and South-East Asia depressing, but West Germany, Italy and Japan have all successfully recreated parliamentary regimes far more stable, for all their problems and imperfections, than before. Japan for the first time has a parliament legally supreme in that it can make or break a Prime Minister without the will of the Emperor or the powers of the army. The Federal Republic of Germany has produced probably the most interesting of the post-war constitutions, a thoughtful blending of American, British and

German practice. The party system has as a rule provided working majorities but coalition was possible without disaster, and the prestige of the parliament and the regime is high. Italy is beset with problems arising from the lack of any party with a clear majority and the instability of the coalitions: government is weak, lacking in consistent parliamentary support. But the experience of the past is vivid, and general support for the constitution is great despite the terrorism. The parliamentary regime does not work well, but that it works at all is worth remarking. Indeed the relatively long history of the parliament, now nearly forty years old, has helped to make even the Italian Communist Party noticeably the most constitutional and national of the major Communist Parties in Western Europe. The old parliamentary republicanism of the young unified Italy survives in the cult of Gramsci, and the more conservative constitutionalism of the Christian Democrats differs from it, but not unworkably. In Spain, even in Franco's lifetime, it was widely assumed that only a parliamentary regime could effectively govern after his death. The army may set limits on the regime, but so do the trade unions; and both seem impressed with either the impossibility or the insufferably high price of trying to govern alone. The Spanish case shows, as in the revival of parliaments in Greece and Portugal, that parliaments are clearly a framework of government, not simply a bourgeois class ideology: both sides think that in the long run they can use this framework, and in the meantime observe reasonable, workable, political compromises.

THE FUNCTION OF PARLIAMENTS

Walter Bagehot's *The English Constitution* of 1867 is worth considering not as an objective description, but as conservative-minded polemic against further extension of the franchise. Yet he realistically argued that democratic reforms could be endured. He identified five basic social functions of parliament. He saw the parliament as an electoral chamber – choosing the prime minister or president (which is not always true). He identified an 'expressive function' – 'it is its office to express the mind of the . . . people on all matters which come before it'. Then he spoke of a 'teaching function' – 'a great and open council of considerable men cannot be placed in the middle of a society without altering the society'. There was also 'the informing function' – 'that to some extent it should make us hear what otherwise we should not'. 'Lastly', Bagehot concluded, 'there is the function of legislation, of which, of course, it would be preposterous to deny the great importance, and which I can only deny to be *as* important as the executive management of the whole state, or the political education given by parliament to the whole nation.' (To admire his acute political sociology surely does not involve agreement with his values.)

A hundred years later we still try to emancipate ourselves from the view that parliaments are failing shadows if they are not themselves making or heavily amending legislation. It is much more realistic to say that only an executive with a large and powerful civil service behind it can produce the kind of complex and mutually consistent legislation needed in modern conditions. The role of the legislature is to gain public understanding of the issues involved in the new legislation, even to get public support for it, not necessarily to defeat it; but also to criticise so strongly, publicly and effectively that it adds, if possible, to the weight of opinion that a government may not be returned at the next election unless it changes its policies. Legislatures can themselves only effectively legislate on relatively small and discrete matters, but they can influence legislation coming from the government, and influence the public for or against the government. Where parliamentary regimes are stable, more and more it is electorates and not parliaments who dismiss or create governments.

The old constitutional theories were developed in terms of what legal powers parliaments should or should not have against executives. But, increasingly, modern practice, in industry as well as in politics, points to the importance of communications as both opportunity and restraint, rather than direct physical or legal sanctions. A parliament is something which stands between a population and its powerful but temporary government, and tells each what the other will stand for. A parliament which in modern conditions itself tries to govern is more likely to destroy the regime than to prevent significant abuses. The fate of the French Third and even of the Fourth Republics is salutory: in both, too much parliamentary power damaged the democratic system. Parliaments are the most important of all the democratic institutions, but they are far from the only ones. Membership of voluntary bodies, the existence of trade unions and business associations, a free press, a speculative and an unregimented education system, all these are part of what the eighteenth century called 'republican virtues of institutions'.

Here the British experience is relevant, but not in absurdly parochial or procedural details. Parliamentary control has never been the enemy of strong and effective government in Britain; it is, rather, its primary condition. Parliament supports as well as restrains governments. The parliamentary system of government has been stable when it has been able to combine strong government with strong opposition. Governments must govern, but they govern best if subject to the kind of scrutiny and criticism that parliaments both provide and focus – focus even when it originates from others, journalists and academics, notably. Social theory should see modern parliaments not as governments, nor as rivals to governments, but as communication systems linking governments and electorates.

Freedom depends on the right to criticise governments, the ability to do so and on *actually doing so*. And freedom works through many more institutions than parliament: it is lost indeed if it all comes to depend on a parliament, but it will not work well without a parliament. What is crucial to a free regime is not the likelihood that a government can be defeated every time it introduces unpopular legislation, but that it can be defeated at the polls and that it will submit itself to polls which will be fairly conducted. The competitive general election is as important as parliament – on that point Schumpeter was right. Governments are restrained as much by knowing that people know, roughly speaking, why they are making a decision, as they are by formal votes. Governments fear public opinion as it begins to crystallise in the form of the prospects for the next election. Parliaments can influence this greatly, far more greatly than they ordinarily can or should influence particular legislation (Beer, 1967).

Parliaments then must be seen as one part, a necessary but not a sufficient part alone, of republican government. After the failures of some parliaments in the 1930s and with the total absence of parliamentary institutions in the lives of most of the world's inhabitants, one must be extremely careful not to claim too much. If the phrase to describe a certain type of regime is 'parliamentary government', we must remember that if government breaks down, no parliament is likely to survive for long: we must reconstrue the phrase as 'regimes of government through parliament'. There is then a very large difference between a government which in order to keep its support has to argue its way through the publicised proceedings of a parliament, and one that can keep its reasons and forecasts, sometimes even its basic intentions, to itself.

More and more, parliaments have to prepare public opinion for steps that governments need to take. They manufacture consent just as much as the one party in a totalitarian regime; but they ordinarily do it more effectively because they proceed by debate and controversy. A person persuaded is more effective than a person commanded against his or her will; and also they are able to report back in time if the persuasion really fails – perhaps then the legislation will be altered rather than, as is sometimes the case, the people (Crick, 1976 and 1973b).

Parliaments now being relatively more concerned with the two-way communications function, what Bagehot called 'expressive', 'teaching' and 'informing' functions rather than legislative ones, it follows that group representation other than by the parties becomes more important. Parties are still of the essence of parliamentary regimes, in keeping some coherence and consistency both in policy and debate. But perhaps they count for relatively less than they used to, and members of legislatures who are known to represent special interests, trade lobbies, reform movements, gain some special attention. The function of interest-group representation and conciliation is now more open, less covert, and the better for it. Some writers in the

1920s, like Sidney and Beatrice Webb, even thought that reformed parliaments should have a functional or syndicalist composition, or one part or house of them anyway, as well as representatives from geographical constituencies. Nowhere has this happened formally, but everywhere in practice it happens to some degree informally.

If the myth of legislative supremacy has been given up, which actually strengthens free institutions, so must the myth of parliamentary sovereignty. The Parliament of Europe is in an early stage of development, but as yet it has few real powers that, in the French or American traditions, would make it worthy of being called a sovereign assembly at all. But in the English tradition, particularly going back to feudal origins, here is an assembly that has the right to debate, that has to be consulted, and whose proceedings are publicised: through these it can have a political effect out of all proportion to its legal powers. However weak the Commission and Parliament of Europe are, their very existence does mean that parliamentary sovereignty, in the legal sense, no longer exists for the other parliaments in the Common Market. Certainly the Treaty of Rome and the powers of the Council of Ministers and of the Commission have removed many things from the control of the national legislatures. But such 'sovereignty' was, in any case, becoming an increasingly weak form of real power. The countries of Europe got together in order to achieve results which they were powerless to achieve separately. The loss of formal sovereignty actually means more real power. And to confuse formal sovereignty with real power and the right to exercise it, is actually to diminish real political power – as the British government discovered in the Falklands crisis. As power passes to European institutions, there is also a tendency in nearly all advanced industrial countries to devolve many functions of government to regions and localities (Thatcherism in Britain may prove an aberration – the change in France is more typical). Formal federalism is not likely to grow, but rather a greater realism about the scale most appropriate to different functions of government – for some of which the traditional national state is too small but for others too large. There is likely to be an increase of representative institutions and their activities both at a national and a supranational level. The national parliaments will be the vital bridges between regional and local government and European government. Modern theories and practices of planning, both economic and physical, share the necessity, not simply the liberal desirability, of increasing public participation in planning. With some exceptions, a new network of representative institutions is arising, strengthening parliamentary government, even if leaving the traditional parliament relatively less important than before – now to be seen as the predominant representative institution, but no longer as the omnipotent one. The traditional powers of parliaments seen as sovereign will diminish; but if looked at realistically as part of a whole complex of representative institutions in highly pluralistic societies in which effective power is not to be found at any single point of a complex system, parliamentary institutions in general are likely to become stronger, not weaker.

THE FUTURE OF GOVERNMENT

What will the future hold? The modern world has been nowhere near as inventive in forms of government as it has been in forms of industrial and agricultural production, in the conduct of war, and in science and technology. Even if we look at the component parts of political systems, what some might strictly call 'institutions', such as parliaments, parties, bureaucracies and electoral systems, we find a paucity of invention. The only original ideas of government in this century have been totalitarianism as a system, the idea of a total control of society (which is now tending to lapse back into something more like old-fashioned autocracy); and party, particularly one party, as the new and unique institution of government. (Parties before this century did not seek actually to govern, only to influence governments.)

A reasonable stability of government amid continuing high rates of technological and social change may be achieved not by new inventions, but simply by application for different purposes of already fairly well-known devices and principles such as parliament and parliamentarianism. Such devices and principles as elections, for instance, or informing the public why decisions are made (unlike in the secret governments of old-fashioned autocracies), will vary widely both in form and in independence. And 'informing the public' can take the form of a government being forced politically by parliament and press to divulge information it would not otherwise divulge (perhaps even about its own security systems) – or it can simply take the form of government propaganda. But modern autocracies or totalitarian regimes cannot ignore the masses, cannot thrive simply on passivity as did old autocracies: they positively need loyal assemblies, elections and propaganda, however deceptive, to mobilise the masses. This is because every population in the world is restless for and believes in the possibility of an increasing standard of living. No one believes now, as mankind believed through most of its history, that the future will resemble the past.

One of the great problems for the future for parliamentary regimes is the concern with size and scale. There is at first sight a clear dichotomy between those who say that efficiency demands the largest units, the world of the superpowers (although even here note how quickly it has changed from two, the USA and the USSR to an emerging five, that is China, Japan and Western Europe as well); and those who see liberty and justice as only secure in the small group, the anarchists, and syndicalists, pluralists and federalists. But the most likely prophecy of common trends in the future is that things will get both bigger and smaller. It will not be the vanishing of central government that is likely, but the devolution to localities, unions, industries or professions of more and more decisions – decisions subject to final central control, but whose initiation and form is local. Housing, town planning, education and welfare policies will become more and more regional, with the state enforcing minimum standards by financial control, but allowing greater variation of practice. At the same time, however, and this is equally important, some functions of government traditionally centred in the national state, are now becoming parts of larger units. Already in Western Europe we see a great concern with administrative devolution, at the same time as some key functions of government have passed beyond the competence of national governments. The situation is not entirely dissimilar in Eastern Europe. Foreign policy, defence and basic monetary, industrial and trading policy are supranationally controlled, but practices and arguments for greater devolution and for greater autonomy of decision-making at the factory level grow stronger and stronger.

Perhaps it is not too rash to say that all large countries in the modern world are trying to solve some of the problems of the reconciliation of order with economic progress, that is, of stability and innovation, in three ways: (1) By allowing the growth and influence of more group representation within the state, that is, groups outside the formal party, parliamentary and electoral systems. (2) By the institutionalisation of these groups so that they begin, even in one-party regimes, to get some relative 'autonomy': they are devices for industrial mobilisation, certainly, but because they are more effective at this than the party or even parties, some freedom for them, some diversity, some political difficulties, have to be tolerated. (3) By informal or formal processes of consultation between governments and these groups before major decisions are taken. Leaders do like to know that they will be followed. For increasingly it is recognised that the kind of economic and social policies needed in the modern state cannot be enforced, or will not prove successful, if the skilled working population and the managers are not convinced, and therefore drag their feet. Industrial changes need some positive response. And if much politics, even in liberal regimes, is, indeed, a matter of what people will put up with or accept rather than what they positively agree to, yet there are limits to what a skilled worker will put up with. Rebellion is not always the ultimate or the realistic sanction against despotic government: rather, it is working slowly, badly, reluctantly, ineffectively – whether we are talking of the skilled worker or the university-trained manager. The Hungarians, the Czechs and Poles have tried different responses to oppression which have all been, perhaps, overly specific, and have appeared as rival powers to the official regime; but looked at in another way, the whole of Eastern Europe represents a vast, informal and unplanned 'go slow' movement, severely limiting the powers of the regimes.

Such pressures arising from the dependence of governments on technologists and experts are not likely to have democratic results in the conventional sense of more and more open political participation. But they may develop something quite as important, also a part of democracy: radical increases in the effectiveness of communications. It seems more likely that what basically restrains governments in advanced industrial societies and makes them serve popular purposes is (i) the knowledge that their decisions become known (as it were, the eighteenth- and nineteenth-century battle against the inefficiency as well as the injustice of arbitrary autocracy); (ii) that the reasons for their decisions will become known (at least among a managerial elite whose intelligent and comprehending skills are needed); (iii) that the consequences of their decisions will be evaluated critically, publicised and popularised intelligently, so that the skilled manual workers (on whom both capitalist and socialist civilisations depend) can be educated, mobilised and integrated into the ruling elites.

There is still a lot to be said for the first general theory of politics. Aristotle put forward two criteria for stability in the *polis* or the citizen-state. The first is famous: that men should rule and be ruled in turn. But the second is less familiar: that the state should be no larger than that the voice of the 'stentor' (or herald) could be heard from boundary to boundary or – he put it another way but meaning the same thing – no larger than that citizens could know each other's characters. We might neglect his second criterion because it would seem to limit democracy, as Rousseau saw, to small groups. But what if part of the modern 'stentor' is the press and radio–television, and 'to know each other's characters' is possible through them, even between states whose populations rarely if ever meet? Some societies may think that they have gone as far as they can in exploring the inferences of Aristotle's first generalisation, but few have begun to appreciate the second, or to translate them into the conditions of mass societies and modern industrial states.

Parliaments will thus be more important than ever before, even if their formal legal powers appear to grow less. They will less and less formulate legislation themselves or be able to stop effective government, but they will be the centre of the whole communications system of modern society, the key element in the feed-back not merely between governed and government, but between all kinds of interest groups and each other. Parties will still be there in parliaments, not always to command in detail but, in Bagehot's phrase, 'to inject a stream of tendency' and to ensure some consistent policy amid such great and ever-growing diversities of interest; but they will count for less than in the first half of the twentieth century. The political influence of parliaments will grow as politicians learn and relearn the hard lessons of history that the strongest governments – those able to do the most in terms of new social policies, not simply to enjoy that negative power that frustrates change and perpetuates the *status quo* – are those governments which can carry with them (as Machiavelli taught) the active support of the people; and the strongest of the strong are those where that support is given willingly and voluntarily, not by propaganda and by restriction of choice. Few countries can now keep their inhabitants from learning how others are governed and none can prevent their administrative or technological elites from gaining such knowledge. And in the long run parliamentary republics are stronger than autocracies because of the power of the people, because of their great flexibility, and because their economic and social plans are open to public criticism and adjustment. It may often be easier to govern without parliaments. Republican Rome, said Machiavelli in the *Discourses*, could have avoided constant tumults and conflicts between the classes if she had suppressed the office of the Tribunes (the representatives of the people). She could have been more peaceful as a purely aristocratic or senatorial republic, but she would, he argued, have thus been less strong. The common people could not have been safely enrolled in the legions had they not felt part of the state. Today the future of civilisation turns not on the citizen-soldier but on the contentment and energy of the citizen industrial worker. The Russians, for example, think it easier to govern in his interests than to let him govern himself. But any state that can harness his allegiance and energies to a free political system is going to be far more full of crises and uproars than the Soviet Union, but far stronger in the ability to carry through new programmes which need popular support, and are popular. Governing through parliaments or popular assemblies is not easy, but in the long run it is the only alternative to either bureaucratic stagnation or ideological oppression. Paradoxically, one of the things that can discredit it is the attempt of parliaments themselves to govern.

This description of the obvious may have been tedious. But there is sometimes a need, as I said at the beginning of my *In Defence of Politics*, to make platitudes pregnant. The sociological attempt to reduce 'liberalism' to an instrumental product of the necessary structures of capitalist society, even in its most subtle and historical formulations contains some truths; but it has badly confused the republican tradition with the liberal, and ends up by throwing out the good with the bad, both morally and theoretically speaking. The theory of parliamentarianism is a synthesis of classical republican with pluralistic feudal ideas. It can be used and modified for many different purposes. It even preceded the competitive party system and could even, to some extent does already, furnish the institutional setting for no-party government or one-party government. Certainly parliamentary institutions can be extended into industry and working life, as to some extent they are (with varying powers and fortunes) into local or devolved government. There is no theoretical reason why existing parliaments should be jealous of extra-parliamentary democracy, nor need extra-parliamentary democracy be anti-parliamentary. Parliaments need not claim sovereignty, perhaps only a minimal co-ordinating primacy. Syndicalists begin by attacking bourgeois parliamentarianism and end by re-creating a national representative assembly.

Freedom is a matter of social relationships, of interactions, not simply of the liberation of individual personality: Marcuse and other modern Rousseauians mislead as much as economic individualists. Freedom needs institutional forms. Talk of 'deinstitutionalising' is either anarchism or else rhetoric for replacing bad institutions with better ones – in which case, the polemicists should specify and show the practical entailments of their theories, however banal.

At the end of the day, if we work with both means and ends (with institutions towards greater freedom, fraternity and equality), what alternatives are there to republican parliaments or assemblies? The concreteness of one-party government (more likely to be ruled by bureaucrats) or the vagueness of 'the movement'? Even if we live in national states (no longer under alien rule) and even if they succeed in raising the living standards of their peoples both absolutely and relatively, do we really believe that they will sustain themselves in the long run without re-creating something analogous to the free assemblies of the republican tradition?[5] Machiavelli was quite clear in *The Prince* why a concentration of power was necessary to create or to restore a state; but he was equally clear in the *Discourses* why power then needs to be spread, why states need to adopt republican institutions if they are to survive through time. Only by a deliberate retreat from normal politics as contaminatory can intellectuals sustain the belief that states of emergency must continue for ever.

Surely the wise theorist, like the shrewd activist (even when they are different people), should be able to distinguish between different levels of theory and different time-scales for action. Not all institutions and ideas uniquely serve the interests of any single social system. Political sociology should deal in conditions, not in causes. It should cease, indeed, to pretend to be simply descriptive; but to drop that pretence is to recognise, before proceeding any further, the primacy of the link between free intellectual inquiry and the values and institutions of republican politics: a minimal value in whatever form they take, but a maximal value in the egalitarian-libertarian ideal of 'the Republic'.

NOTES

1. See the preface to the second edition of Bernard Crick's *In Defence of Politics* (Harmondsworth, Penguin Books, 1972), and the Appendix to the revised Penguin edition of 1982, 'A footnote to rally fellow socialists'.

2. See, for instance, Ralph Miliband, *Marxism and Politics* (Oxford University Press, 1977), which concludes: 'Bourgeois democracy is crippled by its class limitations . . . But the civic freedoms which, however inadequately and precariously, form part of bourgeois democracy are the products of centuries of unremitting popular struggles. The task of Marxist politics is to defend these freedoms; and to make possible their extension and enlargement by the removal of class barriers' (pp. 189–90).

3. Ralph Miliband's *Parliamentary Socialism* (London, Weidenfeld and Nicolson, 1961), by purporting to show that the British Labour Party's original socialism (a state of grace that he assumes rather than demonstrates) lapsed because it embraced parliamentary practices and ideology, infers that this must be generally so – yet on his own detailed argument, the British case is highly peculiar. Would the republican tradition of popular assemblies be open to the same objection? From his more recent writings, it would seem not; and the school of Gramsci have more faith that the historicity of (even) Italian parliamentary institutions are not necessarily incompatible with socialist ideology.

4. See Antonio Marongiu, *Medieval Parliaments: a comparative study* (London, Eyre and Spottiswoode, 1968), and this author's summary of the evidence in the entry under 'Parliament' in *Enciclopedia Italiana*, vol. V (Rome, 1977), on which some of these paragraphs are based.

5. Ernest Gellner, either in very tough-minded mood or setting out to shock us (into thought), argued in his *Thought and Change* (London, Weidenfeld and Nicolson, 1964) that: 'In our time, a social order is valid, has rightful claims on the loyalty of members of the society, under two conditions: (a) It is bringing about, or successfully maintaining an industrial affluent society. (b) Those in authority are co-cultural with the rest of the society' (p. 33).Yet Gellner argues convincingly elsewhere the intellectual and the practical link between freedom and Karl Popper's account of scientific method (see throughout his essays, *Cause and Meaning in the Social Sciences* (London, Routledge and Kegan Paul, 1973) and his *Contemporary Thought and Politics* (London, Routledge and Kegan Paul, 1974)). Even in *Thought and Change*, liberty keeps slipping back in (see pp. 38 and 46 especially). In some ways Bronislaw Malininowski, *Freedom and Civilisation* (London, Allen and Unwin, 1947) contains as convincing a grounding of freedom in social mechanisms of adaptation as Popper's more famous grounding of it in scientific method in his *Open Society and Its Enemies* (London, Routledge and Kegan Paul, 1945). Both were wartime books and a certain amount of rhetoric has to be excused and passed over.

REFERENCES

Anderson, P., 1974. *Passages from Antiquity to Feudalism*. London, New Left Books

Arendt, H., 1958. *The Human Condition*. Cambridge, Cambridge University Press

Beer, S. H., 1967. 'The British legislature and the problem of mobilizing consent', in *Essays on Reform, 1967*, edited B. Crick. Oxford, Clarendon Press

Crick, B., 1973a. 'Freedom as politics', in his *Political Theory and Practice*. London, Allen Lane

 1973b. *Basic Forms of Government: a Sketch of a Model*. London, Macmillan

 1976. 'Participation and the future of government', in J. A. G. Griffith, ed., '*From Policy to Administration: essays in honour of William A. Robson*. London, Allen and Unwin

Finley, M. I., 1966. *The Ancient Greeks*. Harmondsworth, Penguin Books

Hayek, F. A. von, 1960. *The Constitution of Liberty*. London, Routledge and Kegan Paul

McIlwain, C., 1947. *Constitutionalism Ancient and Modern*. Revised edition, Ithaca, New York, Cornell University Press

Macpherson, C. B., 1962. *The Political Theory of Possessive Individualism*. Oxford, Oxford University Press

 1966. *The Real World of Democracy*. Oxford, Oxford University Press

Pocock, J. G. A., 1975. *The Machiavellian Moment: Florentine Political Thought and the Atlantic Republican Tradition*. Princeton, Princeton University Press

5

Marx and the state

RALPH MILIBAND

I

As in the case of so many other aspects of Marx's work, what he thought about the state has more often than not come to be seen through the prism of later interpretations and adaptations. These have long congealed into *the* Marxist theory of the state, or into the Marxist–Leninist theory of the state, but they cannot be taken to constitute an adequate expression of Marx's own views. This is not because these theories bear *no* relation to Marx's views but rather that they emphasise some aspects of his thought to the detriment of others, and thus distort by over-simplification an extremely complex and by no means unambiguous body of ideas; and also that they altogether ignore certain strands in Marx's thought which are of considerable interest and importance. This does not, in itself, make later views better or worse than Marx's own: to decide this, what needs to be compared is not text with text, but text with historical or contemporary reality itself. This can hardly be done within the compass of an essay. But Marx is so inescapably bound up with contemporary politics, his thought is so deeply buried inside the shell of official Marxism and his name is so often invoked in ignorance by enemies and partisans alike, that it is worth asking again what he, rather than Engels, or Lenin or any other of his followers, disciples or critics, actually said and appeared to think about the state. This is the purpose of the present essay.

Marx himself never attempted to set out a comprehensive and systematic theory of the state. In the late 1850s he wrote that he intended, as part of a vast scheme of projected work, of which *Capital* was only to be the first part, to subject the state to systematic study (Marx to Lassalle, 22 February 1858; Marx to Engels, 2 April 1858 in Marx and Engels, 1956, *Selected Correspondence*, hereafter *SC*). But of this scheme, only one part of *Capital* was in fact completed. His ideas on the state must therefore be taken from such historical *pièces de circonstance* as *The Class Struggles in France*, the *18th Brumaire of Louis Bonaparte*, and *The Civil War in France*, and from his incidental remarks on the subject in his other works. On the other hand, the crucial importance of the state in his scheme of analysis is well shown by his constantly recurring references to it in almost all of his writings; and the state was also a central preoccupation of the 'young Marx': his early work from the late 1830s to 1844 was largely concerned with the nature of the state and its relation to society. His most sustained piece of work until the 1844 *Economic and Philosophical Manuscripts*, apart from his doctoral dissertation, was his *Critique of Hegel's Philosophy of Right (Marx/Engels Gesamtausgabe*, 1927) of which only the *Introduction* (Bottomore, 1963), actually written after the *Critique* itself, has so far appeared in English.[1] It is in fact largely through his critique of Hegel's view of the state that Marx completed his emancipation from the Hegelian system. This early work of Marx on the state is of great interest; for, while he soon moved beyond the views and positions he had set out there, some of the questions he had encountered in his examination of Hegel's philosophy recur again and again in his later writings.

II

Marx's earliest views on the state bear a clear Hegelian imprint. In the articles which he wrote for the *Rheinische Zeitung* from May 1842 to March 1843, he repeatedly spoke of the state as the guardian of the general interest of society and of law as the embodiment of freedom. Modern philosophy, he writes in July 1842, 'considers the state as the great organism in which must be realised juridical, moral and political freedom and where the individual citizen, in obeying the laws of the state only obeys the natural laws of his own reason, of human reason' (*Gesamtausgabe*, 1927, vol. I, p. 249).

On the other hand, he also shows himself well aware that this exalted view of the state is in contradiction with the real state's actual behaviour: 'a state which is not the realisation of rational freedom is a bad state', he writes (*Gesamtausgabe*, 1927: vol. I, p. 248), and in his article on the Rhineland Diet's repressive legislation against the pilfering of forest wood, he eloquently denounces the assignation to the state of the role of servant of the rich against the poor. This, he holds, is a perversion of the state's true purpose and mission; private property may wish to degrade the state to its own level of concern, but any modern state, in so far as it remains true to its own meaning, must, confronted by such pretensions, cry out 'your ways are not my ways, and your ideas are not my ideas' (1927, p. 283).

More and more, however, Marx found himself driven to emphasise the external pressures upon the state's actions. Writing in January 1843 on the plight of the wine growers of the Moselle, he remarks that 'in the examination of the institutions of the state, one is too easily tempted to overlook the concrete nature of circumstances [*die sachliche Natur der Verhaltnisse*] and to explain everything by the will of those empowered to act' (*Gesamtausgabe*, 1927, p. 360).[2]

It is this same insistence on the need to consider the 'concrete nature of circumstances' which lies at the core of the *Critique of Hegel's Philosophy of Right*, which Marx wrote in the spring and summer of 1843 after the *Rheinische Zeitung* had been closed down. By then, his horizons had widened to the point where he spoke confidently of a 'break' in the existing society, to which 'the system of acquisition and commerce, of ownership and of exploitation of man is leading even more rapidly than the increase in population' (Marx to Ruge, March 1843 and May 1843 in *SC*; Marx, *Gesamtausgabe*, 1927, vol. I, p. 565). Hegel's 'absurdity', he also writes in the *Critique*, is that he views the affairs and the activities of the state in an abstract fashion; he forgets that the activities of the state are human functions: 'the affairs of the state, etc., are nothing but the modes of existence and activity of the social qualities of men' (1927, vol. I, p. 519).

The burden of Marx's critique of Hegel's concept of the state is that Hegel, while rightly acknowledging the separation of civil society from the state, asserts their reconciliation in the state itself. In his system, the 'contradiction' between the state and society is resolved in the supposed representation in the state of society's true meaning and reality; the alienation of the individual from the state, the contradiction between man as a private member of society, concerned with his own private interests, and as a citizen of the state finds resolution in the state as the expression of society's ultimate reality.

But this, says Marx, is not a resolution but a mystification. The contradiction between the state and society is real enough. Indeed, the political alienation which it entails is the central fact of modern, bourgeois society, since man's political significance is detached from his real private condition, while it is in fact this condition which determines him as a social being, all other determinations appearing to him as external and inessential: 'real man is the private man of the present constitution of the state' (*Gesamtausgabe*, 1927, pp. 498–9; Hyppolite, 1955, pp. 123ff.; Rubel, 1957, pp. 58ff.).

But the mediating elements which are supposed, in Hegel's system, to ensure the resolution of this contradiction – the sovereign, the bureaucracy, the middle classes, the legislature – are not in the least capable, says Marx, of doing so. Ultimately, Hegel's state, far from being above private interests and representing the general interest, is in fact subordinate to private property. What, asks Marx, is the power of the state over private property? The state has only the illusion of being determinant, whereas it is in fact determined; it does, in time, subdue private and social wills, but only to give substance to the will of private property and to acknowledge its reality as the highest reality of the political state, as the highest moral reality (*Gesamtausgabe*, 1927, p. 519).

In the *Critique*, Marx's own resolution of political alienation and of the contradiction between the state and society is still envisaged in mainly political terms, i.e. in the framework of 'true democracy'. 'Democracy is the solution to the riddle of all constitutions'; in it, 'the constitution appears in its true reality, as the free product of man'. 'All other political systems are specific, definite, particular political forms. In democracy, the formal principle is also the material principle.' It constitutes, therefore, the real unity of the universal and the particular (*Gesamtausgabe*, 1927, vol. I, pp. 434–5).

In all states which differ from democracy, the state, the law, the constitution are sovereign without being properly dominant, that is to say without materially affecting the other non-political spheres. In democracy, the constitution, the law, the state itself are only the people's self-determination, a specific aspect of it, in so far as that aspect has a political constitution. (*Gesamtausgabe*, 1927, vol. I, p. 435)

Democracy is here intended to mean more than a specific political form, but Marx does not yet define what else it entails. The struggle between monarchy and republic, he notes, is still a struggle within the framework of what he calls the 'abstract state', i.e. the state alienated from society; the abstract political form of democracy is the republic. 'Property and all that makes up the content of law and the state is, with some modifications, the same in the United States as in Prussia; the republic in America is thus only a purely political form as is the monarchy in Prussia' (*Gesamtausgabe*, 1927, vol. I, p. 436). In a real democracy, however, the constitution ceases to be purely political; indeed Marx quotes the opinion of 'some modern Frenchmen' to the effect that 'in a real democracy the political state disappears' (1927, p. 435). But the concrete content of 'true democracy' remains here undefined.

The *Critique* already suggests the belief that political emancipation is not synonymous with human emancipation. The point, which is, of course, central to Marx's whole system, was made explicit in the two articles which he wrote for the *Franco-German Annals*, namely the *Jewish Question*, and the *Introduction* to a contribution to the *Critique of Hegel's Philosophy of Right*.

In the first essay, Marx criticises Bruno Bauer for confusing political and human emancipation, and notes that 'the limit of political emancipation is immediately apparent in the fact that the *state* may well free itself from some constraint, without man himself being *really* freed from it, and that the state may be a *free state*, without *man* being free' (*Gesamtausgabe*, 1927, vol. I, p. 582). Even so, political emancipation is a great advance; it is not the last form of human emancipation, but it is the last form of human emancipation within the framework of the existing social order (1927, vol. I, p. 585). Human emancipation, on the other hand, can only be realised by transcending bourgeois society, 'which has torn up all genuine bonds between men and replaced them by selfishness, selfish need, and dissolved the world of men into a world of atomised individuals, hostile towards each other' (1927, vol. I, p. 605). The more specific meaning of that emancipation is defined in the *Jewish Question*, in Marx's strictures against 'Judaism', here deemed synonymous with trade, money and the commercial spirit which has come to affect all human relations. On this view, the political emancipation of the Jews, which Marx defends (Avineri, 1964, pp. 445–50), does not produce their social emancipation; this is only possible in a new society, in which practical need has been humanised and the commercial spirit abolished (*Gesamtausgabe*, 1927, p. 606).

In the *Introduction*, which he wrote in Paris at the end of 1843 and the beginning of 1844, Marx now spoke of 'the doctrine, that man is for man the supreme being' and of the 'categorical imperative' which required the overthrow of all conditions in which 'man is a degraded, enslaved, abandoned and contemptible being' (*Gesamtausgabe*, 1927, vol. 1, p. 615). But he also added another element to the system he was constructing, namely the proletariat as the agent of the dissolution of the existing social order (1927, vol. 1, pp. 619ff.). As we shall see, this view of the proletariat is not only crucial for Marx's concept of revolution but also for his view of the state.

By this time, Marx had already made an assessment of the relative importance of the political realm from which he was never to depart and which also had some major consequences for his later thought. On the one hand, he does not wish to underestimate the importance of 'political emancipation', that is, of political reforms tending to make politics and the state more liberal and democratic. Thus, in *The Holy Family*, which he wrote in 1844 in collaboration with Engels, Marx describes the 'democratic representative state' as 'the perfect modern state' (Marx and Engels, 1956, p. 24), meaning the perfect modern *bourgeois* state, its perfection arising from the fact that 'the public system is *not* faced with any privileged exclusivity' (1956, p. 157), i.e. economic and political life are free from feudal encumbrances and constraints.

But there is also, on the other hand, a clear view that political emancipation is not enough, and that society can only be made truly human by the abolition of private property. 'It is natural necessity, *essential human properties*, however alienated they may seem to be, and *interest* that hold the members of civil society together, *civil*, not *political* life is their *real* tie. It is therefore not the state that holds the *atoms* of civil society together ... only *political superstition* today imagines that social life must be held together by the state, whereas in reality the state is held together by civil life' (Marx and Engels, 1956, p. 163). The modern democratic state 'is based on emancipated slavery, on bourgeois society ... the society of industry, of universal competition, of private interest freely following its aims, of anarchy, of the self-alienated natural and spiritual individuality ...' (1956, p. 164); the 'essence' of the modern state is that 'it is based on the unhampered development of bourgeois society, on the free movement of private interest' (1956, p. 166).

A year later, in *The German Ideology*, Marx and Engels defined further the relation of the state to bourgeois society. 'By the mere fact that it is a *class* and no longer an *estate*', they wrote, 'the bourgeoisie is forced to organise itself no longer locally but nationally, and to give a general form to its mean average interest'; this 'general form' is the state, defined as 'nothing more than the form of organisation which the bourgeois necessarily adopt both for internal and external purposes, for the mutual guarantee of their property and interest' (Marx and Engels, 1939, p. 59). This same view is confirmed in the *Poverty of Philosophy* of 1847, where Marx again states that 'political conditions are only the official expression of civil society'; and goes on: 'It is the sovereigns who in all ages have been subject to economic conditions, but it is never they who have dictated laws to them. Legislation, whether political or civil, never does more than proclaim, express in words, the will of economic relations' (Marx, 1936, p. 70).

This whole trend of thought on the subject of the state finds its most explicit expression in the famous formulation of the *Communist Manifesto*: 'The executive of the modern state is but a committee for managing the common affairs of the whole bourgeoisie' (Marx and Engels, 1950, vol. I, p. 35); and political power is merely the 'organised power of one class for oppressing another' (1950: p. 51). This is the classical Marxist view on the subject of the state, and it is the only one which is to be found in Marxism–Leninism. In regard to Marx himself, however, and this is also true to a certain extent of Engels as well, it only constitutes what might be called a primary view of the state. For, as has occasionally been noted in discussions of Marx and the state (Plamenatz, 1954, pp. 144ff.; Sanderson, 1963, pp. 946–55), there is to be found another view of the state in his work, which it is inaccurate to hold up as of similar status with the first, but which is none the less of great interest, not least because it serves to illuminate, and indeed provides an essential context for, certain major elements in Marx's system, notably the concept of the dictatorship of the proletariat. This secondary view is that of the state as independent from and superior to all social classes, as being the dominant force in society rather than the instrument of a dominant class.

III

It may be useful, for a start, to note some qualifications which Marx made even to his primary view of the state. For in relation to the two most advanced capitalist countries of the day, England and France, he often makes the point that, at one time or another, it is not the ruling class as a whole, but a fraction of it, which controls the state,[3] and that those who actually run the state may well belong to a class which is not the economically dominant class.[4] Marx does not suggest that this *fundamentally* affects the state's class character and its role of guardian and defender of the interests of property; but it obviously does introduce an element of flexibility in his view of the operation of the state's bias, not least because the competition between different factions of the ruling class may well make easier the passage of measures favourable to labour, such as the Ten Hours Bill (Marx and Engels, 1953, p. 368).

The extreme manifestation of the state's independent role is, however, to be found in authoritarian personal rule, Bonapartism. Marx's most extensive discussion of this phenomenon occurs in *The 18th Brumaire of Louis Bonaparte*, which was written between December 1851 and March 1852. In this historical study, Marx sought very hard to pin down the precise nature of the rule which Louis Bonaparte's *coup d'état* had established.

The *coup d'état*, he wrote, was 'the victory of Bonaparte over parliament, of the executive power over the legislative power'; in parliament, 'the nation made its general will the law, that is, made the law of the ruling class its general will'; in contrast, 'before the executive power it renounces all will of its own and submits to the superior command of an alien will, to authority';

France, therefore, seems to have escaped the despotism of a class only to fall back beneath the despotism of an individual and, what is more, beneath the authority of an individual without authority. The struggle seems to be settled in such a way that all classes, equally impotent and equally mute, fall on their knees before the rifle butt. (Marx and Engels, 1950, vol. I, p. 300)

Marx then goes on to speak of 'this executive power with its enormous bureaucratic and military organisation, with its ingenious state machinery, embracing wide strata, with a host of officials numbering half a million, besides an army of another half million, this appalling parasitic body which enmeshes the body of French society like a net and chokes all its pores' (Marx and Engels, 1950, vol. I, p. 301). This bureaucratic power, which sprang up in the days of the absolute monarchy, had, he wrote, first been 'the means of preparing the class rule of the bourgeoisie', while 'under the Restoration, under Louis-Philippe, under the parliamentary Republic, it was the instrument of the ruling class, however much it strove for power of its own' (1950, vol. I, p. 302). But the *coup d'état* had seemingly changed its role: 'only under the second Bonaparte does the state seem to have made itself completely independent'; 'as against civil society, the state machine has consolidated its position so thoroughly that the chief of the Society of December 10 [i.e., Louis Bonaparte] suffices for its head' (1950, vol. I, p. 302).

This appears to commit Marx to the view of the Bonapartist state as independent of any specific class and as superior to society. But he then goes on to say, in an often-quoted phrase:

And yet the state power is not suspended in mid-air. Bonaparte represents a class, and the most numerous class of French society at that, *the small-holding peasants*. (Marx and Engels, 1950, vol. I, p. 302)

However, their lack of cohesion makes these 'incapable of enforcing their class interests in their own name whether through a parliament or a convention';[5] they therefore require a representative who 'must at the same time appear as their master, as an authority over them, as an unlimited governmental power that protects them against the other classes and sends them rain and sunshine from above. The political influence of the small-holding peasants, therefore, finds its final expression in the executive power subordinating society to itself' (1950, vol. I, p. 303).

'Represent' is here a confusing word. In the context, the only meaning that may be attached to it is that the small-holding peasants *hoped* to have their interests represented by Louis Bonaparte. But this does not turn Louis Bonaparte or the state into the mere instrument of their will; at the most, it may limit the executive's freedom of action somewhat. Marx also writes that

> as the executive authority which has made itself an independent power, Bonaparte feels it his mission to safeguard 'bourgeois order'. But the strength of this bourgeois order lies in the middle class. He looks on himself, therefore, as the representative of the middle class and issues decrees in this sense. Nevertheless, he is somebody solely due to the fact that he has broken the political power of this middle class and daily breaks it anew;

and again,

> as against the bourgeoisie, Bonaparte looks on himself, at the same time, as the representative of the peasants and of the people in general, who wants to make the lower classes of the people happy within the frame of bourgeois society . . . But, above all, Bonaparte looks on himself as the chief of the Society of 10 December, as the representative of the *lumpenproletariat* to which he himself, his *entourage*, his government and his army belong. (Marx and Engels, 1950, vol. I, pp. 308–9)

On this basis, Louis Napoleon may 'represent' this or that class – and Marx stresses the 'contradictory task' of the man and the 'contradictions of his government, the confused groping about which seeks now to win, now to humiliate first one class and then another and arrays all of them uniformly against him' (Marx and Engels, 1950, vol. I, p. 309) – but his power of initiative remains very largely unimpaired by the specific wishes and demands of any one class or fraction of a class.

On the other hand, this does *not* mean that Bonapartism, for Marx, is in any sense neutral as between contending classes. It may *claim* to represent all classes and to be the embodiment of the whole of society. But it does in fact exist, and has been called into being, for the purpose of maintaining and strengthening the existing social order and the domination of capital over labour. Bonapartism and the empire, Marx wrote much later in *The Civil War in France*, had succeeded the bourgeois republic precisely because 'it was the only form of government possible at a time when the bourgeoisie had already lost, and the working class had not yet acquired, the faculty of ruling the nation'. It was precisely under its sway that 'bourgeois society, freed from political cares, attained a development unexpected even by itself'. Finally, Marx then characterises what he calls 'imperialism', by which he means Napoleon's imperial regime, as

at the same time, the most prostitute and the ultimate form of the State power which nascent middle-class society had commenced to elaborate as a means of its own emancipation from feudalism, and which full-grown bourgeois society had finally transformed into a means for the enslavement of labour by capital. (Marx and Engels, 1950, vol. I, p. 470)

In *The Origin of the Family, Private Property and the State*, written a year after Marx's death, Engels also notes: 'By way of exception, however, periods occur in which the warring classes balance each other so nearly that the state power, as ostensible mediator, acquires, for the moment, a certain degree of independence of both' (Marx and Engels, 1950, vol. II, p. 290). But the independence of which he speaks would seem to go much further than anything Marx had in mind; thus Engels refers to the Second Empire, 'which played off the proletariat against the bourgeoisie and the bourgeoisie against the proletariat' and to Bismarck's German Empire, where 'capitalists and workers are balanced against each other and equally cheated for the benefit of the impoverished Prussian cabbage junkers' (1950, vol. II, p. 290).

For Marx, the Bonapartist state, however independent it may have been *politically* from any given class, remains, and cannot in a class society but remain, the protector of an economically and socially dominant class.

IV

In the *Critique of Hegel's Philosophy of Right*, Marx had devoted a long and involved passage to the bureaucratic element in the state, and to its attempt 'to transform the purpose of the state into the purpose of the bureaucracy and the purpose of the bureaucracy into the purpose of the state' (1927, vol. I, p. 456). But it was only in the early fifties that he began to look closely at a type of society where the state appeared to be genuinely 'above society', namely societies based on the 'Asiatic mode of production', whose place in Marx's thought has recently attracted much attention (Wittfogel, 1957; Lichtheim, 1963; Sawer, 1978).[6] What had, in the *Critique*, been a passing reference to the 'despotic states of Asia, where the political realm is nothing but the arbitrary will of a particular individual, where the political realm, like the material, is enslaved' (*Gesamtausgabe*, 1927, vol. I, p. 438), had, by 1859, become one of Marx's four main stages of history: 'In broad outlines', he wrote in the famous Preface to *A Contribution to the Critique of Political Economy*, 'Asiatic, ancient, feudal and modern bourgeois modes of production can be designated as progressive epochs in the economic formation of society' (Marx and Engels, 1950, vol. I, p. 438).

The countries Marx was mainly concerned with in this connection were India and China, and also Russia as a 'semi-Asiatic' or 'semi-Eastern' state. The Asiatic mode of production, for Marx and Engels, had one outstanding characteristic, namely the absence of private property in land: 'this', Marx wrote to Engels in 1853, 'is the real key, even to the Oriental heaven' (Marx to Engels: *SC*, p. 99). 'In the Asiatic form (or at least predominantly so)', he noted, 'there is no property, but individual possession; the community is properly speaking the real proprietor' (Marx, 1964, p. 79); in Asiatic production, he also remarked, it is the state which is the 'real landlord' (Lichtheim, 1963, p. 94). In this system, he also wrote later, the direct producers are not 'confronted by a private landowner but rather, as in Asia, [are] under direct subordination to a state which stands over them as their landlord and simultaneously as sovereign'; 'the state', he went on,

is then the supreme lord. Sovereignty here consists in the ownership of land concentrated on a national scale. But, on the other hand, no private ownership of land exists, although there is both private and common possession and use of land. (Marx, 1962, vol. III, pp. 771–2)

A prime necessity of the Asiatic mode of production, imposed by climate and territorial conditions, was artificial irrigation by canals, and waterworks: indeed, Marx wrote, this was 'the basis of Oriental agriculture'. In countries like Flanders and Italy the need for an economical and common use of water drove private enterprise into voluntary association; but it required

in the Orient, where civilization was too low and the territorial extent too vast to call into life voluntary associations, the interference of the centralised power of Government. Hence an economical function devolved upon all Asiatic governments, the function of providing public works. (Marx and Engels, n.d., p. 16)[7]

Finally, in the *Grundrisse*, Marx speaks of 'the despotic government which is poised above the lesser communities' (Marx, 1964, p. 71), and describes that government as the

all embracing unity which stands above all these small common bodies . . . since the *unity* is the real owner, and the real pre-condition of common ownership, it is perfectly possible for it to appear as something separate and superior to the numerous real, particular communities . . . the despot here appears as the father of all the numerous lesser communities, thus realising the common unity of all. (Marx, 1964, p. 69)

It is therefore evident that Marx does view the state, in the conditions of Asiatic despotism, as the dominant force in society, independent of and superior to all its members, and that those who control its administration are society's authentic rulers. Karl Wittfogel has noted that Marx did not pursue this theme after the 1850s and that 'in the writings of the later period he emphasised the technical side of large-scale waterworks, where previously he had emphasised their political setting' (Wittfogel, 1957, p. 381). The reason for this, Professor Wittfogel suggests, is that 'obviously the concept of Oriental despotism contained elements that paralysed his search for truth' (1957, p. 387), hence his 'retrogressions' on the subject. But the explanation for Marx's lack of concern for the topic would seem much simpler and much less sinister; it is that he was, in the sixties and the early seventies, primarily concerned with Western capitalism. Furthermore, the notion of bureaucratic despotism can hardly have held any great terror for him since he had, in fact, worked through its nearest equivalent in capitalist society, namely Bonapartism, and had analysed it as an altogether different phenomenon from the despotism encountered in Asiatic society. Nor is it accurate to suggest, as does Mr Lichtheim, that 'Marx for some reason shirked the problem of the bureaucracy' in post-capitalist society (Lichtheim, 1963, p. 110). On the contrary, this may be said to be a crucial element in Marx's thought in the late sixties and in the early seventies. His concern with the question, and with the state, finds expression in this period in his discussion of the nature of political power in post-capitalist societies, and particularly in his view of the dictatorship of the proletariat. This theme had last occupied Marx in 1851–2; after almost twenty years it was again brought to the fore by the Paris Commune, by his struggles with anarchism in the First International and by the programmatic pronouncement of German social democracy. It is to this, one of the most important and the most misunderstood aspects of Marx's work on the state, that we must now turn.

V

It is first of all necessary to go back to the democratic and representative republic, which must be clearly distinguished from the dictatorship of the proletariat: for Marx, the two concepts have nothing in common. An element of confusion arises from the fact that Marx bitterly denounced the class character of the democratic republic, yet supported its coming into being. The contradiction is only apparent; Marx saw the democratic republic as the most advanced type of political regime in *bourgeois society*, and wished to see it prevail over more backward and 'feudal' political systems. But it remained for him a system of class rule, indeed the system in which the bourgeoisie rules most directly.

The limitations of the democratic republic, from Marx's point of view, are made particularly clear in the *Address of the Central Committee of the Communist League* which he and Engels wrote in March 1850. 'Far from desiring to revolutionise all society for the revolutionary proletarians', they wrote, 'the democratic petty-bourgeois strive for a change in social conditions by means of which existing society will be made as tolerable and comfortable as possible for them.' They would therefore demand such measures as 'the diminution of state expenditure by a curtailment of the bureaucracy and shifting the chief taxes on to the big landowners and bourgeois . . . the abolition of the pressure of big capital on small, through public credit institutions and laws against usury . . . the establishment of bourgeois property relations in the countryside by the complete abolition of feudalism'. But in order to achieve their purpose they would need 'a democratic state structure, either constitutional or republican, that will give them and their allies, the peasants, a majority: also a democratic communal structure that will give them direct control over communal property and over a series of functions now performed by the bureaucrats'. However, they added, 'as far as the workers are concerned, it remains certain that they are to remain wage workers as before; the democratic petty-bourgeois only desire better wages and a more secure existence for the workers . . . they hope to bribe the workers by more or less concealed alms and to break their revolutionary potency by making their position tolerable for the moment' (Marx and Engels, 1950, vol. I, p. 101).

But, Marx and Engels go on, 'these demands can in no wise suffice for the party of the proletariat'; while the petty-bourgeois democrats would seek to bring the revolution to a conclusion as quickly as possible,

it is our interest and our task to make the revolution permanent, until all more or less possessing classes have been forced out of their position of dominance, until the proletariat has conquered state power, and the association of proletarians, not only in one country but in all the dominant countries of the world, has advanced so far that competition among the proletarians of these countries has ceased and that at least the decisive productive forces are concentrated in the hands of the proletarians. For us the issue cannot be the alteration of private property but only its annihilation, not the smoothing over of class antagonisms but the abolition of classes, not the improvement of existing society but the foundation of a new one. (Marx and Engels, 1950, vol. I, p. 102)

At the same time, while the demands and aims of the proletarian party went far beyond anything which even the most advanced and radical petty-bourgeois democrats would accept, the revolutionaries must give them qualified support and seek to push the democratic movement into even more radical directions (Marx and Engels, 1950, vol. I, p. 101). It was, incidentally, precisely the same strategy which dictated Marx's later attitude to all movements of radical reform, and which led him, as in the *Inaugural Address* of the First International in 1864, to acclaim the Ten Hours Act or the advances of the co-operative movement as the victories of 'the political economy of labour over the political economy of property' (1950, vol. I, pp. 307–9).

In 1850, Marx and Engels had also suggested that one essential task of the proletarian revolutionaries would be to oppose the decentralising tendencies of the petty-bourgeois revolutionaries. On the contrary, 'the workers must not only strive for a single and indivisible German republic, but also within this republic for the most determined centralisation of power in the hands of the state authority' (Marx and Engels, 1950, vol. 1, p. 106).

This is not only the most extreme 'statist' prescription in Marx's (and Engels') work – it is the only one of its kind, leaving aside Marx's first 'Hegelian' pronouncements on the subject. More important is the fact that the prescription is intended *not* for the proletarian but for the bourgeois democratic revolution.[8] In 1850, Marx and Engels believed, and said in the *Address*, that the German workers would not be able 'to attain power and achieve their own class interest without completely going through a lengthy revolutionary development' (Marx and Engels 1950, vol. 1, p. 108). The proletarian revolution would see the coming into being of an altogether different form of rule than the democratic republic, namely the dictatorship of the proletariat.

In a famous letter to J. Wedemeyer in March 1852, Marx had revealed the cardinal importance he attached to this concept by saying that while no credit was due to him for discovering the existence of classes in modern society or the struggles between them,

what I did that was new was to prove (1) that the *existence of classes* is bound up with *particular historical phases in the development of production*, (2) that the class struggle necessarily leads to the *dictatorship of the proletariat*, (3) that this dictatorship itself only constitutes the transition to *abolition of all classes and to a classless society*. (*SC*, p. 86)

Unfortunately, Marx did not define in any specific way what the dictatorship of the proletariat actually entailed, and more particularly what was its relation to the state. It has been argued by Mr Hal Draper in an extremely well-documented article that it is a '*social description*, a statement of the class character of the political power. It is not a statement about the forms of the government machinery' (Draper, n.d., p. 102). My own view, on the contrary, is that, for Marx, the dictatorship of the proletariat is *both* a statement of the class character of the political power *and* a description of the political power itself; and that it is in fact the nature of the political power which it describes which guarantees its class character.

In the *18th Brumaire*, Marx had made a point which constitutes a main theme of his thought, namely that all previous revolutions had 'perfected this [state] machine instead of smashing it. The parties that contended in turn for domination regarded the possession of this huge state edifice as the principal spoils of the victors' (Marx and Engels, 1950, vol. 1, p. 301). Nearly twenty years later, in *The Civil War In France*, he again stressed how every previous revolution had consolidated 'the centralized State power, with its ubiquitous organs of standing army, police, bureaucracy, clergy and judicature'; and he also stressed how the political character of the state had changed

simultaneously with the economic changes of society. At the same pace at which the progress of modern history developed, widened, intensified the class antagonism between capital and labour, the State power assumed more and more the character of the national power of capital over labour, of a public force organised for social enslavement, of an engine of class despotism. After every revolution marking a progressive phase in the class struggle, the purely repressive character of the State power stands out in bolder and bolder relief. (Marx and Engels, 1950, vol. I, pp. 468–9)

As Mr Draper notes, Marx had made no reference to the dictatorship of the proletariat in all the intervening years. Nor indeed did he so describe the Paris Commune. But what he acclaims above all in the Commune is that, in contrast to previous social convulsions, it sought not the further consolidation of the state power but its destruction. What it wanted, he said, was to have 'restored to the social body all the forces hitherto absorbed by the State parasite feeding upon, and clogging the free movement of, society' (Marx and Engels, 1950, vol. I, p. 473). Marx also lays stress on the Commune's popular democratic and egalitarian character, and on the manner in which 'not only municipal administration but the whole initiative hitherto exercised by the State was laid into the hands of the Commune' (1950, vol. I, p. 471). Moreover, while the communal form of government was to apply even to the 'smallest country hamlet',

the unity of the nation was not to be broken, but, on the contrary, to be organised by the Communal Constitution, and to become a reality by the destruction of the State power which claimed to be the embodiment of that unity independent of, and superior to, the nation itself, from which it was but a parasitic excrescence. (Marx and Engels, 1950, vol. I, p. 472)

In notes which he wrote for *The Civil War in France*, Marx makes even clearer than in the published text the significance which he attached to the Commune's dismantling of the state power. As contributing evidence of his approach to the whole question, the following passage from the notes is extremely revealing:

This [the Commune] was a Revolution not against this or that, legitimate, constitutional, republican or Imperialist form of State power. It was a Revolution against the *State* itself, of this supernaturalist abortion of society, a resumption by the people for the people of its own social life. It was not a revolution to transfer it from one fraction of the ruling class to the other but a Revolution to break down this horrid machinery of Classdomination [*sic*] itself . . . the Second Empire was the final form (?) [*sic*] of this State usurpation. The Commune was its definite negation, and, therefore, the initiation of the social Revolution of the nineteenth century. (*Marx–Engels Archives*, 1934, vol. III (VIII) p. 324)[9]

It is in the light of such views that Marx's verdict on the Commune takes on its full meaning: this 'essentially working-class government,' he wrote, was 'the political form at last discovered under which to work out the economic emancipation of labour' (Marx and Engels, 1950, vol. I, p. 473).

It is of course true that, while Engels, long after Marx's death, did describe the Paris Commune as the dictatorship of the proletariat,[10] Marx himself did not do so. The reason for this would seem fairly obvious, namely that, for Marx, the dictatorship of the proletariat would be the outcome of a socialist revolution on a national scale; the Commune, as he wrote in 1881, was 'merely the rising of a city under exceptional conditions', while 'the majority of the Commune was in no wise socialist, nor could it be' (*SC*, p. 410). Even so, it may justifiably be thought that the Commune, in its de-institutionalisation of political power, did embody, for Marx, the essential elements of his concept of the dictatorship of the proletariat.

Precisely the opposite view has very generally come to be taken for granted; the following statement in Mr Lichtheim's *Marxism* is a typical example of a wide consensus:

His [Marx's] hostility to the state was held in check by a decidedly authoritarian doctrine of political rule during the transition period: prior to being consigned to the dustbin of history, the state was to assume dictatorial powers. In different terms, authority would inaugurate freedom – a typically Hegelian paradox which did not worry Marx though it alarmed Proudon and Bakunin. (Lichtheim, 1961, p. 374)

The trouble with the view that Marx had a 'decidedly authoritarian doctrine' is that it is unsupported by any convincing evidence from Marx himself; and that there is so much evidence which runs directly counter to it.

Marx was undoubtedly the chief opponent of the anarchists in the International. But it is worth remembering that his central quarrel with them concerned above all the manner in which the struggle for a socialist revolution ought to be prosecuted, with Marx insisting on the need for political involvement within the existing political framework, against the anarchists' all-or-nothing rejection of mere politics; and the quarrel also concerned the question of the type of organisation required by the international workers' movement, with Marx insisting on a degree of control by the General Council of the International over its affiliated organisations.

As for the role of the state in the period of transition, there is the well-known passage in the 'private circular' against the anarchists issued by the General Council in 1872, *Les Prétendues Scissions l'Internationale*, and most probably written by Marx:

What all socialists understand by anarchism is this; as soon as the goal of the proletarian movement, the abolition of class, shall have been reached, the power of the state, whose function it is to keep the great majority of the producers beneath the yoke of a small minority of exploiters, will disappear, and governmental functions will be transformed into simple administrative functions. The Alliance [Bakunin's Alliance of Socialist Democracy] turns the thing upside down. It declares anarchism in the ranks of the workers to be an infallible means for disrupting the powerful concentration of social and political forms in the hands of the exploiters. Under this pretext, it asks the International, when the old world is endeavouring to crush our organisation, to replace organisation by anarchism. The international police could ask for nothing better. (Stekloff, 1928, pp.179–80; Freymond, 1962, vol. II, p. 295)

This can hardly be construed as an authoritarian text: nor certainly is Marx's plaintive remark in January 1873 quoted by Lenin in *State and Revolution* that,

if the political struggle of the working class assumes violent forms, if the workers set up this revolutionary dictatorship in place of the dictatorship of the bourgeoisie, they commit the terrible crime of violating principles, for in order to satisfy their wretched, vulgar, everyday needs, in order to crush the resistance of the bourgeoisie, instead of laying down their arms and abolishing the state, they give the state a revolutionary and transitory form. (Lenin, 1933, p. 54)

Nor is there much evidence of Marx's 'decidedly authoritarian doctrine' in his marginal notes of 1875 on the Gotha Programme of the German Social-Democratic Party. In these notes, Marx bitterly attacked the programme's references to 'the free state' ('free state – what is this?') and this is well in line with his belief that the 'free state' is a contradiction in terms: and he then asked: 'What transformation will the state undergo in communist society? In other words, what social function will remain in existence there that are analogous to present functions of the state?' Marx, however, did not answer the question, but merely said that it could only be answered 'scientifically' and that 'one does not get a flea-hop nearer to the problem by a thousandfold combination of the word people with the word state'. He then goes on:

Between capitalist and communist society lies the period of the revolutionary transformation of the one into the other. There corresponds to this also a political transition period in which the state can be nothing but the *revolutionary dictatorship of the proletariat*. (Marx and Engels, 1950, vol. II, p. 30)

This does not advance matters much, but neither does it suggest the slightest 'authoritarian' impulse. In the *Critique of the Gotha Programme*, Marx, as always before, made a sharp distinction between the democratic republic and the dictatorship of the proletariat, and Engels was clearly mistaken when he wrote in 1891 that the democratic republic was 'even the specific form of the dictatorship of the proletariat' (quoted in Lenin, 1933, p. 54).[11] On the contrary, Marx's critical attitude towards the democratic republic in the *Critique of the Gotha Programme* shows that he continued to think of the dictatorship of the proletariat as an altogether different and immeasurably freer form of political power. 'Freedom' he wrote in the *Critique of the Gotha Programme*, 'consists in converting the state from an organ superimposed upon society into one completely subordinated to it' (Marx and Engels, 1950, vol. II, p. 29). This would seem a good description of Marx's view of the state in the period of the dictatorship of the proletariat. No doubt, he would have endorsed Engels' view, expressed a few weeks after Marx's death, that 'the proletarian class will first have to possess itself of the organised political force of the state and with this aid stamp out the resistance of the capitalist class and reorganise society' (*SC*, p. 437). But it is of some significance that, with the possible exception of his remark of January 1873, referred to earlier, Marx himself always chose to emphasise the liberating rather than the repressive aspects of post-capitalist political power; and it is also of some interest that, in the notes he made for *The Civil War in France*, and which were not of course intended for publication, he should have warned the working class that the 'work of regeneration' would be 'again and again relented [*sic*] and impeded by the resistance of vested interests and class egotisms', but that he should have failed to make any reference to the state as an agent of repression. What he did say was that 'great strides may be [made] at once through the communal form of political organisation' and that 'the time has come to begin that movement for themselves and mankind' (*Marx–Engels Archives*, 1934, p. 334).

The fact is that, far from bearing any authoritarian imprint, the whole of Marx's work on the state is pervaded by a powerful anti-authoritarian and anti-bureaucratic bias, not only in relation to a distant communist society but also to the period of transition which is to precede it. True, the state is necessary in this period. But the only thing which, for Marx, makes it tolerable is popular participation and popular rule. If Marx is to be faulted, it is not for any authoritarian bias, but for greatly understating the difficulties of the libertarian position. However, in the light of the experience of socialist movements since Marx wrote, this may perhaps be judged a rather less serious fault than its bureaucratic obverse.

NOTES

This chapter was originally published in *The Socialist Register*, 1965.

1. Since published as *Karl Marx's Critique of Hegel's 'Philosophy of Right'*, ed. J. O'Malley (Cambridge, Cambridge University Press, 1970).
2. Note also his contemptuous reference in an article of May 1842 on the freedom of the press to the inconsistent, nebulous and timorous reasoning of German liberals, who claim to honour freedom by setting it up in an imaginary firmament, rather than on the solid ground of reality (*Marx/Engels Gesamtausgabe*, 1927, p. 220; A. Cornu, *Karl Marx et Friedrich Engels. Leur Vie et leur œuvre*, Paris, 1958, Vol. II, p. 17).
3. See, e.g., *The Class Struggles in France, passim, The 18th Brumaire of Louis Bonaparte, passim.*
4. See, e.g., 'The Elections in Britain' in Marx and Engels, 1953, pp. 353ff.:

   The Whigs are the *aristocratic representatives* of the bourgeoisie, of the industrial and commercial middle class. Under the condition that the bourgeoisie should abandon to them, to an oligarchy of aristocratic families, the monopoly of government and the exclusive possession of office, they make to the middle class, and assist it in conquering, all those concessions, which in the course of social and political developments have shown themselves to have become *unavoidable* and *undelayable*.

5. Marx also notes that the identity of interest of the small-holding peasants 'begets no community, no national bond and no political organisation among them', so that 'they do not form a class' (Marx and Engels, 1950, vol. I, p. 302). For an interesting discussion of Marx's concept of class, see S. Ossowski (1963, ch. 5).

6. See also Marx, *Pre-Capitalist Economic Formations*, with an introduction by E. J. Hobsbawn (London, 1964). This is a translation of a section of Marx's *Grundrisse Der Kritik der Politischen Okonomie (Rohentwurf)* (Berlin, 1953).

7. In *Capital*, vol. II, p. 514, n. 2, Marx also notes that 'one of the material bases of the power of the State over the small disconnected producing organisms in India, was the regulation of the water supply'; also, 'the necessity for predicting the rise and fall of the Nile created Egyptian astronomy, and with it the dominion of the priests, as directors of agriculture' (p. 514, ft. 1): for some further elaborations on the same theme, see also F. Engels (1962, p. 248).

8. It is, in this connection, of some interest that Engels should have thought it necessary to add a Note to the 1885 edition of the Address, explaining that this passage was based on a 'misunderstanding' of French revolutionary experience and that 'local and provincial self-government' were not in contradiction with 'national centralisation' (Marx and Engels, 1950, vol. I, p. 107).

9. I am grateful to Mr M. Johnstone for drawing my attention to these *Marx–Engels Archives* (1934, vol. III (VIII)) notes. Note also, e.g., the following:

> Only the Proletarians, fired by a new social task to accomplish by them for all society, to do away with all classes and class rule, were the men to break the instrument of that class rule – the State, the centralised and organised governmental power usurping to be the master instead of the servant of society . . . It had sprung into life against them. By them it was broken, not as a peculiar form of governmental (centralised) power, but as its most powerful, elaborated into seeming independence from society expression and, therefore, also its most prostitute reality, covered by infamy from top to bottom, having centred in absolute corruption at home and absolute powerlessness abroad. (Ibid., p. 326)

The peculiar English syntax of such passages is obviously due to the fact that they are only notes, not intended for publication.

10. 'Of late', Engels wrote in an Introduction to the 1891 edition of *The Civil War in France*, 'the Social-Democratic philistine has once more been filled with wholesome terror at the words: Dictatorship of the Proletariat. Well and good, gentlemen, do you want to know what this dictatorship looks like? Look at the Paris Commune. That was the Dictatorship of the Proletariat' (Marx and Engels, 1950, vol. I, p. 410).

11. Lenin's own comment is also misleading: 'Engels', he writes, 'repeats here in a particularly striking manner the fundamental idea which runs like a red thread through all of Marx's works, namely, that the democratic republic is the nearest approach to the dictatorship of the proletariat' (1933: p. 54). Engels's phrase does not bear this interpretation; and whatever may be said for the view that the democratic republic is the nearest approach to the dictatorship of the proletariat, it is not so in Marx.

REFERENCES

Avineri, S., 1964. 'Marx and Jewish emancipation', *Journal of the History of Ideas*, 25, July-September

Bottomore, T. B., ed., 1963. *K. Marx: Early Writings*. London, Watts

Draper, H., n.d. 'Marx and the dictatorship of the proletariat', *New Politics*, 1 (4)

Engels, F., 1962. *Anti-Dühring*. 3rd edn, Moscow, Foreign Language Publishing House

Freymond, J., ed., 1962. *La Première Internationale*. Geneva

Hyppolite, J., 1955. *Etudes sur Marx et Hegel*. Paris, Marcel Rivière

Lenin, V. I., 1933. *State and Revolution*. London, Martin Lawrence

Lichtheim, G., 1961. *Marxism*. London, Routledge and Kegan Paul

    1963. 'Marx and the "Asiatic mode of production"', in *St Antony's Papers*, no. 14, Far Eastern Affairs

Marx–Engels Archives, 1934, vol. III (VIII), Moscow

Marx/Engels Gesamtausgabe, 1927. Berlin, Dietz

Marx, K., 1936. *The Poverty of Philosophy*. London, International Publishing

    1959. *Capital* I. Moscow, Foreign Language Publishing House

    1962. *Capital* II. Moscow, Foreign Language Publishing House

    1964. *Pre-Capitalist Economic Formations*. London, Lawrence and Wishart

Marx, K. and F. Engels, n.d. *The First Indian War of Independence (1857–9)*. Moscow

    1956. (*SC*). *Selected Correspondence*. Moscow, Lawrence and Wishart

    1939. *The German Ideology*. New York, International Publishing

    1950. *Selected Works*, vols. I and II. Moscow, Foreign Language Publishing House

    1953. 'The elections in Britain', in *On Britain*. Moscow, Lawrence.

    1956. *The Holy Family*. Moscow

Ossowski, S., 1963. *Class Structure in the Social Consciousness*. London, Routledge and Kegan Paul

Plamenatz, J., 1954. *German Marxism and Russian Communism*. London, Longman

Rubel, M., 1957. *K. Marx: Essai de biographie intellectuelle*. Paris

Sanderson, J., 1963. 'Marx and Engels on the state', *Western Political Quarterly*, 16 (4), December

Sawer, M., 1978. *Marxism and the question of the Asiatic Mode of Production*. Dordrecht, Martinus Nijhoff

Stekloff, G. M., 1928. *History of the First International*. London, International Publishing

Wittfogel, K., 1957. *Oriental Despotism*. New Haven, Yale University Press

6

Mill, Marx and the state

GRAEME DUNCAN

As Mill and Marx ceased writing a century ago, we can hardly expect their critical studies of their own societies to answer questions confronting the 1980s, but some matters on which they disagreed basically remain of great moment, especially the capacity of the state to deal with issues and situations in a neutral or impartial manner, and its power to control events rather than simply respond to them. My central aim here is not to try to determine which of the prevalent theories of the state is most illuminating or useful, or whether there is one correct theory (which would cover what, exactly?), but rather to elucidate the very different assumptions underlying two influential and resourceful theories of the state – those of John Stuart Mill and Karl Marx – and to indicate something of their bearing on current disputes about the state.

As was pointed out – unsurprisingly – in the Introduction, argument over the state is extremely complex, with narrower and more inclusive definitions or conceptions, and with different relations conceived between society/economy and polity, and between sociological and normative analysis. As the sociology of the state was discussed at that point, it remains to add some background comments on normative theories of the state. A normative theory of the state, of the kind presented in traditional political philosophy, is concerned with the relationship between political institutions and human drives, needs, rights, capacities and potentialities. Normally it will consider political institutions as they are taken to exist, in fact, and as they may or should be, and will probably discover a conflict or incompatibility between the two. The demand may be for new worlds or, less grandiosely, for reforms, such as an extension of the franchise or of civil rights. Sometimes a credibility gap emerges, as when a bitter denunciation of diseased and crippling societies is linked with a dream of a world where man will be truly himself, for example, in Marx's savage, if exaggerated, 'realism' in regard to the pretensions of bourgeois society and his utopianism about a communist future.

The same ground is covered by three specific questions which have been central in the historical discussion of the state, and which can be used to

counterpose different views of it: why are there states? What are their functions or purposes? How are they related to human nature, in whatever form
that may be conceived?

Why are there states rather than politically unstructured communities, or
communities without a distinct or separate political apparatus? This is
commonly put either as an historical or as a hypothetical question, though in
both cases it may appear to be somewhat historical. An example of the first
approach is the use by Engels of Lewis Morgan's researches into primitive
societies – whether the dignified term historical is appropriate is another
matter – or in military and conqueror theories of states' origins. The second is
exemplified in Social Contract theory, in which rational and either very
anxious and vulnerable or extremely optimistic creatures unite under a political authority for the furtherance of their common ends. It depicts the natural
or likely relationships between detached individuals in imagined circumstances, and is a speculative – and often delightfully embroidered – psychology. The question why we have states rather than something else thus
leads back to the search for historical origins, or to the invention of logical or
hypothetical models, resting upon assumptions about human nature. Given
optimistic assumptions about man and his environment, it may be urged that
there is no real need for states, which become aberrations, badges of lost
innocence or merely temporary necessities, to be overcome or transcended in
the right circumstances.

What are the functions of the state? The answers to this question are not
now normally sought in historical anthropology or in logical hypothesis or
sheer conceptualisation, but in sociology, political science, political economy
and history. Answers are empirical in the sense that they follow from a
consideration of what in fact those entities which are correctly identified as
states do, but they are theoretically complex as well. Part of the problem is that
states, especially modern states, respond to a great range of pressures and do a
great variety of things, and it is therefore difficult to isolate one function as the
core or basic function of states. Apparently contradictory claims, such as that
states protect the interests of the weak and the disadvantaged, and that they
ensure the continuation of the process of exploitation – both of which might be
true in certain conditions – cannot be simply read off from the activities of
states, but rest within conflicting theoretical schemata, which give sense to
different accounts of the state. Some progress may be made if we replace the
abstract question: 'What are the functions of the state?' by the more incisive
one: 'What do different historical states do?' Common functions or a common
essence can still be sought amidst the apparent diversity. It may be admitted
that the precise functions of the Asiatic, the feudal, the capitalist, the late
capitalist, the state capitalist, the corporatist, and the welfare state vary, and
that there is a difference in the institutional character following from differ-

ences in social structure, resources, conventions and so forth, while claiming that states do certain basic, essential or characteristic things. Such a theory of the state would combine a high level of abstraction or generality with sophistication and subtlety as to the precise historical form which a state might take.

What kind of state, or non-state, best fits men's drives, needs, rights, capacities, potentialities? This is more specific than, but not incompatible with, the grander question: 'Is the state necessary to man?' Answers to this may constitute a legitimation of a particular historical state, as appropriate for or necessary to its citizens, or a justification of a liberal state as against invasive or repressive ones, or an assault upon the state as a destroyer of human development. To a conservative, political institutions – idealised perhaps – are needed to repress and control or civilise and moralise man; to a liberal, particular historical states may inhibit men and prevent the unfolding of their capacities, but this need not be the case, that is, if the state is properly confined according to liberal premises; to others, including Marxists and anarchists, separate political institutions as such mutilate and oppress man, hence the sketch of alternative and ostensibly non-political arrangements consonant with true humanity.

To answer these questions in this order would give a fairly clear structure to theories of the state, as a simplified version of Marxian theory illustrates. However, the questions are not quite distinct from each other, they are not always tackled directly, and it is common to slide from one to the other. A simple Marxian view holds:

(1) The state emerges to manage or resolve the conflict of classes. A more complex formulation is that it arises from – as part of – the functional division of labour, and the associated division and conflict of classes. It emerges, or begins to emerge, once the worker is separated from his surplus. This account of historical origins, whatever its empirical validity or internal consistency, is compatible with the view that the state has no permanent value or place.

(2) The function of the state is to serve as an instrument of class rule, most notably under capitalism, where it sees to the continuation of the capitalist accumulation process. It is both partisan and dependent.

(3) It will disappear with the disappearance of classes and of class rule, when an order arises which is compatible with man's true or emergent nature.

Those who see the state as man's (highest) moral achievement, an embodiment and realisation of his virtue, will disagree with the three parts of the Marxist historical story of the emergence, character and the withering away of the state. One familiar rival view presents the state as the necessary result of man's imperfection or sin, sees its function as that of keeping man in check

and moralising him, and denies that it can ever disappear – human imperfections and divisions render it a permanent and necessary part of our world.
Notions such as exploitation rarely make an entrance in such theories.

These comments establish a background for a critical comparison of Mill
and Marx on the subject of the state. But first, a brief comment on the
historical placing of the argument is required. What we are considering is the
role of political apparatuses and arrangements (legislative, judicial, executive
and peace-keeping authorities) in capitalist societies, the particular historical
context being mid-nineteenth-century England, although neither Mill nor
Marx confined their arguments to this place and period. The argument,
conducted against the background of a relatively free market – the freedom of
which is exaggerated commonly – and a relatively inert state, concerns the
degree to which the economy penetrates and controls the polity and, on the
other hand, the extent to which the polity can influence or run independently
of the economy. One of the difficulties is that the two authors do not list
discrete points or assumptions under the same headings, but develop theoretical systems within which the various components are differently defined and
differently related to each other. Further, neither of them develops a specific
theory of the state, but rather they offer scattered observations. Yet they
appear to be addressing similar problems within a particular historical framework, in the sense that class and in particular the rise of the working class are
central concerns, though their responses differ. And it makes sense at least to
interpret Marx as offering a critique of the kind of theory which Mill
elaborated.

We can best dig into Mill's conception of the state by considering what he
found to attack in existing political institutions. The basic position is simple
and straightforward – there are good states (rare) and bad ones, the bad ones
being distinguished by bad laws, selfish and prejudiced rulers, and unnecessary and destructive intrusions into the lives of individuals and groups. The
ground of attack was that political institutions – not contaminated in their very
nature – were dominated by self-interested groups and individuals. One of his
basic moral–political distinctions is between the general interest and sinister
interest, which is thinner and less penetrating than Marx's class interest, in the
sense that it is the result of removable ignorance and is not structurally
induced. Class, a broad and pejorative term, meant 'any number of persons
who have the same sinister interest . . . whose direct and apparent interest
points towards the same description of bad measures' (Mill, 1960, pp. 254–5).
Sinister interest is linked with ignorance and with selfishness, whereas the
general interest rests upon knowledge and impartiality. Mill fears chaos less
than the use of political power for private or sectional advantage, and thus he
inherited the utilitarian problem of devising 'securities' for good government.
As James Mill had put it: 'All the difficult questions of government relate to

the means of restraining those, in whose hands are lodged the powers necessary for the protection of all, from making a bad use of it' (James Mill, 1937, p. 6). Writing in the preface to the second edition of *The Fragment on Government*, Bentham confessed that he had not realised, when the work first appeared, that governments were 'the elaborately organised and anxiously cherished and guarded products of sinister interest and artifice'. In general, non-representative governments are portrayed by Bentham and the two Mills as tyrannous, brutal and exploitative class governments, controlled only by revolution or the fear of it.

The utilitarian psychological doctrine was wielded most forcefully against the aristocracy. The 'aristocratical principle' (the defence of the leadership claims of an hereditary aristocracy) appeared to be undermined totally by the selfishness, venality and corruption (by power) shown by aristocrats historically. Mill declared that 'we cannot be forced back to the time when rulers were thought not to be made like human beings, but to be free from all the passions and appetites by which other men are misled' (Mill, 1835, p. 243). Other classes could not be trusted as they were. Mill feared legislative class tyranny through the premature admission to the vote of the working class. A purely democratic suffrage would be likely to produce 'a legislature reflecting exclusively the opinions and preferences of the most numerous class' (Mill, 1963, p. 359). Following its immediate and apparent rather than its true and ultimate interest – a familiar and weighty distinction – the working class, given its existing degree of virtue and grasp of reality, would try to raise wages, interfere with contracts, tax machinery. In short, it would introduce 'laws founded on mistakes in political economy' (Mill, 1860a, vol. II, p. 31). That negative judgment on aristocratic, monarchical or working-class domination of the political system is clear and straightforward, and already embodies a model of the good polity. I now turn to the good state as perceived by Mill, and to the assumptions which underly his account of it.

Mill held that ideas, 'the state of the speculative faculties of mankind', constituted the basic – though not the exclusive – power in society. 'It is how men think that determines how they act' (Mill, 1960a, p. 184). Thought was the major source of social progress and of social decay. Intellectual revolutions were more significant than industrial ones, though to have transformative power ideas needed favourable conditions, including increasingly receptive minds, which social policy could help create. Mill's second assumption was that there were true or valid beliefs about political matters, that there were – in principle at least – rational conceptions of the public good or the public interest. These conceptions were uninfluenced by passion, prejudice or egoism, and were in conformity with the objective or real interests of citizens. Of course, Mill had his own views as to the content of many rational beliefs, for whose actual ideological character he has been regularly belaboured from the left (for a defence of Mill against some typical criticisms from the left, see Duncan and Gray, n.d.) and he also envisaged an 'imposing unanimity' of basic ideas once reason ruled.[1] Mill thought it especially important that right reason spread wide, given the growing power of public opinion in his own time. Third, he believed that there were significant differences of intellectual and moral power between ordinary persons and some others, who were specially competent, instructed, virtuous, classless, impartial, unprejudiced. The clear practical consequence of these beliefs was the effort to express and to spread the greatest possible wisdom through carefully designed political and other institutional arrangements. With this in mind, Mill recommended the slow but progressive extension of the franchise, both the secret and the open ballot (at different times), plural voting, the Hare system of proportional representation, competitive examinations for the civil service, the establishment of a commission to draft legislation with the role of parliament being confined to that of discussion, acceptance and rejection, and an upper house, something like the Roman Senate, which would be distinguished by its freedom from class feeling. The general point of these various arrangements was to take full advantage of what skill and virtue there was immediately, but in the longer run to ensure the percolation of skill and virtue throughout the community. Our concern here, however, is not the dynamic if (temporarily) restricted character of Mill's democracy, but the intellectualistic and optimistic assumptions about the state – the nature and efficacy of political knowledge and political institutions – which are interwoven with it.

The most immediate political problem, from a cynical or realistic perspective, concerns the possibility of disinterested rulership. Mill's perception of sinister interest in aristocratic and democratic governments certainly appears sensible, but how, in other circumstances, does he undermine its potency? Like Marx, he managed to tie his moral ideal to particular social groups, though the linkage may not seem at all convincing to an independent observer. In the course of his harsh judgment of aristocracies, Mill made exceptions of the Prussian aristocracy and the East India Company in India, though the latter was not technically an aristocracy. The East India Company remained disinterested because it had little chance to profit from misgovernment – consequently 'it can be kept entirely clear of bias from the individual or class interests of anyone else' (Mill, 1960a, p. 389). The same virtues he found amongst the radicals, or disqualified classes, in England. The self-compliment was commonplace. Mill senior had described the middle rank as 'the chief source of all that has exalted and refined human nature' (James Mill, 1937, p. 72), while Sir James Graham in 1826, after describing the middle ranks as the seat of public opinion, referred to them as 'that numerous class, removed from the wants of labour and the cravings of ambition, enjoying the advantages of leisure, and possessing intelligence sufficient for the formation

of a sound judgment, neither warped by interest nor obscured by passion'
(quoted Briggs, 1967, pp. 56–7).

Mill pictured the true mentors of contemporary mankind emerging
amongst the middle ranks, 'the ascendant power in the present social and
political condition of the kingdom' (Mill, 1960b, p. 143). As they made their
way in the world, often struggling against the advantages conferred by convention and good birth, the enterprising middle classes educated themselves,
developed their capacities, and observed the disasters caused by traditional
power, prejudice and class interest. Amongst their numbers, though certainly
not uniformly throughout the class, Mill found enough rationality, energy and
generosity to support an optimistic view of human possibilities. But although
sinister interest seems to vacate the field of power too readily, Mill did not
tumble into a quite uncritical utopianism. Despite a great deal of tendentious
and proselytising social analysis on behalf of the radicals or the middle classes,
Mill was capable of writing that the distinction in favour of education, 'right in
itself, is further and strongly recommended by its preserving the educated
from the class legislation of the uneducated; but it must stop short of enabling
them to practise class legislation on their own account' (Mill, 1960a, p. 286).
Here at least is a recognition, which should have been blinding to a scion of
Bentham and James Mill, that the psychological truths which he urged so
effectively against the privileged and the powerful could not be simply
shrugged off or forgotten when it came to recommending new rulers. The
claims of apparently disinterested reason may mask the impurity of actual
middle-class politicians. Hence Mill himself was half aware of the difficulties
facing his vision of a classless elite, and offered no strong theoretical support
for his hopes. There seems to be no particular reason why the instructed
should come to hold beliefs which are unanimous or free of class bias, and
Mill's own account of a good society – which includes a purified private
property regime in which economic fallacies have passed into the museum –
leaves, from my own perspective, many of the enemies of impartiality and
disinterestedness intact. He did not elucidate sufficiently the character and
the sources of the capacity for disinterestedness, and assumed too easily that
education would strengthen the moral and social feelings. If we consider the
institutions and arrangements with which Mill held the rationality and impartiality of particular groups and individuals to be compatible, we may find that
he underrated the capacity of even a purified property and market system to
breed values and interests which he deplored, or to have institutional implications which were themselves destructive.

Mill's assumption that the state can be independent is as open to attack as
his assumption that it can be impartial or disinterested. Indeed, a common
voluntarist assumption underlies the conceptions of state neutrality and state
independence. Those who float free from, or transcend, interest and bias are

able to do so because there is no economic or class structure which inevitably ties, forms or inhibits the members of society. To detach the polity from the economy in this way is to enable it to be both just and dominant. Mill clearly believed that political institutions were more than the mere offshoot of economic forces and relationships, more than 'relatively autonomous'. They could be used instrumentally, for the general social good – a general social good which can be both conceived and realised in a society characterised by classes and a free market. In this respect his conception of the independence of the state – if not his desired social outcome – is similar to that of many moderate socialists. R. H. Tawney, justifying social democracy against such enemies of statism as Hayek, wrote:

> The State is an important instrument, hence the struggle to control it. But it is an instrument and nothing more. Fools will use it, when they can, for foolish ends, criminals for criminal ends. Sensible and decent men will use it for ends which are sensible and decent. We, in England, have repeatedly re-made the State, are re-making it now and shall re-make it again. (Tawney, 1966, p. 172)

The underlying assumption in Tawney and Mill – both reforming Englishmen – is that the state is a potent transforming instrument, which can be subjected to various purposes or made to serve various ends, and that it is not part of a structure which forces it to follow a certain line or to maintain certain interests. If the right people were in power they could create the society they wanted. For Mill this was not a simple mechanistic view, however: he noted how different circumstances facilitated or hindered positive development, and did not envisage the state being wiped clean in one dramatic series of events.

The general Marxist position is very different (for more detail, see Duncan, 1982). Superficial agreements between Marxists and liberals are possible over discrete matters, e.g. over the partisan, perhaps class, and repressive character of particular governments, but these are peripheral given substantial differences over state and society and the relationship between them. Conflicting theories of historical causation and social structure are linked with rival views of the independence and the possible neutrality or impartiality of the state within capitalist systems, modified or otherwise.

Throughout his writings Marx insisted upon the dependence of the state on civil society. The natural necessity and interest of civil society, and not the state, hold the members of communities together. Although Marx was to give some role to the state in holding social life together, in the context of class conflict, what is important here is that the early general statements appear to imply a straightforwardly reductionist and materialist theory: the state is not autonomous or creative, but dependent upon civil society, of which it is in some way the expression or outcome. But that basic – and, apparently, very firm – view was to be nibbled away and undermined, both in the processes of empirical research and in the summary statements which Marx and Engels offered from time to time.

The classical Marxist theory asserts a close relationship between two kinds of phenomena – material or economic and ideological – but is imprecise as to their definition or range and to the (historically variable) relationships between them. 'Material' sometimes appears to become a synonym for 'causally significant', which obliterates the problem at a stroke, while making it virtually impossible to elaborate a coherent theory of ideology. It seems impossible to find a general formulation which settles the issue, as any move which allows flexibility or interactionism destroys the rigour of the classical historical materialist vulgarisation. What meanings are to be attached to such notions as 'independence', 'independent variable', 'relative autonomy', 'in the last analysis decisive', 'dependence', 'epiphenomenon' and so on? A hard view will insist upon the independence of certain basic variables or causes, which determine the less significant elements in the social system; a soft view will stress the possible significance of an extensive range of causes, whose weight needs to be explored in each particular case; a middle view will hold that certain forces are in general primary or most significant or 'in the last analysis decisive', but that others have some independence in their processes of development or some power in influencing the various historical outcomes. The second and third views press one towards open-mindedness and detailed historical and other empirical research,[2] while the former may remain a dogma, though it can be defended conceptually.

In relation to the state, it seems to me that Marx's position was closer to the middle one, in that he refused to treat political institutions as either simply dependent variables or independent forces. States resting upon similar economic foundations varied and had some independence, but there were also limits, imposed by the system, to what they could do. Marx observed the variety of state forms in capitalist societies – capitalism, itself historically variable, accommodated different state forms, each with somewhat different potentialities and problems – and the fact that the state could create specific economic conditions or structures and inhibit others. For example, it could reduce national economic difficulties by activity internally and in the outside world (aggressive trading policies, imperialism) and it could inaugurate or at least tolerate reforms which, immediately at least, improved the conditions and the lives of the proletariat. Given this degree of flexibility, is there a distinctive and anti-liberal Marxian theory of the state?

We can begin to answer this question by observing that Marx was concerned essentially with the capitalist state, and that any theory of the capitalist state for him was also a theory of capitalist society and its process of development and dissolution. To theorise about the state was part of theorising about (and acting for) radical social change. If we ask the more precise

question: 'What is the function of the capitalist state?', we get a general answer
– to express the will or the needs of economic relationships or something of the
sort, with the qualification that the state has some independent momentum,
and that the translation from economics to politics is not automatic or simple
or straightforward. This means that the crude capitalist state, the reformist
state, the bureaucratic and the Bonapartist state, are limited by crucial features of the capitalist system. There are certain conceivable things, which may
be the object of social policy, which they cannot do, and other things which
they must do. Their increasing incapacity to do adequately what they must do
is both a source and a sign of the impending collapse of the system.

It is an implication of this that the function of the capitalist state cannot be
decided by asking capitalists or political leaders. It is not a matter of the
subjective intentions or wishes or the declared interests of ruling classes. The
central Marxian assertion about the capitalist state is that, in some way or another,
it serves capitalist interests. And 'in some way or another' is vital to them,
and opens the door to the variety of subtle formulations in different historical
circumstances. Clearly there are times of close congruence between capitalist
interests or the needs of capital and the actual policies of the state – perhaps so
clear that, despite ideological cover-up and evasion, the state does operate as
the executive committee of the ruling class. At other times the separateness or
detachment of the state may build up, dramatically in appearance though to a
lesser degree in actuality. This was the case with mid-nineteenth-century
France, in Marx's view, when Louis Bonaparte gained power on ground made
ready by the divisions and vacillations of the bourgeoisie, who were unwilling
and unable to take power in their own name. They maintained class power at
the cost of losing political power. This inventive piece of analysis has proved
appealing to those who argue that the defence of capital requires a certain
freedom or relative autonomy on the part of the state (the government), to
enable it to protect the bourgeois class against 'its members taken individu-
ally', as well as against the exploited class. In this vein, some Marxist political
economists, observing the contemporary capitalist state, have concluded that,
owing to divisions within the capitalist class, and perhaps also to the irrationality of certain sectors of it, the state must act in support of the logic of
capitalist production or the needs of the system, independently of and in some
cases against the wishes of particular groups of capitalists. The state may then
function – perhaps under the aegis of Social-Democratic governments – as an
'ideal collective capitalist', pursuing capital's general interest in the continuance of the accumulation process against the manifest interests of particular
capitals. In an earlier period this task was achieved essentially by the market.

Further aspects of, and difficulties within, the Marxist theory of the state
are worth noting. Marx's comments on bureaucracy, though undeveloped and
superficial, make it clear that the modern state is characterised by the emer-

gence of a complex and weighty organisational structure with a distinctive personnel, a momentum of its own and perhaps separate interests. Political mediation gains a further level, and radical social change a further enemy. In addition the state develops a variety of supervisory, regulatory and co-ordinative functions which demand state personnel, and which are not related straightforwardly to capitalist needs, nor necessarily confined to them. This raises the issues of the character of the co-ordinating apparatus in the post-capitalist world, and its implications for the possibility of communism.

The diversities and subtleties in Marx's account of the state, and the differences of emphasis in different writings, for example, between conspiratorial and structuralist interpretations of political phenomena, should not blind us to the fact that there must be a strong structuralist assumption underlying it. This means that, according to Marx, there exists a set of institutional relationships, interdependencies or requirements which firmly controls the range of options open to actors (role-bearers), although the severity of the limitations may not be defined with absolute clarity. The underlying assumption is that the logic of capitalist production, the logic or the force of the economy, which is more powerful than that of the polity, requires certain political mechanisms, and that these political mechanisms, such as those which constitute the liberal and representative state, will be brought to heel in so far as they challenge the needs of capital. Presumably this necessary fact is capable of empirical demonstration, though it often happens in the course of such demonstration or elaboration that the notions of capitalism, the needs of capitalism, the ruling class, and so on, become different – and usually looser. As the nature of the capitalist social formation has to be understood in relation to variant historical, geographical and other factors, we must expect variations in the state forms appropriate to it, even without admitting some independent development to political phenomena themselves.

We are now in a position to summarise, in broad terms, the differences between Mill and Marx on the state. Mill was not concerned much with the origins of political institutions; that seemed to him an uncomplicated part of normal human evolution. As for the function of the state, it was used for self-interested purposes by bad and ignorant rulers, but it was not inevitably biassed. It could equally well be devoted to good purposes once the instructed or educated – largely found within the middle ranks of society – were in authority. Its relationship to the society of which it was part was not construed by Mill in anything approaching structuralist terms. He was critical of the free-market and private-property system of his day, finding that they needed purification, but he did not feel that in themselves they challenged or undermined rational public policy, or confined it within particular limits. It is fair, from a quasi-Marxist perspective, to complain that he failed to overcome the great defect of traditional liberal theory, 'which accepted bourgeois society but did not examine the implications of that acceptance' (Macpherson, 1977, p. 231). But that is not the only perspective on the matter: Mill had a different sense of bourgeois society and its implications, a different view of the penetration and power of the economic system. To him, the polity floated fairly free. It was not an expression or servant of the 'capitalist social formation', nor were class and class conflict essential features of the society which he observed about him. Class was admittedly a disruptive force and an abomination, but it is presented in terms of rational principles, as the result of intellectual and moral error. It was a basic object of social policy – through education, population restraint, political engineering, and legislation if necessary – to destroy illusions, perhaps especially illusions of the kind embodied in Marxism, to utilise the formidable strength of right reason, to limit and counterbalance power in case it was abused, and to maximise the uncoerced region of life, which implied a withering of the role of force in maintaining social order. Economic and social divisions and conflicts, sustained by selfish ignorance, challenged his goals, but such challenges could be overcome by good sense and relatively minor reorganisation: bourgeois society was subject neither to a basic and objective conflict of classes, nor to a persisting war between a conservative polity and a dynamic economy. His general assumptions enabled him to claim that the state was an independent social force, and potentially a neutral instrument, capable of serving a genuine common interest within a market society.

For Marx, the class character of the state was its most striking feature, and was revealed in the story of its origins. The fact that it functioned normally as a class instrument could be shown in its activities, including legislation, and was explained through its ultimate dependence upon the economy – specifically, in capitalist society, upon free-market and wage-labour systems, within which exploitation and objective grounds for social conflict were inherent. As capitalist state, its goal was always that of maintaining the established capitalist institutions and fostering the accumulation process, although this did not establish one generally appropriate political form or set of governmental policies. Sometimes the class–state relationship was crude and open, sometimes confused and indirect, owing to complexity or contradiction within the basic social formation itself, or to independent tendencies arising in the development of the political realm, or to both.

And yet Marx, while emphasising the powerful constraints upon politics and political institutions as long as capitalism existed, looked towards a degree of ultimate freedom – including freedom from the state – quite unanticipated by Mill. The reasons why Marx thought the state incompatible with human emancipation and fulfilment are that the state is alienated human activity, and that it is the expression and instrument of class society. The first view, which is associated pre-eminently with the early writings but is not confined to them, presents the state as an ideal and detached embodiment of human needs and powers. It arises out of and presupposes the division of man into citizen and bourgeois, and it gains an independent existence above him. It masks the emptiness of citizenship. Marx wanted an end to the separate realms – ethics, religion, politics, economics – which expressed man's fragmentation: man was to reclaim his missing powers, to discover a new wholeness by reabsorbing those aspects of himself which had been alienated, and this required the abolition of politics and the state, amongst other things. The other main line of argument, treating the state as an epiphenomenon in a class society, simply assumes that once its causes have been removed, it too will pass away. It will have no point, no rationale, no function. That vision, which is summarised often with a misleading simplicity, is far from clear. What will succeed the state remains a controversial question, raised by Marx but not really answered by him. He appears to have envisaged the disappearance of certain of the established functions of the state, and a transformation of the mode in which others are carried out. The coercive or police aspect of the state would disappear, presumably, while persisting political tasks and instrumentalities would be subject to the whole collectivity. The Paris Commune, a harbinger of things to come while yet only a transitional form in circumstances of peculiar difficulty, was characterised by the total and immediate responsibility of its various arms and actors to the whole people. In this sense, both the coercive and the separate character of the traditional state would be overcome. Marx accepted that the tasks of co-ordinating production and managing the affairs of the whole society would persist in the post-capitalist world, though it seems unlikely that they could be done without a distinctive and separate institutional structure. Admittedly such notions as that of society ultimately reabsorbing totally its alienated institutions and functions lead us into a highly complex realm of conceptual and empirical inquiry, but I think that it can be said fairly that Marx did not distinguish with sufficient rigour between the political arrangements functional to class societies and those necessary to any complex technologically advanced societies, and that he failed to indicate clearly – though he made beginnings – why decision-making, the need to choose between options and so forth, would not plant the seeds of institutional structures and divisions of a dangerous kind. Power to a new class was always a lurking possibility.

The different accounts of the state are related to differences in theories of social causation, in the characterisation and evaluation of contemporary societies, and in views of human nature. Mill and Marx characterised economy and polity differently, both generally and in the specific forms of their own time, and they differed over the relations between them: putting it more crudely than it was, Mill's paradigm was essentially political or intellectual, whereas Marx's was essentially economic, asserting the dependence of political institutions and political practice upon productive processes. Hence they differed about the possibilities and the means of social change and improvement, and over the impact of representative government on the capitalist system. To one, its power was decisive, for good or ill, whereas to the other it helped complete capitalism, remaining its appropriate and dependent form despite some subversive elements and possibilities. To Mill, the ignorant and the egotistic, proletarian or otherwise, could destroy capitalism or liberty or culture: to Marx, such a fear underrated the sheer power, the resourcefulness, the range of defences of the dominant class. What was a disaster in Mill's view would have been a working-class achievement to Marx. Finally, they differed about human nature and about the meaning and the conditions of human freedom. Mill's more segregated view of the economic, social and political realms is associated with a readier acceptance of a segmented human being. Although he praised all-round development and, particularly after his 'mental crisis', stressed the importance of emotion, he did not have Marx's extreme sense of the actual fragmentation and possible wholeness of people, and he was certainly prepared to accept institutions which, to Marx, were divisive and deforming. Marx's view of the essential and the ideal interdependence of the different realms is linked with a deep-rooted sense of the whole man, not broken up into discrete and alienated parts, and not subjugated to the institutions and ideas which emerge out of that division. Mill wanted a diminution in the role of the state to allow for wider and fuller self-development, whereas Marx wanted a new world, with which the state was incompatible.

The relevance of these accounts of the state in the late twentieth century is another question. The state is now far weightier and more complex than that which emerged to preside over capitalism in its more vigorous and vital period. But, although its spread has in some ways helped to stabilise capitalism, through the modification of some of the worst features of the unregulated market system and its capacity to iron out crises, critical new problems have arisen. These include the inability of the state to finance welfare systems while providing the necessary incentives for economic growth; the choice sometimes appears to be between meeting electoral claims and satisfying business needs. Within the mixed economy framework of contemporary capitalism, is there a contradiction between the demands which the state must make in order to finance its multifarious activities and the stimulation of the growth upon which those finances depend?

Influential theories of the fiscal crisis (O'Connor) and the legitimation crisis (Habermas) emphasise the problem of financing state functions and the destabilising character of large popular demands, and are concerned with a weakening of civic virtue or the moral basis of capitalism. From one viewpoint, a fat state can temporarily sit athwart a society characterised by high unemployment and low growth, and perhaps inflation as well, balancing and controlling the new divisions and dependencies, but ultimately the whole inverted pyramid will tumble down. From another perspective on the character of the state's crisis, salvation lies at hand if the frontiers of the state can be rolled back, if the shift from market to political decision can be reversed. The source of the current economic plight is seen as 'overloaded government', the growth of capitalism's bureaucratic–political shell, and the consequent weakening of the free market, whose character is idealised and whose power for good is exaggerated by its current champions. Thus Hayek demands that the market be left to do its work while the state confines itself to its legitimate task – that of maintaining the laws and procedures needed for free competition and productive entrepreneurial activity. The state is condemned, not for its class character, but because it is marauding and invasive: that at least suggests the variety of its functions, its growth beyond a simple class instrument.

In grappling with this complex set of problems and choosing between alternative accounts of and responses to them, Mill and Marx – naturally enough – have little specific to contribute. Clearly, Marx addressed our attention to the processes of production and the class structure, and emphasised the dependency of the state. At the very least, it had to maintain the mode of production upon which its revenues, its very existence, depended. But carrying out that function may be compatible with a greater diversity of political forms and a greater degree of working-class advance than Marx imagined. Moreover, as the large state has influenced the nature of class structures and the form and intensity of class conflicts, things are not as they were, and may be harder to read through than they were in Marx's day. My own view is that the state is – and will remain – inevitably partisan, though not as the instrument of a clearly defined and dominant class. The 'general interest' is always defined by particular members of society, and is always the interest of some more than others. The state reflects, though not as a mirror image, the rough balance of social forces (including bureaucratic interests), blurred by traditions and other inheritances from the past, and by ideologies, complex political mechanisms and procedures. It also supports established distributions, in general. Political decision-makers cannot deal impartially with the diverse interests, demands, claims, pressures and ideals of different social groups and individuals, and the reasons for this include scarcity of resources, ignorance and confusion, as well as class division, interest and bias. Marx was closer than Mill to grasping the lean and the limits of the capitalist state, partly because of his solid awareness of the significance of economic life but, underrating the continuing productive capacity of the (increasingly modified) capitalist system, and the complex motivations of both its servants and its masters, he also underrated the power of the state to make genuine reforms. (Some of those reforms are now under threat.) And, while revealing the flaws in some comforting and politically significant myths about the state, he gave little reason for thinking that political apparatuses – which always have repressive and partial aspects – would ever disappear. The claim that formal and distinctive political arrangements are necessary arises, not from optimistic assumptions about the availability of ideal rulers who might govern impartially, but from the persisting facts of diversity, differentiation, complexity and scarcity.

Both Mill and Marx, with their mixtures of critical observation and utopianism, contributed to the task of developing a sceptical and moral typology of states, rooted in historical study. They both identified the state's unnecessarily restrictive features and characterised the form in which it – or its successor – would best serve human ends. At different points we may find their views one-sided or otherwise unconvincing. For the state, and especially the modern state, has several faces, which are more than mere masks, and which shift over time and impress different people differently. That variety of functions and appearances, the fact that the modern state rarely shows itself to be merely a capitalist or merely a repressive state, creates substantial problems for any radical theory of change. Whether current difficulties will lead to its emergence as a blatantly oppressive and class force, or will still allow it to incorporate strategic sections of the working class and to avoid sharp political confrontations, will depend as much on the skills and strengths of political elites as on the nature of the crises and contradictions which challenge it.

NOTES

1. Hence the charge of moral totalitarianism, as in Maurice Cowling's *Mill and Liberalism* (Cambridge, 1963).
2. Examples of work which combines conceptual sophistication and serious and sensitive historical research are Perry Anderson's *Passages From Antiquity to Feudalism* and *Lineages of the Absolutist State*, published by New Left Books.

REFERENCES

Briggs, A., 1967. 'The language of "class" in early nineteenth century England', in Briggs, A. and J. Saville, eds., *Essays in Labour History*. London
Duncan, G. and J. Gray, n.d. 'The left against Mill', *Canadian Journal of Philosophy*, supplementary volume 5
Duncan, G., 1982. 'The Marxist theory of the state', in *Marx and Marxisms*, G. H. R. Parkinson, ed. Cambridge, Cambridge University Press
Macpherson, C. B., 1977. 'Do we need a theory of the state?' *Archives européennes de sociologie*, 18 (reprinted in this volume, pp. 15–32)
Mill, James, 1937. *Essay on Government*. Cambridge, Cambridge University Press
Mill, J. S., 1835. 'Law of libel and liberty of the press', *Westminster Review*, 30 (July)

1860, 'Democracy in America', J. S. Mill, *Dissertations and Discussions*, vol. II. London

1960a. *Representative Government*, in *Utilitarianism, Liberty and Representative Government*. London, Everyman

1960b. *On Liberty*, in *Utilitarianism, Liberty and Representative Government*. London, Everyman

1963, 'Recent writers on reform', in G. Himmelfarb, ed., *Essays on Politics and Culture (J. S. Mill)*. New York, Doubleday

Tawney, R. H. 1966, 'Social democracy in Britain', in *The Radical Tradition*. Harmondsworth, Penguin Books

7

Max Weber and the capitalist state

TOM BOTTOMORE

What is important in Max Weber's political theory is not simply his analysis of the concept of power, which has been widely debated, but his specific model of the modern state. In the present essay I propose to examine the main component parts of that model – Weber's conceptions of the nation state, bureaucracy and democracy – and to consider the practical political orientations which are implicit in it, or explicitly derived from it.

Weber was, as Wolfgang Mommsen (1959, 1974) in particular has made clear, a passionate nationalist and imperialist who 'never envisaged any other world than his own, which was largely characterized by the rivalry of nation states' (Mommsen, 1974, p. 37). In his Inaugural Lecture at Freiburg in 1895 Weber formulated the basic principle of his political theory as being the 'absolute primacy of the interests of the nation state' which constitute an 'ultimate standard of value' in both politics and economics (Weber, 1895, pp. 14–15). He went on to argue that following the creation of a German national state by the preceding generation the supreme task facing his own generation was to promote the expansion of German power and influence, and as a means to that end to help create a capable and vigorous political leadership; for 'we should realize that the unification of Germany was a youthful folly committed by the nation in the old days, which it would have been better not to undertake at all, in view of its cost, if this was to be the conclusion, and not the starting point, of Germany's striving to become a world power' (1895, p. 23).

In his later political studies Weber never abandoned this criterion of the interests of the German state, and the value-laden notion of 'effective political leadership' which he constantly invoked always meant that kind of political leadership which would most successfully promote, in the given international conditions, the interests of Germany as a world power. Thus, in his monograph of May 1918 on 'Parliament and Government in a Reconstructed Germany' (1918a, pp. 305–443) he analysed bureaucracy and democracy primarily in relation to the need for strong political leadership, and he concluded his lecture on socialism, delivered in June 1918 to a group of army officers in Vienna, by saying: 'The question is only whether this socialism will be of such a kind that it is bearable from the standpoint of the interests of the state, and in particular at the present time, of its military interests' (1918b, p. 517). During the last two years of his life Weber's attitude to the revolutionary movement in Germany was determined by the same considerations, namely, that a revolution would weaken Germany still further in relation to the victorious allied powers, whereas the most urgent need was to re-establish a strong state.[1]

Weber was the intellectual voice of the German bourgeoisie[2] in the period of rapid growth of German capitalism between the 1880s and 1914. His theory of the modern state is a theory of the capitalist nation state in the age of imperialism; not only, or even mainly, in the sense of analysing the social and historical characteristics of this form of state,[3] but in the sense of formulating as the central problem of political sociology the most effective possible development of bourgeois rule and of German participation in the struggle for world power. In short, Weber's model of the nation-state is also an ideal. This appears most clearly if we contrast his analysis with that of Rudolf Hilferding, who examined from a very different standpoint the same phenomenon of German capitalist development. In the final part of *Finance Capital* (1910) Hilferding analysed the 'struggle for economic territory' resulting from the growth of capitalist monopolies, and observed in particular the rivalry between Britain and Germany in the export of capital to colonial or dependent countries, a rivalry which was the principal factor creating the danger of a European war. For Hilferding, therefore, rational and effective political leadership did not consist in strengthening the power position of Germany in world politics, but, on the contrary, in organising working-class opposition to the militarist and expansionist orientation of the German bourgeoisie – which Weber's doctrine helped to reinforce – and formulating a strategy to achieve a new international economic order which would be both pacific and just.

It is in no way surprising, given the character of Weber's basic model, that in discussing bureaucracy and democracy he should have concentrated his attention almost entirely upon their relation to the interests of the nation state. In the case of bureaucracy, it is true, there is also a larger theme concerning the rationalisation and 'disenchantment' of the modern world brought about by the development of capitalist production with its increasing specialisation of tasks, and an ever more pervasive and sophisticated money economy, which diffuses the 'specifically modern calculating attitude' through all spheres of social and cultural life.[4] But in examining the political context of bureaucracy, Weber was concerned only with two questions: the extent to which the power of the state bureaucracy impeded the development of an 'effective political leadership' serving German national interests; and the significance which could be attributed to bureaucracy in his general argument against the socialists.

For Weber, the political problem in Germany consisted in the fact that since Bismarck's eclipse (but also because Bismarck had left Germany in a condition of complete political immaturity)[5] the direction of the nation's affairs had fallen into the hands of the state bureaucracy, which had become a distinct social stratum with its own particular interests and values, while on the other hand the bourgeoisie had been excluded from political involvement and rendered incapable of assuming a leading political role. Hence Germany, largely as a result of the alliance between the Emperor and the high officials against parliament, presented an extreme example of bureaucratic domination or rule by officials (*Beamtenherrschaft*), where officials had assumed functions (in particular as cabinet ministers) for which, in Weber's view, they were quite unsuited. The absence of real political leadership was responsible, Weber later argued, for the disastrous foreign policy pursued from the end of the nineteenth century up to 1914 which 'helped to create a world coalition against Germany' (1918a, pp. 369–82). It was largely as a response to this bureaucratic domination that Weber formulated the alternative of charismatic leadership, but this idea was closely related to his peculiar conception of democracy and will be better examined in that context.

The growth of bureaucracy also provided the ground for one of Weber's principal objections to socialism.[6] In his view a socialist regime would be obliged to rely, as did capitalism, upon an extensive bureaucracy as the most rational form of administration, and bureaucratic domination would in fact be strengthened by the merging of public and private bureaucracies.

A progressive elimination of private capitalism is no doubt theoretically conceivable . . . although it will certainly not be the outcome of this war. But assuming that it eventually happens, what would that mean in practice? The destruction of the iron cage of modern industrial labour? No! Rather that the administration of nationalized or 'socialized' enterprises too would become bureaucratic . . . If private capitalism were eliminated the state bureaucracy would rule *alone*. The public and private bureaucracies which can now, at least in principle, counterbalance each other and hold each other in check, would then be welded into a single hierarchy. (1918a, pp. 331–2)

The changes taking place in modern society, according to Weber, indicated an advance towards the 'dictatorship of the official' rather than the 'dictatorship of the proletariat' (1918b, p. 508).

This interpretation of the relation between bureaucracy and socialism is open to criticism on several counts. First, it is only 'in principle', as Weber himself says, that the public and private bureaucracies in a capitalist society counterbalance each other; in practice, in the conditions of advanced capitalism where the economy is dominated by large corporations (including the banks), it is much more likely that the two sectors will reinforce each other, and the situation is made worse by the fact that private bureaucracies elude any effective democratic control. Second, the historical experience of the USSR since 1917 and of the state socialist societies in Eastern Europe since 1945 indicates clearly, in my view, that they have been dominated, not by a bureaucracy, but by a political party which possessed at various times the charismatic leadership qualities which Weber saw as the alternative to bureaucratic domination. If those societies are to become less authoritarian in the future it will not be through the restoration of large-scale private ownership of productive resources and the recreation of private bureaucracies, but through the decentralisation of political power, the emergence of independent centres of political thought and action, and the restoration of democratic control over policy-making. Finally, it seems scarcely plausible any longer to contrast 'dynamic capitalism' with 'bureaucratic socialism', as Mommsen (1974, ch. 3) suggests that Weber is doing. For the present-day Western capitalist societies are anything but dynamic, in either an economic or a cultural sense; on the contrary, they are now characterised by economic stagnation and cultural decline, while dynamism in the assertion of new values and commitment to political ideals, sometimes in opposition to the authoritarianism of the ruling groups, has been more evident in some socialist countries (in China at least until the death of Mao Tse Tung, Yugoslavia, Czechoslovakia until the military occupation of August 1968, Poland until the imposition of martial law in December 1981) as well as in a number of socialist-oriented, developing countries.

Weber's own solution to the problem of bureaucratic domination had two elements: the first – which I have just discussed – was the strengthening of private capitalism against the encroachment of socialism; the second, the creation of conditions in which it would be possible for 'charismatic' political leaders to emerge within the framework of a limited democratic system. Mommsen has suggested that 'Weber's charismatic personalities have much in common with Nietzsche's great individuals who set new values for themselves and for their followers' (1974, p. 79); and it is undoubtedly the case that Weber's later thought was strongly influenced by Nietzsche.[7] But this influence is most apparent in the emphasis which he placed upon the 'will to power' and the inevitability of struggles for power (which he interpreted almost exclusively in terms of the conflicts among nation-states). On the other hand, Weber's conception of charismatic leaders is very much narrower than Nietzsche's idea of 'superior individuals' who would bring about a 'transvaluation of all values'; for the role of Weber's political leaders is not so much to create new values as to uphold effectively traditional bourgeois values – private capitalism and the power interests of the capitalist nation-state.[8] Sorel's vision of the proletariat as the creator of new values, 'confronting the bourgeois world as an irreconcilable adversary, threatening it with a moral catastrophe much more than with a material catastrophe' (Sorel, 1898) might be interpreted as a more authentic expression of the Nietzschean doctrine.

It is in his discussion of democracy, mainly in the writings of his last years, that Weber reveals most clearly his obsession with political leadership by exceptional individuals. Western democracy, for Weber, is in no sense rule *by* the people,[9] but simply a useful arrangement, in the form of parliamentary government, for the recruitment and training of political leaders. In *Economy and Society* he argues that 'direct democracy' (i.e. effective rule by the people) is only possible in associations or societies which are small (not more than a few thousand members), have no need for specialised administration, and have no permanent party organisations engaged in a struggle for offices (1921, pp. 170–1). Beyond this stage some kind of representation is unavoidable, and in the case of the modern Western societies Weber conceives it as a 'representation of interests' which has to be analysed largely in terms of the situation of various classes and status groups (1921, pp. 171–6). At the same time, representation produces a sharp distinction between leaders and followers, and the subordination of the latter (1921, pp. 667–8).

Consequently, according to Weber, the modern 'mass democracies' can only take the form of 'plebiscitarian leader democracies'; that is to say, political regimes in which charismatic leaders of party organisations compete for the popular vote: 'There is only a choice between leader-democracy with a "machine" and leaderless democracy – that is to say domination by professional politicians without a calling, without the inner charismatic qualities which make a leader' (1919, p. 544). In the whole of Weber's discussion of plebiscitarian leader democracy there is an ambiguity about the basis of legitimacy in such a regime; whether what exists is rational – legal domination (depending upon the popular vote) or charismatic domination (depending upon the personal qualities of the leader). But Weber's inclination was to emphasise the latter. In *Economy and Society* he observed that

'Plebiscitarian democracy' – the most important type of leader democracy – is, in its genuine sense, a kind of charismatic domination which conceals itself behind a legitimacy that is formally derived from and sustained by the will of the governed. The leader (the demagogue) rules in fact by virtue of the devotion of his followers and their trust in him as a person. (1921, p. 156)

and in his articles on the future form of the German state he expressed himself in favour of a *plebiscitarian* President of the Reich as head of the government (1918c, p. 482), rather than a purely parliamentary system.

Weber's preoccupation with charismatic leaders – politicians *with* a 'calling' – had two main sources. One was his concern with the 'overwhelming tendency towards bureaucratisation' (1918a, p. 333) – in political parties as well as in the state and the economy – and its probable outcome in a severe restriction of the sphere of free individual activity and an ossification of Western society, which he saw both as an eclipse of 'dynamic capitalism' and as a cultural decline, a routinisation and disenchantment of the world. But the second source, as I have argued above, was his conviction that Germany needed political leaders who, unlike the bureaucracy, would effectively promote the power interests of the nation-state. Many commentators on Weber's political theory have drawn attention to the vague and unsatisfactory character of his conception of a 'charismatic leader', whose personal qualities – which are supposed to entitle him to this exalted role – are left entirely undefined and unanalysed. In fact, the normally hidden content of this notion was from time to time revealed when, as in his Freiburg lecture or in the lecture on socialism, Weber related the political capacity of various classes and status groups, and of the leaders who rose to prominence within them, solely to the probable consequences of their actions for the interests of the nation-state. The 'charismatic leader' is the politician who can most effectively arouse nationalist fervour and set, or keep, the nation on its path of glory.

Democracy as a political idea, and as a social movement inspired by that idea, which is valuable in its own right, finds no place whatsoever in Weber's thought. A sharp contrast is drawn between 'direct democracy' which can exist only in small-scale, undifferentiated societies, and modern 'mass democracies' in which the people cannot possibly govern themselves and the only feasible system is 'leader democracy'. Any intermediate position is ignored, as is the idea of a gradual broadening of democracy which was historically the fundamental element in the whole modern democratic movement. Democracy is thus reduced to a mechanism for the selection and training of political leaders through a competitive struggle for the popular vote,[10] and any other view of a democratic political system is dismissed as 'utopian' – utopian because, according to Weber, there is no way in which the people can effectively control either the leaders for whom they have voted or the expert officials who administer the complex apparatus of a modern industrial society.

But even leaving aside any consideration of the intrinsic value of such utopian thought which, while it may never lead to a complete attainment of its goal, may none the less push society closer to the goal, it is not difficult to criticise Weber's sweeping denial of the possibility of any real and direct democratic participation in policy-making. In the first place, democratic organisations in many different spheres, and at different levels, can and do control the actions of their officials in a more or less effective way, though there is undoubtedly scope for much more extensive study (which a Weberian stance on the issue would systematically discourage) of how democratic control can be progressively improved in large organisations. Furthermore, as Paul Hirst has suggested in a discussion of this question, democratic participation may not only provide adequate control, but may actually increase the efficiency of bureaucratic administration, particularly in the sphere of production; as he argues (and the argument applies more widely) 'the more antagonistic the separation between manager and managed, the greater the labour devoted to supervision and the less efficient the means of coordination ... In contradiction to Weber, efficiency is only possible when the production workers do *not* play the part of cogs in a wheel' (1976, pp. 120–1). No doubt at the level of national government (and of regional and international organisations) it is much more difficult for the people and their elected representatives to ensure that it is their own policies which are carried out rather than those of the permanent high officials, who are certainly able to exert a very great influence on policy making,[11] but the problem is widely recognised, and there are numerous ways in which control over the actions of officials can be strengthened, among them being, again, greater direct participation by the people who are the consumers of public services.

The second important issue concerns the degree of control which the people can exercise over their elected representatives and party leaders. Here Weber took the same one-sided view as was expounded by Michels (1911) in his formulation of the 'iron law of oligarchy', according to which a small group of leaders is bound to dominate the unorganised majority of the party members or the electorate.[12] Robert Brym (1980), however, has recently noted that 'Michels, of course, never bothered to specify those forces which might counteract the iron law of oligarchy', and has proposed an alternative conceptualisation which 'transforms a constant (the "inexorable" drift toward oligarchy and élitism) into a variable (the ebb and flow of oligarchical and democratic tendencies)', bringing evidence to demonstrate 'that in some cases the iron law of oligarchy does not apply, and even that the distribution of power within political organizations may on occasion be such as to allow us to speak of an "iron law of democracy"' (pp. 41–2). The conceptions of Michels and Weber were probably influenced very greatly by the generally authoritarian climate of German politics, but in Weber's case something more is involved too; he espoused as a value commitment the idea of a strong authoritarian capitalist nation-state, and spoke with contempt of 'leaderless democracy', such as he thought was implicit in the aims of the German revolutionary movement. Yet the cult of leaders which he expounded is itself an indication of political immaturity and a servile cast of mind; and the advocacy of strong 'charismatic' leadership itself operates as a social-psychological force which increases the propensity to authoritarianism on one side, servility and political irresponsibility on the other. In practice, there are many methods – all of which could be greatly improved beyond their present effectiveness – by which the power and pretensions of political leaders can be regulated: elections, scrutiny of the performance of elected representatives (as is suggested in recent Labour Party discussions on the reselection of MPs), a free and critical press and television (such as exists as yet only imperfectly even in the Western countries), and the deliberate encouragement and the extension of practices of self-management in all spheres of society, from the economic to the cultural. These matters – involving a continual struggle to achieve an ever greater degree of genuine rule *by* the people – are infinitely more significant for the well-being, and indeed the survival, of humanity in the next few decades than is Weber's obsession with charismatic leaders and the power of the nation state, which in the present age is little more than a dangerous irrelevance.

It is astonishing to my mind that after the horrible and senseless slaughter of the First World War Weber himself should not have felt a need to reconsider his early beliefs about the paramountcy of national interests and of the 'struggle for existence' among nation states. In fact, he clung to these beliefs, retained his faith in bourgeois values, and by his interpretations of the post-war political situation in Germany helped to sustain that conservative nationalism and militarism which in due course, destroyed the Weimar Republic. He remained to the end a fervent nationalist, a half-hearted democrat, and an implacable opponent of socialism.

NOTES

1. Weber is said to have replied to a student who asked him what his political plans were after the signing of the Versailles peace treaty and its ratification by the National Assembly in July 1919: 'I have no political plans except to concentrate all my intellectual strength on the one problem, how to get once more for Germany a great general staff' (quoted in Mayer, 1956, p. 107).

2. He himself made this clear in his Inaugural Lecture of 1895: 'I am a member of the bourgeois class, regard myself as a member, and have been educated in its view and ideals.' His criticism of the bourgeoisie was that it had not yet demonstrated its political capacity to rule and to direct national policy effectively towards making Germany a world power.

3. There is indeed very little critical or comparative analysis of the modern nation state in Weber's political writings, and as Mommsen suggests he largely took for granted the late-nineteenth-century world of imperialist rivalries.

4. From the standpoint of an interpretation of modern culture in the capitalist world the concept of rationalisation is no doubt a fundamental theme in Weber's work, as Karl Löwith argued in his monograph on Weber and Marx (Löwith, 1932). A similar theme occupies a prominent place in Simmel's analysis of modern culture, especially in his study of money (Simmel, 1900).

5. See Weber's analysis of Bismarck's 'political legacy' in 'Parliament and Government in a reconstructed Germany' (1918a, pp. 311–19).

6. Weber's general argument against socialism – which is set out in fragmentary form in several of his political essays (1895) and in a more connected way in *Economy and Society* (1921) and the lecture on socialism (1918b) – had three main elements: (i) that a socialist economy would be deprived of the means of rational calculation, in so far as it involved physical allocation of resources rather than the use of money and a price mechanism (1921, esp. pp. 53–8); (ii) that socialism would result not in government by the people, but in an extension of bureaucratic power; and (iii) that the existing socialist movement in Germany was incapable of providing competent and effective political leadership for the nation. In the present context I am concerned only with the second element.

7. See especially E. Fleischmann (1964).

8. H. P. Bahrdt notes, quite correctly in my view, that Weber's fundamental conviction, as expressed for example in his lecture on socialism, was that 'the property-owning entrepreneurial bourgeoisie was the only group capable of providing the leadership to maintain a dynamic society' (Bahrdt, 1965, p. 126).

9. Already in a letter of 1908 to Roberto Michels (cited in Mommsen, 1959), Weber asserted that 'any idea which proposes to eliminate the domination of man by man through an extension of "democracy" is utopian', and further 'Such concepts as "will of the people", authentic will of the people, have long since ceased to exist for me; they are *fictions*.'

10. This view was later elaborated by Schumpeter (1976, part IV) in his study of capitalism, socialism and democracy.

11. Their influence is generally greater when governments themselves are weak and short-lived; hence the considerable discussion about the role of high officials during the period of the Third Republic in France. However, there may well be a tendency for the power of officials to increase steadily, unless checked, in present-day societies, as is suggested by critical accounts of the 'rule of the *Enarques*' (high officials trained since the war at the National School of Administration, ENA) in France, and by Mr Tony Benn's recent comments on the role of higher civil servants in Britain.

12. Roberto Michels, *Political Parties* (1911, English trans. 1962). On the relations between Weber and Michels, see Wolfgang J. Mommsen, 'Max Weber and Roberto Michels', *European Journal of Sociology*, 22 (1), 1981: 100–16; and on the development of Michels' own views, see Beetham, David, 'Michels and his critics', ibid., 81–99.

REFERENCES

Bahrdt, H. P., 1965. 'Contribution to discussion on "Max Weber und die Machtpolitik"', in Otto Stammer, ed., *Max Weber und die Soziologie heute*. Tübingen, J. C. B. Mohr (Paul Siebeck), pp. 124–30

Brym, Robert J., 1980. *Intellectuals and Politics*. London Allen and Unwin

Fleischmann, E., 'De Weber à Nietzsche', in *Archives Européennes de Sociologie*, 5: 190–238

Hilferding, Rudolf, 1910. *Finance Capital: A Study of the Latest Phase of Capitalist Development*. English trans. London, Routledge and Kegan Paul, 1981

Hirst, Paul Q., 1976. *Social Evolution and Sociological Categories*. London, Allen and Unwin

Löwith, Karl, 1932. 'Max Weber und Karl Marx', in *Archiv für Sozialwissenshaft und Sozialpolitik*, 66: 53–99, 175–214. English trans. London, Allen and Unwin, 1982

Mayer, J. P., 1956. *Max Weber and German Politics: A Study in Political Sociology*. 2nd rev. and enlarged edn. London, Faber and Faber, 1956

Michels, Roberto, 1911. *Political Parties*. English trans. New York, The Free Press, 1962

Mommsen, Wolfgang J., 1959. *Max Weber und die deutsche Politik 1890–1920*. Tübingen, J. C. B. Mohr (Paul Siebeck), 1959

    1974. *The Age of Bureaucracy: Perspectives on the Political Sociology of Max Weber*. Oxford, Basil Blackwell

Schumpeter, J. P., 1942. *Capitalism, Socialism and Democracy*, 5th edn., with a new introduction. London, Allen and Unwin, 1976

Simmel, Georg, 1900. *Philosophie des Geldes*. 2nd enlarged edn. Munich and Leipzig, Duncker and Humblot, 1907; English trans. London: Routledge and Kegan Paul, 1978

Sorel, Georges, 1898. Preface to Saverio Merlino, *Formes et essence du Socialisme*. Paris

Weber, Max, 1895. 'Der Nationalstaat und die Volkswirtschaftspolitik' [Inaugural lecture at the University of Freiburg], in *Gesammelte Politische Schriften*. 3rd enlarged edn., Tübingen, J. C. B. Mohr (Paul Siebeck), 1971, pp. 1–25

    1918a. 'Parlament und Regierung im neugeordneten Deutschland', in *Gesammelte Politische*

Schriften (1971), pp. 306–443. English trans. in *Economy and Society*. 3 vols. New York, Bedminster Press, 1968. Appendix to vol. III

1918b. 'Der Sozialismus', in *Gesammelte Aufsätze zur Soziologie und Sozialpolitik*. Tübingen, J. C. B. Mohr (Paul Siebeck), 1924, pp. 492–518. English trans. in J. E. T. Eldridge, ed., *Max Weber: The Interpretation of Social Reality*. London, Michael Joseph, 1970

1918c. 'Deutschlands künftige Staatsform', in *Gesammelte Politische Schriften* (1971), pp. 448–83

1919. 'Politik als Beruf', in *Gesammelte Politische Schriften* (1971), pp. 505–60. English trans. in H. H. Gerth and C. Wright Mills, eds., *From Max Weber: Essays in Sociology*. New York, Oxford University Press, 1947, pp. 77–128

1921. *Wirtschaft und Gesellschaft*. Tübingen, J. C. B. Mohr (Paul Siebeck), 1921. English trans. *Economy and Society*. 3 vols. New York, Bedminster Press, 1968

8

The state and legitimation: the work of Jürgen Habermas

PHILIP K. LAWRENCE

More than a decade has elapsed since the publication of Habermas's *Legitimation Crisis*. During this period the politics of advanced capitalist societies has undergone profound changes. Indeed, the specific social and political characteristics of the early 1970s appear now as alien; features, almost of a forgotten age. For in the early 1970s *Legitimation Crisis* was one work, amongst many of a neo-Marxist and humanist complexion, which anticipated radical and positive social change in the West. At the same time neo-conservative theories emerged which were highly pessimistic. They proclaimed a 'crisis of governability' and prophesied the death of liberal democracy. Seemingly, then, there was a remarkable degree of consensus at this time concerning prognoses of social change. However, the predictions appear not to have been borne out. The last ten years have seen a vital resurgence of conservative philosophy and practice and the prospects for progressive radical change seem almost nil.

In the light of these reactionary developments it is, I believe, an apposite moment to cast a glance backwards at theories which had anticipated a political crisis of capitalism. To this end I will examine the analysis in *Legitimation Crisis* because it was the most theoretically sophisticated of the 'cultural crisis' school of thought which emerged in the 1970s. Therefore the purpose of this chapter is to reassess Habermas's work against the background of recent political change and to judge if it invalidates his theories, or whether the categories developed in *Legitimation Crisis* can be accommodated to the new political reality of advanced capitalism.

An implicit focus of my analysis will be an assessment of the degree to which a democratic challenge to the authority of the state has been a feature of recent years. This, of course, was something which Habermas and others had anticipated (e.g. Wolfe, 1977). However, as I shall indicate below, these theories underestimate the continuing effectiveness of mainstream capitalist ideologies. At the same time they exaggerate the destabilising effects of new cultural and social practices. In particular I believe Habermas relied too heavily on Weber's theory of the rationalisation of traditional values. But, as I shall demonstrate, this does not demolish his analytic framework of a crisis of legitimation.

I

In assessing the prospects for the continued existence of the capitalist state Habermas begins by reflecting on the meaning of the concept of crisis (Habermas, 1973, pp. 1–6). As I shall demonstrate, his arguments at this stage are vital to his subsequent analysis – a fact which is often neglected in interpretations of his work. He maintains that 'crisis' always evokes both objective and subjective connotations and that this is clear in medical and aesthetic usages. (The patient loses his subjective powers while under the influence of disease and the actor, caught up in a fateful process that appears as objective, is subjectively involved because personality affects the final outcome.) However, in its usage in the social sciences crisis often appears as entirely an objective process. In particular the conception of society as a 'system' has led to the view that a 'crisis' refers to measurable processes which indicate breakdowns and malfunctions. But in Habermas's view this is inadequate because when a society breaks down or disintegrates a vital factor is the subjectivity of the social actors themselves. Thus whether given objective disturbances in a society's functioning represent a crisis depends on what these mean to social actors. In other words, the key question is, do such changes affect collective social identity? As a result, when we designate change as representing a transformation or revolution we depend on individuals and groups believing that they are in a new situation which is distinct from the previous *status quo*: 'only when members of a society experience structural alterations as critical for continued existence and feel their social identity threatened can we speak of crisis' (Habermas, 1973, p. 3).

The inclusion of a 'social life world' element in the concept of crisis has implications, not only for our designation of a social process as a crisis, but also for which factors we isolate as causes. As a result Habermas maintains that social culture – key norms and values – plays a vital role in the maintenance or collapse of institutions. Thus, objective disturbances such as war, unemployment and business bankruptcies will only spark off crises if they become coupled with patterns of social consciousness which spark off an identity crisis. In *Legitimation Crisis* the meaning of this is left rather obscure, but, in my view, what it signifies is that the members of a society must begin to experience their dominant institutions as unviable. In other words, the manner in which institutions function contradicts social expectations which are based on dominant norms and values.

By focussing on social/psychological factors as well as objective and measurable indicators of breakdown, Habermas has developed a concept of crisis which is more sophisticated than many of the crude notions often invoked by social scientists. In the last two decades the concept has almost become synonymous with problem or hiatus and has been deployed far too readily. A major advantage of the conception used in *Legitimation Crisis* is the strict adherence to a rigorous yet broad definition. As a result it becomes easier to explain national variations in reactions to economic dislocation because cultural factors are brought into the analysis as independent variables. In consequence political crises become somewhat difficult to predict, because they can no longer simply be deduced from economic dislocations. Here, then, is a clear rejection of the orthodox Marxian position which attempts to 'read off' political consequences of economic malfunctions in a deterministic fashion. In Habermas's view political and cultural factors are vital to the question of the continuation of capitalism. Therefore the degree of economic disturbance which the capitalist state can tolerate is an empirical issue which cannot be determined in advance.

From the arguments outlined above it should be clear what Habermas's central concerns are. If we cannot predict how economic developments will constrain state actions then clearly we need to look elsewhere. In his view the ultimate determinant of state power is legitimation and as a result the crucial issue is whether the capitalist state will be able to legitimate its necessary mode of functioning: 'But, if we do not wish to fall back on theorems of economic crisis, governmental activity can find a necessary limit only in available legitimations' (Habermas, 1973, p. 69).

Although collective social identity is central to Habermas's model of crisis, it is important to note that he is not advocating an idealist conception of social change. Obviously the members of a society do not simply think themselves into a transformation. In his analysis the objective elements in the process are the state and the system of social labour (including education) and changes in these spheres are vital to his overall assessment. However, he does decisively reject the view that the socio-cultural and political realms are a reflex of the capital/wage-labour relationship. In other words he dismisses the mode of argument which reduces the state to an epiphenomenon of the economic base. As I shall show, Habermas advocates a model of the state which stresses autonomy and is far removed from traditional Marxian conceptions. Indeed, it is a contentious issue whether the theories he has developed move within the Marxian sphere of influence at all.

II

In *Legitimation Crisis*, the nature of the autonomy of the state is explored by assessing the crucial differences between liberal capitalism and advanced capitalism. In the former the state merely creates and maintains the boundary conditions within which the market economy functions.[1] Therefore the main steering mechanism for the social system is the market, which simultaneously defines the goals which the economy and society are directed towards and also generates the structure of social stratification, i.e. the class structure. In this instance it is appropriate to speak of a separate state and economy and also to assume that the political sphere is determined by the logic of forces emanating from a privately constituted economic system. A major consequence of this is that the effective political nexus of the system – the class structure – is de-politicised. The market perpetuates the decisive yet anonymous hegemony of the bourgeoisie and economic existence is merely a natural fate to which societal members succumb. However, in advanced capitalism the state is the control centre of the society. Therefore it self-consciously acts to avoid dysfunctions; a strategy which Habermas terms 'reactive crisis avoidance'. The suggestion here is that the state – *qua* organism – has undergone a learning process whereby developments which had previously created social disintegration are adapted and controlled so as to be neutralised. Obviously, given the history of capitalism, the decisive watershed in this respect was the 1930s when economic collapse engendered political revolution in Europe, but was managed and contained in Britain and the United States. The learning process is thus manifest in an attempt to 'iron out' the peaks and troughs of the business cycle and also to engineer politically what Habermas terms a 'partial class compromise' (Habermas, 1973, p. 55).

As I have shown above, the view Habermas takes of liberal capitalism is an orthodox Marxian one. But in his assessment of advanced capitalism the Marxian categories are displaced because of three decisive changes. First, the class structure is political, in that the state increasingly displaces the market as the determining factor in the distribution of life chances. As he expresses it, 'class struggle must be maintained over the administratively mediated distribution of increases in the social product. Thus the class structure can now be affected by political disputes as well' (Habermas, 1973, p. 52). In addition Habermas cites the fact that wage levels, especially in the state sector and in large private companies which depend on state expenditure, are set 'quasi politically', in that the work-force can be paid at levels higher than would accrue from the market. As Habermas sees it the main point of this is to 'mitigate the opposition between wage labour and capital and to bring about a partial class compromise' (Habermas, 1973, p. 57). The second factor which obviates the value of traditional Marxian categories is simply that the state has supplanted the market as the dominant steering mechanism of the society. Of course economic logic retains a major impact, but there is a 'political counter-control in which a displacement of the forces of production finds expression' (Habermas, 1973, p. 56). Finally, Habermas contends that the labour theory of value, which previously explained a 'tendential fall in the rate of profit', is inadequate in its account of the 'reflexive' value created by science and technology. Thus the unproductive labour of scientists and teachers actually heightens the productivity of labour in general. As a result analysis based on the labour theory of value can no longer predict, *a priori*, the inevitability of economic collapse. For it is 'an empirical question whether the new form of production of surplus value can compensate for the tendential fall in the rate of profit, that is, whether it can work against economic crisis' (Habermas, 1973, p. 57).

As I have already suggested Habermas's conception of advanced capitalism is markedly at odds with orthodox Marxism. What is clear from the three positions outlined above is not just a rejection of the labour theory of value, but also of the traditional understanding of the base/superstructure relationship, which according to Habermas is only appropriate to liberal capitalism.

Notwithstanding any deeper theoretical confusions,[2] it is clear that Habermas regards the state in advanced capitalism as the self-conscious control centre of society. In a more literal vein he speaks of governments setting themselves the declared target of steering the economy so as to avoid the more unfortunate contingencies of the market system. Naturally this is a significant goal in itself, but it is even more important when it is coupled with the desire to avoid disintegration – political crisis – and also the need for growth and adaptation. Thus the state is geared to the survival needs of the social system which include the reproduction of labour, technology, markets and capital etc., and rivalry with other states in economic, political and military spheres.

Although Habermas does not grasp the state as a reflex of class structure he does understand the programme of goals which the state pursues as a function of the inherent instability of capitalism. Thus the state is not just attempting to engineer a *modus vivendi* amongst any contending factions which happen to emerge: it is directed to contain class conflict which is viewed as structural. He writes, 'To ward off system crisis, advanced capitalist societies focus all forces of social integration at the point of the structurally most probable conflict – in order all the more to keep it latent' (Habermas, 1973, p. 38). Pursuing this line of argument Habermas suggests that the wages and conditions in the state sector and the private oligopolistic sector, where unions are most powerful, have created a situation where class conflict is externalised into other areas of the labour market where workers are less well organised. The costs of securing this class compromise are filtered downwards on to immigrants, the elderly, the sick and the unemployed, etc. As a result class consciousness becomes increasingly fragmented and the likelihood of a working-class revolution, on the lines anticipated by Marx, is increasingly diminished.

If the activities of the state serve to forestall economic collapse and class conflict this is not achieved without heavy costs. Habermas contends that the potential economic crises which capitalism faces and which are managed and contained by the 'political counter control' of the state are not expelled from the social system, but merely displaced into other spheres. Thus the traditional view of the market system as anarchical and unplanned is applied to the process of governmental administration. In other words he considers it plausible that the unstable dynamics of the market economy reassert themselves in the planning process and that, in consequence, the state exhibits a crisis of rationality – simply an inability to produce sufficient effective decisions. However, despite a brief consideration of theories of rationality crisis it is clear that Habermas does not regard this as the heart of the matter. If we think back to the reflections on the nature of crisis itself and the contention that the concept must encompass the duality of social-system and social-life world perspectives, then the rationality theory can be viewed as too objectivistic. We cannot stipulate in advance the degree of planning disorganisation which the state can tolerate. Indeed, unlike economic failures which have a direct manifestation in unemployment, liquidations and inflation, rationality dysfunctions become apparent gradually in increasing social disorganisation. Whether such disorganisations will spark off a crisis cannot be decided by reference to perspectives which highlight the contradictions of different planning perspectives. In other words the social system perspective is inadequate. Therefore the crucial issue is the degree of legitimation which the state can muster. Thus the central problem which *Legitimation Crisis* poses can be formulated in the following question: can the capitalist state manage and co-ordinate an economy still based on the logic of private accumulation while simultaneously maintaining political legitimacy? In other words Habermas is seeking to know whether the political and social culture of advanced capitalism is still compatible with the imperatives of the politically managed accumulation process. As we shall see the ingenious nature of his answer lies in the view that the very political actions which serve to ward off crises trigger political and social expectations which call the system into question. Therefore the crisis displacement is not merely a shift from the economy into the administrative system: it moves into the social-value system as well.

III

The pressure for legitimation which will validate the authority of the state has two interrelated sources. First, there are simply the values which emerge in a democratic polity. In Habermas's view even bourgeois democratic theory contains equalitarian ingredients, but these are, in the main, applied formalistically to legal status and the franchise. However, with the emergence of working-class parties the concept of citizenship changes to include the rights of health care, education and freedom from poverty. Thus expectations which cluster around the need for a welfare state cannot simply be swept away, for they have become central ingredients in democratic politics. Secondly, the state's involvement in the economy has, in his opinion, re-politicised the relations of production. This is of great significance because in liberal capitalism the most effective ideology was the market theory of justice. Here the laws which determine the distribution of life chances are entirely impersonal and anonymous. But because in advanced capitalism there is a large public sector, state-regulated pay controls, state determination of social benefits and general expectations concerning the steering of the economy, life chances now appear as directly determined by political decisions. There is, then, to use Daniel Bell's phrase, a 'public household' (Bell, 1976, p. 220). However, if the state's use of public resources appears as merely a duplication of the priorities of the system of private and unequal wealth accumulation, this will not be compatible with expectations of justice and equality. But this is precisely the pattern of intervention the state must follow – within certain limits – if the logic and meaning of capitalism are to remain intact. As we have seen, any generosity shown to the best-organised labour groupings is paid for by the relative impoverishment of other sectors. Therefore what the state must avoid at all costs is the development of a collectivised orientation towards justice. In other words the limiting effects of the political democracy are real enough, but really radical demands which could emerge from the polity are kept latent or diffused.

In addition to the general reflection that state-regulated capitalism politicises class relations Habermas also ponders whether capitalism has a political culture which can justify the new level of intervention. As Raymond Plant has written, 'The central question is: are there normative resources in society on which the state can draw to justify and sustain the degree of intervention required to avoid some of the dysfunctional effects of the economic market?' (Plant, 1981, p. 2). This, of course, is a theme which is reminiscent of right-wing analysis. Here the cry is usually that the state is over-loaded because of exorbitant demands for welfare expenditure and subsidies. Daniel Bell has suggested that the solution lies in the generation of a new code of restraint and public duty underpinned by morality (Bell, 1976, p. 278). However, Habermas is thinking along different lines. In his view a genuinely participatory democracy could set the criteria by which political interventions would be judged, but this would probably call capitalism into question. Indeed, it is precisely the type of polity the state must not confront. Therefore the lack of binding obligations which would justify the level of state intervention, is a necessary pre-condition for a pattern of involvement which must eschew public scrutiny: 'In the final analysis, the *class structure* is the source of the legitimation deficit' (Habermas, 1973, p. 73).

In the light of this it is obvious that the real motives behind planning and intervention must be screened out of political discussion. According to

Habermas this is achieved by separating the administrative and legitimatory functions of the state. Thus an attempt is made to focus public attention on the symbolism of politics – pageantry, juridical pronouncements, personalisation of substantive issues which obscures underlying themes, and also explicit manoeuvres aimed at manipulating and garnishing prejudice – while real participation by citizens in decisions which are contentious is avoided. However, Habermas perceives this 'ideology planning' as a double-edged weapon because if the process of manipulation is transparent it becomes self-defeating. His reasons for adopting this view are, in fact, rather complex and, as with many arguments made in *Legitimation Crisis*, they are not adequately explained. In essence he maintains that cultural traditions which bind individuals together in structures of common meaning immediately lose their power of integration when the state adopts them as objects to be purposively deployed for political ends. In other words the force of such traditions lies precisely in their unconscious and natural character. If this still remains obscure then I would suggest that the crux of the argument is really a contrast between Weber's concepts of traditional and rational-legal authority: the idea being that the purposive use of tradition is an epistemological impossibility. As Habermas puts it, albeit rather cryptically, 'The structural dissimilarity between areas of administrative action and areas of cultural tradition constitutes, then, a systematic limit to attempts to compensate for legitimation deficits through conscious manipulation' (Habermas, 1973, p. 71).

The fact that the social culture is, to some degree, immunised from instrumental political manipulation would not, in itself, generate legitimation problems if it were not for two conditions present in advanced capitalism. First, the state needs increasing supplies of legitimation to secure mass loyalty for its new functions and, second, the state has expanded to encompass areas that were previously in the domain of civil society. Thus, if we think again in terms of a disjunction between traditional rationality and purposive rationality the latter is seen to be growing at the expense of the former. In Habermas's view this inevitably leads to increasing problems in the sphere of legitimation because the rationalisation and scientisation of traditional culture destroy integrative meaning. The thesis is that the prior strength of the system lay in traditional value systems which were not, in a direct sense, touched upon by the instrumental actions of state planning agencies. Thus, while once the nature of the family, education, the use of land, access to health care and the pattern of inequalities was explained by reference to sets of uncontested assumptions, these 'facts' of existence have now become contingent. In Habermas's words,

Administrative planning produces a universal pressure for legitimation in a sphere that was once distinguished precisely for its power of self-legitimation ... The end effect is a consciousness of the contingency, not only of the contents of tradition, but also of the techniques of tradition, that is, of socialisation. (Habermas, 1973, pp. 71–2)

Now this is, of course, an argument which is heavily dependent on Weber's thesis concerning rationalisation. However, unlike Weber, who saw no difficulties posed with respect to legitimation by the spread of rational-legalism, Habermas sees the consequence as a crisis of meaning. Although it is not presented in the form of an argument about civil society and the state I would suggest that Habermas is contending that the effective line drawn between the state and civil society in liberal capitalism ensures that any pressures for legitimation do not spill over into the public realm. In other words the level of social problems which the state is deemed to be responsible for is relatively low. But as civil society shrinks, its content – religion, privatism, and fatalism, etc. – is absorbed into the public realm in a changed form, that is, in a manner which is critical and requires answers to pressing questions. In consequence the state in advanced capitalism is forced into a dialogue with large numbers of citizens on a plethora of contentious issues – income differentials, defence, welfare provisions, the education service, taxation, devolution, ecology, to name but a few – therefore, again the question is: will the expanded and increasingly active public realm call into question the economic system of private wealth?

I am reminded again at this point of the conservative arguments which crystallise around the idea of the overloaded state (e.g. King, 1975). But whereas these simply posit that the citizenry have been seduced by welfarism, Habermas, as we have seen, has a far more sophisticated explanation. For him the expanded public realm is the cost of the attempt to side-step the economic crisis. But is this growing political sphere really such a problem for the state? Looking back one can see why writers saw, in the late 1960s and early 1970s, clear signs of increased politicisation. After all, industrial conflict, the anti-Vietnam War protests, the civil rights movement and student protests were objective features on the political landscape. However, these have proved to be temporary and peripheral phenomena, whereas what Habermas has in mind is a permanent manifestation of legitimation problems. For him the reality is a permanent politicisation of issues which the capitalist state finds problematic to resolve. Thus he sees the necessary functional separation of legitimatory and administrative processes as breaking down. Again, in a manner which is somewhat obscure, Habermas implies that one consequence of this is the increasing significance of material rewards as a replacement for other means of securing legitimation: if the state inadvertently destroys meaning systems it must find a function replacement. Hence, 'The fiscally siphoned-off resource "value" must take the place of the scanty resource meaning' (Habermas, 1973, p. 73). What this amounts to, I believe, is the thesis that as the polity becomes increasingly active because of new pressure groups, citizens' initiatives and the plethora of experimental social alternatives in church, school, university and the arts, the state is burdened with the costs of funding these new social demands. The consequence of this is that, even though such groups may not believe in the intrinsic 'goodness' of the political order, they accept it on pragmatic grounds because it 'delivers the goods'. However, as Habermas is aware, there is a paradox here which could have significant political consequences in the longer term. This lies in the fact that the state may be funding activities which are underpinned by values antagonistic to capitalism. In other words the state may sponsor a culture which is a 'foreign body' within the system. As a result the possibility of a legitimation crisis rests on two distinct developments. On the one hand the state may run short of revenue with which to 'buy' claimants off and on the other it may be confronted by demands which cannot be met by material rewards. It is my contention that the latter is, in fact, the more significant because it may signify a growing commitment to alternative models of how economy and society should be organised. However, one should also add a note of caution, for amongst theorists who are seeking signs of radical social developments there has been a tendency to exaggerate the implications of seemingly novel cultural practices. As we have seen, Habermas declines to argue that there are clear limits to the degree of economic dislocation which the state can tolerate and I would assert that the same applies to the level of cultural pluralism which capitalism can incorporate. The point is that the political significance of social and cultural changes depends on whether these are coupled to wider conceptions of property distribution and democracy and also on the strategic significance of the groups who adopt new styles. Much of the interest in such groups stems, of course, from the fact that the working class have not fulfilled their expected role as agent of radical change. This may be, but in comparison their designated replacements – students, feminists, blacks, draft dodgers and artists – lack political weight and substance. More significantly, if such groups were to constitute a real political counter-weight to the state then the cultural pluralism I mentioned above would have to break down. Thus the groups which Habermas believes have become active in the public realm would, somehow, have to merge together. But in recent years this has not happened;[3] the success of conservatives in Germany, Great Britain and the United States being as much because of the fragmentation of the opposition as their own numerical strength. Finally, we should also bear in mind that many of the strata whom writers such as Marcuse (1972), and Habermas perceive as radicals are materially advantaged within the current state of affairs. Therefore, one does not need to be entirely cynical to assume that such individuals may come to a pragmatic accommodation with the state. As McCarthy has perceptively indicated there are many half-way houses between complete acceptance and rejection of state authority (McCarthy, 1978, p. 375). At this point let me clarify and condense the arguments above.

I follow Habermas in his view that the manner in which the state/civil society line has been redrawn in advanced capitalism leads to legitimation problems. The public realm has expanded and it lacks an ideological core which would bind it to the integrated state-economy network. However, I do not believe it is inevitable that this legitimacy vacuum will be filled by a political culture which demands radical change. On the contrary, it may be that the state can coexist with this vacuum and hence cope with a 'legitimacy deficit', or it may shore up its authority with ideologies which were supposedly moribund. Alternatively, the state/civil society line may be redrawn again to reduce the interface between governmental actions and economic and social demands.

I shall argue below that a mixture of the three aforementioned tendencies has been characteristic of advanced capitalist states in recent years and that this explains the success of conservative political strategies which have sought to 'roll back the state'. However, I have not yet explicitly assessed the implications of this for Habermas's fundamental assumptions. Thus far we have seen that in his analysis the crisis is displaced from the economic and administrative spheres into the authority structure of the polity. But if no solution is to be found here there is one final sub-system where the crisis can be resolved: the social culture itself.

IV

When we speak of legitimacy, from a normative point of view, we assume that a political order lays claim to validation in terms of criteria such as justice, freedom and equality. Thus legitimacy pin-points, hypothetically, a dialogue between state and citizens in which normative assessments are paramount. However, the extent to which any such dialogue takes place in the real world depends on a number of factors. Do citizens actually believe in these values? Are there any mechanisms which make transparent deviations from cherished norms? Are such values so subjective that their meaning is always contested? Finally, there is the possibility that the whole process is a façade. What if citizens could be made to believe anything which the state regarded as functionally necessary? In fact it is just this 'brave new world' scenario which Habermas considers at the conclusion of his arguments. Thus the likelihood of a legitimation crisis depends, in the final analysis, on whether the value system of capitalism can be manipulated in line with state needs or whether it holds firm. In Habermas's words

This reflection supports my thesis that only a rigid socio-cultural system, incapable of being randomly functionalized for the needs of the administrative system, could explain a sharpening of legitimation difficulties into a legitimation crisis . . . A legitimation crisis, then, must be based on a motivation crisis. (Habermas, 1973, pp. 74–5)

As David Held has pointed out, the concept of a motivation crisis plays a key role in Habermas's arguments, but is actually given a brief and somewhat cryptic explanation (Held, 1982, p. 188). In fact what Habermas does is to separate into two categories – legitimation and motivation – a set of arguments which are normally joined together. Thus in Habermas's view we cannot simply talk of the interface between the state and the political culture; rather we must trace back the source of political demands and expectations to fundamental syndromes of motivation in the social culture which generate meaning. His specific designation of a motivation crisis is a situation where the state's control and management of strategic institutions, i.e. government bureaucracy, business and commerce and education, requires a pattern of behaviour from citizens which citizens cannot be motivated to perform. In other words he presupposes that the loyalty of societal members to a regime depends on the regime demonstrably fulfilling the realisation of central norms and values. To the extent that there is a crisis it lies, then, in changing values which generate expectations which the capitalist state cannot meet. Held (1982) questions whether this is realistic and suggests that Habermas's preconditions for political stability are too strict. He writes, 'social integration, when tied to the generation of a shared sense of "the worthiness of a political order to be recognised" (legitimacy), is not a necessary condition for every relatively stable society' (Held, 1982, p. 188). There is, I believe, some force in this criticism; indeed, I have already suggested that Habermas neglects the mid-points between ideal legitimacy and collapse of authority. However, Held neglects two key points. First, Habermas is not concerned with 'every . . . stable society', but with advanced capitalism; a system which explicitly claims democratic validation for its management of economy and society. Thus over time norms which demand universal rights have shifted from a formal legal domain into substantive social and economic expectations. Moreover, the 'social welfare-state democracy' explicitly eschews direct coercion as a means of securing order. Therefore the use of more coercion is damaging to the self-image of the system: an image which itself secures legitimation. Hence I support Gouldner's assertion that: 'Never before in a class society did the security of a ruling class depend so much on the presence of belief-systems appropriate to its rule' (Gouldner, 1978, p. 231). Secondly, Held errs in seeing the motivation crisis as a discrepancy between the declared values of the state and political values held by citizens. Rather Habermas is thinking of basic social values which only generate the most abstract of political ethics. In consequence the crisis looms when such values change in a manner which threatens de-politicisation. Habermas has thus assumed that dominant patterns of motivation in capitalism have steered citizens away from political participation. Civil privatism, which he regards as a key attitudinal syndrome, has thus directed attention away from substantive politics and corresponds to dominant conceptions of democracy in the West which have stressed elitism and the need for rulers to govern independently of specific motives of citizens. Paradoxically, Held (1982) suggests that the real foundations of order lie in mixtures of fatalism, deference and false consciousness. But, as regards the working class, this is precisely what civil privatism makes possible. In effect it helps secure legitimacy by default.

The second vital pattern of motivation which Habermas cites is 'familial-vocational privatism'. This is the positive counterpart to civil privatism because it stipulates what fills the empty spaces in the political culture. The lack of public politics is thus complemented by an intense interest in family, leisure, occupation and consumption. In the middle classes it is underpinned by the achievement ethos and deferred gratification. In the working classes it is based on fatalism, uncoerced obedience and hedonism and in both cases it serves to minimise political participation.

In Habermas's view both these sets of attitudes are being destroyed by the state, modern ideologies and changes in the social structure. In this regard a central factor is that the meaning of these traditions rests on values which are pre-capitalist, in other words traditional conceptions of authority and religion. As we have seen already these are seen as incompatible with the dominant structures and ideologies of capitalism which simultaneously scientise, rationalise and commercialise social, economic and political intercourse. The result is a loss of meaning; therefore economic competition is no longer predicated on the Protestant ethic and work, seen as an end in itself, sheds its aura of a redemption from sin.

These arguments, which crystallise around the Weberian rationalisation thesis, are vital to Habermas's position. However, they are incorporated into the analysis in a manner which presents them as self-evident. In my opinion they represent the first serious flaw in the general assessment of capitalism which Habermas provides. The idea of the rationalisation of tradition and religion is, of course, a powerful one, but it can give us no more than a tendential indication of changing values. Thus it cannot be used as a factual claim which amounts to the view that instrumental-purposive rationality is hegemonic in capitalist societies. Indeed, while certain states in the West are unambiguously secular, Great Britain for example, others such as Italy, Germany and the United States have potent national religions. In the realm of legitimation we should not discount the role of such religions, especially the relationship between Christianity and conservatism in the US. In a wider sense the general resurgence of conservatism also rests on beliefs and prejudices which, according to Habermas, have long been demystified. I have in mind here the teleology inherent in American nationalism, the significance of traditional symbols of authority which generate patriotism in Great Britain, the racial and cultural prejudice inherent in European nationalism and the unbelievable simplicity of conservative social and economic slogans which again unite work with the ideas of sobriety and frugality. In addition such processes are underpinned by ideologies which work on an international plane. Today the new cold war helps to create a climate where rational discussion of politics is fatally contaminated. As Halliday has remarked, 'Patriotism, warmongering and strategic paranoia combine well with piety and domestic repression' (Halliday, 1983, p. 115).

The error which leads to the assumption that the modern citizen is impervious to the appeal of tradition and religion, with their attendant prejudices, lies in positing the existence of 'the integrated consciousness'. Today the citizen acts out many roles where meanings are, so to speak, horizontally discrepant: that is they pursue courses of behaviour in family life, business, politics, leisure and other spheres which are based on values which conflict. However, this does not mean that the individual has a consciousness, articulated at the level of a world view, of these contradictions. Such an achievement, in fact, necessitates a reflective subject who becomes distanced from all roles in order to construct a general life assessment. In reality, such research as there is reveals the opposite: namely confusion, the lack of any integrated philosophy and, indeed, a reluctance to construct one.[4]

If the argument above is correct, values which in a schematic sense are pre-capitalist can survive today alongside the imperatives of administration and science and technology. Historically the paradigmatic instance of this was Hitler's Germany, which combined the rational use of science, technology and administration with xenophobic nationalism and *völkisch* mysticism. Thus in my view the rationalisation thesis has been greatly exaggerated.

In addition to the fact that capitalism can no longer rely on integrative values which are legacies of a former age, Habermas also maintains that core elements of bourgeois ideologies are themselves made meaningless by recent developments. In essence these changes undermine the achievement principle, possessive individualism and orientation to exchange value. The achievement ideology, which grasps social placement as a consequence of the meritocratic self determination of life changes is being undermined by: (1) the demise of the ideology of the free market; (2) the loosening of the relationship between educational and occupational success; (3) the increasing number of jobs where assessments cannot be made of productivity and effectiveness in individual terms; (4) the spread of new technologies into white-collar occupations which destroy intrinsic work satisfaction, and (5) the reduced motivation towards working for material rewards if (a) there is no competitive pressure in the labour market and (b) lower levels of wages are no higher than rewards which accrue from social security and welfare payments.

The ideology of possessive individualism, which understood the social creation of wealth as the mere addition of individual achievements is, according to Habermas, made redundant by the growing significance of the infrastructure and collective commodities within the modern economy. Thus today our material life can no longer be understood as a personal achievement. Moreover, the notion of a privately determined pattern of consumer preferences, which indicates 'freedom', is now patently absurd. Try as we might, we consume the same standardised products as the rest of the population.

Finally, Habermas considers that the socialising impact of the market has been weakened in advanced capitalism. Increasing numbers of individuals who are dependent on grants, state benefits, direct income from the state etc., can thus be regarded as outside a framework where life chances depend on the ebb and flow of economic contingency. In consequence the material basis of such individuals' existence is a question of concrete political expectations, whereas traditional bourgeois ideologies always stressed the competitive and fortuitous aspects of prosperity. In addition the growth of leisure pursuits in capitalism indicates a demand for goods which are not commodities, that is, positional goods, such as peaceful countryside, quiet cottages and empty beaches etc., and these, of course, have a fixed supply and cannot be distributed on the basis of market criteria without excluding most of the population from access.

In the context of the contemporary resurgence of conservatism the observations above seem overtly flawed. The supposed death of bourgeois ideologies has not come about. Indeed, the intriguing feature of neo-conservatism today is the explicit proclamation of central tenets of capitalism which for four decades were disguised beneath concepts which emphasised the caring and social aspects of the system. But now the profit motive, self-interest and private accumulation are again paraded as self-evident virtues in Great Britain and the United States. Moreover, they seem to have caught the public imagination and hence they furnish the success of conservative parties. As I suggested at the beginning it is almost as if the decade of radical protest had never existed.

But why was the period of radical protest so transient? Certainly the Conservative Right feared its consequences, especially when it was coupled with industrial unrest and demands for more social expenditures. But today the relationship between state and society is again one in which the Right feels at ease. Why is this so?

In the first place the anti-bourgeois radicalism obviously depended on the success of the bourgeois economy. In other words, the middle-class radicals who held the system in contempt were actually secure within it. While such individuals would not necessarily take employment in traditional enterprises they could find work in a plethora of new occupations – the arts, education, the culture industry, publishing, the media and other service industries. Superficially such occupations are less repressive than other typical capitalist ones; however, they are still embedded within the capitalist economy. Thus while the activities of such individuals indicated a denial of certain bourgeois values – sobriety, conservatism, frugality, etc. – they did not really challenge the underlying premises of ownership and control. But, more significant than all else, prosperity and growth have been replaced by unemployment and inflation. In other words the material conditions which allow youth to be confident and even arrogant are gone.

The series of slumps in Western economies is, of course, even more germane to the decline of working-class protest. The effectiveness of strikes is reduced when demand for labour drops. Moreover, the sanctions of work discipline are more telling when the prospect of unemployment is real. In addition, the ideological terrain has altered to the disadvantage of labour and its political supporters. Today the success of conservative interpretations of state and society is not just the consequence of material changes, it is the result of a deliberate and aggressive right-wing offensive. If Habermas were correct, the level of unemployment in Europe and cuts in the welfare budget should have brought a clamour for radical change. However, as we have seen, his analysis offers a pessimistic accommodation to these negative developments. Is it, then, that the culture of the West can be manipulated easily in line with the needs of the state? Or is it that his assessment of the demise of bourgeois ideologies was false? In fact, I shall argue that political reality today indicates a mixture of the two.

In the first place, as I have begun to indicate, the claim that core elements of bourgeois ideology have been dissolved is misleading. It may well be that material conditions imply that such ideologies are nonsense, but surely a central aspect of ideology is its power to misinterpret reality. Today this feature of ideology is not even controversial, for as the state develops more power and autonomy it is understood as shrinking in power and scope and as key economic resources become yet more concentrated the values of individualism and market competition are reinstated. Thus democracy in the West today is premised on a perverse misunderstanding of the facts of political economy.

The underlying reason for this myopia lies in an astounding political failure and reveals that bourgeois liberalism lives today essentially by default. Quite simply political values which have arisen to challenge bourgeois capitalism have never held a secure place in the political cultures of the majority of Western states. All the efforts of the Left, reformist labour parties and the cultural radicals have failed in this respect. Thus the welfare state, the provision of a social infrastructure and public ownership have not been adequately underpinned by a non-capitalist ideology. Thus it could be argued that it is not just capitalist ideologies which are exhausted, but their alternatives as well.

In the light of this, the appeal of private consumption versus public investment becomes easier to understand. Individuals are attracted by the proposition that they will have personal control of their income rather than no control over how income is used by the state. At the same time they are vulnerable to the claim that this increases freedom because of how they have actually experienced state institutions. Needless to say the whole process is really an illusion, because the private alternatives to state provisions are beyond the means of most individuals, or in some cases simply do not exist. As for the decline of the infrastructure this becomes apparent only gradually and in any case is only really catastrophic for the poor. Thus the new economic privatism is possible because its costs are initially invisible and really only effect those who lack a political voice.

As social expenditures are reduced and state agencies made even more coercive, conservative political leaders can claim to preside over a system in which they have no faith. The result is further justifications for 'rolling back the state'. Naturally, though, in the context of the increasingly Hobbesian world which results there is a need for more effective law and order. In other words, as one arm of the state shrinks, the other expands in order to police the increasing social disorganisation. In terms of our discussion of the relationship between civil society and the state the result is that the state is less vulnerable to the claims emanating from the civil society for care and welfare and freer to control civil society by means of direct coercion.

If the argument above is valid, Habermas's basic concept of crisis displacement is correct. The state is seeking to stabilise the system as a whole by forcing the citizens to accept new interpretations of the meaning of politics. However, this is not because concrete expectations of justice are simply pushed to one side. The point is that such expectations have always been fragile and were never underpinned by a cohesive ideology. Of equal importance is the fact that the renewal of liberal capitalist principles has rested on political attitudes which are of long standing. I refer here to fatalism, which has been united very successfully with the refurbished philosophy of the minimal state. Here the state's failure to counteract economic crisis, which has a positive gloss in the slogan 'non-intervention equals freedom', also finds a negative justification in the fatalistic view that the basic determinants of economic well-being are beyond political control. Again, this conception is aided by the lack of an alternative discourse about politics and economics: unemployment and poverty simply become incontrovertible facts of life.

Although I have suggested that the cultural content of civil society has not changed as much as Habermas suggests, it is important to realise that his arguments carry a degree of truth. In objective terms possessive individualism and the achievement principle are increasingly meaningless in the context of advanced capitalism. The former seems a nonsense in the wake of the concentration of economic resources in fewer and fewer hands. Yet as society becomes more collectivised and dominated by larger and larger institutions we are asked again to subscribe to an individualist philosophy and to believe in the intrinsic 'goodness' of the market.

A significant cause of the lack of theoretically informed debate about the social process as a whole also lies at the heart of liberalism: namely the primacy of the private over the public. In Habermas's view this privatism is breaking down, but in fact it is much more ingrained than he believed. In part it is reinforced by default because the underlying premises which underwrite public institutions seem immune from human assessment. As Schaar argued, the organs of control in modern societies grow in power and anonymity simultaneously (Schaar, 1981, p. 15). At the same time the aspects of public life which appear as human cause increasing dismay: what one sees are violence, poverty, dereliction, drug addiction and other vestiges of modernism which culminate in nihilism. Small wonder, as a result, that there is a desire to retreat from serious analysis of the pressing issues which confront us and a need to withdraw into the private realm. In the light of this the cause of the success of other Rightist slogans becomes more comprehensive. Today conservative ideologies receive great support because of the law-and-order issue. While little effort is made to protect ordinary citizens in public places, we are encouraged to make our private and domestic worlds safer through our own efforts. More generally the 'autonomy of process' which characterises Western politics creates a protest potential which only the Right can use advantageously. Thus political leaders who skilfully reveal their own distaste for bureaucracy and large corporations and who touch citizens with homely aphorisms about the family, religion and morality can feed off a fear of institutions which actually underpin their power. Paradoxically, then, leaders can stipulate aspects of the system, which they and the citizens find inhuman and inefficient, even though such leaders preside over the institutions in question. This is, I believe, the reason for the survival of the attitudes, prejudices and values which Habermas regards as moribund. In essence nothing has emerged to take their place and in a context of fear and misunderstanding the strident proclamation of the old virtues – individualism, the nuclear family, authority, work and self-help – is enough to secure their survival.

In practice the conception of bourgeois ideology which highlights the gap between such beliefs and contemporary political experience misses a crucial point: ideologies do not have to adequately mirror reality. Obviously there is a point at which the disjuncture between a belief system and the real world creates change, but this is impossible to predict. Moreover, this mirror-like representation of the relationship is misleading; essentially ideologies interpret experience, rather than describe it. Again, the point at which an interpretation loses credibility cannot be stipulated in advance. What is clear is that the specific ideologies of bourgeois capitalism, even though they may be catch-words, are not yet a spent force. If my argument is correct their continued effectiveness is really a result of default. However, there are aspects of bourgeois theory, which cluster around freedom and choice, which are not devoid of content and which have found some resonance in the needs of citizens in the 1970s and 1980s. Thus there is a fear of statism, even under the guise of welfarism, which has fed the revival of individualism in recent years.

V

The elements of the arguments concerning a 'crisis of motivation' which we have so far dealt with are negative; that is, they concern what is moribund. However, it is in certain remnants of the bourgeois world view that Habermas detects a pattern of motivations which will challenge the authority of the state. These residues are science, modern art and universal morality.

The most important of these belief systems is universal morality. This, in fact, is where Habermas places the real emphasis, because it combines his political assessments with wider aspects of his general social theory. Thus at this stage we can see clearly the implications of Habermas's variant of critical theory for political praxis because moral universalism is the basic ethic underlying all of his normative theory.

Habermas maintains that the moral and legal codes which developed alongside the material evolution of capitalism share one fundamental principle: universalism. In his view this is no accident, for normative structures follow a developmental logic which moves from the concrete and particular to the abstract and general. Historically normative structures which were based on substantive ethics – as in feudalism – could engender legal norms which gave privileges and rights to certain strata, but denied them to others. However, such structures depend for their validity on world views which presuppose either divine revelation or objective values. Needless to say, such traditions were undermined by the belief systems which emerged with liberalism and which shattered the epistemological bases of medieval ethics. In consequence, all moral systems developed by bourgeois theorists could only find justification in the principle of universalism because the grounds for a differentiated moral code no longer existed. Thus the principle of universal equality was not a political gift bestowed on society, but the result of the exhaustion of alternatives. In addition, the mode of economic activity characteristic of capitalism necessitated a universalist justification because the state proclaimed the free-market system as a self-legitimating agency of equal opportunity. As a result the principle of universal justice became enshrined in the material activities of the capitalist economy under the ideology of the 'exchange of equivalents' (Habermas, 1973, p. 87).

As we have seen above, the façade of free-market justice is broken by the collapse of liberal capitalist systems in the 1930s and the visible and palpable political determination of economic life by the state in advanced capitalism. In other words the demand for universalism is retained while the specific mechanism for promoting the image of universal justice in practice is dismantled. Underlying this contradiction is another which is also rooted in liberal philosophy, for in liberal capitalism the domain of law which applies to the public sphere of the state is complemented by a private moral zone where action is sanctioned by the principles of conscience. Thus in theory there may be a contradiction between actions which could be sanctioned by the authority of conscience and those demanded of the citizen by the state. To the extent that the strict demarcation of moral and legal realms breaks down then we may expect parallel conflicts between the two spheres. Again, this illuminates a discussion we have dealt with above, because it indicates why the capitalist state needs to incorporate civil society, but simultaneously to maintain the ideology of privatism. Thus the state seeks to neutralise, rather than embrace, what was previously private. From Habermas's perspective, then, it is quite plausible that groups of citizens should engage in political dissent because the state appears as immoral. In the past there has been evidence of this in critiques addressed against the Vietnam War, the denial of civil rights to blacks, the immorality of incumbents of high political office, the subversive use of intelligence agencies, and the general fact of behaving immorally to other states. Thus the state has often been seen to lag behind governmental commitments to universal human rights. However, in order for this perspective to have a more explosive impact it would need to be focussed on the issue of the distribution of the social product viewed as a systematic defect of welfare-state democracy. But such evidence as there is suggests that in the West perceptions of the failure of institutions to behave morally are tied to dissatisfaction with specific incumbents of offices and specific corporations and not to the systematic view that liberal democracy or the business community are illegitimate *per se*. Empirical evidence which could support this thesis is thus in short supply.[5]

A further feature of Habermas's general theory which adds to the political significance of his claim about universal morality lies in the fact that he assumes that the moral self-development of the individual mirrors the historical evolution of the normative structures of social systems. Thus the attainment of a moral consciousness where action is judged by universal principles is feasible for all individuals. However, the evolution of the developmental logic of morality is interwoven with the concrete process of social and political socialisation, which may stabilise moral identity at a point where there is correspondence between the official morality of the nation-state and the morality of individual citizens. Thus, for youth to transcend the limiting socialisation of family, peers and the community, some period of freedom and reflection is necessary so that an escape from the traditional agencies of socialisation can be made.

In advanced capitalist societies Habermas believes that this 'psycho-social moratorium' is actually occurring, because increasing numbers of children experience an extended period of schooling where they are free from traditional socialisation. In addition, as well as the improvement in cognitive capacities which results, there is also a trend towards more egalitarian family structures and the possibility of more experimentation in social and sexual relationships. Thus conditions have been generated which allow certain strata amongst the young to explore the potentials of autonomy in contexts isolated from orthodox agencies of socialisation. In Habermas's view this makes possible the achievement of a state of mind which Keniston – drawing on William James – has termed a second birth; that is a process of re-socialisation where central values are subjected to intense criticism (Keniston, 1971, p. 387).

From the comments above it should be clear that the most likely groups to enact the mode of critique stipulated are young radicals, students, feminists and anti-war protesters, etc. While this, in itself, indicates a considerable schism between Habermas and Marxism the real gap is even greater because those groups most likely not to reach the level of moral consciousness which embraces universalism are the working classes. Indeed, the educational and work experience of the manual working class represents a zone of immunity from the liberating tendencies inherent in middle-class education and experimental life styles.

Whatever the truth of the thesis of the differential class basis of moral development, it is the case that Habermas locates the ground of critique in the likely activities of young radicals. To do this he is highly dependent on the work of Keniston (1971) and Döbert and Nunner. However, their studies – as he realises – are really a very fragile basis upon which to erect a substantive prognosis of likely political actions. We have already seen that the activities of such groups are really peripheral and also that the tempo of protest has slowed down. But really this is not the issue, for what is abundantly clear in Habermas is that the potential for political action which his theory isolates is not located in the situational–empirical space which a social group occupies, but rather in the nature of truth. In fact the concept of legitimation developed by Habermas is not a social/psychological one which ascertains whether real belief systems secure legitimacy; rather his conception indicates whether a regime fulfils substantive imperatives of a social morality which he believes is the only moral system left to man which is still plausible. Thus from his vantage point capitalism is illegitimate in its political sphere even if this is not widely recognised. But of course Habermas believes that the mechanics of domination, which are anonymous in liberal capitalism, become more transparent in state-regulated regimes and that the perceived gap between dominant norms – universalist – and material actions – particularist (favouring specific interests) – grows wider.

As McCarthy recognises, Habermas's critical theory is not addressed to any specific groups at all; as I have suggested it is there to be grasped by anyone who seeks the truth (McCarthy, 1978, p. 384). Obviously this generates serious weaknesses and Habermas is often criticised for the half-hearted nature of his political commitments. However, it also carries benefits when one avoids pinning the normative content of a political theory to the shirts of a given class or group: there are discrepancies between truth and action. In consequence, Habermas's theory could never entail the absurd assumption that the proletariat necessarily carries the torch of enlightenment for the whole of mankind. Thus I would contend that the conception of the working-classes interests as universal, merely because of the profound nature of their suffering, is a serious flaw within Marxian political theory which results from a normative content being deduced from a situational ethic of praxis.

In the light of these comments the marginal nature of those who might take up the imperatives of critical theory is irrelevant. Nevertheless, there are real dilemmas which arise from this formulation which we must consider. As Habermas knows, the Kantian variant of moral universalism generated a seemingly intractable contradiction, for the moral actions indicated by the nature of a pure practical reason and categorised as duty could conflict with material inclinations of a subject interested in pleasure. Precisely because the realm of duty is grounded in a non-material subject, Kant could not explain why the inclination to behave morally exists. Habermas has attempted to overcome this by, first, claiming a material basis for reason and, second, projecting the content of the moral conscience outwards from the individual towards others in the form of an inter-subjective ethic of communication. However, even in this formulation the norms of duty which may even have been an object of a public discourse could still be cynically pushed to one side. Thus individuals could know that the system was immoral, that the state exploited other poorer and weaker states and that benefits accruing to some were denied to others and still support the regime. And this is, of course, more likely because the groups who have adopted this morality are materially advantaged.

As well as the fact that morality lacks the force to determine action there is also the problem involved in expecting people to behave morally when the network of relations around the individual is immoral. Should we expect individuals who are treated as means to treat others as ends? Naturally citizens could engage in a critique of the state from a universalist vantage point, yet still follow the dictates of the economic system and still take their place in the hierarchy of privilege. But this smacks of hypocrisy; more problematically, the true ethics which Habermas maintains would result from a dialogue between equals necessitates that the participants are no longer speaking to each other across class barriers. To employ a familiar analogy, could the master and the slave undertake a dialogue to reconstitute their relationship on the grounds of equality if they begin the discussion as incumbents of the roles of master and slave?

A final difficulty inherent in identifying the motive forming power of universal ethics is that what really counts is not the values which individuals hold, but the way in which convictions are made. For Habermas's point to stand, the mode of critique must be more than a passing fashion and must be aimed at the system in general and not dissatisfaction with specific events. Hence to show empirically that groups committed to universal political ethics actually existed, involves more than pointing to the substantive ends being pursued: it must also grasp the epistemological basis of the critique.

VI

Because the twists and turns of the argument above have followed rather diverse paths, I would like to conclude with a somewhat schematic and stylised assessment of Habermas's arguments. In the first place, any tendential and predictive aspects of the theory seem not to have been confirmed. However, the programme of hypotheses in *Legitimation Crisis* was never really meant as a simplistic set of predictions, therefore this is not a significant test. What matters far more is if the developments of recent years indicate basic theoretical errors in Habermas's formulation of categories. In fact the idea of crisis displacement fits the changing political reality of recent years very neatly because it indicates the mutually substitutable elements of advanced societies which can be manipulated in order to forestall crisis. In the United States the de-legitimacy of the political order – shaken by Watergate, Vietnam, economic recession and reverses in foreign policy – has been recouped by a mixture of ideological offensive and stunning economic recovery. In Britain the stubborn persistence of recession has not ignited a high level of protest and it has been quite apparent that the political system has been 'baled out' by the culture. The relationship of the state to civil society has also changed in a manner which increases coercion and reduces welfare and community. Today the 'overloaded' state has distanced itself from urban social disorganisation and, free from the fetters of a responsibility to care for the sick, the old and the poor, it merely leaves them to their own devices.

Despite being able to accommodate these features of contemporary politics, some aspects of the crisis theory – as specific empirical arguments – are false. Traditional values have not completely evaporated, for citizens can be moved by other means than purposive rationality, science and law. Thus the role set of the modern individual seems able to contain a variety of epistemological assumptions.

Another set of attitudes which remains potent clusters around individualism, egoism, competition and materialism. Thus the specific arguments advanced to the effect that bourgeois attitudes have been exhausted are also false. In fact, it may be the case that derivatives of these have become plausible for groups who previously understood their lives in collectivist and solidaristic terms. I refer here, of course, to the collapse of working-class communities which were rooted in traditional industries and the extended family. Today it is no longer even controversial to assume the allegiance of working-class groups to the new conservatism in Britain and the United States. Finally, one should note some surprise at Habermas's belief that the public realm in contemporary capitalism has become enlivened by substantive debate over distribution and justice. In earlier works, where he continued the somewhat pessimistic traditions of critical theory, he laid down the precise means whereby the system of asymmetrical rewards and political domination could adequately disguise its true nature. Here politics had become scientised, consciousness of defects had succumbed to technocratic rationalisations and, as Adorno and Marcuse showed, blows directed against the dominant consciousness seemed to be miraculously absorbed (Habermas, 1974).

In reality these perspectives were too negative; the monolithic systems of science, technology and administration being granted the capacity to neutralise all critique. However, why a belief in real radical change should be advanced in *Legitimation Crisis* is impossible to judge. It may be, as McCarthy (1978) suggests, that the truth content of Habermas's theories is now less dependent on historical/political references and relies more on systematised theorising of a formalised nature. In other words the Kantian elements in his theories may be coming to prominence at the expense of Marxian and Hegelian motifs.

At the beginning I placed a heavy emphasis on Habermas's inclusion of a hermeneutic dimension within the concept of crisis. If the tendency towards a formalised derivation of the grounds of de-legitimation is characteristic of Habermas's work, then it appears to me that his conclusions have not adequately incorporated the 'actionist' dimension. Of course what he assumes is that the process of the construction of culture and the reference points of truth are interlinked. However, to be empirically accurate, I would say that the adoption of principles, norms and ideals is rooted in a belief in truth, rather than truth itself. Thus the analysis in *Legitimation Crisis* is an idealisation; it tells us what the presuppositions of the concept of crisis must be. It is, then, a work of political philosophy and not political sociology. In consequence its true value does not depend on actual political development, but on whether it heightens our theoretical and moral sense of the political dilemmas of the contemporary period.

NOTES

1. By boundary conditions I mean the minimum prerequisites necessary for a market to function. This is a significant designation for Habermas and is counterposed to state operations which supplant the market.
2. This is problematic because base/superstructure is central to Marxian meta-theory. Thus to accept that it applies adequately to liberal capitalism, but not elsewhere, is to say that Marxian meta-theory is historically relative.
3. A possible exception is the peace movement which has carried on some of the radical traditions of the 1970s.
4. This is manifested in M. Mann's important article, 'The social cohesion of liberal democracy', *American Sociological Review*, 35 (3), 1970: 423–39.
5. For example the evidence in R. E. Lane's 'The legitimacy bias: conservative man in market and state', in B. Denitch (ed.), *Legitimation of Regimes*, London, Sage, 1979, pp. 55–80. Also the arguments in D. P. Conradt, 'Political culture, legitimacy and participation', *West European Politics*, 4 (2), 1981: 18–34.

REFERENCES

Bell, R., 1976. *The Cultural Contradictions of Capitalism*. London, Heinemann
Berger, P., 1977. *Facing up to Modernity*. Harmondsworth, Penguin Books
Berger, P., B. Berger and H. Kellner, 1973. *The Homeless Mind*. Harmondsworth, Penguin Books
Brittan, S., 1975. 'The economic consequences of democracy', *British Journal of Political Science*, 5: 129–59
Clark, G. L. and M. Dear, 1984. *State Apparatus*, London, Allen and Unwin
Connolly, W. (ed.), 1984. *Legitimacy and the State*. Oxford, Basil Blackwell
Gouldner, A. 1978. *The Dialectic of Ideology and Technology*. London, Heinemann
Habermas, J., 1973. *Legitimation Crisis*. London, Heinemann
    1974. *Theory and Practice*. London, Heinemann
    1976. *Communication and the Evolution of Society*. London, Heinemann
Halliday, F., 1983. *The Making of the Second Cold War*. London, Verso
Held, D., 1982. 'Crisis tendencies, legitimation and the state', in D. Held and J. B. Thompson, eds., *Habermas: Critical Debates*. London, Macmillan, pp. 176–89
Hirsch, F., 1976. *The Social Limits to Growth*. London, Hutchinson
Keniston, K., 1971. *Youth and Dissent*. New York, Harcourt Brace Jovanovich, Inc.
King, A., 1975. 'Overload: problems of governing in the 1970s', *Political Studies*, 23
Lane, R. E., 1979. 'The legitimacy bias: conservative man in market and state', in B. Denitch, ed., *Legitimation of Regimes*. London, Sage, pp. 55–79
Mancias, P., 1974. *The Death of the State*. New York, Putman
McCarthy, T., 1978. *The Critical Theory of Jürgen Habermas*. London, Heinemann

Marcuse, H., 1972. *An Essay on Liberation*. Harmondsworth, Penguin Books

O'Connor, J., 1973. *The Fiscal Crisis of the State*. New York, St Martin's Press

Offe, C., 1976. 'Political authority and class structure', in P. Connerton, ed., *Critical Sociology*. Harmondsworth, Penguin Books, pp. 388–421

Plant, R., 1981. Jürgen Habermas and the idea of a legitimation crisis, Political Studies Association Conference, Hull

Schaar, J., 1981. *Legitimacy in the Modern State*. Transaction Books

Wolfe, A., 1977. *The Limits of Legitimacy*. New York, Free Press

9

Fabian socialism, democracy and the state

JOHN CALLAGHAN

> I once rashly joined in the search for a suitable name and in
> *New Fabian Essays* called the new society 'statism'. But, it
> was, on reflection a bad choice. (Crosland, 1956)

The 'bad choice' Crosland refers to was not confined to questions of nomenclature, if other Fabian socialists are to be believed. Richard Crossman, writing in the same year as Crosland, called attention to the dangers of centralised planning and the extension of state ownership: even though these measures were already associated with his own party, the Labour Party, Crossman thought that the bureaucracy they entailed posed a threat to democracy (Crossman, 1956). A quarter of a century later a growing chorus of socialist critics argued that Labour's statist version of the doctrine was responsible for its flagging support and electoral defeats (see Hain 1983; Hodgson, 1984; Hall, 1978; Seabrook, 1978). More fundamentally, mainstream socialism, whether social-democratic or communist, was held guilty of a complacent faith in the efficacy of state planning and the ability of experts to advance 'working-class interests'. Both traditions evinced a naive rationalism when it came to the matter of a state-directed economy as well as a deep-seated paternalism. Moreover these doctrines privileged the objectives of economic growth, efficiency and planning, either to the detriment of democratic and cultural goals or in the conviction that such non-economic ends would be reached as desirable side-effects of the growth of productive forces (see Selucky, 1979; Nove, 1983).

My examination of Fabianism in this chapter will focus on the writings of G. D. H. Cole, Harold J. Laski and R. H. Tawney. All three took an early anti-statist stance in their theoretical work and represented the leading figures in the second generation of Fabian intellectuals. They also occupied influential positions in the Labour Party yet were unusually aware of the dilemmas of its reformist strategy. But their chief interest for us in this context is as early critics of the collectivism which the Labour Party actually came to embrace. In examining their ideas, then, it may be possible to say something of why the

Fabianism which intellectually inspired the Labour Party was not that of Cole, Tawney or the early Laski. Considering the influence of Fabianism in the Labour Party since 1945 it is of some interest to take a close look at the issues and debates which absorbed it in the Party's formative period. In so doing we may shed light on the current ambivalence of socialists on the questions of state and democracy.

THE SOCIALIST SAMURAI AND BUREAUCRATIC COLLECTIVISM

The early Fabians were influenced more by positivism and Benthamism than by any specifically socialist tradition. Sidney Webb, who revealingly preferred the term 'collectivist' to 'socialist', fought against *laissez-faire* with the very philosophy on which it was supposed to rest – utilitarianism. Like the later J. S. Mill, his acknowledged mentor, Webb believed that the constructive work of collectivism was essentially a civil-service task which left little place to democratic initiative. The greatest happiness of the greatest number required the reorganisation of society by the state under the direction of experts. Only in this way could the Fabians reconstruct society 'in accordance with the highest moral possibilities', as Pease once put it (see M. Cole, 1949, p. 17). A common conviction of late Victorian intellectuals whether positivists, new liberals or Fabians concerned the crucial role of what J. S. Mill had called the 'secular clerisy'. 'Society may be said to be in its *natural* state when worldly power and moral influence are habitually and undisputedly exercised by the fittest person whom the existing state of society affords.' For Mill this meant a dominating role for professional civil servants over the 'uninstructed mass' (see Greenleaf, 1983, p. 115).

This emphasis suited Sidney Webb, the ex-civil servant, very well. It has been observed that despite their notorious immersion in sewage, gas, and municipal politics the Fabians showed no impatience in drafting their first detailed plan for nationalisation. This is instructive because, during the first twenty-five years of their existence, the Fabians were so preoccupied with the extension of the existing regulatory and protective functions of the state that any specifically socialist measures were neglected (McBriar, 1966, p. 107). Any kind of state activity was sufficient to win Fabian approval as evidence of the collectivist trend of society and so 'their gospel was summed up in the largest possible extension of state powers' (Gray, 1944, p. 387). This statist ideology is particularly emphatic in Sidney Webb's contribution to *Fabian Essays*, even though he specifically denied that socialism implied 'a rigidly centralised national administration of all the details of life' a year later (see S. Webb, 1890, pp. 109–10).

Fabian Essays testifies to Webb's satisfaction with the British political system even before the advent of universal suffrage. The Fabians had welcomed the suffrage reforms of 1884–5 principally in the expectation that they would accelerate existing collectivist trends which were in any case held to be working for the transformation of the state from a police power to mere housekeeping on a national scale. By 1889 their common conviction 'of the necessity of vesting the organisation of industry and the material of production in a state identified with the whole people by complete Democracy' did not dispose them to consider this democracy as in any way problematic (Fabian Society, 1889, pp. xxxix–xl). Sidney Webb never considered theoretical questions concerning the nature of state power and though Shaw did he concluded that the extension of the vote to the working class would enable government to dominate the other state institutions. Thus while Webb merely assumed the essentially benign character of state activity and perceived every extension of it as an instalment of socialism, Shaw, in 1896, declared the Fabians content with the existing democratic machinery of England, which would become 'a first-rate practical instrument of democratic government'

when the House of Commons is freed from the veto of the House of Lords and thrown open to candidates from all classes by an effective system of Payment of Representatives and a more rational method of election is introduced. (Shaw, 1896)

Neither Webb nor Shaw expected or desired massive institutional change on the road to socialism. Nor did they require the transformation of personal and societal values. While the Fabians could envisage the state 'enrolling every able-bodied man directly in the service of the community', as Sidney Webb phrased it in *Socialism: True and False*, this did not involve equality of official status, authority and hours of labour. These were found to be impediments to that general 'equality of subordination to the common interest' which Shaw – that 'instinctive elitist' (see Lichtheim, 1975, p. 206) – reckoned to be 'fundamental in modern socialism' (Shaw, 1896). Just how this 'common interest' would be established is never discussed, but from the foregoing it is clear that only minor adjustments to the British political system were required by the early Fabians who would then, presumably, announce the arrival of the general will. In fact the real issue which concentrated Fabian minds was that of efficiency rather than the intricacies of political representation. Beatrice Potter had early-on established that ordinary workers had neither the managerial ability nor the discipline necessary for the attainment of industrial efficiency: henceforth the Webbs found any talk of industrial democracy anathema. Likewise it is clear that political democracy is low on the Fabian list of priorities, because the linkage which really mattered to the intellectual leaders of the Society was that between efficiency, order and expertise.

One of the first to recognise the authoritarian implications of Fabian socialism was L. T. Hobhouse, who contrasted the values of freedom, humanism and individualism with 'either a Fabian or a Marxist dictatorship' (Weiler,

1982, p. 20). It was the absence of an ethical or spiritual dimension to Fabianism which repelled Hobhouse rather than a fear of collectivism *per se*. Indeed he regarded Fabianism as a distortion of collectivism and a religion of experts and efficiency. In his view, in Fabian hands 'all that was human in Socialism vanishes out of it' (Hobhouse, 1972, p. 227 and pp. 228–9). This is not an unkind judgment of the early Fabians for whom, as we have seen, the extent and depth of liberty in Britain was nearly right. The problem they addressed was capitalist waste. It is for this reason that their vision of socialism was a peculiarly desiccated thing. They were not animated by the cultural or the democratic vision of socialism: indeed it seems to have been for them what Natural Law was for Bentham – 'nonsense on stilts'. Sidney Webb made the Fabian version of collectivism perfectly plain when he said that:

the perfect and fitting development of each individual is not necessarily the utmost and highest cultivation of his own personality, but the fitting, in the best possible way of his humble function in the great social machine. (Fabian Society, 1889, p. 54)

It was, as Shaw avowed, an identification of people and state, for:

The Socialism advocated by the Fabian Society is State Socialism exclusively . . . England now possesses an elaborate democratic State machinery . . . the opposition which exists in Continental Monarchies between the State and people does not hamper English Socialists. (Shaw, 1896)

As the tone of this statement reveals, even the absence of universal suffrage is not seen as a pressing problem in the attainment of Fabian state socialism.

ANTI-STATISM

The Fabians imagined that a selfless intellectual elite of state bureaucrats could organise the capitalists for collective ends even if they could not 'moralise' them as the positivists believed. But from a number of vantage points this Fabian ambition looked suspiciously authoritarian. Distributists such as Hilaire Belloc and G. K. Chesterton believed that the collectivist provisions already extant after the 1906 Liberal government had done its work threatened to increase the regulation and subordination of the lower orders while leaving the power of the capitalists unimpaired. Similarly if the labour unrest after 1910 was connected with disappointment in that same Liberal administration for not going far enough with its reforms, the emergence of syndicalism testifies to a growing awareness that the powers of the state were increased out of all proportion to any gains that organised labour may have won. Even now a case can be made for the democratic credentials of the early Fabians only by ignoring the disproportions between the massive increase in state power required to achieve their objectives and the slight adjustments in the level of popular control which they advocated (e.g. Radice, 1984). In fact the actual experience of an encroaching state both before and during the First World War demonstrated that an interventionist regulatory state was perfectly compatible with the continued predominance of the capitalists. Such experience reinforced suspicion of any socialist proposing to employ the existing state machinery in the service of socialism and cast doubts on the nature of nationalisation in particular.

Indeed the Marxist journal *Plebs* argued that the measures advocated by Fabians such as Ramsay MacDonald could only produce state capitalism (Walton-Newbold, 1918). The Socialist Labour Party argued that Fabian policies were nothing less than 'the very life blood and method of the most militant and aggressive Imperialism' (Hinton, 1973, p. 47) while William Paul denounced them as 'the future of competitive capitalism' (Paul, 1917). The implication of all these Left critiques of Fabianism was that its policies would merely hasten existing trends toward state capitalism. It was the rise of bureaucratic collectivism and the decline in simple individualism which also stimulated a revival of interest in voluntary groups and associations which seemed to represent late-Victorian ideals of community and service. The attraction for many thinkers consisted in the potential which a plurality of such groups had for the attainment of social justice while preserving individual liberty. This philosophical pluralism, as it became known, was a reaction against both the doctrine that society is simply an aggregate of discrete individuals as Spencer claimed and the statist claim that a community is only welded by state power.

This pluralism can be traced to work of historians of political thought such as F. W. Maitland whose critique of the Austinian theory of sovereignty was concerned to repudiate the idea of the omnicompetent state and assert the right of groups to claim comparable allegiance from their members. The argument was taken up by Figgis, who claimed in 1905 that the growth of a centralised state had recently made the development and spread of autonomous societies and groups more necessary as a counter to centralised collectivism. In the intellectual ferment of these years the advocates of pluralism drew on the sociology of Durkheim and Bosanquet's emphasis on associations as well as the work of Figgis and Maitland. Socialist variations of these arguments derived many of their positions from the work of William Morris and the earlier Owenite tradition of socialism, both of which stressed the ideal of co-operative democracy. Guild socialism brought together many of these strands including elements of the romanticist critique of capitalism found in Carlyle's and Ruskin's writings. Arthur Penty began this fusion in *The Restoration of the Guild System* in 1906 but it was the conversion of another Fabian, A. R. Orage, which enabled the argument to be advanced effectively in the pages of the *New Age*. Guild socialism became an intellectual force and won the support of Bertrand Russell (see Russell, 1970), R. H. Tawney, Harold

Laski and G. D. H. Cole – culminating in a major split inside the Fabian Society when around 500 members left in 1915 to form the National Guilds League.

GUILD SOCIALISM

Cole first argued for the 'functional democracy' desired by guild socialists in *The World of Labour* which was published in 1913, before he actually thought of himself as one of its advocates. His focus in that work was industrial democracy, a theme which was then exercising practical influence within British trade unionism as it would continue to do until the post-war slump began in 1921. The demand for workers' control, which was heard frequently in these years, underlined the extent to which the leading Fabians willingly embraced the wage system and found little to complain of in capitalist relations of production, the division of labour and the nature of factory work generally. Inspired by Rousseau and William Morris, Cole, however, was increasingly persuaded of the centrality of precisely such issues as these in determining the character of social systems whether capitalist or, in the future, socialist.

It was Cole's conviction that capitalist industry was governed autocratically by a minority of large property owners. He was enough of a Marxist to reason that the economic power thus wielded enabled the capitalists to exercise a disproportionate influence over the state, which was shaped by the interplay of economic forces over which it exercised little real control. Accordingly any serious attempt to change the nature of the state must also change the dictatorial rule of the capitalists in industry (Cole, 1917, pp. 2–6).

Despite these borrowings from Marxism, Cole, like the pluralist Laski, was convinced that the state was 'nothing more or less than the political machinery of government in a community' (1917, p. 1). If, as Laski posed it, 'a theory of the state . . . is essentially a theory of the governmental act' (Laski, 1925, p. 28), socialists who took this view could still regard government as the dominant element in the state apparatus. Thus for both Cole and Laski it was possible to believe that the priorities of economic power holders set the limits of state activity when Liberals or Tories were in government, but also to contend that a democratically elected socialist government could help to abolish capitalism. Cole believed that the advance of political democracy in Britain had already modified the state but this process had not gone far enough to prevent it from 'faithfully reflecting the social and economic structure of capitalism'.

Nevertheless, in his view the state was already something more than the mere expression of property interests because the working class was now able to exert pressure (Cole, 1915, p. 3). Further progress along the road of the abolition of capitalism would serve to emancipate the state from the dis-

tortions imposed by a class-divided society. Only with the complete elimination of capitalism could the state fulfil its 'true purpose' of representing
general rather than sectional impulses. Thus, contrary to Engels's idea, Cole
believed that once the class system was abolished only the coercive functions
of the state would wither while those functions serving the general interest
would for the first time come into their own (Cole, 1918, pp. 182–7). Until
then the state would remain a pale reflection of the economic base of society.

In Cole's view, the theory of representation which the modern bourgeois
state claimed to embody was simply absurd. Capitalist society was increasingly
composed of a multitude of functional associations representing specific
aspects of men, yet the state claimed that it alone could represent all these
facets of the citizenry. Thus while sovereignty was *de facto* divided between the
many voluntary associations of civil society the state was still formally held to
be the only legitimate power centre. In Cole's view the danger was that this
theory of sovereignty would be used to justify the 'Great State' prefigured in
liberal collectivism and in wartime controls which threatened to engulf the
individual and destroy liberty (1918, p. 189). For Cole capitalist democracy
was all the more vulnerable to this danger because it restricted participation to
a specifically political arena and denied it elsewhere. In 'politics' the citizen
was further confined to a choice between rival rulers who, once elected, were
submerged in the real business of safeguarding the interests of capital rather
than those of the individual voter. Yet this one MP was supposed to represent
the voters' interests in relation to every conceivable question put before
parliament. Cole argued that this was simply untenable but, what was worse,
the electors were left with no control over MPs when the day of elections had
passed, thus vindicating Rousseau's taunt that the British were free only
during elections (Cole, 1920a, p. 22).

Guild socialism was based on the idea that the problems outlined above
could be remedied by a strategy of encroaching control of industry by organised labour. The Storrington Document which set out guild socialist principles in 1915 envisaged the abolition of capitalism by the combined activities
of industrial unions pursuing workers' control and a parliamentary majority of
socialists enacting nationalisation of the key industries (see Briggs and Saville,
1971). The strength of this strategy seemed to lie in its recognition of the
primordial significance of economic power and of civil society as the basis for
the organisational diversity and range of functional representations which
alone could guarantee the compatibility of democracy, individual liberty and
collectivism which all socialists wanted but which few had actually thought
about. Moreover it seemed realistic because capitalist industry itself had
forced workers to organise in trade unions and these powerful functional
associations would provide the impulse and the organisational basis for industrial democracy. Cole believed – and contemporary events seemed to confirm

this – that the unions were objectively impelled to challenge for managerial prerogatives; even the bread-and-butter concerns of workers were permanently imperilled if they did not. But for anyone subscribing, like Cole, to a participatory democracy it was also tempting to believe that a latent communal spirit could be tapped once the reorganisation of industry was set in motion (Cole, 1920a, p. 46).

But Cole also believed, in common with Fabians from the Webbs to Laski and Tawney, that the rise of professional associations and the organisations of skilled and technical workers embodied an ethic of service inimical to the continued preponderance of the profit motive. In this view, the spread of scientific work and professionalism created workers more receptive to the idea of the general good and hostile to the profit-maximiser whose gain was based on exploitation. It is curious that this idea should have been so widespread among socialists, especially since liberals such as Hobhouse saw this same middle class as a contributor only to 'collective selfishness' and suspected 'suburban villadom' as a political obstacle devoid of the healthy corporate life which made trade unionism the 'arm of the democratic movement' (Hobhouse, 1972, pp. 68–9). But in all probability the idea appealed because it fitted into an evolutionary and optimistic way of thinking which dominated British socialism before 1914 and was found all the more congenial because so many socialist intellectuals were themselves from this sort of professional background.

In any case the idea played only a minor part in Cole's thinking, which was shaped by the conviction that 'the emancipation of Labour must be the work of Labour' – a phrase of Marx's which, as Cole said, was often repeated but rarely understood (Cole, 1917, p. 137). Cole's advocacy of encroachment was an attempt to put this right. It was intended to find a close correspondence between the ends and means of socialism. For if socialism was to be based on participatory democracy it was necessary to adopt a strategy which would enhance the capacity of the working class for self-government. Like Marx, Cole stressed the educative dimension of struggle but he also envisaged industrial struggle leading to workers' participation in the management of capitalism. This 'common responsibility', however, would not lead to the co-option of the workers but would rather sharpen the taste for more control. As the experience of control deepened the knowledge and broadened the practical know-how of the workers, Cole believed that this greater awareness would make them more conscious as a class with definite interests incompatible with the survival of capitalism. For Cole the one certainty was that only such a prolonged school of management under capitalism would develop the skills and experience necessary for democratic socialism.

Cole was less persuasive when it came to outlining the division of powers and functions that would characterise Guild Socialism. Though the self-managing factory was its fundamental unit, he regarded the state as the necessary representative of the citizens as consumers. He rejected syndicalism just as he rejected Fabian collectivism – indeed they were inverted reflections of each other where sovereignty was concerned, with the one vesting it in the Trades Union Congress and the other placing it in the state. In Cole's alternative vision there would be two assemblies: one for the guilds, the other – the surviving elements of the old state – for the consumers. Here it must be said that Cole vacillated over the role of the old state, sometimes affirming its significance for the traditional communal functions (health, education, defence, law), at other times ignoring or downplaying it. The best that can be said of his scheme for guild socialism is that two parallel federations of consumers and producers would provide the basic forms of functional representation corresponding to the basic roles of individuals as Cole saw them. The success or failure of this system would depend on the positive wills, not the passive consent of the citizenry (Cole, 1918, p. 206). And the objective – freedom – is realised in and by these individuals while the precise institutional arrangements are a matter for practice and experiment. The real principle in all of this for Cole is that sovereignty rests inalienably with the whole people and cannot be transferred to any representative governmental institutions (Cole, 1918, p. 200).

In fact Cole could provide no institutional guarantees against the kind of degeneration of the guild organisations associated with parliamentarism, which he professed to despise. For one so concerned with the idea of 'function', moreover, it is surprising that Cole imagined that the separation of production and consumption was possible for practical purposes. Obviously separate parliaments along these lines would soon act as one, with policy dictated by whichever controlled fiscal matters.

This type of criticism, however, supposes none of the elements which Cole regarded as vital to Guild Socialism. Central to his vision is the image of a new type of man created in the school of struggle over a considerable period of time. Cole's citizens are organised, politically active and knowledgeable – their political judgment having been formed through the reflective experience of communal self-government. This is the basis of Cole's optimism concerning the preservation of liberty under guild socialism, not the separation of powers which his critics seized upon. And it is the dialectic of ends and means in Cole's socialist thought which contrasts most sharply with the thinking of other gradualists.

Apart from the early Fabians, whom we have already discussed, there were other currents in mainstream socialism which showed a mistrust of working-class political initiatives in almost equal measure. Kautsky's Marxism for instance was as committed as Bernstein's revisionism to the capture of the existing state machinery by means of a parliamentary majority. Both regarded the masses as unpredictable and believed that working-class consciousness had to be subordinated to the planned projections of the party centre. Like the Fabians they took the view that the complexity of public affairs required experts and paid functionaries and regarded bureaucracy as a necessary and unproblematic feature of socialism (Salvadori, 1979, pp. 153–61). After 1918 Kautsky viewed the Weimar Constitution in much the same way as the Webbs saw the British system. The German Social Democratic Party abhorrence of putschism extended to any form of direct action, industrial or otherwise, prior to the political takeover. Electoral democracy was an end in itself, the victory of socialism assured by evolutionary movements of an 'invisible-hand' character (see Guttsman, 1981).

Advocates of participatory democracy were in truth a small minority within European socialism. Cole's critique of Fabianism forced some concessions (mainly verbal) from the Webbs (see Webb, S. and B., 1920) but the prospects for the guild socialist approach deteriorated rapidly after 1921 for two main reasons. First, the industrial slump which lasted for the rest of the inter-war years forced trade unionism into defensive postures from which it rarely escaped and thus ended the innovative militancy which had supported encroachment. Second, the Bolshevik revolution attracted radicals to the newly formed Communist Party. Not only did this draw leading guildsmen away from the movement; Leninism changed the questions and answers of radical socialist debate and theory. The principal focus henceforth was the state, crudely analysed as 'bodies of armed men' and the chosen instrument of its destruction was to be the vanguard party (which might also be described as 'bodies of armed men', such was the militarism of its language, imagery and organisation). After 1917 socialism came to mean for many the system of power in the USSR. And here, it was noted, the political ascendancy of the working class coexisted with Taylorist industrial practices, bonus wage-payments, and hierarchical managerial structures. Now it was possible for British Marxists to argue that as long as the Bolshevik party-state existed these 'superficially capitalist' industrial forms were of no consequence (Dobb, 1923, pp. 169–71). Anyone who doubted that the Bolshevik dictatorship was the same as the proletarian dictatorship first had Lenin, later Stalin, to warn that this testified to 'the most incredibly and hopelessly muddled thinking'.

Cole immediately noted that the Bolsheviks opposed industrial democracy as incompatible with workshop discipline and productive efficiency. Workers' control meant the collective class-control of the proletarian dictatorship (that is the Bolshevik Party), for the Leninists. Cole also observed that a marked preference for centralism, bigness and power characterised their approach. These features of Bolshevik power were not simply the result of factors peculiar to the Russian experience but were sought after as intrinsic to the socialist project. But perhaps the most disconcerting aspect of the Bolshevik approach for Cole was their imitation of capitalist methods in the factories where, as Sirianni has recently noted, even the most barbaric features of German capitalism were replicated in the belief that these represented the highest development of emancipatory technique (Sirianni, 1982, p. 253). This underlines the Bolshevik tendency to regard the cultural development of the working class as a mere effect of economic developments, whereas guild socialism was sensitive to the independent significance of political and social dimensions in the struggle for socialism.

However the guild strategy depended on circumstances conducive to strong and confident trade unionism but the reality, of course, was the very opposite for most of the inter-war years. This necessarily forced attention back to politics, parties and the state, and since some guild socialists had always had their doubts about encroachment, the Leninist success in Russia led leading guildsmen like Robin Page Arnot and William Mellor to help found the British Communist Party. In so far as the movement for industrial democracy retained any vigour after 1921 it did so with the kind of arguments and language which R. H. Tawney provided (Barker, 1975).

A CHRISTIAN SOCIOLOGY

Tawney's Christian socialism owed a good deal to disciples of T. H. Green, such as Bishop Gore and Edward Caird, especially in regard to Green's theory of the positive functions of the state in the fulfilment of individual personality. But he shared with the guild socialists the conviction that institutional change required the extension of the democratic idea into those areas of society which had escaped its influence. Because of this he was never convinced by the Webbs' socialism, in which he detected autocratic consequences. By 1914 he was convinced that the great influence of Fabianism in British socialism owed much to the absence of a moral ideal. It was this absence which allowed proposals to adjust the minutiae of social arrangements (while leaving the old, discredited system intact) to dominate the movement (Winter and Joslin, 1972, pp. 51, 56). It is symptomatic of the stability of Tawney's thought, derived as it is in great measure from his belief in God, that in his last public address he complained that socialism had become dehumanised and feared that the measures taken by the 1945 Labour government might prove to be further steps towards the Servile State (Greenleaf, 1983, p. 463).

Tawney was unusual among members of the Fabian Society in trying to think of a socialist transformation based on a comprehensive change in values generated by the working class itself. Graham Wallas was more typical when he complained of the absence in Britain of 'a Socialist clergy such as the German social democrats had created, charged with the duty of thinking for the working class' (quoted by Miliband, 1982, p. 90). Tawney, like Cole, wanted the working class to think for itself. A self-reliant, self-determining socialist movement was required to bring about the cultural revolution necessary to restore fraternity and fellowship. Only a great educational experience – partly understood in terms of formal education but principally created through democratic advance – could create the hegemonic force which Tawney perceived as the precondition for lasting structural changes spearheaded by the Labour Party (see Terrill, 1974). This was because:

An appeal to principles is the condition of any reconstruction of society because social institutions are the visible expression of the scale of moral values which rules the minds of individuals and it is impossible to alter institutions without altering that valuation. (Tawney, 1921, p. 10)

Such a change in values was the condition for any genuine socialist community, since an authentic community is based on a common culture. Nothing approaching a common culture could be secured unless the foundations of social organisation embodied the principle of equality. In Tawney's view something like this had existed before the advent of capitalism for

whatever the future may contain the past has shown no more excellent social order than that in which the mass of the people were the masters of the holdings which they ploughed and the tools which they worked. (1921, p. 64)

But this was a nostalgia for the equality, fellowship and common culture destroyed by industrialism rather than a call to return to medievalism. Tawney saw that the lost values could only be constructed on a modern basis through widespread participation, devolved power and economic equality.

In *Religion and the Rise of Capitalism* (1929), as in his other historical studies, Tawney sees the transition to capitalism as marked by generations of moral change involving the rise of the motive of personal gain at the expense of the idea that the significance and measure of institutions and practices was the common end to which they were related. The self-adjusting mechanism of political economy replaced the idea of mutual obligation. The language of rights expressed the practice of the bourgeois system which denied that those rights were contingent on social responsibility. The result of this was that the functionless property-owning rich were able to exercise dictatorial power in industry over a subordinate mass of wage earners. In Tawney's mind this made class struggle inevitable but it also ensured that though politically free the mass of mankind live under rules imposed by property owners whose rights are secured by the state (Tawney, 1921, pp. 43 and 92). Property in things had become sovereignty over persons.

Tawney wrote history as if the economic and social structure of a society was determinant in shaping the practical operation of political institutions. He even asserted this in his work on social theory (Tawney, 1931, p. 78), but otherwise proceeded as if Marxism was irrelevant when it came to analysing contemporary political problems. However, this did not prevent him from arguing that political democracy was unstable so long as it tried to coexist with social oligarchy and the class system (1931, p. 30). This arrangement always left democracy vulnerable to the magnates of industry and finance, whose interests may clash with it. Hence democracy needed to be extended into these other areas (1931, p. 167). Earlier, Tawney had justified industrial democracy on grounds of civil liberty, economic efficiency and social harmony (Tawney, 1918, p. 120). He had then supposed that it would be realised by a combination of trade-union encroachment and the action of a state concerned to encourage the principle of service. This Fabian idea appears also in his 'guild socialist' work, *The Acquisitive Society*, where he recognises that the elimination of the capitalist from 'highly organised trades' would demand state action rather than trade-union encroachment. But if he was prepared to advocate nationalisation he did not regard it as synonymous with bureaucratic administration, nor did he want to see it impinge on experiments in 'self-government'. Nationalisation, argued Tawney, was not an end in itself nor was its object to establish the state management of industry (Tawney, 1921, p. 119). Tawney hoped that it would be confined to the 'great foundation industries' and even there he believed that its real strength would reside in its power to enlist the latent forces of professional pride by providing for as much rank-and-file power as required to generate a sense of responsibility (1921, pp. 140–55).

Tawney recognised the need for a hierarchy of authority in industry but believed this could be made to serve the common good as long as three conditions maintained. First, economic relations ought to be governed by settled rules based on social needs rather than company profit. Second, many managerial prerogatives 'must in future be the subject of common determination'. And third, the formulators of economic strategy must be accountable to the public (1931, p. 174). On this last point Tawney appears to have subscribed to the Fabian fiction that parliamentary control over a minister responsible for appointing or overseeing the board of a public corporation would actually constitute 'democratic control' when, in fact, parliament does not even control the government. However, unlike the Webbs, he assumed that on matters of economic strategy, industrial amalgamation and 'the closing of uneconomic factories and pits', 'complete equality between managers and unions would pertain' (1931, p. 179). In fact, of course, when nationalisation came in 1945 it did so in the absence of these conditions, as was vividly demonstrated in the miners' strike of 1984–5. On that occasion the principle of community before profit was not uppermost in the policy of the National Coal Board, though it was still possible for the government to claim that a larger community interest would be served in the long run, which the lesser mining communities resisted. This would not have persuaded Tawney, the radical decentraliser.

Tawney hoped that nationalisation would be accompanied or preceded by the enlargement of trade-union powers and responsibilities. To be genuine this had to be the work of the unions themselves though the state could encourage the process (1931, p. 179). Although this emphasis is consistent with Tawney's focus on a change of values as the basis for real institutional movement towards socialism it betrays the idealism and naivety of one who supposed that identifying the common ends required to unite society was unproblematic. He tended to overlook class and institutional obstructions as well as the whole question of power. In a decade which witnessed the rise of fascism and the consolidation of Stalinism, a thinker like Tawney was necessarily eclipsed.

Despite his awareness of the contradictions in the liberal-democratic state, Tawney was essentially confident in the efficacy of a Labour government working within the parliamentary and bureaucratic machinery for socialism. In this regard he agreed with the Webbs. Yet unlike them he saw in the Labour Party's theoretical poverty its gravest weakness and referred to the 'decorous drapery of political democracy' behind which stood 'the economic power wielded by a few thousand' (Tawney, 1953, p. 60). Tawney realised that any 'strategy for equality' which failed to overcome the ideology or, as he termed it, the 'religion' of inequality was doomed to failure (see Le Grand, 1982). Though he believed in a parliamentary transition to socialism – arguing that ultimately the state is simply an instrument which can be used either sensibly or foolishly, depending on those who control it – he did not suppose that state action was sufficient without fundamental ideological change from below. His optimism concerning such change was, like that of most Fabians, derived from the conviction that the growth of professions signalled the rise of social responsibility and the exclusion of 'speculative profit' from the motives of a growing proportion of the intellectual workforce (Tawney, 1921, pp. 106–7).

Cole and Laski also made much of this purported retreat of 'functionless property' before the advance of salaried managers, technicians and other scientific workers. According to Tawney these groups had already been converted to 'a cautious and doctrineless trade unionism' such as took place among manual workers in the nineteenth century. Cole argued for an enlarged definition of the proletariat to account for these new intermediate groups and maintained that their social power was sufficient to make or break the socialist movement (Cole, 1920b). Indeed it was the absence of this layer from Russia which in Cole's view explained the peculiarity of the Bolshevik road to power and rendered that strategy inapplicable in Britain (Cole, 1932, pp. 576–8). Cole also reasoned that the scientific demands which were made on this new salariat made them more receptive to the socialist critique of capitalism with its waste, its disorder and its irrationality (Cole, 1935, p. 250). Even in the catastrophic thirties, then, echoes could still be heard of the philosophical pluralism of an earlier, more optimistic, period; indeed Laski managed to combine elements of both, claiming, in the year of Hitler's accession to power, 'whatever . . . be the forms of the modern state, the character of its society is increasingly democratic' (Laski, 1933, p. 30).

THE ROAD TO STATE SOCIALISM

Laski's early concern was that the belief in state sovereignty placed the state above the moral law and the conscience of individuals. The actual growth of state power in the first two decades of the twentieth century threatened the destruction of democracy (Laski, 1920) which he believed to be inconsistent both with paternalism in particular and the sovereign state in general. In Laski's view advanced societies were increasingly characterised by a federalism of functions as the growth of voluntary associations enabled men to find expression and representation of the many particular facets of themselves without subscribing to the false omnibus representation claimed by the state. Thus Laski claimed to see a contradiction between the evidence in civil society of a growth in functional associations and the evidence of a growing state machine seeking to regulate and control that society. His espousal of pluralism was intended to safeguard and extend democracy and individual liberty in the face of the threat to these which he saw in liberal and Fabian paternalism.

These ideas made Laski at first an enemy of that 'rigid collectivism' which saw the answer to a well-ordered community in the transfer of industry to government. Instead he believed in the necessity for an extension of democracy to industry, in order to destroy the plutocracy from which Britain suffered (Laski, 1919, p. 38). It was this propertied minority which was responsible for the irreconcilable conflict between labour and capital 'for the ultimate object of labour activity is democratic self-government in industry' (1919, p. 87). Like Cole and Tawney, Laski was deeply impressed by the apparent revolt in sections of British industry, arguing that 'it was in the workshop and factory that the new ideas were being forged'. It was here that he detected a movement for participatory democracy concerned with the 'vastest problems of the age' – from the sheer scale of contemporary life to the de-humanisation of work represented by Taylorism and the narrow pursuit of efficiency which fetishises centralisation. All these issues had their source in the corruption of the state by the industrial autocracy of the capitalists since

the State . . . is in reality the reflexion of what the dominant group or class in a community believes to be politically good . . . and it is reasonably clear that political good is today for the most part defined in economic terms. It mirrors within itself, that is to say, the economic structure of society. (1919, p. 81)

It would seem then that even in his pluralist period Laski, like Cole, was persuaded that political ideas in class societies, ideas such as the sovereignty of the state and the particular idea of justice embodied in law, are all manifestations of the imposition of the consciousness of the ruling class because they disguise and facilitate class exploitation.

By the mid 1920s Laski had renounced the Guild Socialist and Fabian measures which he had earlier proposed as solutions to these problems (Laski, 1925, p. 82). Thus he no longer believed in the efficacy of twin legislatures to cater respectively for consumers and producers (an idea also canvassed by the Webbs). But the death of the workers' control movement is also reflected in Laski's change of mind concerning the importance of industrial democracy: from having enthusiastically supported the most sweeping changes in the structure of power in industry, Laski now advocated parliamentary control over the boards of nationalised industries. Workers' participation was reduced from a fundamental 'directive' role to the work's committee which makes suggestions and discusses grievances (see 1925, pp. 444–53: compare Laski 1919, p. 91 with 1925, p. 439). This change of mind can be explained in terms of Laski's new optimism concerning the power of functional associations: this was now such that 'the sovereign state becomes . . . little more than a machine for registering decisions arrived at elsewhere' (Laski, 1925, p. 53). Thus Laski's former fears in regard to the Servile State were now completely dispelled and he was even enthusiastic about the nationalisation of industry without workers' control. This is all the more remarkable given the general retreat of trade unionism during the same interval.

But Laski was now convinced that in Western Europe 'democratic government has become a commonplace beyond discussion' (1925, p. 16). However, he continued to insist on the corrupting influence of big property owners. The difference was that he now had faith in the power of parliament to deal with these magnates without trespassing on the liberties of other citizens. Laski was already, by 1927, trying to reconcile a Marxist analysis of British capitalism with faith that Britain would prove in practice the possibility of achieving socialism by constitutional means (Laski, 1927, p. 182). Hence he showed sympathy with the Marxist theory of the state – in reality the Lenin–Engels formulation – while hoping that Britain would prove exceptional. At this time Cole was also converted to the idea that the state – which he had earlier castigated as the agent of capitalist interests – would now provide measures of reform advantageous to the working class. This may represent more than just Cole's acknowledgment that the economic crisis had effectively nullified the working class as an important lever for social change at the same time as the agenda of reforms was becoming overloaded. Under these circumstances both Cole and Laski apparently believed that state action was the only alternative. But in Cole's case confidence in the efficacy of such state action may have been derived from a growing conviction in Keynesian economics. Certainly his arguments in the late 1920s urged a distributionist fiscal policy on the state which he believed, thus armed, could then control industrial policy (Cole, 1929). In March 1931, months before the collapse of the Labour government Cole established the New Fabian Research Bureau and it was here that Evan Durbin and Hugh Gaitskell did most of the theoretical work to justify the Labour Party's post-war commitment to the mixed economy (see Durbin, 1985).

These developments were concealed by the reaction to the collapse of the MacDonald government. Faith in the inevitability of gradualness was now shattered and socialist rhetoric and debate moved decisively to the Left. Even the Webbs, increasingly besotted with Stalinism, expressed their doubts about the parliamentary road to socialism. Laski began to expound an essentially Leninist analysis of international affairs but persisted in his belief that Britain could prove an exception where violent revolution was not necessary. There was no real theoretical rationale for this exceptionalism, because Laski reasoned that a feature of the imperialist epoch was precisely the destruction of parliamentary democracy which alone made a peaceful transition to socialism possible. If the lesson of fascism was, as he argued, that class antagonisms could only be settled by force it was clear that democracy could only be defended by a violent assault on capital. For

it is clear that fascism . . . is simply the expedient adopted by capitalism in distress to defeat the democratic political foundation with which it could be successfully linked in its period of creative expansion. (Laski, 1934, p. xxxi)

Democracy was everywhere in retreat as the state adopted authoritarian forms appropriate to an epoch of wars and economic crises (Laski, 1933, p. 233). Parliamentary democracy had only ever been possible in the expansionary competitive phase of capitalism – the present phase of economic decline was only compatible with dictatorship.

Laski found the liberal theory of the state wanting in two fundamental respects. First, the kind of order maintained by the state does not provide a technique of peaceful change, because the state is the tool of vested interests prepared to reverse existing democratic gains in order to stabilise capitalism. Second, such a state cannot, as liberal rationalisations of state power suggest, maximise utilities, because it acts to safeguard a system of gross inequalities (Laski, 1938, p. iii). Laski was now satisfied that the Marxist theory of the state 'holds the field' and that his earlier pluralism was but a stage on the way to realising it.

The stark choice which Laski put before his readers was socialism or fascism. Yet when it came to the case of Britain Laski fell back on his long-standing conviction that the deep constitutionalism of the British people ruled out the insurrectionary strategy of Bolshevism. Moreover, despite his acute awareness of the depths of the world crisis Laski continued to give credence to the Fabian faith in the civilising mission of the professions. These, he argued, embodied the values of public service which continued to encroach on the capitalist realm of self-interest. Though yet in the embryonic stages of a revolt against the standards of 'capitalist democracy' their special significance as a rising caste resides, reasoned Laski, in the fact that they are especially prominent among the corps of government officials. Thus 'in a realm promoted by the businessman for his own private purpose', Laski claimed to detect the most effective pressure against capitalist values (Laski, 1933, pp. 59–62).

CONCLUSIONS

It is now possible to identify the principal reasons for the dominance of statist conceptions of collectivism in British socialism. The socialist critique of statism depended for its force on economic circumstances conducive to a confident and political trade unionism concerned with the question of power in industry. Guild socialist and pluralist ideas withered in the harsh climate of the long inter-war recession because the economic slump undermined the strategy of encroachment. Moreover this economic crisis and the Bolshevik successes in Russia persuaded most radicals to the Left of the Labour Party that Leninist doctrine was a more realistic and relevant body of theory than the pluralist ideas which preceded it. Thereafter British Marxists were concerned with different issues – moving, in particular, away from the problem of how democracy and collectivism could be made compatible to the question of state power and its conquest.

Meanwhile crisis conditions made the Fabian approach more, not less, relevant. Even during the First World War it became apparent that the Webbs were best equipped to aid the Labour leaders in finding policies to meet the special problems it had created (see Winter, 1974). With their detailed knowledge of social problems, the Webbs were better placed than their opponents to formulate definite policies for the peace. Furthermore the constitutionalist Labour leaders were necessarily inclined to consider *how* the state could be used to address these problems (rather than *whether* it should be so used) in a context in which the state's powers were growing anyway. Once issues such as mass unemployment, poverty, and bad housing came to dominate the scene – as they did with the onset of the industrial depression in 1921 – it was clear to most socialists that only further extensions of state powers and responsibilities could provide the means to deal effectively with them. Thus socialist thought turned away from the issues of principle which characterised the guild and pluralist debates to questions of technique. A general accommodation to collectivism took place on the Left as is evinced by the evolution of Cole's and Laski's thinking.

Other pressures also worked in favour of Fabian collectivism. Cole, Tawney and Laski were wrong to think that the growth in voluntary associations would result in the state conceding ground and losing power as it was rendered superfluous in one area of life after another. On the contrary, this very process of politicisation of groups which they welcomed provided a reason for more, not less, state intervention. As the highest association the state was necessarily interested in such matters and when, once, for example, industrial relations became 'political', the state intervened in order to create forums for containing the new demands – the so-called Whitley Councils. In fact trade-union legislation grew in parallel to the growth of political trade unionism between 1906 and 1913.

The early anti-statist ideologies made the mistake of regarding state activity purely as a form of interference with individuals. In fact the state became a major source of goods and services in the same period and, especially after 1945, individuals often stood in a contractual relationship to it. Voluntary groups were more likely to respond to these developments by competing for the scarce resources which the state increasingly supplied than to adopt a communitarian perspective as the anti-statists imagined. State activity of this sort, moreover, was apt to be self-sustaining since the provision of goods and services generated its own demand. Thus even when economic circumstances were more propitious for the adoption of a guild socialist perspective, as during the period of full employment in the 1950s and 1960s, group behaviour showed no such indications. Instead the trend was to 'overload' the state with demands and thereby encourage its further growth.

The critique of statism took the form of an assault on the concept of sovereignty. But I have already suggested that the claims of other associations – which our maverick Fabians championed – far from logically leading to a curtailment of the state actually enhanced its role. Laski and Cole were wrong to make sovereignty synonymous with power. By doing so they thought that the growth of powerful groups would undermine the all-powerful state. But in fact the growth of associations reinforced the state's claim to be the protector of the public interest and underlined its role as adjudicator between sectional and selfish impulses. Thus the claims of the sovereign state were reinforced because its real strength has always been in connection with the idea of a public interest which it is its responsibility to promote. The anti-statist critique of sovereignty was thus self-defeating.

Of course Cole, Laski and Tawney made much of the state's incapacity to protect the general interest because of its connection with 'vested interests'. Here, however, there is no coherent account of the problem or of how to deal with it. Cole and Laski in particular veered from functionalist explanations of the capitalist state to those consistent with a reformist perspective. Laski drifted from the view that only community mattered to the idea, after 1925, that only the state could serve the community interest via ownership of the means of production. The one consistent strand in all of this was the dissolution of the distinction between community and state (a strength, incidentally, of the concept of sovereignty). Pluralism, in fact, served to draw attention away from the state by apparently reconciling statist and anti-statist perspectives and may thereby have 'allowed the state to slip out of political discourse and become the greatest unstudied feature of twentieth century British politics' (Barker, 1978, p. 103).

Laski's egalitarianism recognised no legitimate bases of authority other than those associated with the efficient performance of office. He was therefore forced to rely on the traditional Fabian stress on the authority of technical knowledge and expertise. In different ways this is characteristic of all three of our radicals. All shared a naive evolutionist view of society in which the elements representing public service and social responsibility are identified with the professions, the technicians and the scientists. Ultimately only Cole provides an antidote to this peculiarly Fabian elitism by virtue of the assumption that expertise will itself be democratised by the experience of self-government in industry. Likewise his critique of sovereignty was on securer ground than Laski's because it was focussed on the Webbs' notion that the state could adequately act as the agent of representation of consumers. In analysing the bogus nature of this representation he was able to undercut such claims and thereby provide an argument for some degree of producers' self-government. Otherwise the anti-statist socialism which we have analysed here shares too much in the constructionist rationalism of the Webbs to be an adequate alternative to it.

REFERENCES

Barker, R., 1975. 'Guild socialism revisited?', *Political Quarterly*, 46
    1978. *Political Ideas in Modern Britain*. London, Routledge and Kegan Paul
Belloc, H. 1913. *The Servile State*. London
Briggs, A. and J. Saville, eds., 1971. *Essays in Labour History*, vol. II. London, Macmillan
Cole, G. D. H., 1915. *Labour in Wartime*. London, G. Bell and Sons
    1917 and 1972. *Self-Government in Industry*. London, Hutchinson
    1918. *Labour in the Commonwealth*. London
    1920a. *Guild Socialism Re-Stated*. London, L. Parsons
    1920b. *Chaos and Order in Industry*. London, Methuen
    1929. *The Next Ten Years in British Social Policy*. London.
    1932. *The Intelligent Man's Guide Through World Chaos*. London, Gollancz
    1935. 'Marxism and the World Situation Today', in J. Middleton Murry, ed., *Marxism*. London, Chapman and Hall
    1937. *What Marx Really Meant*. London
    1938. *Socialism in Evolution*. London

Cole, M., ed., 1949. *The Webbs and their Work*. London, Muller

Crosland, A., 1956. *The Future of Socialism*. London, Jonathan Cape

Crossman, R., 1956. *Socialism and the New Despotism*. Fabian Tract 298

Dobb, M., 1923. 'The Webbs, the state, and the workers', *Plebs*, 15(4)

Durbin, E., 1985. *New Jerusalems*. London, Routledge and Kegan Paul

Fabian Society, 1889. *Fabian Essays*, ed. G. B. Shaw. London

Gray, A., 1944. *The Socialist Tradition*. London, Longmans Green

Greenleaf, W. H., 1983. *The British Political Tradition*, vol. II. London, Methuen

Guttsman, W. L., 1981. *The German Social Democratic Party*. London, Allen and Unwin

Hain, P., 1983. *The Democratic Alternative*. Harmondsworth, Penguin Books

Hall, S., 1978. 'Authoritarian populism', in A. Hunt, ed., *Marxism and Democracy*. London,
    Lawrence and Wishart

Hinton, J., 1973. *The First Shop Stewards Movement*. London, Allen and Unwin

Hobhouse, L. T., 1972. *Democracy and Reaction*. Brighton, Harvester

Hodgson, G., 1984. *The Democratic Economy*. London, Penguin Books

Laski, H. J., 1919. *Authority in the Modern State*. New Haven, Yale University Press

    1920. *Political Thought in England From Locke to Bentham*. London, The Home University
    Library of Modern Knowledge

    1925. *A Grammar of Politics*. London, Allen and Unwin

    1927. *Communism*. London, Williams and Norgate

    1933. *Democracy in Crisis*. London, Allen and Unwin

    1934. Preface to 3rd edition of *A Grammar of Politics*

    1935. *The State in Theory and Practice*. London, Allen and Unwin

    1938. Introduction to 4th edition of *A Grammar of Politics*

    1948. *Communist Manifesto: Socialist Landmark*. London, Allen and Unwin

Le Grand, J., 1982. *The Strategy of Equality*. London, Allen and Unwin

Lichtheim, G., 1975. *A Short History of Socialism*. London, Fontana Press

McBriar, A. M., 1966. *Fabian Socialism and English Politics 1884–1918*. Cambridge, Cambridge
    University Press

Miliband, R., 1982. *Capitalist Democracy in Britain*. London, Penguin Books

Nove, A., 1983. *The Economics of Feasible Socialism*. London, George Allen and Unwin

Paul, W., 1917. *The State: Its Origins and Functions*. London

Pimlott, B., 1977. *Labour and the Left in the 1930s*. Cambridge, Cambridge University Press

Potter, B., 1891. *The Co-operative Movement in Great Britain*. London

Radice, L., 1984. *Beatrice and Sidney Webb*. London, Macmillan

Russell, B., 1970. *Roads to Freedom*. London, Unwin

Salvadori, M., 1979. *Karl Kautsky*. London, New Left Books

Seabrook, J., 1978. *What Went Wrong*. London, Gollancz

Selucky, R., 1979. *Marxism, Socialism, Freedom*. London, Macmillan

Shaw, G. B., 1896. *Report on Fabian Policy*. Fabian Tract 70

Sirianni, C., 1982. *Workers' Control and Socialist Democracy*. London, New Left Books

Tawney, R. H., 1918. *The Conditions of Economic Liberty in the Radical Tradition*. Republished,
    1964. London, Allen and Unwin

    1921. *The Acquisitive Society*. London, Bell

    1931. *Equality*. London, Allen and Unwin

    1953. *The Attack and other Papers*. London, Allen and Unwin

Terrill, R., 1974. *R. H. Tawney and His Times*. London, André Deutsch

Ulam, A., 1951. *Philosophical Foundations of English Socialism*. Cambridge, Mass., Harvard
    University Press

Walton-Newbold, J. T., 1918. 'Socialists and the state', *Plebs*, 10 (Jan 1918)

Webb, S., 1890. *Socialism in England*. London

1894. *Socialism: True and False*. Fabian Tract 51

1937. 'The Future of Soviet Communism', in G. D. H. Cole, ed., *What is Ahead of Us?* London

Webb, Sidney and Beatrice Webb, 1920. *A Constitution for the Socialist Commonwealth*. London, Longman

Weiler, P., 1982. *The New Liberalism*. London, Garland

Winter, J. M., 1974. *Socialism and the Challenge of War*. London, Routledge

Winter, J. M. and D. M. Joslin, 1972. *R. H. Tawney's Commonplace Book*. Cambridge, Cambridge University Press

Wright, A. W., 1979. *G. D. H. Cole and Socialist Democracy*. Oxford, Clarendon Press

1983. *British Socialism*. London, Longman

CAPITAL AND LABOUR

Amongst the most noticeable trends in advanced capitalist countries this century have been the widening and deepening of state activities and a significant increase in the number of state employees. These developments have altered class structures, capitalist arrangements, and, by definition, the role and character of the state itself. Theoretical difficulties have emerged for Marxists, liberals and pluralists – how are these trends to be understood, and related to established categories and to enduring political goals? – and democracy has seemed once more a problematic if not impossible ideal. At the very least it has been reconceptualised in relation to the new circumstances. The following chapters examine, at varying levels of abstraction, the changing structures of advanced capitalist societies and seek to relate the new analyses to popular struggle and to democratic values and goals.

In addition to the increase of state activities and of public employment, Fairbrother emphasises the emergence of a more centralised and cohesive state apparatus, with government adopting a more directive role over the different elements making up the state, and the development of a state labour process, which is a distinctive form of capitalist employment. In Britain this century there has been a huge increase in state employment, especially after 1938, and more especially during the 1960s and 1970s, with the expansion being most marked in the welfare field. There has been a great increase in female part-time state employment though – not surprisingly – these low-paid and often casual workers have suffered disproportionate losses with the cut-backs. Fairbrother's is in no sense a simple story. Even before the reversal of long-term trends in the 1980s, there had been falls in particular areas of state employment, for example, the most significant shift during the last half century was the absolute and relative decline in the armed forces, and there has also been a notable decline in the proportion employed in public corporations. Fairbrother underlines the complex internal structure of the capitalist state while seeking to identify a particular class position for state workers, as 'wage labourers subject to control and exploitation'. That control has grown recently, with the increase of managerialism and of government centralisation, particularly with the assault on local authorities.

The development of the new state proletariat of administrative, clerical and semi-professional workers suggests new possibilities of collective action to Fairbrother. Not that he ignores difficulties, for example, the important distinction between manual and non-manual workers, the existence of employment units whose employees are represented by different unions, as in schools or local government, and the problems of industrial action for wage labourers who are also providing a service – industrial action may simultaneously hurt the clients and save the employer's (state) expenditure. But despite the obvious problems of unity and cohesion, and despite the general decline in union membership in the 1980s, and other setbacks, Fairbrother claims that the changes in the structure and organisation of state work which he has analysed, have laid the foundation for the emergence of a proletarian consciousness amongst non-manual state workers. That suggests new possibilities of collective action, a more campaigning and direct style by public-sector unions, learning from their manufacturing fellows. More militant action may be provoked by government programmes, and may become distinctly political rather than merely economistic. Fairbrother remains tentative about such an achievement, but even his cautious hopes sound very optimistic in present circumstances.

Street's basic concern is the effects of technology upon the practice of state control and upon democratic ideals. His discussion focusses on two examples of high technology in Britain – nuclear power, which is inevitably very close to the state, and microelectronics, which is generally left to the private sector but which raises more serious questions about democratic and political control. The development of nuclear power is in the immediate interest of the state, which plays a crucial role in producing the conditions for capitalist accumulation and production. The nuclear-power industry may seem susceptible to political control because of its dependence upon state initiative and support, yet, as Benn discovered when Minister for Energy, the supply and the character of information and the power structure of the industry conspired against the democratic goal of controlling technology. The experts were devious, partisan and well protected. Politicians remained dependent on the industry for advice and information, and tended to follow rather than direct changes in the industry. On the face of it, microelectronics is even less susceptible to political and democratic control, as it is understood appropriately in terms of markets and capitalist interests rather than those of the state – though the 'state' sees it as vital to national growth and generously subsidises it. While dependent on state funding, bodies such as Inmos resemble private companies as much as public corporations (and the chiefs did become millionaires very quickly). Central government forgoes a directive role, allowing autonomy to private companies.

Street's analysis leaves him pessimistic about the possibility of democratic control of technology. The old socialist notion of democratic control through public ownership, in the form of nationalisation, was and remains irrelevant to actual practice, partly because such structures were never democratic from the bottom, partly because the notion of general political oversight was a very loose one. The difficulties in the way of democratic control, even by committed and theoretically conscious Ministers, were clearly revealed in the case of Benn. We are left, not with any gesture towards democracy, but with a dual vision of the possibilities of technology: on the one side there is the image of isolated citizens facing a dominant state, which is armed with expert knowledge, management control techniques, and new means of surveillance, and on the other a liberating potentiality of technology, lying in its capacity to spread information and to increase the powers of individual citizens. If technology was to be used to free people, governmental commitment to greater democracy would be needed, and Street's study of two cases of high technology provides little ground for optimism about that.

Cawson's refinement of corporatist theory assumes that existing theories of the state require a rigorous theory of corporatism (rather than vice versa) and that corporatism must be placed within a theory of the state rather than of party government. In Schmitter's early concept of 'interest intermediation', the central idea was a reciprocal or contractual relationship between groups and the state, which sharply separates corporatism from pluralism. In corporatist theory, organisation is an important element in the constitution and definition of interests. The focus is on the specific structures of intermediation beween state actors and interest organisations, and the *how* is of course crucial. Privileged access to the state may occur at different levels, which leads Cawson to distinguish between macro-corporatism, meso-corporatism and micro-corporatism. In macro-corporatism political exchanges are concerned with major distributive questions which are vitally relevant to class interests, claims and organisations. Meso-corporatism involves negotiations within defined policy areas, specific sectors or product branches, and these have no necessary class basis. Micro-corporatism concerns the negotiation of semi-binding contractual arrangements with individual firms. The existence of these two latter forms of corporatism underly one of Cawson's major claims – that the dominant organised interests in major policy-making areas of many capitalist democracies are not reducible to class. At this point the distinction between class and sector is central.

The corporate universe is presented as 'largely non-competitive and hierarchically ordered'. Interests, especially the class and sectoral interests of producers, are organised into corporate and collusive arrangements expressed less in the electoral parliamentary process than in political side-channels. The public and the private penetrate each other, subverting that crucial liberal distinction. The corporate world is contrasted with a sphere of competitive politics – shades of James O'Connor – where we find the excluded interests, disorganised and fluid, consumers rather than producers, takers rather than makers.

This theory of corporatism, unlike pluralism, points to the crucial role of the state in promoting political exchanges, which are not just the outcome of inter-group bargaining. Unlike traditional Marxism, it presents sectoral interests as sometimes more compelling than class divisions and interests, and it stresses the way in which the state creates sectoral constituencies and interndencies which cut across class divisions. Although he claims that the democratic character of the state is no mere façade, Cawson does not explore directly what democratic forces and instruments exist in this increasingly corporatist world. The complex relations between democracy and corporatism are taken up more seriously by Boreham, Clegg and Dow. But first, what analysis of the modern state do they offer?

The three authors present the state, formally, as 'a complex of organisational resources', which 'structures the fundamental social relations of modern societies'. The adoption of an organisational perspective enables them to emphasise the complex and often internally contradictory and inconsistent character of the institutions which constitute the state. The capitalist state, like other organisations, suffers from rigidities, bureaucratic inertia, and caution. It cannot impose a unitary logic over policy-making deliberations. The characteristic state form in OECD countries is seen to be liberal-democratic – something different from a repressive apparatus, though it is far from a benignly neutral instrument. It acts for capitalism only in a very broad sense, for example, in preserving privately property relations, and it does act against particular capitals. Significantly, state apparatuses are the sites of a constant, historically patterned struggle between different organisations of capital and labour for control of the resources they have available to them. And the outcome is not settled. The working class can gain from state interventions through mobilising political resources, which makes the state problematic for the capitalist class. Indeed, not only may state interventions fail to be optimally reproductive, they may even be non-reproductive, in the sense that they transform the underlying organisational principles of both capitalism and the state.

The refusal to adopt simple structural or instrumental terms, and the use of an organisational perspective, leads to a recognition of the relative autonomy of the state and of the limits imposed by its operating environment. Within the underlying society – though the liberal distinction between state and civil society has become blurred through state interventions – the authors see a growth of corporatist mechanisms. Assuming that political agency will at least sometimes be stronger than structural determination, they adopt a positive interpretation of corporatism. Whereas corporatism normally implies consensus and an opposition to change, it can be seen constructively if it provides a forum for conflictual politics. The authors follow Jessop in seeking 'a new productivist orientation to left economic policies', and seeing a democratic corporatism as a means of extending economic democracy and deepening political representation. Impressed particularly by the example of Sweden, they look toward the replacement of market mechanisms and market rationality for resource allocation by political mechanisms which may be best embodied in 'corporatist' structures. These structures would be democratic, responsive and open, unlike the typical tripartite structures of the present. Yet the fate of the excluded remains a problem.

The final chapter in this section explores the practice and the ideals of industrial democracy in relation to the capitalist state. Carter begins with the familiar problem that, depending on how it is defined, on how far it is participation and how far control, industrial democracy can be capitalist or socialist. In its capitalist form participation or consultation would be emphasised and the goal would be good labour relations, achieved by minor involvement by workers, the discovery and notification of grievances and so on. Such minor democratic mechanisms might be expected to increase efficiency and productivity. A socialist form of industrial democracy would involve much more significant worker control, well beyond that hitherto achieved in Yugoslavia.

Carter sees four leading models of political democracy – elitist, liberal, pluralist and participatory – as also appropriate to industry. The liberal form, she thinks, best describes the moves toward industrial democracy in Western Europe, including co-determination in West Germany, while participatory democracy is more in tune with a socialist society. She has few illusions about the power holders, who will manoeuvre to prevent implementation of anything approaching workers' control, and will seek to draw the teeth of even mildly radical recommendations, for example, those contained in the Bullock Report. On the other side, workers may not be interested in achieving industrial democracy – better wages and working conditions may matter far more to them – or they may be excluded from full involvement in board business and/or co-opted. Her conclusion is that a realistic advancement of workers' claims is more likely through extension of the rights and powers of trade unions to influence company policy, with their ability in the last resort to challenge economic and institutional power through civil disobedience and direct action. That might broaden and deepen our somewhat emasculated parliamentary democracy.

10

State workers: class position and collective action

PETER FAIRBROTHER

Over the last two decades the class position of workers in the contemporary capitalist state has changed, with important implications for collective action by these workers. Specifically, state workers have increasingly displayed a capacity to organise and act in ways that indicate a recognition – still generally embryonic and hesitant – of their subordination as waged workers. This has occurred in the context of a major restructuring of state work. At a general level, the occupational structure of state work has been transformed, involving a massive increase in state employment and the recomposition of the work-force, particularly with the increased employment of women and the increase in part-time and, more recently, casual employment. These changes have been particularly evident in local and central government and have resulted in the emergence of more militant forms of trade unionism. Increasingly, the formerly quiescent state-sector unions have adapted themselves to the new circumstances and experience of state work, the restructuring of the state apparatus and the implementation of government policies aimed at redefining and redrawing the contours of state institutions. In responding to these developments, state-sector unions have tended to model themselves organis-ationally, in terms of activity and union objectives, on the prevailing images and practices of industrial unions, particularly those in the manufacturing sector. At the same time, there are signs that in the course of defending their members' interests these unions have begun to reconsider these traditional methods of organisation and to adopt more campaigning styles of trade unionism. But to date this has been a limited achievement, although there is a continuing prospect that these unions could develop in innovative and novel ways.

STATE WORKERS AND THE STATE LABOUR PROCESS

This essay develops an argument about the character and significance of state work in advanced capitalist societies, specifically with reference to the United Kingdom. There has, in recent decades, been a burgeoning of literature about the capitalist state, much of it concerned with a classification and analysis of the character of the capitalist state. There has, however, been surprisingly little examination of the internal organisation of the institutions that make up the state apparatus, and hence only brief consideration of state employment. One consequence of this narrow focus has been that there is very little discussion or debate about state workers and their trade unionism. It is the intention in this essay to develop an argument about the contemporary capitalist state through a consideration of the class position of state workers, their location in the state labour process and the implications of the recent restructuring of this labour process for trade unionism.

In the extensive literature on the capitalist state it has been usual to focus on the internal organisation of the state in terms of the role and activity of the senior layers of the state apparatus – senior civil servants, judges, senior officials in local government, senior administrators in statutory corporations, and military and police officials (e.g. Miliband, 1969, 1982 and Poulantzas, 1973). The emphasis has been on the way such officials are decisive in policy determination and implementation, the assumption being that their position and actions indicate the organisation and operation of a relatively cohesive apparatus. While it is important to examine the role and part played by senior levels of the state apparatus, drawing attention to inter-connections and relations between these groups of state officials, restricting the analysis in this way results in an oversimplification of the way the state is organised and operates.

To substantiate this claim it will be argued that state institutions have been restructured so as to compose a state labour process. State workers have come to occupy class positions as wage labourers subject to control and exploitation. This has resulted in a recomposition of non-manual areas of state work with the lower grades of administrative, clerical and semi-professional workers comprising a 'new' state proletariat (Crompton and Jones, 1984, pp. 34–41, 236–9). At the same time, and as part of this process, state management has been redefined in more precise ways than in the past, with a reaffirmation of supervision and control and other managerial aspects of middle and senior levels of non-manual employment. These developments have had important implications for the consciousness of state workers, in particular the possibility that the structural redefinition of the managerial and 'proletarian' boundary will be accompanied by the development of a managerial and a 'proletarian' consciousness respectively. Such a transformation in the social relations of state employment could have important implications for collective action and unity by state workers, and may give rise to a major division between state worker unions, depending upon the class position of their memberships.

The argument in this essay is predicated on the assumption that state employment is a distinctive form of capitalist employment. Unlike employment in other sectors of the economy, it is not directly or exclusively defined by the labour–capital relation. It is a form of employment that is distinctive in at least two respects. First, major sections of state employment are characterised by a structural contradiction whereby workers sell their labour power for wages, on the one hand, and produce use values or the means for others to participate in exchange relationships, on the other. Second, and related, the state apparatus in a liberal democracy is moulded as both a representative and a managerial structure. It is with regard to these two distinct features of state employment that the argument about state workers and their trade unionism will be developed. The thesis will be advanced that in recent decades the restructuring of the state apparatus has served to underline the common position of state workers as waged workers which has had major consequences for trade unionism in the state sector.

THE EXPANSION AND CONTRACTION OF STATE EMPLOYMENT

The state sector (compared with other sectors in the economy) is the major employer in advanced capitalist societies (Therborn, 1984, pp. 33–5). Throughout this century state employment has expanded, although in the last few years there has been a contraction and a reorganisation of the occupational structure as governments have adopted the view that state employment is a major economic problem. In the United Kingdom this has meant that state employment increased more than fivefold this century, with the major period of expansion after 1938; although in the 1980s these long-term trends were reversed. If a long view is taken of the trends in state employment the most significant shift in the patterns of state employment has been the absolute and relative decline in the armed services. Figures show that 70.5 per cent of state employees in 1851 were employed in the armed forces and related colonial services (Abramovitz and Eliasberg, 1957, p. 16). In the main, this was a consequence of Britain's position during the nineteenth century, as an imperial power and as a country which effectively occupied Ireland and indeed Scotland. By 1959, with the relegation of Britain to the status of a secondary world power and with the gradual weakening of Britain's economy, only 9.8 per cent of the state workforce were in uniform (Department of Employment and Productivity, 1971, p. 298, Table 152). Subject to adjustments at the margin with respect to British involvement in military alliances, particularly NATO, this position has been maintained throughout the two subsequent decades.

In line with the trends in the armed services, throughout the 1940s and 1950s there was a steady decline in the absolute figures for civilian state employment (Department of Employment and Productivity, 1971, p. 298,

Table 152). During this period, a major part of the decline in state employment was accounted for by a decrease in central-government civilian employment of 13.6 per cent from 1949 to 1959. Alongside this trend, public corporation employment was stabilised and began to decline, against an increase in this employment until 1952. The initial increase in this employment was in part accounted for by the founding and expansion of public corporations, particularly in the period 1945 to 1951 under Labour governments. Even so, public corporation employment displayed an overall increase during this period, 4.0 per cent from 1949 to 1959. More significantly in the long term, there was during this period a marked increase in local-government employment, altogether 18.8 per cent from 1949 to 1959 (Department of Employment and Productivity, 1971, p. 298. Table 152).

The pattern up to 1959 was just the prelude to the massive growth in state work which occurred during the 1960s and continued on into the 1970s. In this period, overall state employment increased from 5,800,000 in 1961 to a high point of 7,400,000 in 1979 and 1980 (Semple, 1979; Morrison, 1983). This represented a relative increase in state employment from 23.7 per cent of those in total employment in 1961 to 29.4 per cent in 1980. The major increase in state employment took place in local government, which increased by 57.8 per cent between 1961 and 1980 – an increase of 1.2 million persons. This increase occurred even though some areas of local-government employment were shifted to either central government (local-government health services: 1974) or public corporations (sewerage and sewerage-disposal functions, local-authority-owned water undertakings, and statutory harbour boards and authorities in England and Wales: 1974). There was an equally important although slightly less dramatic increase in central government civilian employment during the same period, an increase of 53.8 per cent between 1961 and 1980, altogether 700,000 persons. Over the same period, public-corporation employment fell by 9.1 per cent, a decrease of 200,000 persons. This was part of a long-term trend away from such employment, paradoxically unaffected by the re-nationalisation of steel in 1967 and the nationalisation of aerospace and shipbuilding in 1977. More importantly, this trend represented a major change in the composition of state employment, so that in the 1940s and 1950s public corporations accounted for the largest proportion of state employees, on average 44 per cent from 1949 to 1959, whereas in the 1960s and 1970s local government employed the largest proportion of state employees, on average 41 per cent from 1970 to 1980.

From the mid 1970s state employment has been questioned as governments attempted to stabilise the level of state employment and then reduce it. While these policies were formulated and implemented first by a Labour government (1974 to 1979) it was not until the 1980s, under a Conservative government, that they began to have an effect on aggregate employment levels when state employment fell by just over 936,000 between 1979 and 1985, a decline of 12.6 per cent (Richardson, 1985). The largest percentage decrease occurred in the public corporations, where employment fell by 803,000 between 1979 and 1985, a decline of 38.9 per cent. Local-government employment fell by 106,000, a decline of 3.5 per cent; while central-government employment fell by 27,000, a decline of 1.1 per cent, although there were sharper reductions in particular areas. While this represents a massive decline in a very short time period, it must be noted that a proportion of these jobs were transferred to the private sector under the privatisation policies of the Conservative government, the most notable being the transfer in 1984 of British Telecom plc to the private sector, involving about 250,000 workers.

Moving beyond the aggregate numbers and considering specific areas of employment, the following picture emerges for the late 1970s into the 1980s (Richardson, 1985). Within local-government employment the decreases were accounted for by education (7.1 per cent between 1979 and 1985) and other local-government employment, apart from the police and social services, which increased by 6.2 per cent and 9.3 per cent respectively for the period 1979 to 1985. Within central government there were, over the same period, increases in National Health Service employment (about 6.2 per cent between 1979 and 1985) and in the armed forces (3.8 per cent between 1979 and 1985) and reductions in other central government employment, 11.9 per cent between 1979 and 1985. But on the other hand it should be noted that the numbers employed in local government and central government, excluding the National Health Service and the armed forces, increased slightly between 1984 and 1985, accounted for by a more general move toward part-time and casual employment in these areas. This could signify the beginning of a major recomposition of the occupational structure of the state in these areas.

Two features of the pattern of state employment are particularly noteworthy – the incidence of part-time work and the gender of state workers. There has been, in general, a massive increase in female part-time employment in the state. In 1985, female workers accounted for approximately three-fifths of those employed by the state in central and local government areas, and only a seventh of the public corporation employment (Richardson, 1985). The major part of this employment in central and local government was in education, health and social services, 35.6 per cent of all state workers in 1985, over half of whom were part-time, altogether 53.4 per cent. To appreciate the recent origins of this employment it is necessary to note that by 1978 female part-time workers accounted for twice their proportion of state workers in 1961, an increase of 2 million persons, most as a result of increased female part-time work. But with the elaboration and implementation of more comprehensive policies of restructuring state expenditure there is evidence to indicate that part-time women workers, for example, in local government manual grades, have suffered disproportionate job loss, although elsewhere the evidence suggests that part-time paid employment is being substituted for posts that were previously full time.

THE CHANGING TERRAIN OF STATE WORK

In the period following the Second World War, there has been considerable change in the way the capitalist state has organised and operated. This has occurred in two principal ways. First, as noted above, the scope and range of state activities have been expanded and extended. Second, there has been a process of reinforcing control both between and within state institutions, with the result that the state apparatus has become more centralised and cohesive than was the case in the past. For state workers, these two developments have meant a changing terrain of state work.

The most notable change in the state apparatus in this century has been the enormous expansion of welfare activities (Therborn, 1984, pp. 26–9). In particular, this development is associated with the establishment in 1948 of a comprehensive public-health system, the National Health Service, which has become the largest single employer in the United Kingdom. But it is equally important to note the other areas of welfare activity in local and central government, especially education, housing and a wide variety of social services. Not only has this meant employment of specialist workers – nurses, teachers and the like – but it has also meant increased employment of ancillary and auxiliary staff as well as large increases in clerical and administrative workers. To appreciate the class position of these workers it is necessary to consider the structural contradictions of their place in capitalist society (cf. Offe, 1984, pp. 126–8). On the one hand, workers in the welfare areas sell their labour power for wages – as teachers, nurses, administrators, or clerical workers – and on the other hand, these workers are employed in contexts where the 'immediate purpose' of their labour is to produce use values – knowledge, health, shelter – or to provide the means for participating in exchange relationships, through income maintenance. In view of the contradictory position of these workers, it becomes a possibility that there will be disputes about who controls these institutions and to what ends, and under what criteria they should operate, exemplified by the debates about the privatisation of welfare services. At the same time, and as part of the debate about these services, the terms and conditions of employment of these workers may become subject to dispute and conflict.

Sections of the state have long been involved in the production of goods and services. This has been the case with the provisions of gas, water and electricity, originally the responsibility of local government and currently the concern of statutory authorities. More recently, since the Second World War, the state has extended its activities in this direction through nationalisation and the extension of state ownership in specific industrial enterprises. With regard to nationalisation, coal (1948), steel (1948, 1968), aerospace and shipbuilding (1977), or parts thereof, have been incorporated as part of the state apparatus. Through purchase and acquisition of shares, state ownership has also been extended, as exemplified in the car and oil industries. In part, this recent extension of state activities has been a response to an unwillingness of capital to sustain these industries in a situation of relative economic decline and industrial restructuring; in part, it has been the outcome of campaigns by the labour movement to extend the direct involvement of the state in the economy. But, for the workers in these areas, state ownership and control has not signified any structural change in their class position: they continue to sell their labour power for the purpose of production in a market context. It did, however, mean that the state as employer continued to be concerned with the mechanisms of production, productivity and output, and market conditions. It also meant that reorganisation, relocation and redundancy characterised these areas of employment as the state attempted to meet the problems engendered by a declining capitalist economy.

Within state institutions there has been a trend toward the consolidation and centralisation of the state apparatus. This is well illustrated by the proliferation of regional administrators replacing locally based structures, such as the regional water authorities, health authorities and economic planning bodies; increased controls over local authorities, particularly through the operation of the Rate Support Grant or more recently the block grant system; and the extension of quasi-governmental agencies, such as water and sewerage (Duncan and Goodwin, 1982; Hodgwood and Keating, 1982; Barker, 1982). The impetus for these developments has been the concern of successive governments to assume a more directive role over the different elements that make up the state. As a result it is now more likely that uniform employment arrangements and co-ordinated state policies will be implemented than was the case previously. In some areas of the state, particularly in local government, a consequence and also a spur to this development has been a restriction of electoral accountability to minimise the impact of electoral resistance to state policies.

But what began as a process of centralising state institutions and restricting state expenditure has become a way of controlling state workers. This is reflected in the steady introduction of managerial controls into areas of state work notable for the absence or imperfect operation of such controls, especially in local government (Cockburn, 1977). These controls may be characterised as business-management techniques where the manufacturing and financial world is regarded as the model of how the state apparatus should be organised. In state corporations, these procedures of management have long been evident in the restructuring of such corporations so that they can operate in a market context. Dating from the 1960s, management structures were introduced in local authorities (Bains Report, 1972; Pattison, 1973; Cockburn, 1977), the National Health Service (Klein, 1983) and the civil service (Garrett, 1980). As part of this reorganisation, techniques typical of private industry, such as work study and job evaluation, have been implemented in local government and the National Health Service. This has been complemented by the commissioning of studies by management consultants to extend further the reorganisation of the state apparatus, exemplified by the Rayner studies in the civil service. The consequence is that mechanisms of control over workers have been extended, with respect to increasing output of state institutions from fewer workers and by subjecting state workers to more direct forms of supervision.

These trends towards centralisation and managerialism must be qualified in one important respect, namely with reference to the representative procedures and practices evident in the state sector. At a general level, the state apparatus in a liberal democracy is distinguished by systems of representation entailing forms of accountability and participatory practices; in practice, these procedures may be highly mediated and, indeed, structured in ways that minimise accountability and participation. Even so, electoral politics are significant in a number of respects. At the national level, the periodic change of government does have consequences for state employment and the experience of that employment, albeit within the parameters of the trends referred to above. This is illustrated by the difference in legislative foci and emphasis on union and employment rights under the Labour government of 1974 to 1979 and the subsequent Conservative governments. But, more significantly, it is with respect to local government that representation has come to be associated with an aspect of local state autonomy, thereby constituting an important counter-tendency to the general patterns of development in the state sector. There has, as noted above, been a centralisation of local government structures and the introduction of managerial control and practice. This has been accompanied by an attempt to consolidate and extend central-government control over local government, with implications for electoral accountability at a local-government level. At the same time, local-government authorities have been able to maintain a degree of autonomy from central government, through local electoral politics, the maintenance of some degree of financial discretion, and the local provision of goods and services to the community. What this means is that the employment experience of local state workers may be different from other state workers to the extent that elected local-government bodies may attempt to implement policies which run counter to the centralising and managerial trends elsewhere (Boddy and Fudge, 1984). None the less, the constraints on local 'autonomy' and initiatives will ensure that such developments will remain limited in scope and scale.

The structure of state employment in local and central government, the National Health Service and some statutory corporations, such as the Post Office, has long been characterised by low pay, part-time and casual labour, as noted above. This work is often done by women, who have been used as a reserve army of labour drawn into the workforce in accordance with the changing demands for labour. Women make up the vast majority of workers in clerical and typing, cleaning and catering jobs in local and central government and in nursing and ancillary work in the National Health Service. This pattern of female employment is part of a broader long-term pattern of occupational segregation between the male and female labour force both within and beyond the state sector (Hakim, 1979). But, as noted already, the impact of recent state policies toward employment has fallen more heavily on women workers and is likely to continue to do so. Where women work full time in large numbers, particularly in the clerical and administrative areas, the introduction of micro-technology is likely to affect adversely the numbers employed. And, as part-time and casual employment increases relative to full-time jobs held by women, these state workers will experience a continuing deterioration in the overall terms and conditions of employment.

A further feature of the deterioration of the terms and conditions of employment has occurred with reference to pay. If the period following the Second World War is taken as a whole then there is extensive evidence to support the view that state workers have experienced a relative decline in their earnings, particularly during the successive incomes policies introduced by Conservative and Labour governments (Clegg, 1982, pp. 4–7). In part, this is because the effects of incomes policies have had unequal impact upon state workers compared with private-sector workers. All the same, within the state sector there is considerable unevenness in earnings levels, signified by the relative improvement of manual-state-worker pay levels compared with private-sector counterparts during the 1970s; the persistence of low-paid employment; the privileged position of firefighters and the police, particularly after 1978 with the introduction of pay indexation arrangements; and the preferential pay levels for nurses, compared with ancillary and non-manual health workers in 1984. For some sections of the state workforce, comparability arrangements were introduced, covering the non-industrial civil servants, doctors, dentists, armed forces and the most senior levels of the state workforce. But the history of these arrangements has been far from straightforward, with different systems 'inaugurated, abolished, suspended and renewed' as governments reconsidered the basis and desirability of such arrangements (Clegg, 1982, p. 8). Most recently, cash limits and government-determined wage levels have been used to hold down state workers' pay levels.

State policies and state restructuring have had important consequences for the way that state workers experience employment. At the level of institutional arrangements the basic conformation of the state has been maintained, but with a massive expansion in welfare activity and organisation. One important implication of this latter development has been to underline the contradictory basis of a capitalist state increasingly structured to provide welfare services. Alongside this, and effective in all areas of state activity, state institutions have been reorganised with the introduction of further refinement of management practices and procedures of control and work organisation. This has had the effect of introducing a degree of uniformity in control and work practice in all areas of state activity and laid the basis of a 'state' labour process. As part of this development, non-manual state work has been structurally redefined so that this work has taken on features of 'proletarian' work, with the development and extension of state labour processes contributing to and sustaining the complex social arrangements associated with capital accumulation. It is in terms of these experiences that state workers have come to play a part in the trade-union movement.

THE BASIS OF TRADE UNIONISM IN THE STATE SECTOR

Whether state workers join trade unions and act as part of a trade-union collectivity depends to a large extent on their location in the state apparatus. At a general level, jobs are clustered in a number of parallel and rigid hierarchical managerial structures so that state workers are distinguished by employer (statutory corporations, central government, local government) and division within the employment structure (civil service departments). State workers are further defined by type of work (manual or non-manual) as well as a complex hierarchy of grades within the manual and, in particular, the non-manual range. Superimposed upon these general patterns of employment, there is a further set of divisions with reference to gender, so that in the non-manual areas of employment women are concentrated in the lower grades as well as being employed predominantly in the lower levels of each grade band. Such patterns of employment have had a major impact on the trends and structure of trade-union organisation in the state sector.

It is apparent that state workers face a very complex class situation, out of which an attempt is made to build unity and cohesion; failing this, the prevailing divisions tend to be confirmed. The most obvious circumstance of such employment is that workers are distinguished and, as a consequence, divided by the jobs they do. In a single workplace, a school for example, there are many different jobs: ancillary, maintenance, clerical and teaching. While it is possible, and indeed important, that the common concerns and interests are pointed to in these clusters of jobs, it is also the case that the way workers perceive and recognise their interests differs from one set of jobs to another. Such uncertainty and differentiation arises out of the way these varied jobs and associated relationships are experienced by workers, the most obvious being the way in which jobs are grouped into managerial structures, part of the aim of which is to distinguish one set of jobs from another. More precisely, while officially a school is managed by a local authority, in practice it is managed by a head teacher acting within guidelines set by the education department of a local authority. At the same time, ancillary workers and teachers are supervised by head teachers, but both groups of workers may be answerable to different sections of management in the education department. Further, general education policy and practice is the responsibility of the Department of Education and Science, part of central government. While there has been a move towards national determination and direction of education policy, it still remains the case that education workers must build unity out of the diverse, complex and contradictory relationships that characterise the education sector.

One of the most important features of employment in the state and other sectors, with major implications for trade unionism, is the distinction between manual and non-manual work. This distinction has been institutionalised and perpetuated through grading structures, promotion paths, and the terms and conditions of employment, as well as by different levels of pay. With the increasing bureaucratisation and nationalisation of the state apparatus, as well as the growing importance of the state for capital accumulation, state employment structures which formerly served to reinforce the differences between manual and non-manual work have begun to break down. Non-manual work has increasingly been recomposed and redefined as part of a state labour process, concerned with such activities as clerical work, book-keeping, records, the organisation and administration of state policy, guarding or controlling law-breakers, caring for patients, and teaching and instructing others. One further development has been that as state work has increasingly become the object of government policy the relatively privileged position of state employment, with its well-defined and extensive promotion paths, particularly for non-manual males, has been undermined and is now characterised by considerable uncertainty and insecurity of employment.

There has been a recent development in state policies which has had major consequences for trade unions in the state sector, namely the reintroduction of management practices into the civil service and the health service. If the period is examined overall, it is reasonable to conclude that there has been a marked 'proletarianisation' of these areas of employment. In part, this has meant that middle-level grades in the civil service and health service acted as co-ordinators and facilitators of work tasks, with minimal substantive discretionary authority over lower grades. In the process, these grades of workers, particularly in the civil service, came to see that they had interests in common with the lower grades of worker. These trends, however, have recently been reversed, principally through rearrangements regarding financial control and expenditure. A cluster of policies has already been implemented, creating regional financial centres and giving middle levels of management responsibility and discretion for expenditure, although on a limited scale.

To extend the argument further, the changes evident in the structure and organisation of state work have laid the foundations for the emergence of a 'proletarian' consciousness among non-manual state workers (cf. Kelly, 1980, particularly pp. 138–45). As state work has been redefined as proletarian work, with the routines and relationships characteristic of such work, it has become much more likely that the status consciousness characteristic of state workers of the past will be qualified and compromised as the new circumstances of work and employment are confronted. State work has become an object of state policy, exemplified by state policy towards teaching, and it is in these conditions that state workers are most likely to be able to articulate a consciousness as wage workers, experiencing exploitation and subordination alongside other wage workers. If this is so, then it follows that state workers now may be more willing than in the past to engage in trade unionism, sometimes of a militant nature.

It is also under these circumstances of increased employment uncertainty and increased government intervention in pay bargaining that both manual and non-manual workers have looked to their trade unions as one way of confronting these developments. While state employment, particularly in the manual and clerical areas, has long been an area of low pay and part-time work, it is the recruitment of large numbers of women workers that has provided the impetus for the enormous growth of many state-sector unions and their increased involvement in major disputes. Women workers have long been politically and economically segregated from better-paid men workers; they have been employed at the lower levels of the state hierarchy, seemingly with little 'political' muscle or interest in trade unionism. But with the expansion of women's employment in these areas – in the health service, local and central government – in the 1960s and 1970s and an increased recognition by women that they are a 'doubly' oppressed section of the workforce, as workers and as women, there has developed a consciousness that employment rights and concerns are not gender specific; to the extent that they are seen to be so by workers they must be redefined. This has meant that women workers in the state sector have campaigned for and sought access to hitherto 'forbidden' areas of employment and promotion pathways (Crompton and Jones, 1984, pp. 129–66). To illustrate, low pay, which is a feature of most women's employment in the state sector, has become an issue among the trade unions representing state workers. While low pay is not confined to women workers or the state sector, it would appear to be the case that low pay as a 'political' issue has in part been defined by the experience of women working in the state sector.

State workers face considerable difficulties in organising and acting collectively, in joining trade unions and confronting the realities of employment in a capitalist society. At base, the work relationships of state workers are characterised by divisions and separations which are partly overcome through union organisation and action. It is unions which, in the first instance, give some content to the possibility that state workers will challenge the organisation and operation of the state. This is so because unions represent a moment of collectivity in circumstances where state workers are individualised and fragmented. This individualisation occurs through the jobs people do, the employment structures they are grouped in and their places of work, and is expressed through the ideologies that surround their work. Further, at different times in their lives, state workers find themselves relating to the state in ways that are the same as other workers, as patients, claimants, voters, law-abiding or law-breaking citizens. In these circumstances, without unions state workers remain divided and separated from each other; with unions unity and cohesiveness become a possibility, albeit on a limited scale.

THE STRUCTURE OF UNION ORGANISATION

There has been a long tradition of union organisation among state workers. In many instances this dates back to the turn of the century, although non-manual state workers have tended to join trade unions more recently than manual workers. The patterns of union recruitment reveal some very important differences between unions in the state sector, some of which make unity and co-operation between unions difficult. Some unions recruit almost wholly in the state sector, like the National Union of Public Employees (NUPE) and the National and Local Government Officers' Association (NALGO); others recruit in the state sector and elsewhere, like the giant Transport and General Workers' Union (TGWU). In addition some unions, such as the Iron and Steel Trades Confederation (ISTC) have members in the state and non-state sectors, principally as a result of government policies and decisions. Cutting across these patterns, there are unions which only recruit particular occupations, for example the Institute of Professional and Civil Servants (IPCS), or functions of employment, such as the Inland Revenue Staff Federation (IRSF).

These patterns of union organisation are the outcome of the specific history of trade unionism in the state sector. In the main, unions in local and central government were founded as staff associations, representing the interests of particular sections of the workforce, with reference to grades, occupations or areas of work. A major impetus to the development of such organisations was the establishment of Whitley arrangements for major sections of the state apparatus. The Whitley system of negotiation and consultation for the civil service was established in 1918–19 for non-industrial grades, in part because the government accepted that their employees should be subject to the same arrangements as they were advocating for the private sector (see Beaumont, 1981, pp. 21–5; Parris, 1973, ch. 1). In local government, particularly in the non-manual areas, the process of establishing a Whitley system of negotiation and consultation was long drawn out but no less important for unionisation with union campaigns, in the form of lobbying for a Whitley system, providing the rationale for local-government non-manual unionism from the 1920s to the 1940s (Spoor, 1967, pp. 80–244). A key feature of this form of development is that these embryonic unions mirrored the structure of management, in terms of organisation and in the way issues were examined and considered. Subsequent history has involved mergers between these unions, in part indicating a move towards more comprehensive and more adequately resourced unions. Even so, the sectional base of these organisations has meant that co-ordination between these unions has been difficult to achieve.

Alongside this, the patterns of union density (the proportion of workers eligible to join unions who become union members) in the state sector also point to some important variations in trade unionism in different areas of the state. When the main sections of state employment are compared with each other, the following picture emerges. Unions in central government (excluding health services) have been able to increase their membership to very high levels of union density, from 52.9 per cent in 1948 to 91.3 per cent in 1979. In comparison, the unions recruiting health service workers have had lower levels of union density, 42.6 per cent in 1948 rising to 73.7 per cent by 1979. It should be noted that there is some evidence to suggest that unions in the health service were more successful in raising the density of their membership in the 1970s, in spite of very high levels of worker turnover, especially amongst the ancillary levels, with union density rising from 43.4 per cent in 1970 to 73.7 per cent in 1979. Unions in local government, including education, have been able to maintain relatively high levels of union density, 69.4 per cent in 1948 and 77.5 per cent in 1979. In the public corporations unions have increased their density, illustrated by the railways, where union density rose from 88.7 per cent in 1948 to 97.8 per cent in 1979 and, even more dramatically, by water authorities, from 57.0 per cent in 1948 to 92.7 per cent in 1979 (Bain and Price, 1980, p. 77 and Bain and Price, 1983, pp. 14–15).

The increased density of union membership, particularly in local and central government unions, may be explained by a series of developments conducive to an increase in trade union membership. First, in the period from 1960 to 1980, successive governments generally encouraged the use of state-sector industrial-relations machinery and the participation of unions in that machinery. This favourable climate for union participation in negotiation and consultation procedures was, in part, the result of the view government took that, as employer, it should aspire to treat its employees in the manner advocated for other sectors. This recommendation was advanced on the assumption that difficult industrial relations problems could be dealt with under the Whitley and related industrial relations arrangements in the state sector. In effect, this meant giving some substance to the long-standing recognition by government of trade unions in local and central government, as well as imposing a duty on nationalised enterprises to recognise and indeed bargain with the relevant unions in these industries (Kahn Freund, 1954, p. 54; Spoor, 1967, chs. 9, 16, 17). Under these circumstances, unions were able to extend their membership coverage and density.

Second, and related, it is reasonable to assume that with the increased visibility of union involvement in the industrial relations procedures of the state sector, state workers would look to their unions for improvements to their terms and conditions of employment. It is possible that state workers sought to influence and indeed have a say in the way in which their unions were developing and operating in the negotiating structures. In part, this is on the assumption that even in highly centralised unions membership carries with it an ability to influence policy and activity. In support of this claim there is evidence to suggest that where unions have appeared to be effective or active in their pursuit of members' claims, many non-unionists are likely to reconsider their non-membership (Heritage, 1983).

Conversely, as unions become more actively concerned with industrial relations and bargaining, as has been the case in local and central government throughout the 1970s, then unions may become concerned with recruitment and raising the density of their membership. This process was particularly evident towards the end of the 1960s and into the 1970s as unions deliberately set out to recruit women workers, following the increased employment of women in state employment during this period. To illustrate, by 1978 NUPE had 457,000 women members, a 989 per cent increase on 1950, most of whom were concentrated in education (cleaners and school meals), local government (home helps and residential workers) and health services (ancillary workers). A substantial proportion of these were part-time workers. Over the same period, the proportion of women NUPE members rose from 30 per cent to 60 per cent, a remarkable transformation in the gender composition of union membership. Although not on the same scale, similar developments occurred in other unions recruiting state workers, particularly in central and local-government areas. Nevertheless, it must be noted that while attention was given to the recruitment of women workers by unions such as NUPE and the Civil and Public Services Association (CPSA) this was not immediately accompanied by a reconsideration of union policies and objectives. Under such circumstances, union membership for many women workers was a sign of commitment to trade unionism rather than a response to specific union policies directed towards women workers.

In the 1980s, and in line with the contraction of state employment, there has been a marked decline in the absolute levels of union membership in some areas. The decline in union-membership levels in local government has been quite marked, as indicated by the two major unions: the membership of NALGO fell from a high point of 784,297 in 1982 to 766,390 in 1984 and that of NUPE fell from 702,159 in 1982 to 673,445 in 1984 (Trades Union Congress (TUC) records). The decline in union membership in central government, as indicated by the two largest non-industrial civil-service unions, has been more long-term, with CPSA membership falling from 223,884 in 1979 to 149,782 in 1984 and Society of Civil and Public Servants (SCPS) membership falling from 108,697 in 1979 to 85,597 in 1984 (TUC records). Before considering the reasons for this, it is worth noting that this collapse in union membership has been part of a general decline in union membership in the United Kingdom, in both the private and the public sectors of employment. More specifically, the restructuring of the state apparatus in the 1980s has had an impact on union membership. This is especially evident in the case of the civil-service unions referred to above, both of which lost substantial sections of their membership with the privatisation of British Telecom plc. At the same time, it is clear that the general decline in staffing levels and the increased employment of casual and part-time workers has adversely affected union-membership levels. There is also some evidence from union sources to suggest that union density has decreased in some areas of state employment during the 1980s, although unions such as the SCPS have begun to target their recruitment campaigns in more effective ways to meet the reluctance to join the union.

The bargaining and consultation arrangements evident in most sections of state employment, and particularly in local and central government, are predicated on a particular form of union involvement which has had major consequences for the patterns of union organisation and activity. Union participation in the extensive committee and consultative arrangements in the state sector has had the effect of creating generations of union activists whose experience of trade unionism has been largely defined by their experience and involvement in elaborate and complex committee procedures and organisation. Further, the range of facilities provided for this purpose, particularly time-off agreements, has in effect promoted a dependency relationship between many union activists and management. It is on the basis of an acceptance of these bargaining arrangements that facility time is granted. This has had two specific consequences. This system of negotiation has served to educate trade-union leaders in the problems of management as well as providing the basis for remote and non-participative forms of union organisation. While these features of union practice are not inevitable or indeed invariable, the pressures toward these forms of trade unionism have been, historically, quite compelling. The recent developments amongst state trade unions represent, in part, an attempt to go beyond this history.

STRUGGLES IN THE STATE

In the 1970s the pattern of British trade unionism shifted in a dramatic and fundamental way. It was during this period that state-sector unions emerged as unions prepared and, at times, able to challenge government policy and practice. This was a period when local and central-government workers began to organise and campaign against the attempts by successive governments to impose wage restraint and to reduce public expenditure. During this period the majority of national union campaigns and struggles involved state workers, located in the local and central-government areas of employment. With the exception of the steelworkers' strike of 1980 and the more significant miners' struggle from 1984 to 1985, this pattern of union activity has continued into the 1980s. For many state workers, particularly in local and central government, this has meant involvement in union collective action for the first time in their employment lives. While these developments signified a restructuring in the pattern of union activism in Great Britain, in particular the advent of a more active and campaigning trade unionism in the state sector, it is nevertheless the case that these unions have embraced traditional forms of union struggle, particularly emphasising 'economistic' concerns and objectives.

The patterns of union militancy in the state sector have changed, so that in the 1970s and into the 1980s it was more likely that local and central-government workers were involved in principal stoppages (that is, disputes of 50,000 strike days or more) than were public corporation and statutory authority workers (with the exception of the mineworkers). In the 1960s and into the 1970s manual workers, particularly from the statutory authorities and public corporations, were involved in principal stoppages (dock workers 1960, 1961, 1962, 1972, 1975; mineworkers 1961, 1968, 1969, 1970, 1974). Towards the end of the 1960s, state workers who had not been involved in principal stoppages during the earlier part of the decade participated in such stoppages (bus workers 1967, 1968, 1970, 1974, 1978; refuse-workers 1969; teachers 1969, 1974). But, of more significance, it was during the 1970s that many local and central-government workers were involved in principal stoppages for the first time (local-authority manual workers 1970 and 1979; non-industrial civil servants 1973 and 1979; and local authority non-manual workers 1974 and 1978/9). Other state workers with a past history of participation in stoppages, although not in principal stoppages during the 1960s, were also involved in such disputes during the 1970s (steelworkers 1970, 1971, 1972, 1973, 1974, 1976, 1977; post-office workers 1971; gas manual workers 1973; local-authority electricians 1975; airport workers 1977; and firefighters 1977). These trends seemed to come together in 1979, with a threefold increase in striker days, a total of 29,051,000, some 20 million more than the previous year. Although a wide range of workers was involved in strike activity in 1979, a significant proportion of these workers were employed by the state, including railway-workers, hospital ancillary workers and local-authority manual workers (*Employment Gazette*: various issues).

These trends have continued into the 1980s, with state workers becoming more and more likely to participate in principal stoppages (steel workers 1980; teachers 1980 and 1985/6; non-industrial civil servants 1981; nurses and ancillary workers 1982) although there were some notable exceptions to this pattern, such as the print-worker disputes. Alongside this pattern of strike activity, a number of unions have been involved in campaigns and demonstrations which have complemented the strike trends identified above. Nurses, for example, participated in demonstrations in 1974 as part of a national dispute. From the mid 1970s onwards, a number of unions organising in local and central government propagandised, lobbied and demonstrated against the Labour government's policies of public-expenditure cuts. While some of the momentum behind such campaigns has died away over the last six years, with the advent of a Conservative government seemingly impervious to such appeals, they will remain part of the state unions' repertoire of collective activity. This is symbolised by the fruitless years of lobbying and campaigning by university lecturers against the government's higher-education policies (including pay policies), which in 1986 resulted in the first official national strike by university lecturers.

Unions in the state sector have tended to rely on traditional forms of union struggle: strikes, overtime bans, walk-outs, work-to-rules, and the like. On occasion these forms of action have been questioned by union members with regard to their effectiveness and desirability, partly because some action does not have any great impact on the employer. To use an obvious example, a walk-out by a group of recreation workers does not produce an immediate impact on the employer or, for that matter, the community. In contrast, some action can be very effective, although the impact is on those who are dependent on state services rather than on the employer, so that a strike in the Department of Employment may stop claimants receiving unemployment benefit and may, paradoxically, represent a saving through unpaid wages. In these circumstances, some unions have rejected strike action, particularly since many state workers remained ambivalent about such action, and looked to alternatives such as work-ins, parliamentary lobbies, and various types of local demonstrations. For some unions, particularly non-manual unions, this has meant an emphasis on symbolically important rather than economically effective action. In these various ways, state unions have attempted to move beyond an exclusive reliance on traditional forms of union struggle.

The disputes of the 1970s and early 1980s were concerned principally with pay and related issues, and to this extent these struggles appear to conform to the traditional pattern of 'economistic' unionism. This, however, is to overlook the social content of disputes about pay and conditions of employment in two important respects. First, while the increased union activity of state workers in local and central government stemmed primarily from a concern with pay and related matters, it is also the case that this activity brought into question, if not challenged, a fundamental feature of government policies. For at least three decades incomes policies, formal and informal, have been a central feature of the economic policies of successive governments. Although unions tended to define their campaigns and disputes in narrowly 'economistic' ways, the action often undermined and brought into question government plans and policies. Second, and related, union activity has also acquired a broader significance as unions have campaigned to defend the terms and conditions of employment in circumstances where government policies have been directed towards a major restructuring and reorganisation of state institutions. In effect, this has meant that state-sector unions have come to question the rationale and procedures of this restructuring, particularly with reference to the Conservative governments' privatisation policies.

But the increased prominence of state-sector unions in the local and central-government areas has not been without problems. Along with increased involvement in negotiations and industrial disputes, some unions have displayed a concern with their patterns of organisation. It has not always been easy for unions in the state sector to effect a unity within their unions and between unions. While this is not an unusual problem, it acquired a particular urgency for state-sector unions as governments began to implement common policies towards the vast majority of state workers, particularly with regard to the terms and conditions of state employment as well as the detail of state restructuring. As noted above, it has been common for unions to organise in relation to divisions in management structures, so that unions recruiting central-government workers are often organised by government departments. For instance, the largest non-industrial civil-service union, the CPSA, is organised into a number of sections: Department of Health and Social Security Section, Ministry of Defence Section, and so on. While this form of organisation was regarded as adequate in the past, this union, in conjunction with other civil-service unions, has begun to consider ways of establishing inter-section as well as inter-union links between analogous union sections for the specific purpose of facilitating union action in disputes. Unions have also tended to organise in relation to broad occupational bands, as indicated by grading structures, so that in local government NALGO recruits non-manual workers and NUPE recruits manual workers. All the same, the events of the past twenty-five years have brought these arrangements into question and resulted in the establishment of embryonic links between the two unions. At a more specific level, occupational hierarchy has been reflected in union organisation and structure so that it has been relatively common for senior local-government officials to hold branch office in NALGO. But even this practice has come to be questioned through the increased propensity of lower-grade government workers to seek nomination and election to branch office. The difficulties of achieving union co-operation have been addressed, albeit tentatively and cautiously.

It is against this background of issues that union democracy has become a question for many state-sector unions. In general, unions in the state sector are highly centralised, with limited membership participation and leadership accountability. In part, this mode of organisation has reflected the ways in which these unions have been incorporated into negotiating and bargaining structures and, in these circumstances, indicates a union preoccupation with a style of organisation that facilitates centralised negotiations rather than one based on membership involvement in union policy-making. As a corollary, locally based participative activity has tended to be devalued and subordinated to centralised union structures and concerns. Nevertheless, union organisation and membership involvement has become a consideration in some unions, especially when confronted with the need to mobilise memberships to prosecute union claims and to defend past union achievements.

In recent years, there have been moves in central and local-government unions to include some provision for local negotiations, in part to facilitate the development of more actively involved union memberships. One such example occurred in 1978 when NALGO social workers campaigned for a month to obtain the right to negotiate directly with their own employers and so create the possibility of local negotiations: the result was a framework agreement for local negotiations. This approach to bargaining, however, has not been embraced by all unions, as illustrated by civil-service unions, which have campaigned against local and regional agreements on the grounds that these would open up the possibility of regional pay bargaining with the prospect of regional differentials. At the same time, it should be noted that there have been long-standing arrangements for local bargaining in statutory authorities and public corporations, with respect at least to the terms and conditions of employment, if not to pay. But even in these areas of employment there has been considerable debate and discussion about such arrangements, particularly when they give rise to local and regional earnings differentials, as has been the case in the productivity agreements in the mining industry towards the end of the 1970s. Thus the very degree to which such agreements may facilitate more localised union involvement in the context of centralised bargaining and consultation arrangements may also be the foundation for division within the unions.

The disputes and campaigns of the 1970s have provided the impetus for some unions to take steps to reorganise so as to enable a more widespread involvement and participation in the determination and implementation of union policies. While for the national leaderships in such unions the motive may be largely instrumental, to allow the unions to pursue centrally determined policies more actively and, it is assumed, more effectively, any provisions for more comprehensive membership participation may lead in the long term to a challenge to the long-established centralised leaderships in these unions. Two unions stand out in this respect, NUPE and SCPS, both of which commissioned inquiries (in 1974 and 1979–82 respectively) and as a consequence undertook substantial reorganisation, particularly through the introduction and establishment of systems of workplace representation (Fryer, 1974; Drake *et al.*, 1980, 1982). In the case of NUPE, its subsequent prominence as a relatively active state-sector union was facilitated, at least in part, by the 1974 reorganisation. Other unions have also undertaken to reorganise their structures, through the provision for locally based systems of representation, the most notable being that of NALGO, which was initiated in the 1970s.

For many state workers who identify with state policy and practice, the developments of the last two decades have been unwelcome. Given the position of many local and central-government workers, it is frequently the case that they will argue that industrial action represents the negation of the objectives of their jobs; industrial action may hurt the very people who are most dependent on these workers. For example, Department of Employment workers often deal on a routine basis with unemployed people who are receiving benefits and may be involved in training programmes of various sorts. This practice may be the basis of a scepticism on the part of these workers about certain types of industrial action or even a hostility to the suggestion that they should strike or engage in similar action. Such differences of opinion have often been evident amongst workers employed in the health service, particularly during the 1982 nurses' and ancillary-workers' dispute. This reveals an uncertainty and division amongst many state workers about their trade unionism, a feature of the cultural and ideological patterns of their employment and which may serve to inhibit militancy on their part. Nevertheless, such views and outlooks have been partially negated in the course of the development of active forms of trade unionism during the 1970s and into the 1980s.

In short, over the last two decades, the patterns of union organisation and action in the state sector have changed, particularly in local and central-government areas. The responses by state workers to government pay policies, deteriorating conditions of employment and the reorganisation and restructuring of the state have transformed the structure of union organisation and activity, with state-sector unions beginning to challenge key features of government policies. There have, however, been important differences in the responses which signify the embryonic and tentative character of trade union-ism in this sector of employment. The response of central- and local-govern-ment workers in the last decade has been to resort to trade-union action principally over wage levels and related conditions of employment. So in the early 1980s nurses and ancillary workers and civil servants were each involved in major disputes with the government over wage issues. With regard to reorganisation and job loss, the concern of state workers, with the notable exception of mineworkers, has been restricted to less direct action in the form of campaigns, including demonstrations and lobbying. Nevertheless, it is important to note that while such issues have not been to the forefront of strike and related activity by these workers they have constituted part of the back-ground to these disputes. In view of the continued prospect that state workers will face these problems again in the future, it is probable that militant action against government plans to restructure the state apparatus will occur more frequently than in the past. This is made even more likely with government proposals to further subordinate local government to central-government control and direction as well as the continued adherence to the policy of transferring state services to the private sector.

THE SCOPE AND LIMITS OF STATE TRADE UNIONISM

The pattern of trade unionism identified above is one that is rooted in the way that state employment has been restructured and reconstituted as part of a state labour process. Important segments of non-manual work have been proletarianised, and the boundary between management and proletarian forms of work has been redrawn. These developments have meant that the class position of state workers can be identified more precisely than has been the case in the past, and they have meant that this 'newly' proletarianised workforce has been more likely to embrace trade unionism than in the past. All the same, the advent of more active forms of trade unionism has been part of a more broadly based development involving manual and non-manual sections of the state workforce and including large numbers of part-time women workers, particularly in the areas of health, social services and education.

None the less, while there has been a general development towards more active forms of trade unionism, it is necessary to note that it has been accompanied by tentativeness and hesitancy on the part of many state workers. For many state workers there is a dilemma in acting as trade unionists pursuing their concerns about pay and employment conditions and at the same time being employed as the providers of socially necessary goods and services. Although this dilemma may not always be acknowledged or even recognised, it is still the case that trade unionism in the state sector confronts this dilemma in a variety of ways. The problem becomes even more acute in situations where unions have often found themselves unable to do much more than defend the basic employment rights of members. While this need not be an inevitable circumstance of union organisation, it is as well to recognise that it is, at least, one important feature of the way many unions have organised.

This examination of state workers and their trade unions indicates a problem with much of the literature about the contemporary capitalist state. As noted above, there has been a tendency in this writing either to ignore the internal organisation of state institutions and the position of state workers in these institutions or, where this has not been the case, to emphasise the degree of interconnectedness and unity between and within state institutions (e.g. Miliband, 1969, 1982 and Poulantzas, 1973). The result has been to ignore the class character and basis of the state apparatus and the institutions that constitute it. It has been argued in this study that to understand the class position of state workers it is necessary to examine the way the state apparatus has been reorganised so as to comprise a state labour process. As this has occurred, managerial boundaries have been redrawn and state workers increasingly have come to occupy class positions as wage labourers.

The argument presented in this essay suggests that a comprehensive account of state employment in a capitalist society requires consideration of the following. First, to go beyond the one-sided emphasis in the literature, it is essential to examine the way in which the state labour process is based on a contradiction between contributing directly to capital accumulation and providing for social needs. Second, and in line with arguments about the restructuring of the capitalist state, it is material to the analysis to render systematically the way the distinction between managerial and proletarian work has been redrawn with major implications for the way state workers are located in the state apparatus. Third, in order to appreciate and understand the dilemmas and prospects of state trade unions it is important to locate the patterns and structures of unionism in the context of the state labour process and the way that process has been restructured and recomposed. Such considerations of the capitalist state are a necessary part of providing an assessment and evaluation of the changing patterns and structures of collective action by state workers over the last two decades.

It has been a theme in the literature on the capitalist state to focus on the social and political unity of the state apparatus. Although it is necessary to consider the degree of interconnectedness and unity both within and between state institutions, it is equally important to examine the complexity of the internal organisation of the state. Such a consideration involves an examination of the contradictory character of the state apparatus, the systematic tensions between subordination to capital and the provision of needs, between work as waged labour and work as service. This in turn requires a consideration of the differential bases of state work, the complex division of labour evident in state institutions and the competition and division between different sectors of the state, as well as the examples of individual and collective resistance by state workers (London–Edinburgh Weekend Return Group, 1980).

An indication of the significance of the patterns and trends in state work is obtained by considering the state as the key form of political domination in advanced capitalist societies, the state being a particular form of the capital relation (see Holloway and Picciotto, 1977, 1978 and cf. Frankel, 1983). In this view, the state is integral to the organisation and operation of capitalist society. On the one hand, the state functions to provide the means for productive activity, through direct intervention in the economy and through a complex of welfare and coercive measures and practices. On the other hand, the state is organised to respond to and meet social needs, albeit in highly mediated ways. Following on from this, and in line with theses about the basic contradiction of the capital relation, there is a prospect of frequent change and reorganisation of the state apparatus as the circumstances and conditions for capital accumulation alter. To illustrate, the patterns of expansion in state employment evident throughout the post-war years were the outcome of a major structural transformation of the capitalist state. This transformation had the effect of consolidating the centrality of the state for the processes of capital accumulation, particularly in the 'welfare' areas of the state apparatus (cf. Therborn, 1984, pp. 25–9). Such a development meant that the increase in state employment during the post-war period constituted the restructuring of the state itself and, as a corollary, the recent contraction of state employment signifies a further restructuring of the state. Such restructuring, however, is no simple and determinate development, but is the outcome of a complex of development involving political parties and government policies, the dominance of capital, and patterns of resistance both within and beyond the state apparatus.

It is within the context of restructuring and in view of the distinctive features of state employment that there has been some questioning of state policies and practice by unions in the state sector. To counter the trends in state restructuring, some unions have begun to move beyond the narrowly economistic preoccupations of the past. One example where union innovation and initiative has seemed possible has been in the local-government area. It is at this level of state organisation that tentative steps have been taken to redefine the experience of state workers and the role of unions with reference to the relationship between unions and local electoral representatives, and between local-government workers and the community. In this respect the form and character of local government has, in part, provided an opportunity for unions to develop and extend their repertoire of concerns in new and distinctive ways. But to date this has largely remained a possibility. There has, for example, been no sustained and extensive attempt to redefine union structure and modes of operation so as to meet the opportunities that may have been provided by the attempt on the part of some local authorities to introduce modern variants of municipal socialism. Even so, the constraints on local government and the continuing trends towards further centralisation and control suggest that this opportunity may be short-lived, although it is likely to remain an issue in local government, and possibly elsewhere.

As to the future, it can be expected that unions in the state sector will increasingly come to occupy the forefront of the union stage. This, however, will not be without difficulty and will require that these unions address some very difficult questions. To date, unions have tended to accept an 'economistic' definition of union concerns and objectives. Indeed, it could be argued that this has been a source of strength, as these unions have made the transition from relative quiescence and non-participation to more active forms of trade unionism. But there are clearly limits to this mode of organisation and activity, especially in circumstances where a major restructuring of state institutions is occurring. It would seem that one option before these unions is to embrace a 'political' definition of union concerns and objectives and address the contradictory nature of state employment in a direct and immediate way. In turn this would require that unions in the state sector reassess their reliance on traditional modes of collective action, such as strikes and the like, and begin to look at tactics which may begin to challenge the social relations of capitalist production, including the part played by the state in affirming and sustaining these relations.

At present, innovative developments in the modes of union organisation and activity would appear to be extremely unlikely. But it should not be forgotten that the advent of more active forms of unionism in the state sector is very recent and has meant that these unions have occasionally gone beyond boundaries of traditional union organisation and have begun to question the predominant patterns of union organisation and activity, albeit in a limited way. In part, such developments indicate that it is in the state sector, particularly in local and central government, that unions may be able to step beyond the economistic preoccupations of most unions and to reconsider the forms and patterns of union organisation and action. This is not to suggest that unions outside the state will become irrelevant or inactive but it is to submit that the very distinctiveness of state employment may provide the opportunities for development of imaginative and innovative forms of union organisation and action. For these reasons, it remains a possibility that these unions could eventually come to occupy a strategic position in the struggle between labour and capital.

REFERENCES

Abramovitz, M. and V. Eliasberg, 1957. *The Growth of Public Employment in Great Britain.* Princeton, Princeton University Press

Bain, G. and R. Price, 1980. *Profiles of Union Growth: A Comparative Statistical Portrait of Eight Countries.* Oxford, Basil Blackwell

   1983. 'Union growth: dimensions, determinants and destiny', in G. Bain, ed., *Industrial Relations in Britain.* Oxford, Basil Blackwell

Bains Report, 1972: Study Group on Local Authority Management Structure. *The New Local Authorities, Management and Structure.* London, HMSO

Barker, A., ed., 1982. *Quangos in Britain.* London, Macmillan

Beaumont, P., 1981. *Government as Employer – Setting an Example.* London, Royal Institute of Public Administration

Boddy, M. and C. Fudge, 1984. *Local Socialism? Labour Councils and New Left Alternatives.* London, Macmillan

Clegg, H., 1982. 'How public sector pay systems have gone wrong before', in J. Gretton and J. Harrison, eds., *How much are public servants worth?* Oxford, Basil Blackwell

Cockburn, C., 1977. *The Local State.* London, Pluto Press

Crompton, R. and G. Jones, 1984. *White-Collar Proletariat: Deskilling and Gender in Clerical Work.* London, Macmillan

Department of Employment, *Employment Gazette*, various issues

Department of Employment and Productivity, 1971. *British Labour Statistics: Historical Abstract 1886–1968.* London, Her Majesty's Stationery Office

Drake, P., P. Fairbrother, R. Fryer and J. Murphy, 1980. *Which Way Forward? An Interim Report for the Society of Civil and Public Servants.* Coventry, Department of Sociology, University of Warwick

Drake, P., P. Fairbrother, R. Fryer and G. Stratford, 1982. *A Programme For Union Democracy: The Review of the Organisation and Structure of the Society of Civil and Public Servants.* Coventry, Department of Sociology, University of Warwick

Duncan, S. and M. Goodwin, 1982. 'The local state and restructuring social relations: theory and practice', *International Journal of Urban and Regional Research,* 6: 157–86

Frankel, B., 1983. *Beyond the State? Dominant Theories and Socialist Strategies.* London, Macmillan

Fryer, R., A. Fairclough and T. Manson, 1974. *Organisation and Change in the National Union of Public Employees.* Coventry, Department of Sociology, University of Warwick

Garrett, J., 1980. *Managing the Civil Service.* London, Heinemann

Hakim, C., 1979. 'Occupational segregation', *Department of Employment Research Paper,* no. 9

Heritage, J., 1983. 'Feminisation and unionisation: a case study from banking', in E. Gamarnikow, D. Morgan, J. Purvis and D. Taylorson eds., *Gender, Class and Work.* London, Heinemann

Hodgwood, B. and M. Keating eds., 1982. *Regional Government in England.* Oxford, Clarendon Press

Holloway, J. and S. Picciotto, 1977. 'Capital, crisis and the state', *Capital and Class,* 2: 76–101 eds., 1978. *State and Capital: A Marxist Debate.* London, Edward Arnold

Kahn Freund, O., 1954. 'Legal framework', in A. Flanders and H. Clegg, eds., *The System of Industrial Relations in Great Britain: Its History, Law and Institutions.* Oxford, Basil Blackwell

Kelly, M., 1980. *White-Collar Proletariat: The Industrial Behaviour of British Civil Servants.* London, Routledge and Kegan Paul

Klein, R., 1983. *The Politics of the National Health Service.* London, Longmans

London–Edinburgh Weekend Return Group, 1980. *In And Against The State.* Rev. ed., London, Pluto Press

Miliband, R., 1969. *The State in Capitalist Society*. London, Weidenfeld and Nicolson
   1982. *Capitalist Democracy in Britain*. Oxford, Oxford University Press

Morrison, H., 1983. 'Employment in the public and private sectors 1976 to 1982', *Economic Trends*, 352 (February), 82–9

Offe, C., 1984. 'Theses on the theory of the state', in C. Offe, ed. by J. Keane, *Contradictions of the Welfare State*. London, Hutchinson

Parris, H., 1973. *Staff Relations in the Civil Service*. London, George Allen and Unwin

Pattison, I., 1973. *The New Scottish Local Authorities: Organisation and Management Structures*. Edinburgh, Scottish Development Department, Working Group on Scottish Local Government Management Structures

Poulantzas, N., 1973. *Political Power and Social Classes*. London, New Left Books

Richardson, I., 1985. 'Employment in the public and private sectors 1979 to 1985', *Economic Trends*, 386 (December): 90–8.

Semple, M., 1979. 'Employment in the public and private sectors 1961–78', *Economic Trends*, 313 (November): 90–108.

Spoor, A., 1967. *White Collar Union: Sixty Years of NALGO*. London, Heinemann

Therborn, G., 1984. 'The prospects of labour and the transformation of advanced capitalism', *New Left Review*, 145 (May–June): 5–38

Trades Union Congress 1979, 1980, 1981, 1982, 1983, 1984, 1985. *Report of [year] Annual Trades Union Congress*. London, Trades Union Congress

11

Controlling interests: technology, state control and democracy

JOHN STREET

One of the most distinctive features of the capitalist state has been its ever-increasing links with modern technology. Both the technology and the state have grown in their dependence on each other. Analysts of very different political persuasions have observed the way in which technological development has relied on state support for the funding of research and for the creation of a suitable infrastructure; while, at the same time, the state has come to depend on technological innovation for its own political goals and for attempts to maintain its legitimacy (Galbraith, 1974; Marcuse, 1968; Ellul, 1964). Such commentators have also suggested that advances in technology have seemed to exert a controlling influence on the direction and character of political change. However, although such observations are commonplace their implications have received rather less attention. Political theorists, for example, have been slow to consider the consequences of technology for the idea of democracy. And students of policy-making and political institutions have yet to devote much attention to the ways in which high technology constrains and influences the state and its agents. These two issues are the concern of this chapter. They can be combined into a single question: how does technology affect the ideal of democracy and the practice of state control?

No single chapter can, of course, do justice to this large topic. I shall, therefore, limit my reflections to Britain and to two particular recent, important examples of high technology, nuclear power and microelectronics. Nuclear power is caught in a web which involves substantial state subsidy, national and international markets, and a complicated network of agencies, all of which claim some responsibility for the industry's management. In the case of microelectronics, the state appears to make little or no effort to control policy directly, preferring instead to leave such matters to the private sector. Paradoxically, although the case of microelectronics appears to fall outside the ambit of state control, it perhaps raises more fundamental questions about the relationship between democracy and the state than does nuclear power. Each example illustrates a different connection between the state and the technology, and thereby raises different questions about what democratic control involves. And yet they share much too. Both nuclear power and micro-electronics are technologies with long lead times, requiring considerable advance investment and state involvement. Both examples raise important issues for those concerned with the need to ensure a democratic society. Is it possible for these technologies to be subjected to democratic state control? Can the principles of democracy – responsible government, the accountability of politicians, the implementation of the popular will – be applied to the everyday behaviour of the state? Or is there a divide between democratic theory and actual practice which requires a change in expectations for democracy and definitions of it? Or should the role of the state be changed to comply with the democratic ideal? My own concern here is to examine the problems that technology poses for those who seek a modern, democratic state, and to give an assessment of some of the solutions. Before considering the technologies themselves, it helps to consider the principles which have traditionally shaped reformist thinking on the nature of the democratic state. Only then can we understand the nature of the problems which technologies pose and the background out of which the reforms emerge.

THE IDEA OF DEMOCRATIC STATE CONTROL

British socialist ideas of democratic state control are typically tied to discussion of public ownership (Weiner, 1960). The familiar words of the Labour Party's Clause IV suggest that socialism is, *inter alia*, 'the common ownership of the means of production, distribution and exchange, and the best obtainable system of popular administration and control of each industry and service'. Giving practical form to these words has occupied the British Labour movement for most of this century. Gradually, democratic socialism has come to be thought of in terms of public ownership, and in the institutional form of nationalisation. This was the interpretation of Clause IV which was argued out in the 1930s and implemented by the 1945–51 Labour governments (Street, 1981).

Democracy, understood as the popular will, was said to be expressed through the elected government. Nationalisation was the means by which that government could plan and manage the economy, the means by which the popular will could be enacted. Public ownership was seen by socialists to embody the spirit and reality of democracy. This belief was based on the assumption that the running of an industry was a scientific matter, and that managerial decisions were a matter of logic and not politics (Webb, 1920; Clegg, 1951). If management was a science, it could be assumed, first, that the policies adopted would simply reflect the information put before it; and second, that once told what its general policy objects were, management could be freed of any direct political involvement.

This kind of argument informed the case made by Herbert Morrison, one of the chief architects of democratic–socialist ideas of public ownership. Morrison (1933) suggested that the best type of public ownership was one which combined state ownership with traditional forms of management and with limited political oversight. Removing the incentive for private profit, and replacing it with the idea of public good, was sufficient. The workforce would be consulted, but would not substitute for management. The workers would simply act as a useful source of additional information. Participation was not necessary to ensure their commitment and efforts; these would be guaranteed by the fact that the workers were now working for public rather than private interests. Successful management of public enterprises depended on disinterested experts working under the general direction of the elected leaders. Despite considerable dispute within the labour movement, the Morrisonian version of public ownership triumphed and was the model for the immediate post-war nationalisation programme (Chester, 1975).

There were, therefore, five features of democratic control established within the idea of public ownership: (1) the emphasis on the government as the main actor in the democratic process; (2) the view of government as embodying a collective popular will; (3) the belief in the need for centrally planned forms of social and economic control; (4) the separation of political and managerial responsibility; (5) the distinction made between political and managerial or administrative responsibility, which rests on the assumption that objective decision-making is a realistic possibility.

Even a cursory examination of Britain's nationalisation programme suggests that the ideas and the practice were flawed. The formal rules suggested a demarcation between 'general policy' and 'day-to-day administration'. This distinction, which Morrison made much of (Morrison, 1933, p. 280), was intended to separate the work of the national board from that of the responsible minister or department. Ministers were required to appoint the board, approve capital and research investment, control borrowing and use of reserve funds, and to set general guidelines for the board to follow. The board, in turn, was responsible for the everyday operations of the industry (Sloman, 1978).

Such distinctions are more suitable for formal purposes than for practical ones. It is not intuitively obvious where administration ends and general oversight begins, and yet this was the separation envisaged by the constitution of nationalised industries. And it is quite obvious that that distinction remains largely one of political convenience. Not only is the autonomy of management ignored when short-term political wishes are to be met, but also the function and activities of nationalised industry are largely determined by their role in servicing the demands of the wider national and international economy, and owe little to the popular will (Redwood, 1980; O'Connor, 1973; Holland, 1975). However we characterise the activities of nationalised industry (and, of course, no easy generalisation can be made to cover all forms of public ownership or all types of publicly owned industry), no simple congruence can be found between actual practice and ideas of democratic state control. The publicly owned enterprise attempts to manage competing market interests and state interests, while it also tries to serve its own bureaucratic interests. Herbert Morrison himself recognised these conflicting pulls. 'The public corporation', he wrote, 'must be no mere capitalist business, the be-all and end-all of which is profit and dividends' (Morrison, 1933, p. 156). But he expected the nationalised industry to meet other economic criteria: 'it will, quite properly, be expected to pay its way' (Morrison, 1933, p. 157). Morrison's prescription for public-service and economic efficiency captures one of the main tensions within public ownership. The political legitimation for such enterprises has to meet criteria of democracy and of economic efficiency, but the conditions under which nationalised industries have to operate, and the management structure which orders their activities, make it almost impossible for them to call upon the allegiance of those whom the industries are intended to serve. While the democratic rationale remains part of conventional socialist wisdom, it is constantly threatened and undermined by economic and administrative realities (Offe, 1984; Habermas, 1976). And if this is true for the conventional object of state control, then it is even more true for the new objects of state control and of democratic socialist reforms.

NUCLEAR POWER

Although the development of the nuclear-power industry was only possible by virtue of politically directed state initiative, its actual management has, in fact, been beyond the officially recognised sources of political control, and may, in principle, be beyond democratic control.

The origins of Britain's nuclear power industry lie in the Attlee government's decision to develop an independent nuclear weapon (Gowing, 1964 and 1974). The fuel for the weapons programme had to be home-produced, and for this it was necessary to build atomic piles. These were devices which were able to create radioactive uranium in sufficient quantities and of sufficient quality to serve in the weapons. Initially, the atomic pile had no purpose beyond this. However, the same process that created military fuel could be used for civilian purposes. Indeed, in the beginning it had been assumed by scientists that the only use for nuclear fission was civil, and that the atom bomb was technically impossible. The Manhattan Project changed this, with the result that, for Britain, civil nuclear power was a by-product of military goals (Gowing, 1964).

The development of civil nuclear power arose from two particular concerns. First, it had a public-relations role: to appease popular worries about the dangers of nuclear technology, and to present nuclear power as benign and socially useful. Second, it appeared to offer a source of cheap energy. For the 1950s, it was the former role that was most evident. The first power stations, though presented as machines for making 'free' energy, were in fact much less efficient than other, existing forms of energy generation (Gowing, 1974, ch. 19; Patterson, 1976, pp. 49–55). Their design made this inevitable, since it was guided by the particular needs of weapons-fuel creation.

Not only was the design shaped by the initial military needs which nuclear power was to service, its persistence within the British nuclear power industry was ensured by the internal structure of the nuclear power decision-making process (Williams, 1980). The original design, for military, geographical and technical reasons, was based on the use of a gas-cooled technology. And it was in this particular technology that the relevant nuclear institutions – the United Kingdom Atomic Energy Authority (UKAEA), the Central Electricity Generating Board (CEGB), etc. – developed their expertise. The 'problems' they addressed themselves to were those of producing a more efficient gas-cooled reactor – hence Britain's commitment in the late 1950s to the Advanced Gas-Cooled Reactor (AGR). The possibility of alternative designs (not to mention alternatives to nuclear power) were effectively ruled out by the corporate interests which were established by the creation of a nuclear power community (Williams, 1980, ch. 2). Only as the shortcomings of the gas-cooled technology became increasingly obvious (and increasingly public) did a lobby emerge for an alternative, pressurised water reactor (the PWR). But the appearance of this new policy was almost entirely dependent on the politics of the nuclear community, and the AGR programme was continued long after its inadequacies had been exposed (Williams, 1980, pp. 197–230). Not that the PWR option was necessarily any better. Support for it derived from the bureaucratic interests of those within the nuclear industry and from the financial interests of the General Electric Company (GEC) who were keen to manufacture the British PWR (Cannell and Chudleigh, 1983).

It can be argued that the history of Britain's nuclear-power policy owes as much to the internal divisions within the nuclear industry as to the overall context of state planning or economic conditions. It is equally clear that politicians have been obliged to follow, rather than direct, changes within the nuclear industry. They have always been dependent on the nuclear industry for advice and for the options open to them (Sedgemore, 1980, ch. 4). It is difficult to see the government as an independent actor in the emergence of nuclear-power policy. Not surprisingly, the emergent policy resulted from the competition between claims and aspirations of a variety of interested parties, whose own fortunes fluctuated according to their relative position within the network of institutions and corporate interests which make up the nuclear community. In these circumstances what can we say about state control and democracy?

Some socialists are tempted to argue that the problems of control posed by nuclear power are, in fact, problems of capitalism; that changes at the level of the economic system will eliminate the difficulties posed by nuclear power (Spence, 1982). It has been suggested that the evolution of nuclear policy, and the state's role in it, can be explained in terms of the overriding importance of capitalist interests in the process. There are a number of reasons for supposing this to be the case. There is, for example, the leaked Cabinet minute which revealed that the Conservative government's decision to develop a large PWR programme was specifically intended to break the hold of the power workers, and particularly the miners (Bunyard, 1981, p. 55). Similarly, much might be made of the role played by GEC and its former chairman, Sir Arnold Weinstock, in the lobbying of the Department of Energy. GEC were substantial shareholders in the National Nuclear Corporation (NNC), the conglomerate responsible for the manufacture of nuclear-power reactors. GEC were very keen to see Britain adopt the United States's PWR rather than the British AGR, because only the former seemed to offer the prospect of substantial overseas sales and profits. And when Tony Benn, as Secretary of State for Energy, decided in favour of the AGR, GEC cut back its investment in the NNC substantially, forcing the government to carry yet more of the financial burden (Sedgemore, 1980, pp. 118ff.). However, such evidence, though revealing, does not make the case that nuclear-power policy simply served capitalist interests. As Wolfgang Rudig (1983) argues, emphasis on capitalist interests tends to obscure the role played by the state and to distract attention from the military priorities which underlay the development of nuclear power.

Rudig suggests that the central agent in the development of nuclear power has been the state. The development of nuclear power depended on 'the coincidence of essential insights in atomic physics and the Second World War' (Rudig, 1983, p. 118). Further, the survival of the nuclear industry has relied upon the support of government precisely because of the difficulty of establishing it as an economically viable proposition (Elliott, 1978). This latter argument is sustained by comparison of the performance of the state in countries such as West Germany, America, France and Britain. Only in countries where nuclear power has received the backing of the state has it survived. As a capitalist venture nuclear power has proved peculiarly unsuccessful. There are areas in which profits can be made (uranium mining and fuel fabrication), but for the most part the 'nuclear industry has made tremendous losses' (Rudig, 1983, pp. 120–8).

If we accept the integral role played by the state, we are then left to ask why the state is interested. There are a number of explanations to be offered. First, there is the weapons connection. The state's interest in military defence and nuclear weapons created a strong incentive for the development of a nuclear-power industry. Second, this initial decision created an institutional lobby within the state which it found difficult to resist. Third, while the use of nuclear power to break groups like the miners may not be attributed directly to 'capitalist' reasoning, it does seem to fit within a view of the state which sees it as intent upon increasing its own security and authority. Fourth, as Rudig suggests, there are further state-related security interests: 'energy security' (1983, p. 129). Without acting as a capitalist, the state is required to provide the conditions for capitalist accumulation and production. The sponsorship of nuclear power is an example of the state seeking to promote a new area of industrial production.

If nuclear power is only tangentially connected to capitalism, then the focus of those concerned with democratic control turns to the state itself. This is Tony Benn's argument, itself a consequence both of his commitment to democratic socialism and his experience at the Department of Energy. For Benn, nuclear power, just like any other area of government responsibility, must be subject to parliamentary scrutiny and popular control, since technology is central to the way we live and since important decisions 'must ultimately be made by the people as a whole' (Benn, 1982, p. 101). Any failure to ensure democratic control over technology leads to 'institutional obsolescence' (Benn, 1980, p. 109).

While at the Department of Energy in 1976, Benn was expected to make a number of crucial decisions about Britain's nuclear-power programme. Although he had little opportunity to question the desirability of nuclear power itself, he was called upon to choose between the competing reactor designs. In making the choice, Benn felt himself unable to carry out what he considered to be his democratic function. In evidence to the Sizewell Inquiry, Benn said:

I had a meeting with all my officials, and they were unanimous under the permanent secretary we should adopt the PWR, and I declined to accept that, and as a result they refused to draft a paper for me to say what I wanted. (Benn, 1983, p. 19)

But a recalcitrant civil service was not his only problem. He had also to contend with the lobbying of the vested commercial interests and their allies within Whitehall, not least of whom was the Department of Energy's Scientific Adviser, Sir Walter Marshall (who later was to pioneer the introduction of the PWR from his new post as head of the CEGB). These pressures were compounded by the minister's lack of direct control over bodies like the CEGB. Benn felt he had no option but to include a prototype PWR in the new programme.

It is this kind of experience which informs Benn's view of what is necessary for democratic control of nuclear technology. One of his main targets is, not

surprisingly, the civil service's control over the information available to ministers. As he told the Sizewell Inquiry, 'if I had known in 1977/78 what I now
know about the sale of plutonium for American weapons, I would have
conducted the argument completely differently' (Benn, 1983, p. 20). His
argument is clear: 'It is very difficult even for Ministers to get all the information necessary, and this does make it hard, therefore, to retain and develop
democratic control' (Benn, 1983, p. 15). Benn's prescription for democratic
decision-making places considerable emphasis on information; in *Arguments
for Democracy* he lists ten questions which Ministers must put to scientists and
technologists – about benefits to the community, about the risks and the
vulnerable groups, about resource demand and employment prospects, about
the alternatives, and about the problems of stopping the project once begun
(Benn, 1982, pp. 96–7).

Accompanying his demand for greater information, Benn also anticipates
greater ministerial power. For this, decision-making power is to be centralised, and the autonomy presently enjoyed by organisations like the CEGB
is to be curtailed. Beyond this, Benn appears to have few specific proposals.
Perhaps this is not altogether surprising; his commitment to popular mandates
and the power of argument seems to obviate the need for substantial structural
reforms in the particular area of nuclear power (Benn, 1985). Democratic
decisions about nuclear power seem, for Benn, to pose no special problems
which cannot be solved by his general programme of reforms.

Clearly, the instances of civil-service disobedience and deception represent
obvious targets for reform. It is equally clear that in an ideally democratic
world we would want answers to Benn's 'Ten Questions for Scientists'.
However, it is also true that, on the one hand, reform of the civil service may be
inadequate, and that, on the other, the questions may make impossible
demands.

This scepticism is warranted, in part, by the nature of nuclear technology
itself. Even with hindsight and with a wholly impartial civil service, it is not
obvious which reactor would be most appropriate. The present disagreement
between the English and Scottish electricity boards over just this question
neatly expresses the dilemmas involved (Fairhall, 1985): if those with direct
knowledge of the technology cannot decide, how can a popularly elected
representative, however well informed, make a better decision? Anyway the
ideal of impartial advice is undermined by the conditions under which knowledge is acquired. Knowledge of the merits of a PWR or AGR derives from
experience of working on and with them, not by means of some independent
vantage point above the scientific fray. In high technology, expertise and
partiality are almost inevitably linked (Williams, 1980).

In the same way, high technology depends on state finance, and the state
depends on organisations like the Atomic Energy Authority and GEC for the

implementation of its projects (Rudig, 1983). In creating this dependence relationship, governments inevitably restrict their freedom of action and find themselves part of a corporatist network in which early policy decisions set the precedent for later ones. Alternative sources of energy or conservation policies become increasingly costly or increasingly risky, given the decision to invest in nuclear power. These are simple facts of policy-making, but they seem to be ignored by Benn's reforms. Put crudely, it is not clear that a Bennite democracy would have taken substantially different decisions about nuclear power than the undemocratic decisions of actual governments.

Benn's response to the need to secure democratic control over nuclear power does not differ greatly from the model of democratic control applied to nationalised industry. The structure of the industry and the nature of the technology remain unchanged, and the only modifications are to the involvement of elected politicians. Little attempt is made to match the technical to the political cycle. Nor are any questions raised about the nature of expertise or the character of knowledge upon which the politician relies. Further, no suggestion is made about the power structure of the nuclear industry either in terms of worker participation or the nuclear 'club'.

The technology of nuclear power poses considerable difficulties for democratic control. At the same time, the fact that it is vitally dependent on state support and initiative, and cannot be understood in purely capitalist terms, suggests that the opportunity for democratic control through the state does exist. The same, it seems, is not true for microelectronics, where both the technology and its relationship with the state make it much less susceptible to politically or, more importantly, democratically directed control.

MICROELECTRONICS

The public ownership model of state control and democratic accountability fits no more easily with the example of microelectronics than it does with nuclear power. Indeed, where in the case of nuclear power the state has an identifiable, if ambiguous, relationship with the emergent policy, in the case of microelectronics the connections are much more loosely drawn. But though the links are tenuous, the impact of microelectronics on the state is considerable, affecting its power, its responsibilities and its democratic character.

Government rhetoric has suggested that microelectronics, and particularly information technology (IT) will guarantee either Britain's economic recovery or survival. In 1982, Kenneth Baker, then Minister for Information Technology, said,

Without doubt it [information technology] will be the engine of economic growth for at least the rest of the century. Britain's economic prosperity depends on the success with which we manufacture its products and provide and exploit its services. (Department of Industry, 1982)

This rhetoric has been given practical support in two main ways. First, governments, through the National Enterprise Board (NEB), have become directly involved in the creation of those industries necessary to the development of microelectronics. One such industry was Inmos, for which the NEB provided 75 per cent of the funds (the other 25 per cent being provided by the two experts hired to lead Inmos). Inmos's task was to build a new generation of microprocessors, the element at the centre of the 'microelectronics revolution', which would be able to compete with Japanese and American products (Benson and Lloyd, 1983). More recently, Inmos has been rather overshadowed by the Alvey project, another form of direct government intervention in the development and implementation of microelectronics. Under the Alvey programme, the government provides half the research costs for existing large companies (Plessey, GEC, International Computers Ltd, and Racal) to work on projects which are either of obvious commercial or administrative value (speech-driven word-processors, factory automation, the computerisation of administration, and mobile traffic information systems). The Alvey programme fits between the government's first strategy – direct intervention – and its second – enabling initiatives. The second strategy was to create favourable conditions for the use of microelectronics technology. This involved the provision of generous subsidies and an extensive propaganda campaign.

Though Inmos was dependent for its existence on government funds, the links between it and government were not bounded by the constitutional principles and practices which characterised other nationalised industries. In many ways, Inmos resembled a private company as much as a public corporation. Inmos was the first state-funded industry to make its two chiefs into millionaires. Now that Inmos has been privatised, the transformation into a private enterprise is complete. However, for our purposes, it is its earlier existence that must concern us. To understand this, we need to look at the conditions under which it worked.

Inmos was intended to provide a way for Britain to compete in the lucrative world of microprocessor technology and to provide British industry with a source of microchips (Benson and Lloyd, 1983, pp. 140–1). The microprocessor is at the heart of the microelectronics world. It is the device which enables all the more obvious, physical changes to take place: the bank cashpoint; the home computer; the word-processor; and the factory robot. Essentially, it is a quarter-inch square computer. The competition within the microprocessor industry is over the size, sophistication and cost of the computer that can be etched on to one quarter of an inch of silicon. This competition was dominated by the Japanese and the Americans. Furthermore, the demand for microchips always threatened to outstrip the supply, so that while the US and Japan could furnish their home markets, other countries went begging (Hills, 1984a). This problem was particularly acute for Britain whose consumption of microelectronics was considerably greater than that of its European neighbours.

In this world, and with these prospects, the development of an indigenous microelectronics industry seemed very necessary. For Britain, this need was made all the more pressing as its traditional industrial base appeared increasingly less competitive. Only the state could initiate such a project. The risks and costs alone argued for this. But the lack of expertise or a previously established base also argued for the need to import US talent, and the character of the market argued for a company which operated independently of direct political oversight.

Whatever the losses to democracy incurred by these demands, they have to be set against the alternatives, in particular, the consequence of US domination of Britain's domestic market. For Jill Hills, the history of the last twenty years in the European electronics sector has been 'a struggle to retain some measure of domestic power against the overwhelming superiority of American industry' (Hills, 1984b, p. 2). It is a domination that is perhaps most vividly illustrated by the controls exercised by the US government over the movement and use of American-manufactured technology within Britain. Hills concludes that 'European governments have little option but to give in to American demands and American dominance in electronics' (Hills, 1984b, p. 14). This is an opinion reinforced by Sir Ieuan Maddock, former Chief Scientist to the Department of Industry, who argued that if British governments failed to maintain the indigenous microprocessor industry, Britain would become 'a technological colony of large offshore companies who will determine what products are made, where, and when, and how high or low the national standard of living should be' (Large, 1984).

In this context, the decision to privatise Inmos involved more than the loss of a national asset; it entailed a loss of national sovereignty. At the same time, the conditions which led to the creation of Inmos, and the form the enterprise took, both worked against the possibility of direct state control and of retaining sovereignty. The competition, the technology, the distribution of the relevant expertise, the costs and risks, meant that, if Britain was to survive in the microelectronics market, it would depend largely on the government's willingness to finance it, and on outside experts to organise it. The kind of solution that nationalising the coal industry represented to the Labour government in 1945 was not on the agenda for its namesake in 1975. Once the state committed itself or was committed (and the element of choice is a moot point) to developing a British microelectronics industry, it had little alternative but to establish an organisation like Inmos which served to prime the pumps, rather than to offer any direct control over the future economic and industrial character of Britain.

The Alvey programme, like Inmos, is part of a similar industrial strategy, inspired by similar incentives and limited by similar problems. It is based on a belief about the importance of IT to Britain's future economic development and the need to compete in IT markets with the US and Japan. The Alvey programme is an attempt to create the conditions for this market victory. The government finances research undertaken by private companies who are responsible for the direction of that research. This partnership is partly a consequence of political choices – the wish of a 'non-interventionist' government not to be seen to be 'meddling' – and partly a consequence of the technology itself, which makes dependence on outside agents an inevitability. The result, as Jon Turney (1985) has pointed out, is that central government is unable to direct the projects because of the autonomy it allows to the private companies. Furthermore, as with nuclear power, the decision-making process tends to be corporatist and club-like, involving only the powerful, interested parties within industry and government (Williams, 1984; Turney, 1985).

But state involvement with microelectronics does not end with its sponsorship practices. The technology also has repercussions for the way government itself operates and for the opportunities for democratic control. One of the Alvey projects, for example, involves designing a computer to incorporate legislative changes immediately into the Department of Health and Social Security's administrative system. Indeed, the impact of microelectronics extends beyond its effects upon the operation of government into the relationship between citizens and government, to the heart of the democratic process.

The CSE Microelectronics Group (1980) has argued that the development of the new technology has served the state in many of its central functions. The use of computers within the state bureaucracy has, for instance, increased the possibility of management control and decreased employment in the public sector. The computerisation of data sources – from the Police National Computer to the Driver Vehicle Licence Centre – has allowed the state to acquire and correlate information on its citizens. Finally, the CSE group claims that microelectronics has been used to restructure industry 'in an attack on the basis of one of the most concentrated areas of working class power' (1980, p. 109). Similar conclusions are reached by the CIS Report, *The New Technology*, which suggests that the government's promotion of new technology was intended to boost productivity, 'regardless of the social consequences' (1979, p. 22). State involvement with microelectronics, then, may be more than mere 'pump-priming' exercises.

In the same way, the accompanying propaganda campaign, the second arm of the state's overt policy for microelectronics, is about more than promoting a particular range of products or techniques. Underneath campaigns like 'The Year of Information Technology' lies a particular vision of how society should be organised, which fits both with a distinct ideology and with a particular view of the interests of the state. Wherever microelectronics is to be applied, the underlying ideal is of a privatised, individualistic nirvana in which all needs are met at the press of a button. The centre of human activity in this 'ideal' world is the home. It is from here that work, banking, shopping, learning and relaxing, are organised.

The political consequence of such a strategy, it is argued, is to isolate individuals and thereby to make them more vulnerable to state control (Burnham, 1983). The likelihood of this is increased by the de-skilling effects of microelectronics in the factory and in the office, by the extension of state powers of surveillance (Jordan, 1981; Jones, 1982; Weeramantry, 1983). The overall picture is one of increasingly isolated citizens and of an increasingly powerful state. Webster and Robins write:

[Information Technology] will result in the intrusion of capital across a very wide range of social relations: the extension of capitalist planning, rationality and social management; a more intensive and aggressive exploitation of the sphere of leisure and the further penetration of the private sphere. (1981, p. 251)

Whatever the accuracy of such analyses, and there is a danger in microelectronics of confusing government and manufacturers' propaganda with reality, there are some things of which we can be sure.

Developments in microelectronics, besides drawing the state into new areas of sponsorship, will also have a direct impact on the nature of the state itself. These changes have clear repercussions for the possibilities for democracy. In respect of direct state intervention, democratic control has to confront two particular sets of difficulties: first, the problems of controlling the indigenous industry, and second, the problems of controlling the market itself.

The obstacles posed by the industry are similar to those experienced with nuclear power: dependence on external expertise, long lead times, and so on. But microelectronics is different from nuclear power in respect of market forces. Where nuclear power's development can best be explained in terms of the state's immediate interests, microelectronics has to be analysed in terms of the market and capital interests (CIS Report, 1979; Hills, 1984a). In so far as IT's development is determined by market competition, the opportunities for state control, let alone democratic control, seem limited. There are no points at which democratic pressure can usefully be applied, and as a consequence, the British Left has divided between those who have looked either to the emergence of an international socialist order and a planned world market (CSE Microelectronics Group, 1980), or to the imposition of trade barriers and tariffs (Cripps *et al.*, 1981). Outside this broad divide, there have been those on the left who regard attempts to avoid or eliminate the market as futile. They have argued that a more coherent attempt to serve the public interest, albeit without major advances in control, is to find new markets and to form trade links with new, less overbearing partners (Hills, 1984b).

The question of democratic control also arises in respect of the application of microelectronic technology. Those who understand the technology's development in market terms apply the same argument to the technology's impact. The cause and effect of microelectronics are linked by the market. Information technology, according to this view, serves to enhance the power of those interests already dominant in society. Two conclusions follow from this analysis: either that changing the system will alter the technology, which, in turn, will serve new (democratic-socialist) goals; or the technology will remain the same, while the system changes, and thereby alters the uses to which the technology is put. In each case, the technology itself poses no problems for democratic control. It is merely a symbol of the existing distribution of power, not a cause of it, and, therefore, of little interest to the democratic reformer.

Other writers, with the same concern for democracy, have adopted a radically different approach. They have suggested that the technology works to *improve* the prospects for democracy. Tom Stonier (1983), for example, has argued that IT acts to decentralise power and undermine attempts to monopolise the means of social control. Because IT introduces new means of communication and because their use cannot be fully monitored (while every newspaper can be censored, not every phone can be tapped), citizens can create their own systems of communication independently of the authorities. The same case is made by John Garratt and Geoff Wright (1980) who argue that the miniaturisation and mass production of computers makes available a new, decentralised, accountable political system. They write:

The [new] communication networks should allow decision-making to be faster, more responsive to events, and theoretically enable *all* members of a unit to be consulted rather than just one delegate. Politics could become the day-to-day occupation of the many rather than the personal gamesmanship of the few. (Garratt and Wright, 1980, p. 493)

What is distinctive about these views is that the changes are seen as resulting from the technology, rather than from conventional political initiatives: 'Our main point', say Garratt and Wright, 'is that through the development of mainstream technology, the present social and economic system is producing a structural crisis' (1980, p. 495).

Interestingly, although the Left has produced these very divergent views on democracy and the new technology, they agree on one thing. They all seem to regard the technology itself as outside the concern of democrats. Either the technology operates in an entirely determinist fashion, advancing or undermining democracy; or its function is dependent on its context. The parallel between these attitudes and those that informed socialist thinking on democratic state control is obvious. Instead of the objectivity of scientific management, there is the objectivity of the technology – it sets the conditions around which democracy is to be ordered. Similarly, the state remains the focus of political attention, and democracy is organised around traditional forms of political representation.

CONCLUSION

In this chapter, my concern has been to examine the problems which high technology poses for democratic state control. This has involved both exploring existing state relations with technology and assessing the reforms which have been suggested by democratic socialists. Here I want to draw out the main points of this survey.

One condition of the development of high technology, with its long lead times and high costs, is the involvement of the state. Without state initiatives and support, such technologies would be unviable. On the other hand, it is clear that there are considerable market and political pressures on the state to support high technology. Though the option of a self-sufficient, low-technology society may exist, the likelihood of its being adopted is slight. Those who seek a democratic state have, therefore, to work with high technology. But while many reformers recognise this, it is not clear that their reforms acknowledge the problems involved. It is noticeable how many proposals appear as recycled versions of traditional public-ownership models of democratic state control, based on the separation of politics and administration. Experience of high technology suggests that such solutions are inadequate.

The long development time of high technology conflicts with the short electoral cycle required for accountable government. Similarly, the expertise required in the design of new technology conflicts with the 'amateurism' that is admired in representative democracy. Furthermore, the expertise created in the development of new high technology tends to result in the emergence of an internal lobby which both influences subsequent thinking and advances its own interests. These tensions are compounded by the problems of assessing a high-technology policy: its qualities or failings become known only when it has been implemented and is therefore beyond control. Finally, it is evident that high technologies can have a profound effect upon the character of society, and thereby alter the conditions under which democracy itself operates.

All of the issues have to be addressed by those who are committed to a democratic state, but who are, unlike the Green movement, also committed to the development of high technology. Indeed, even if the 'Green' solution were adopted, and only manageable, soft technologies were introduced, considerable problems would remain: first, in identifying those technologies which are susceptible to democratic control; and second, in devising forms of management which are democratic. It would seem, therefore, that questions of the design, development and consequences of technology are inescapable features of any attempt to describe a 'democratic state'.

ACKNOWLEDGMENTS

Bob Alford, Graeme Duncan, John Zvesper and the participants in the Wolverhampton–East Anglia mini-conference all helped to turn my half-formed ideas into something slightly more respectable. They deserve the credit, while I take the blame, for what remains.

REFERENCES

Benn, Tony, 1980. *Arguments for Socialism*. Harmondsworth, Penguin Books
 1982. *Arguments for Democracy*. Harmondsworth, Penguin Books
 1983. *Transcript of Sizewell B Public Inquiry*, Day 150
 1985. 'Who dares wins', *Marxism Today*, 29(1): 15–18
Benson, I. and J. Lloyd, 1983. *New Technology and Industrial Change*. London, Kogan Page
Bunyard, P., 1981. *Nuclear Britain*. London, New English Library
Burnham, D., 1983. *The Computer State*. London, Weidenfeld and Nicolson
Cannell, W. and R. Chudleigh, 1983. *The PWR Decision*. London, Friends of the Earth
Chester, D. N., 1975. *The Nationalisation of British Industry*. London, HMSO
CIS Report, 1979. *New Technology*, London, CIS
Clegg, H. A., 1951. *Industrial Democracy and Nationalisation*. Oxford, Basil Blackwell
Cripps, F., J. Griffith, F. Morrell, J. Reid, P. Townsend and S. Weir, 1981. *Manifesto: A Radical Strategy for Britain's Future*. London, Pan Books
CSE Microelectronics Group, 1980. *Microelectronics*. London, CSE Books
Department of Industry, 1982. *Information Technology Year 1982*. London, HMSO
Elliott, D., 1978. *The Politics of Nuclear Power*. London, Pluto Press
Ellul, J., 1964. *The Technological Society*. New York, Vintage
Fairhall, D., 1985. 'US reactor "would not doom British nuclear design"', *The Guardian*, 6 February
Galbraith, J. K., 1974. *The New Industrial State*. 2nd edn, Harmondsworth, Penguin Books
Garratt, J. and G. Wright, 1980. 'Micro is beautiful', in T. Forrester, *The Microelectronics Revolution*. Oxford, Basil Blackwell
Gowing, M., 1964. *Britain and Atomic energy 1939–45*. London, Macmillan
 1974. *Independence and Deterrence*. 2 vols., London, Macmillan
Habermas, J., 1976. *Legitimation Crisis*. London, Heinemann
Hills, J., 1984a. *Information Technology and Industrial Policy*. London, Croom Helm
 1984b. Dependence and electronics: is there an alternative for Europe? Paper to PSA, University of Southampton
Holland, S., 1975. *The Socialist Challenge*. London, Quartet
Jones, B., 1982. *Sleepers, Wake*. Brighton, Wheatsheaf
Jordan, B., 1981. *Automatic Poverty*. London, Routledge and Kegan Paul
Large, P., 1984. 'Sense is putting cash where your chips are', *The Guardian*, 17 April
Marcuse, H., 1968. *One-Dimensional Man*. London, Sphere
Morrison, H., 1933. *Socialisation and Transport*. London, Constable
O'Connor, J., 1973. *The Fiscal Crisis of the State*. New York, St Martin's Press
Offe, C., 1984. *Contradictions of the Welfare State*. London, Hutchinson

Patterson, W., 1976. *Nuclear Power*. Harmondsworth, Penguin Books

Redwood, J., 1980. *Public Enterprise in Crisis*. Oxford, Basil Blackwell

Rudig, W., 1983. 'Capitalism and nuclear power: a reassessment', *Capital and Class*, 20 (Summer), pp. 117–56

Sedgemore, B., 1980. *The Secret Constitution*. London, Hodder and Stoughton

Sloman, M., 1978. *Socialising Public Ownership*. London, Macmillan

Spence, M., 1982. 'Nuclear Capital', *Capital and Class*, 16 (Spring), 5–40

Stonier, T., 1983. *The Wealth of Information*. London, Methuen

Street, J., 1981, Trade-union attitudes to worker participation in nationalised industry, unpublished D.Phil. thesis, University of Oxford

Turney, J., 1985. 'The fifth generation game', *New Socialist*, 24, February: 14–16

Webb, S. and B., 1920. *A Constitution for the Socialist Commonwealth of Great Britain*. London, Longmans

Webster, F. and K. Robins, 1981. 'Information technology: futurism, corporations and the state', *Socialist Register*. London, Merlin Press, pp. 247–69

Weeramantry, C. G., 1983. *The Slumbering Sentinels*. Harmondsworth, Penguin Books

Weiner, H. E., 1960. *British Labour and Public Ownership*. London, Stevens

Williams, R., 1980. *The Nuclear Power Decisions*. London, Croom Helm

1984. 'British technology policy', *Government and Opposition*, 19(1): 30–51

12

Is there a corporatist theory of the state?

ALAN CAWSON

INTRODUCTION

A spectre is haunting the theory of corporatism: the spectre of the state. From the earliest attempts to refashion the concept of corporatism in order to comprehend developments in the organisation of interests in liberal-democratic polities, corporatist theorists have identified the state as central to the phenomenon of interest intermediation. At the same time, however, exactly what is meant by 'the state' has been left ill defined, and critics such as Leo Panitch have argued (Panitch, 1979, p. 124) that corporatist theory is notable for its 'critical lack of a rigorous theory of the state'.

Panitch's observation was based on the view that corporatism should be interpreted within a class theory of the state, and should be seen as a strategy by the dominant class to subordinate labour through mechanisms such as incomes policies, social contracts and the like. This view contains two assumptions which can be questioned from the standpoint of corporatist theory, and the pursuit of these questions can help to clarify the nature of the task of constructing a corporatist theory of the state.

The first assumption is that it is possible to fashion a single general theory of the state which explains state activities by reference to its class character, or location within a given system of production. According to this view corporatism is one means among many others of handling the class tensions and conflicts endemic to capitalist society; the state has no independent effect on the substance of corporatist arrangements, but appears as a hollow shell into which the cement of class domination is poured. The counter-argument from within corporatist theory is that the relationship of the state to its social base is not constant but varies according to the functions that interest organisations perform, and whether or not those functions are incorporated within the policy-making processes of state agencies.

The second assumption contained within the argument that corporatism can best be understood within the framework of a class theory of the state is that interest categories are to be seen as projections onto the surface of society of underlying class relations, so that 'who benefits' from corporatist arrangements is always predetermined by the state of the class struggle. A focus on the strategic decision-making of interest organisations, by contrast, emphasises the calculus of political exchange in which the costs and benefits of collaboration in policy-making may be weighed. Moreover, these organisations may or may not be formed around economic class categories: corporatist theory draws attention to the significance of organisational closure around 'vertical' partitions as well as 'horizontal' class relationships.

This chapter seeks to stand Panitch's observation on its head by advancing the view that what existing theories of the state require is a rigorous theory of corporatism. Organised interests which are *not* reducible to class have come to dominate major areas of policy-making in many capitalist democracies, and the interpretation of their significance requires a major reassessment of state theory. Moreover, their presence as intermediaries between the state and the primary social groups which comprise civil society is sufficient to erode the central plank of the neo-Marxist platform, which is that social classes emerging from the relations of production are the determining forces behind political conflicts and the activities of the state.

This will involve the argument that corporatist theory provides a *structural* account of non-class forces, and the basis for a dualist theory which implies that a fundamental contradiction in late-capitalist societies, as significant as the class polarisation between bourgeoisie and proletariat, is that between the sphere of society in which interests have been organised into corporatist and collusive arrangements, and those disorganised and competitive interests which have been excluded. These processes, it is argued, can best be captured in the development of a state theory which is a creative synthesis located, as Friedland (1982, p. xxvi) put it, 'in the erogenous zone between Weber and Marx'.

My chapter begins with a brief review of theories of corporatism, their divergent approaches and common problems. It goes on to develop a distinction between the structural categories of class and sector, and shows how these provide opportunities and constraints for different varieties of interest-based politics. The argument locates corporatism as one possible form of the articulation between the state and the range of interests in society, and makes the argument that corporatism coexists with a sphere of competitive politics. The chapter concludes by discussing the implications of this dualism for the theoretical concept of the state.

RECENT THEORIES OF CORPORATISM

Schmitter's (1974) essay, 'Still the century of corporatism?', is often seen as the starting pistol for the race to develop a modern theory of interest politics as an alternative to the neo-Marxist critique of pluralism (Miliband, 1969, ch. 5). This may be so, but some of the runners were already on their blocks: Beer's 'Epilogue' to his *Modern British Politics* (Beer, 1969) contains a discussion of 'quasi-corporatism' which links the growing power and interdependence of functional interest organisations to those interventionist activities of the state, notably macro-economic management and the development of the welfare state, which had been traced in detail in the first (1965) edition of the book. Nigel Harris's *Competition and the Corporate Society* (Harris, 1972) showed how the Conservative Party's orientation to industry and economy was shaped by a conflict between the neo-corporatist Macmillanite analysis of industrial capitalism, and the neo-liberal approach which has now become the dominant ideological strand in Thatcherism.

Schmitter, however, provided the first rigorous attempt to define the concept in contradistinction to pluralism, monism and syndicalism (Schmitter, 1974, pp. 93–8). The different ideal types referred to systems of interest representation, where under corporatism the constituent units were limited in number, hierarchically ordered, based on differentiation of function, and, most importantly, entered into a contractual relationship with the state. Under the terms of this contract their integration into policy formation was conditional on the capacity of interest organisations to control their membership and deliver their part of the bargain. It was this reciprocal relationship between groups and the state that was the essence of Schmitter's concept of 'interest intermediation' (Schmitter, 1982).

Recent critics (Heisler, 1979; Almond, 1983; Martin, 1983; Jordan, 1983) have claimed that there is not much that is new in such a concept, and that its proponents' view that it differs sharply from pluralism is based on a failure to understand pluralist theory, and in particular arguments about the development of 'corporate pluralism'. If this were true, why should so many disaffected pluralists (and not a few disaffected Marxists) find the corporatist paradigm so attractive? There may well be an element of academic fashion in the surge of writing on corporatism (see Cawson and Ballard, 1984, for a bibliography), but the differences in approach remain profound. The crucial point that pluralist critics overlook is that their 'process' notion of the political system implies a characterisation of the state as reactive and responsive, and denies the state any capacity to shape the recognition and organisation of interests. In corporatist theory the structured and selective relationship between corporate groups and the state is at the heart of the concept, rather than the process of spontaneous interaction between all groups, public and private, which is characteristic of pluralism.

Martin's (1983) suggestion that pluralism and corporatism can best be seen as points on a continuum devalues the significance of the qualitative shift that takes place in the relationship between the state and organised interests. In addition, as Crouch (1983) argues, Martin ignores the importance of the manipulation and control over members' behaviour exercised by interest organisations. In corporatist theory organisation is more than the aggregation and 're-presentation' of existing interests; it is an important element in the constitution and definition of those interests. The development of oligopoly in the political market-place is not a spontaneous process, but is itself in part a consequence of state activity. By licensing and privileging specific groups, conferring what Offe (1981) calls 'public status' on certain groups and denying it to others, the state in effect erects 'barriers to entry' in political competition. The central focus for corporatist theory is on the specific structures of interaction, or better intermediation, between state actors and interest organisations. Under what conditions and with what consequences for both parties do 'political exchanges' take place?

Of course if this view were universally accepted within the corporatist literature, then the latter would have far more theoretical coherence and empirical focus than it actually displays. Critics are right to point to the lack of agreement on the nature of the concept, but wrong if they imply that this is unique to corporatism. After all pluralists have had rather longer to define their central concepts, and have had no more success!

Within the corporatist debate one can find the suggestion that corporatism is a new form of political economy beyond capitalism and socialism (Winkler, 1976); a new state form within advanced capitalism (Jessop, 1979); a new system for organising industrial relations within capitalism (Crouch, 1977) which amounts to a strategy for subordinating the working class (Panitch, 1979; Strinati, 1979); or may develop into a new form of ordering social relationships in addition to the traditional ones of community, market and the state (Streeck and Schmitter, 1984). Whilst this diversity has given a certain richness to the literature, its costs are evident in the increasing elasticity of the concept as it is continually stretched to encompass new observations (Wilson, 1983, p. 108). Before it snaps, it is incumbent on corporatist theorists to be able to specify which processes in industrial societies are not corporatist, as well as to show which are. As Beer (1969, p. 428) correctly observed, 'corporatism cannot constitute a complete polity'. The focus on the relationship between the state and organised interests is not by itself enough if we cannot explain the mechanisms of the state itself, or the processes through which some interests are organised into corporatist politics whilst others are organised out (to amend slightly Schattschneider's (1960, p. 30) celebrated observation about the 'mobilisation of bias').

One way of clarifying the nature of corporatism (and 'non-corporatism') is to distinguish between different levels according to the scope of the interest associations involved (for elaboration, see Cawson, 1986). Much of the work concerned with tripartite representation, policy concertation and the role of 'peak' class associations has been addressed to the *macro-level* where the content of political exchange has covered national planning, tax and incomes policies, social pacts, contracts and the like. It is this 'macro-corporatism' which has attracted speculation about the emergence of a 'corporate state', or wildly deterministic theorising about the inevitability of a post-capitalist corporatist order (Winkler, 1976).

But it is also at the macro-level that there have been important comparative studies based on an attempt to quantify corporatist developments. Wilensky (1976) provides evidence to substantiate the hypothesis that macro-corporatist developments can explain the different reactions in industrialised countries to the crisis of welfare budgets. He suggests that some countries have experienced a low level of 'tax-welfare backlash', and concludes that 'what makes [their] sensible tax policies possible is a corporatist cast to political life and social policy' (Wilensky, 1976, p. 21). Schmitter (1981) examines the proposition that 'ungovernability' is not a consequence of 'overload' in party and electoral systems, but is related to the development of societal corporatism. He provides measures of 'citizen unruliness', governmental instability and fiscal ineffectiveness in fifteen industrialised countries, and argues that whilst his indices of societal corporatism cannot predict governmental instability, they are reliable negative predictors of citizen unruliness and fiscal ineffectiveness. 'What seems to count', Schmitter argues, 'is not *whether* everyone is getting organised for the pursuit of specialised class and sectoral self-interest but *how* they are doing so' (Schmitter, 1981, p. 312). Schmidt (1982) tests a number of hypotheses (including corporatist ones) concerning the explanation of the different rates of unemployment in twenty-one capitalist democracies, and concludes that 'corporatism is the best single predictor for differential rates of unemployment' (Schmidt, 1982, p. 251).

The results are impressive, but not conclusive in view of the difficulty of constructing reliable operational measures of corporatism, and the familiar problem of possible spuriousness in the observed correlations. What seems to be happening is that, often under the aegis of strong social-democratic parties in government during periods of economic growth, a subsidiary system of organised political exchange develops alongside the electoral–parliamentary channel (Lehmbruch, 1982). This system institutionalises bargaining with the peak associations over economic and social policies, and this has at least to a certain extent carried over into periods of economic recession, reducing the influence of electoral and party influences and reducing the need for severely deflationary policies. Nevertheless, the eventual breakdown or dispersion to other levels of even the most highly institutionalised macro-corporatist arrangements alerts us to the dangers of seeing macro-corporatism as the product of some new stage of capitalist development, and has proved to be an effective antidote to some of the earlier more speculative writing.

By focussing on the reciprocal nature of the exchange between corporate groups and the state, corporatist theory highlights the conditions under which interest organisations might submerge short-term immediate interests beneath the expectation of a non-zero-sum outcome if other 'social parties' and state agencies do likewise. Here the state's role is crucial in promoting such political exchanges: they do not emerge spontaneously from the interplay of group pressures, but depend upon the configuration of power relations. Part of this refers to the pay-offs in terms of the state's capacity to provide rewards for participation, but equally important is the ultimate threat of coercion if 'voluntary' agreements fail to materialise. Fear of the consequences of failing to agree – that is, regulation through legal means – can be a powerful inducement to participate.

Such multipartite bargaining at the macro-level has been an important focus for corporatist research, but the basic concept refers to bipartite state–group relations, from which tripartism or multipartism can be a possible extension. When confined to a specific sector or product branch, for example in export promotion or milk marketing, corporatist practices can develop where there is no necessary class base for interest organisation, and where there is no necessity for trans-class collaboration. This level of interaction between state agencies and organised interest associations can be usefully identified as *meso-corporatism* (Wassenberg, 1982; Cawson, 1985). The content of political exchange is not concerned, as is macro-corporatism, with major redistributive questions which affect encompassing class organisations, but rather with negotiation within defined policy areas. In certain cases this amounts to the devolution of entire policy areas, for example in industrial standards, to private-interest organisations, and the term 'private-interest government' (Streeck and Schmitter, 1984) is gaining increasing currency as a description of these kinds of arrangements.

There is another level of corporatist practice about which much less has been written, but which may also be of increasing significance. *Micro-corporatism* is a useful term with which to refer to the negotiation of semi-binding contractual arrangements with individual firms, in which public policies are pursued by those firms agreeing to follow investment, employment, location or pricing strategies which differ from the outcomes which would have followed from unfettered adjustments to market conditions. There are as yet few well-documented studies of this (but see Jowell, 1977 on British land-use planning, and Estrin and Holmes, 1983 on French industrial policy). Such agreements are not enforceable in the courts, and indeed may be repudiated by the courts, as has happened in British planning. Unlike cases of class collaboration at the micro-level in the form of plant bargaining, which are sometimes referred to as micro-corporatist, planning agreements such as these involve the presence of the state and monopolistic private-interest bodies, and so are properly to be seen as a variety of corporatism.

Micro-corporatist bargaining involves discretionary state intervention, and tends to occur where meso-corporatist industrial associations which defend a collective 'sectoral' interest are inappropriate instruments for permitting discretion in favour of individual firms. An alternative policy mode for such intervention has been the quasi-governmental body, which acts as a channel for discretionary assistance; for example, the National Enterprise Board and the regional development agencies. If it were possible to interpret such developments within the framework of pluralist or neo-Marxist theory, then such conceptual elaboration would be superfluous. But the relationship between the state and such interests is non-competitive, exclusionary and interdependent, involving an element of coercion even if only latent (hence, the invalidity of pluralist assumptions), and at the same time the interests are sectorally rather than class-defined (hence, the limitations of neo-Marxism). This distinction between sectoral and class interests requires further elaboration, and this is the task of the following sections.

INTERESTS, INTEREST GROUPS AND POLITICAL ACTION

One of the most persuasive objections to pluralist theory lies in its conception of interests as individual preferences (Connolly, 1972; Saunders, 1979, ch. 1). Pluralism denies structure and depends on an individualistic methodology which sees individuals as the constituent units of society, and recognises social groups only as aggregates of individuals. Group interests emerge through the process of 'interest aggregation' as the sum of member preferences: the whole can never be more than the sum of the constituent parts. Ideology, for example, is thus atomised and its existence only recognised in terms of its observable behavioural effects. Lukes's (1974) classic essay on *Power: A Radical View* provides an effective critique of pluralist theories of decision-making, and his insights on the different dimensions of power can be used to clarify the nature of interests.

Interests can be seen as expressed through individual preferences, but as existing and persisting by virtue of organisation. The interest organisation both shapes the preferences and controls the behaviour of its members. If membership in groups were wholly voluntary, one would have to agree with the pluralist view of groups as the simple sum of the already formed preferences of their members. Individuals who did not agree with the actions of the group would simply leave it and join or found another one more congruent with their preferences. But whilst pluralists interpret *all* groups, and sometimes even the state in this way, Marxist, neo-elitist and neo-corporatist critics have raised powerful objections. To the extent that for certain groups, segments, categories etc. membership has become semi- or even totally compulsory (*de facto* or *de jure*), one must concede that individual preferences and behaviours may be effectively subordinated to organisationally defined interests.

Neo-Marxists have built their critique of pluralism on the foundation of a class view of society, in which the supposed competition of pluralistic interest groups is vitiated by the structural advantage accruing to capital. This advantage is built into the structure of the state, which then becomes the ultimate guarantor of capitalist prerogatives. But if we accept this proposition, we are forced either to accept the view that all interests in capitalist society derive from class position, or at least to concede that class interests are *fundamentally* more important than non-class interests.

I would suggest that a resolution of this problem can be found by distinguishing different kinds of interest groups along a number of dimensions. Claus Offe argues that there are three perspectives from which interests can be viewed:

(1) the level of will, consciousness, sense of collective identity, and the values of the *constituent* members of the interest group; (2) the level of the socio-economic *opportunity structure* of the society within which an interest group emerges and acts; and (3) the institutional forms and practices that are provided to the interest group by the *political system* and that confer a particular *status* as its basis of operation.

(Offe, 1981, pp. 123–4, emphasis in original)

Pluralist theory, he argues, fails to take account of the second and third elements. I would suggest that a developed neo-corporatist theory of the state has to be built around the second and third dimensions, but that the first is also important, particularly for the study of groups which are outside corporatist networks.

At the second and third levels, we can identify groups which, often as a result of their relationships with state agencies, have achieved 'public status', which implies amongst other things that the interests of the organisation amount to more than the sum of the interests of its parts. Members are not completely free to 'exit', because such a course imposes intolerable or unacceptable costs on them, or because the organisation has the power to sanction defectors. I will refer to such groups as *corporate groups* to distinguish them from purely voluntary associations, which I will call *preference groups*. Most corporate groups take their identity and interests from a function performed in the socio-economic division of labour, but this is an empirical generalisation rather than a defining characteristic.

At the third level, that of the system, we can say that the structure of the corporate group universe is largely non-competitive and hierarchically ordered: a *corporate sphere* of the political system. Here public and private are difficult to distinguish, since the most important corporate groups at the macro-level take on the character of 'governing institutions' (Middlemas,

1979). This is at the same time an extension of the private into the public and an extension of the public into the private. The crossing of the state threshold by private interest organisations compromises the 'essential unity of the state' claimed in some neo-Marxist theories, and leads to a process of fragmentation. But a second consequence of public–private interpenetration is the inverse of this: private groups are forced to acquire an element of state- or public-regardingness in their definitions of their interests. The separation of politics and economics in liberal theories is belied, at least in the sphere of production, by the increasing politicisation of economic decision-making, which tends to hold political authorities increasingly accountable for economic success or failure (Habermas, 1976).

To concentrate exclusively on economic interests and the corporate sphere would be to give an unduly economistic interpretation of the political process. Moral and ideological issues – 'popular democratic struggles' in Jessop's term (1979, p. 194) – which are centrally concerned with political citizenship and social identity, are resistant to the corporatist mode of interest intermediation. It is in a *competitive sphere* that the familiar pluralist processes of group competition tend to prevail, and where group membership depends on the coincidence of the association's objectives with the individual preferences of its members. Many of the most important social and political issues of contemporary societies are fought out in this arena: nuclear disarmament, abortion law reform, environmental campaigns and the like. The natural basis of these groups is parliament, whose representative basis is the individual citizen.

It is not possible to argue that *all* corporate groups are *always* more powerful than *all* preference groups, despite the valid observation that in specific issue areas producer interests often prevail over consumer interests. The state is not simply a collection of functional agencies each bargaining with corporate groups; its democratic character is not merely a façade, and the problem of legitimating corporatist policy-making in a hostile liberal culture is ever-present. Liberal democracy provides an 'opportunity structure' for preference groups to become social movements and thereby extract quite decisive policy shifts over a short period. But over the longer term the requirements of policy-making and policy-implementation tend to lead towards mutually supportive and exclusive relationships between the state and organised *producer* interests.

SECTORAL INTERESTS AND CLASS INTERESTS

If we concede that interest groups organise within a set of opportunities and constraints, within a structure, then we need to explore what this is. Pluralist theory can ignore this question, because it sees the resultant collective action as exclusively the product of spontaneously generated preferences and voluntary actions. This raises the old and thorny issue of structure and agency, and the dialectical relationship between the two. Marxist theory poses this issue clearly, but confines the analysis of social structure to class forces. Class is both a structural concept ('class-in-itself') and a concept at the level of social action ('class-for-itself'). Classes do not act politically as such, but through organisations based on class interest. The link between structure and agency arises from class awareness and class consciousness, which are necessary but not sufficient conditions for class-based political action.

The important theoretical basis for understanding the link between structure and process can be developed further through a recognition that there are structural opportunities and constraints which *cannot* be reduced to class. In the transition from feudalism to capitalism, old forms of structure based on political and economic status obligations were replaced by new ones derived from a novel system of capitalist production. With the development of capitalism both the structure of capitalist markets and the role of the state undergoes a decisive transformation. The state ceases to act simply as guarantor of the conditions under which market processes take place, but becomes implicated in the organisation of production itself. State intervention creates *sectoral* constituencies and interdependencies which cut across class divisions.

Class structuration results in a 'horizontally' stratified society, whereby class organisations form in defence of subordinate and superordinate positions of power based on property. Sectoral structuration comprises 'vertical' cleavages characterised by *interdependence* between sectors within an extended and increasingly complex division of function. The basic sectoral distinctions are those between production and consumption, with a crucial vertical division arising from the effects of state intervention. Thus within the sphere of production there is an important cleavage of interest between those employed in the public sector (who have a vital interest in maintaining levels of state expenditure) and those employed in the private sector (who see state expenditure as a burden on private productive activity). Similarly the effects of state intervention in the sphere of consumption lead to a cleavage of interest between those (e.g. home owners, car owners) who achieve provision of their consumption need through the market, and those (e.g. public sector tenants, public transport users) who are dependent on state provision (Dunleavy, 1980). Sectoral theory is an attempt to recognise the central role of state power in determining life chances, by compensating for the excessive attention paid in earlier stratification theory to the role of private property and the market.

Sector is not simply an analytic distinction, but is reflected in political practice and interest organisation. Groups such as farmers, doctors and steel-producers fashion their interest organisations in a context where state subsidies or collective consumption programmes define the 'rules of the game'. Class conflict within a sector may be muted where sectoral interests are perceived in relation to state intervention, and form the basis for interest organisation. Changing economic processes and new technologies constantly revise the structure, and, often with a time lag, the perceptions of sectoral interests in the sphere of production. Likewise, dramatic changes in consumption, for example in the spread of owner-occupation and car ownership, change both the opportunity constraint structure and the perception of consumer interests. But, as we have argued above, there is no automatic link between structure and practice; it depends upon consciousness and organisation.

In analysing these factors, we can find a partial explanation for the disparity in political power between organisations based on sectoral production interests, and those based on consumption ones. The social organisation of production in the factory/office system affords greater opportunities for interest organisation than does the dispersal of consumers across the whole society, so that the most frequent basis for consumer-interest organisation is territory: neighbourhood, community, city and so on. This is a partial explanation for the greater impact that consumption-based interest organisations have at the local level, although the different potential of producer and consumer groups in terms of corporatist exchanges is more significant.

The link between sectoral organisation and corporatism should by now be apparent. Capital and labour (in private industry) or management and labour (in the public sector) may find a common sectoral interest more compelling as a motive for co-operation than their class differences are a reason for conflict. To the extent that their sectoral interests are threatened by industrial decline, or public expenditure cuts, they may be willing to bargain with state agencies, even if it means suppressing or forgoing a wider class identification.

The key to these processes is organisation, and herein lies the mobilisation of bias and the profound consequences of corporatism for traditional conceptions of liberal democracy. Those who are not producers – the old, the young, the unemployed, the non-unionised among the employed, the small producers who are subordinate to the market, and so on – are left out of such processes. In Claus Offe's words, they are the 'policy-takers' rather than the 'policy-makers' (Offe, 1981, pp. 138–9). They are particularly dependent economically on the level of state expenditure, and the effectiveness of state regulation of the market. There is, of course, the possibility that such groups could be 'incorporated' through the creation of monopolistic interest associations for each category, but as Schmitter (1982, p. 272) points out, the inspiration for such a process would have to come from the state, and there is no reason to suppose that those already privileged within the corporate sphere would willingly forgo their privileges in the name of greater equality and participation.

The organisations present in policy-making and political processes at the meso-level will be an amalgam of corporate and preference groups, and of sector- and class-based ones. There is no necessary correspondence between these two distinctions, and both class and sectoral groups will be found in the competitive sphere as well as the corporate sphere. The key difference arises from their respective relationship to the state, with preference groups adopting classic pressure-group tactics, dependent on private contributions of resources and effort, and trying to obtain access to state institutions to have their preferences prevail in public policies. Corporate groups, by contrast, whilst obtaining privileged access, are also to a certain extent dependent on maintaining their relationship to the state, having traded-off at least some of their capacity for autonomous action. Given that the state is clearly central to both the definition of corporatism, and more importantly to the structure of the corporate sphere, we need now to turn our attention to the state side of the relationship, and to the contribution to our understanding of it that existing theories of the state are able to make.

WHAT IS DISTINCTIVE ABOUT THE STATE?

This seems to be one of the most important, but least frequently posed questions in writings about the state. Given that one of the major thrusts of the reaction to pluralist theory (which failed to ask any questions about the state) has been the observation that public and private spheres of society are becoming increasingly difficult to disentangle, some kind of stocktaking appears to be in order. An older, normative tradition of writing about the state was in no doubt about this question: the state was the only institution 'above society', and was the guardian of the public interest and the national purpose. But as Macpherson (this volume) has convincingly argued, unless one is a 'philosophic liberal' with a fixed and minimalist conception of the state, the need for explanatory clarity is pressing.

Consider the following activities which might be held to be the sole prerogative of the state: law-making, taxation, guaranteeing the currency, upholding private-property rights. In each of these, on inspection, it turns out that the state has no effective monopoly. The existence of 'private governments' which set rights and duties for their members disposes of the first. Of course this is not to say that the relative importance of 'public' and 'private' government is equal, but to point out that we cannot distinguish the state by its unique capacity to generate generally binding norms. Likewise, many semi-compulsory organisations exact levies on their members which amount to a form of private taxation. In some countries, such as the United States, the currency is controlled by a formally private and autonomously constituted private body (the Federal Reserve Bank). In many others, governments have found state power inadequate for the task of controlling the supply of money, partly because the older unambiguous definitions of money have disappeared (for the first time one form of money is now a minute electric current transmitted in milliseconds between banks). Finally, state activities have infringed on so many private-property rights that propertied groups have come to see it as performing the reverse function! On very close inspection it becomes extremely difficult to identify any particular defining characteristic, which is of course not to jump to the conclusion that the state is just another organisation.

Re-examining Max Weber's writings on the state (Weber, 1968), it is possible to identify a 'bottom line' of state monopoly power, although the circumstances under which it can be employed are subject to various constraints. Having rejected the view that the state can be distinguished on the basis of *what* it does, Weber emphasised two aspects: territory and force. The modern state is still pre-eminently a *nation-state* (notwithstanding weak forms of supranational policy co-ordination such as the EEC), although to some extent its sovereignty has been weakened by the development of multinational economic forms. But the locus of the political relationships implicit in the concept of citizenship is still firmly the nation-state.

The second aspect of the state stressed by Weber is the monopoly of the legitimate use of force in society. Although we have been stressing negotiated exchanges between the state and organised interests, these are always underpinned by the implied threat that the state's coercive power may be deployed if arrangements break down. Weber's qualifying adjective 'legitimate' is crucial for the discussion of the underlying role of coercion in corporatism, because of the extent to which the legitimacy of the state is grounded in democratic principles of accessibility and accountability. Corporatist policy circuits are relatively closed and inaccessible, and depend for their effectiveness on the extent to which potentially destabilising competitive interests can be organised out. Coercion is a problematic weapon for states to deploy in their negotiation with corporate groups, because legal regulation involves opening up closed arenas to competitive forces, with potentially adverse consequences for state actors in terms of their loss of control over policy implementation.

If the state is to be interpreted as a system of domination, then clearly it is important to understand the balance of forces within the state. As well as contending class pressures, this must include the relative importance of corporatist versus electoral–partisan policy networks, and the extent to which the shift towards corporatism has contributed to the increasing difficulty of legitimating state activity. Procedural democratic norms are not, of course, the only basis for the state's legitimacy and the decreasing significance of these may be offset by the capacity of the state to deal effectively with its policy problems. As we have seen earlier, there is some evidence that, with respect for example to employment policy, corporatist structures help to enhance this capacity.

MARXIST THEORIES OF THE STATE

Marxist theories of the state seem to neglect the aspect of the divisions and contradictions within the state system in favour of examining the external forces which act on the state, although as we shall see below, recent arguments put forward by Miliband go some way towards remedying this neglect.

The common thread within Marxist theory is the link between the state and capitalism, whether the latter is seen as constituting a mode of production or a social formation. This is not the place to explore the issue of whether the objective of state theory is to generalise about the state in capitalist society (Miliband, 1969) or the capitalist state (Poulantzas, 1973; Jessop, 1982). Indeed, as the next section will show, it is in my view a fool's errand to search for a single general theory of the state at all. One approach, commonly referred to as the 'state derivation' approach (Holloway and Picciotto, 1978), seeks to uncover the specificity of the capitalist state by deducing logically what is required for a capitalist mode of production to operate. The result is argued to be a structure which is required to perform certain functions, such as the provision of a common currency, the passage of laws in defence of private property, the enforcement of contracts and so on. The major objection to this effort is that it takes an ideal-type construct of the capitalist mode of production, and derives from it an ideal-type conception of the state. The objection is not to the use of ideal types as such, but to the failure of this school to recognise the necessity for grounding them in empirical observations. After all, Weber and Marx arrived at their abstract concepts only after a massive empirical and historical inquiry. The results were clearly to some extent tied to the stage of economic and social development existing at the time. Unless we are to assume, in the case of Marx and the state derivationists, that no significant changes have taken place over the last 120 years or so, then the theory of the state so derived is only of historical interest.

A second, and far more significant Marxist approach to the theory of the state, concerns the relationship between the state and the class structure of capitalist society. In the more deterministic and structuralist accounts (especially in the work of Poulantzas, 1973) the state *qua* state is held to exercise no power at all, but to be a 'terrain' on which the class struggle takes place, and state policy registers the current state of play. In spite of the obvious differences, it is striking to compare this view with the accounts of government policy in some pluralist writing, where the outcome is seen as a result of the interaction of group pressures. The state is argued to have no autonomous source of power, its so-called 'relative autonomy' being the consequence of the state of play of the class struggle. This is especially clear in Poulantzas's (1973) interpretation of Marx's *Eighteenth Brumaire*, and has provoked the common criticism of Poulantzas that he attempted to construct a general theory of the capitalist state from an analysis of an exceptional one. In considering the relevance of this approach for understanding corporatism, it is important to note that the theory contains no distinction between state power and class power, and hence no concept of state action or state interests independent of class. This distinction is refused even where, as in Jessop's formulation, the reduction of all political forces to class forces is avoided. 'Whatever the relation between political categories and classes and/or between the twin determinations of the state as class and as popular domination, state power is a mediated effect of the balance among *all* forces in a given situation' (Jessop, 1979, p. 192, emphasis in original).

Miliband's more accessible and empirically grounded theory of the state (as developed in Miliband, 1969, 1977, 1983) makes the distinction between class power and state power quite explicit. In his earlier work Miliband sought to explain the class bias of the state in terms of the recruitment and socialisation of the state elite, and the superior power of business as an organised interest. Later (Miliband, 1977, pp. 71–3), having accepted something from the structuralist offensive mounted by Poulantzas (1973, 1975), Miliband conceded the importance for the understanding of state policy of the impact of 'structural constraints' inherent in the requirements of managing the capitalist economy. In doing so he provided a workable concept of the 'relative autonomy of the state' (Miliband, 1977, p. 83) which consists in the room for manoeuvre available to state actors, which depends upon the stringency of the fiscal pressures consequent on the rate of capital accumulation at any given time. That this relative autonomy properly belongs to the state, and not to any government in office, should be evident from the extent to which expenditure constraints, in Britain as elsewhere, operate independently of the party in power.

The development in Miliband's latest work (Miliband, 1983) of the concept of a partnership between state power and class power is worthy of close attention. Clearly such a partnership is contingent and not necessary, and the sources of state power and class power are quite distinct. State power is not simply the power of those who occupy the upper positions in the state apparatus as a social category, although this should not be discounted, but is related to the legitimation of state activity through democratic mechanisms. The change in emphasis from *The State in Capitalist Society* (1969), where democracy was seen primarily as a means of mystifying class rule, to *Capitalist Democracy in Britain* (1982) is striking, and part of the increasing tendency within Marxism to take democracy seriously. There remain, however, problems with the concept of a partnership because of the implication that it is primarily through the democratic mechanism that non-class forces impinge on the political process. The argument above concerning sectoral and class forces suggests that the idea of partnership may be used to analyse the relationship between the state and sources of power apart from class. At the theoretical level the need is for a partnership between state theory and corporatist theory!

The third major, and more 'capital-theoretical' Marxist approach to state theory is a development of the view that capitalist states exist in a particular, and structurally constraining, relationship to the process of capital accumulation. As the conditions under which accumulation takes place change with the evolution of industrial capitalism, and particularly with the development of an oligopolistic sector of large corporations, state intervention in the sphere of production becomes more extensive at the same time that concessions to organised labour in the form of enhanced welfare benefits increase claims on the state budget. The resulting *Fiscal Crisis of the State* (O'Connor, 1973) becomes a major constraint on state policy-making. The theoretical basis for this account is the view that the state can be defined by its twin (and contradictory) functions of accumulation and legitimation. The former function produces state expenditures in the form of social investment and social consumption, both of which indirectly contribute to capital accumulation. The latter function requires social expenses which are a drain on capital. O'Connor's work has been widely influential, and his distinction between the monopoly sector and the competitive sector within advanced capitalism is one source for the corporate/competitive distinction made above. Offe's (1975) distinction between the productive and allocative activities of the state bears some similarity, although his approach is not marred by the instrumentalism involved in O'Connor's insistence that the accumulation function is prioritised by a 'class conscious political directorate' at the heart of the state (O'Connor, 1973, p. 67).

CORPORATISM, COMPETITIVE POLITICS AND THE 'DUAL STATE'

The crucial insight that is found in this work is the distinction between a political process centred around production (policies concerned with private sector profitability, investment and infrastructure, etc.), and that concerned with consumption (involved in the collective provision of social consumption resources, such as health care, education and housing). Recent Marxist work has emphasised the politics of production (although it has neglected the significance of sectoral organisation within it) and has alerted us to the importance of state activities which have extended into private sector production.

Abandoning any attempt to build a single, general theory of the state, we can concentrate on 'middle range' theories which seek to explain different aspects of state policy-making according to distinct social and political processes, without the prior assertion that there is a 'class conscious political directorate' which 'in the last instance' will guarantee a determinate and predictable outcome.

An important question then becomes whether there are different social bases and modes of political organisation in different spheres. We have already pointed to the distinction between corporate and competitive spheres of the polity. In the former sphere politics is dominated by the bargaining relationship between corporate functional groups and state agencies which is well insulated from disturbances from unincorporated groups. To the extent that corporatisation occurs around the class and sectoral interests of producers, the politics of production is dominated by corporatist politics. In the politics of consumption, the structural base is consumption category and knowledge- or skill-related class (in the form of professionalism or managerialism). Social closure around consumption categories is much harder to achieve than that around producer or class interests, and consumption-based interest groups inhabit a fluid, competitive and constantly shifting environment.

The thesis does not claim that corporatism is restricted to the politics of production, and competitive politics confined to consumption processes, although for some countries like Britain there is a relatively good 'fit', in that collective consumption provision is delivered through state bureaucratic structures at the local level which are relatively accessible to influence from client groups. What it does claim is that the structural base for interest organisation is different in the two spheres, and hence the *form* that corporatist processes take also differs. In collectively provided consumption services, the providers are able to achieve social closure around technical and professional skills, and are in a strong position to co-manage the services in a way which undermines the mechanisms of democratic accountability. The state is involved in a financial and regulatory capacity, but for some services, like health and higher education, policy-making is parcelled out to 'private-interest governments' dominated by the professions (Cawson, 1982). The most important state powers are financial ones, whereby it establishes expenditure ceilings which may be more closely tied to electoral and budgetary pressures. But here also sectoral interests (in maintaining the level of health or education budgets) can lead to alliances and struggles which cut across class lines.

In the sphere of production, the social bases for interest organisation are class, based on property relations, and sector, emerging from the pattern of state intervention. Unlike consumption processes embodied in the idea of the 'welfare state', where the prevailing ideology is universalist, production politics is dominated by the themes of private property and the market. Macro- and meso-corporatist processes are determined by the interplay between sector and class, and by the predisposition of governments to intervene in market processes. The parliamentary–electoral process, which aggregates individual interests on a territorial basis, ill suits the functional constituencies required for production policy-making, and parliamentary structures are rarely able to monitor these processes effectively, let alone control them.

Overarching political and economic changes, such as the election of a government deeply suspicious of corporatism and eager to achieve a return to the competitive market, or the necessity for adjustment to worldwide recession, can send shockwaves through the elaborate structure of corporatist networks. This may result in the breakdown of corporatist arrangements at the macro-level, and the displacement of corporatism to meso- and micro-levels where more limited sectoral bargaining may be achieved more readily. These developments underline the need to locate corporatism within a theory of the *state*, rather than within a theory of party government, because the relationships involved are the product of an interplay between structural opportunities and constraints, and organisational and social action, and are not simply the product of voluntaristic, partisan-structured and electorally monitored choice. The converse is equally important: state theory needs to be sensitive to the extent to which different parts of the state system are grounded in distinct social bases and forms of mobilisation.

REFERENCES

Almond, G. A., 1983. 'Corporatism, pluralism and professional memory', *World Politics*, 35: 245–60
Beer, S. H., 1969. *Modern British Politics*, 2nd edn. London, Faber and Faber
Cawson, A., 1982. *Corporatism and Welfare: Social Policy and State Intervention in Britain*. London, Heinemann Educational Books
      1985. 'Varieties of corporatism: the importance of the meso-level of interest intermediation', in A. Cawson ed., *Organised Interests and the State: Studies in Meso-Corporatism*. London, Sage Publications
      1986, *Corporatism and Political Theory*, Oxford, Basil Blackwell
Cawson, A. and J. Ballard, 1984. A bibliography of corporatism. European University Institute Working Paper 84/115
Connolly, W., 1972. 'On "interests" in politics', *Politics and Society*, 2: 459–77
Crouch, C., 1977. *Class Conflict and the Industrial Relations Crisis: Compromise and Corporatism in the Policies of the British State*. London, Heinemann Educational Books
      1983. 'Pluralism and the new corporatism: a rejoinder', *Political Studies*, 31: 452–60
Dunleavy, P., 1980. *Urban Political Analysis*. London, Macmillan
Estrin, S. and P. Holmes, 1983. *French Planning in Theory and Practice*. London, Macmillan
Friedland, R., 1982. *Power and Crisis in the City: Corporations, Unions and Urban Policy*. London, Macmillan
Habermas, J., 1976. *Legitimation Crisis*. London, Heinemann Educational Books

Harris, N., 1972. *Competition and the Corporate Society: British Conservatives, the State and Industry 1945–1964*. London: Methuen

Heisler, M. O., 1979. 'Corporate pluralism revisited: where is the theory?', *Scandinavian Political Studies*, n.s., 2: 278–98.

Holloway, J. and S. Picciotto, eds., 1978. *State and Capital: A Marxist Debate*. London, Edward Arnold

Jessop, B., 1979. 'Corporatism, parliamentarism and social democracy', in P. C. Schmitter, and G. Lehmbruch, eds., *Trends Toward Corporatist Intermediation*. Beverly Hills and London, Sage Publications

1982. *The Capitalist State*. Oxford, Martin Robertson

Jordan, A. G., 1983. 'Corporatism: the unity and utility of the concept', *Strathclyde Papers on Government and Politics*, no. XIII

Jowell, J., 1977. 'Bargaining in development control', *Journal of Planning and Environment Law*: 414–33

Lehmbruch, G., 1982. 'Introduction: neo-corporatism in comparative perspective', in G. Lehmbruch and P. C. Schmitter, eds., *Patterns of Corporatist Policy-Making*. Beverly Hills and London, Sage Publications

Lukes, S., 1974. *Power: A Radical View*. London, Macmillan

Martin, R. M., 1983. 'Pluralism and the new corporatism', *Political Studies*, 31: 86–102

Middlemas, R. K., 1979. *Politics in Industrial Society: The Experience of the British System Since 1911*. London, André Deutsch

Miliband, R., 1969. *The State in Capitalist Society*. London, Weidenfeld and Nicolson

1977. *Marxism and Politics*. Oxford, Oxford University Press

1982. *Capitalist Democracy in Britain*. Oxford, Oxford University Press

1983. *Class Power and State Power*. London, Verso

O'Connor, J., 1973. *The Fiscal Crisis of the State*. New York, St Martin's Press

Offe, C., 1975. 'The theory of the capitalist state and the problem of policy formation', in L. Lindberg, R. Alford, C. Crouch, and C. Offe, eds., *Stress and Contradiction in Modern Capitalism*. Lexington, Ill., D. C. Heath

1981. 'The attribution of public status to interest groups: observations on the West German case', in S. Berger, ed., *Organizing Interests in Western Europe: Pluralism, Corporatism and the Transformation of Politics*. Cambridge, Cambridge University Press

Panitch, L., 1979. 'The development of corporatism in liberal democracies', in P. C. Schmitter and G. Lehmbruch, eds., *Trends Toward Corporatist Intermediation*. Beverly Hills and London, Sage Publications

Poulantzas, N., 1973. *Political Power and Social Classes*. London, New Left Books

1975. *Classes in Contemporary Capitalism*. London, New Left Books.

Saunders, P., 1979. *Urban Politics: A Sociological Approach*. London, Hutchinson

Schattschneider, E. E., 1960. *The Semi-Sovereign People*. Hinsdale, Ill., The Dryden Press

Schmidt, M. G., 1982 'Does corporatism matter? Economic crisis, politics and rates of unemployment in capitalist democracies in the 1970s', in G. Lehmbruch, and P. C. Schmitter, eds., *Patterns of Corporatist Policy-Making*. Beverly Hills and London, Sage Publications

Schmitter, P. C., 1974. 'Still the century of corporatism?', *Review of Politics*, 36(1): 85–131

1981. 'Interest intermediation and regime governability in contemporary Western Europe and North America', in S. Berger, ed., *Organizing Interests in Western Europe: Pluralism, Corporatism and the Transformation of Politics*. Cambridge, Cambridge University Press

1982. 'Reflections on where the theory of neo-corporatism has gone and where the praxis of neo-corporatism may be going', in G. Lehmbruch, and P. C. Schmitter, eds., *Patterns of Corporatist Policy-Making*. Beverly Hills and London, Sage Publications

Streeck, W. and Schmitter, P. C., 1984. Community, market, state – and associations? The prospective contribution of interest governance to social order. European University Institute Working Paper, no. 94

Strinati, D., 1979. 'Capitalism, the state and industrial relations', in C. Crouch, ed., *State and Economy in Contemporary Capitalism*. London, Croom Helm

Wassenberg, A., 1982. 'Neo-corporatism and the quest for control: the cuckoo game', in G. Lehmbruch, and P. C. Schmitter, eds., *Patterns of Corporatist Policy-Making*. Beverly Hills and London, Sage Publications

Weber, M., 1968. *Economy and Society*. Ed. G. Roth and C. Wittich, 2 vols. New York, Bedminster Press

Wilensky, H. L., 1976. *The New Corporatism, Centralization and the Welfare State*. Beverly Hills and London, Sage Publications

Wilson, F. L., 1983. 'Interest groups and politics in Western Europe: the neo-corporatist approach', *Comparative Politics*, 16: 105–23

Winkler, J. T., 1976. 'Corporatism', *European Journal of Sociology*: 17(1): 100–36

13

Political organisation and economic policy

PAUL BOREHAM, STEWART CLEGG AND GEOFF DOW

INTRODUCTION: THE STATE AND POLITICS

Civil society is the terrain upon which definitions of the possible are given presence, condensed, materialised and fought over by classes and other bases of social mobilisation. A crucial resource to be fought for, over and within is the state. The state may be conceived as a complex of organisational resources oriented to the construction of the economy and of civility in various determinate modes. These modes centre on diverse forms of representation, intervention and regulation. As a centre of representation, intervention and regulation, it exhibits a degree of centredness and inclusivity which is unique amongst the organisational apparatus of modern society. The state structures the fundamental social relations of modern societies.

It cannot be deduced from such formal definitions that the state is necessarily an external, coercive phenomenon *vis à vis* its citizens. Initially state power developed not to oppress its citizens but to constitute them as such, as *citizens*, under its protection; protection against other competitive powers aspiring to similar strategies of 'organisation' of a populace. (The organisation of state power can take diverse forms. Historically, it has ranged from plunder, through to slavery, subjugation, exploitation, etc.) It is not that there are 'the people' and there is 'the state', the former under the yoke of the latter. There are simply different state forms for organising a populace into a people. Hence, conceptions of the state which invoke it as an external interference in the 'normal' functioning of civil society are necessarily mistaken. State intervention and regulation, of one sort or another, are necessarily pervasive. They have been ever since the construction of the state as an organisational complex for safeguarding the interests of its constituent associations during princely absolutism. Monopoly over the means of violence always has the potential for use against citizens of the state in question, but has its origins more especially defined against the citizens of other states or the people of other territories, in pursuit of issues constructed as being in the 'national interest'.

This is not to argue that the authoritarian, repressive state is absent from the modern world, any more than is state terror. However, the dominance of the 'repressive apparatus' (as Althusser, 1971, termed it) is not typical of the state form of the advanced societies in the post-war period. The state form which could be regarded as being more characteristic of the major OECD nations is that of 'liberal democracy'. Liberal democracy was developed in states where liberal practices based on private property and wage labour emerged long before they were democratic. Democracy came only after prolonged struggle by those excluded from the liberal state, a state which was narrowly founded on the enfranchisement of propertied males. Progressively, under pressure from below, usually accompanied, as Therborn (1977) suggests, by external pressure on the state during warfare, the franchise was extended to the male working class, women, blacks and other groups disenfranchised on the basis of some salient status attribute.

In the struggle for the franchise, it was collective action by groups such as workers, women and blacks which won the issue. What was won was entry into an electoral contest in which the status of citizen was uniquely privileged in the ritual of most people's active participation in politics. Through the act of voting, one's individual status as a citizen apparently becomes compelling. Whatever qualities are inscribed in one's other statuses in civil society are abstracted away in the solitary act of representation by voting, in favour of the socially and economically naked individual.

Voting has become increasingly plebiscitary in character as electoral contests have become a competition between two or more active elites, organised in parties, and the mass of passive citizenry 'choosing' between political identities constructed none the less as specific individuals seeking mandates to represent the passive mass. The process of identity-construction, of course, has become a highly complex matter of psychology and public relations. The infrequent, secret, ritualistic casting of the vote thus becomes the high-note of politics, obscuring the political context of this 'public performance politics'.

The political context of these public performances operates through the field of political 'issues', which in a modern state, are overwhelmingly those of 'the economy'. But this 'economy', the site of class relations, appears, as both Wells (1981) and Emmison (1983) have argued, as a 'fetish'. The economy, in a liberal democracy where citizenship does not extend to the right of universal participation in key macro-economic decisions, is none the less presented as a national issue. In reality these problems of 'the nation' *are* problems of citizens; but only the capitals which operate within it have direct and immediate influence over broad outcomes. The involvement, on the basis of economic democracy or the rights of labour, of the entire citizenry is denied, even while responsibility can be attributed to a whole populace deemed to be 'living beyond its means'. Market ideology is an important means of deflecting attention from this gap between power and responsibility. 'By defining the contradictions of capital as national problems, and voters as abstract citizens in relation to these national problems, liberal democratic elections enable capital to appear as identical with the national interest' (Wells, 1981, p. 159). The basis for this is inherent in the class relations of capitalist production. It is seemingly through capital, and capital alone, that labour power can be used to generate growth, accumulation and employment. The national interest, standing mystically outside of and over those people whose actions comprise it, requires a formal homology between, on the one hand, alienated workers and voters, and on the other hand, a reified economy and politics, fused in the representation of all abstract individuals. It is this ritual of representation that sanctions, even within the context of anti-statist, anti-interventionist market liberalism, a conception of nation that permits centralised administration and technical, rational–legal state structures.

The unity of physical protection and legal regulation circumscribes the specific complex of organisations which, in Urry's (1981, p. 104) words, implement policy 'through the application of predetermined rules by hier-archically organized bureaucrats' with 'little possibility of innovative action' beyond that demanded by legitimated pressure groups. Such people are generally regarded as the more-or-less ideal embodiment of the bureaucratic type identified by Weber in *Economy and Society*. This type was organised around what Wilson (1983, p. 154) has referred to as three basic clusters of characteristics. The scalar cluster comprises principles of hierarchy, dis-cipline, formal authority and rule orientation; the functional cluster demar-cates spheres of competence, principles of selection and advancement and the technical bases for identifying these; finally, the career cluster provides the formally meritocratic rationale for submission to bureaucratic work, with its principles of free selection and contract, the separation from the means of administration of the official, with a career defined in terms of a full-time, salaried and revokable appointment. Collectively, these principles have been seen as an appropriate means for achieving efficient and formally equitable administration. They are the bedrock for any view of the state as an apparatus of neutral, technical and apolitical efficiency in its means of achieving goals which are politically defined elsewhere, by a party.

The traditional neutral view of the state depended upon a conception of civil society which was, in fact, subsumed to the competitive market (Poggi, 1978, p. 129). There were two reasons for this. First, the competitive market (at least as it appeared in its representation in economic theory) was self-equili-brating; it did not require any regulation and intervention by the state. Second, for as long as the market remained competitive it produced no power relations among economic actors other than a generalised dependency of all upon impersonal equilibrating mechanisms. Thus the state could appear as the only leviathan in the nation (the church/state battle having been fought and won by the state). However, the fiction of self-equilibrating markets could hardly survive the growth of centralised and concentrated business power in firms which maximised not only profits, but also control over markets, one another and the wider society. Consequently, with the increasing dependence of civil society as a whole upon the success or failure of these giant enterprises, the state, of necessity, has to attempt to achieve some degree of control over what can no longer be assumed to be self-equilibrating. Consequently, as conservatives such as Durkheim feared, the liberal distinction between state and civil society does become blurred by both contested and uncontested state interventions; but these are an effect of the grossness of the economic actors rather than the 'external' coercion of the state itself.

The view of the state as a benignly neutral instrument is now generally regarded as archaic, more ideological than real, and even as somewhat whimsical. In its place, however, stands no clear alternative. Indeed, the concept and theory of the state has been one of the most contested areas of debate within social science in the recent past.

THEORIES OF THE STATE

Most conservative characterisations of the state tend to overemphasise the autonomy of politics (narrowly defined) and to underemphasise the politics of administration. On the other hand, many recent Marxist theories have understated both by collapsing the distinction between the state as a custodian of social relations and the state as a complex of organisations into a theory of the state *per se*, without reference to the components of the state in anything other than functional terms.

The genesis of this 'collapsing' may be located, despite the differences of emphasis, in the classical Marxist texts (Jessop, 1977, 1978). The earliest of these derive from 1842–3 when Marx sharpened his ideas in the context of *A Critique of Hegel's 'Philosophy of Right'* (1970) and 'A Contribution to the Critique of Hegel's *Philosophy of Right*' (1975). Hegel had developed a theory of the state as the universal synthetic institution created through a series of mediations between civil and political society. Marx envisaged this function being redundant in a genuine democracy: thus he regarded the present state, in which the bureaucracy functioned sectionally rather than neutrally, as a parasite on the people. In his later writings this view was elaborated into a conception of the state as an instrument of class rule: it 'is nothing more than the form of organization which the bourgeoisie necessarily adopts both for internal and external purposes, for the mutual guarantee of their property and interests' (Marx and Engels, 1964, p. 59). It is this theme which Lenin developed when he defined the state as the oppression of one class by another in *The State and Revolution.* The state is an instrument of power which develops with the emergence of class exploitation and which finds expression in a body of officials functionally specialised in administration and repression.

Later analyses by Althusser (1971) and Poulantzas (1973) took this theme but gave it a distinctively structuralist impetus. This was derived from the centrality in their work of a particular conception of Marx's *Capital* (Althusser and Balibar, 1970). In this interpretation *Capital* is an analysis of the concept of a 'pure' mode of production as an abstraction. However, as experience has shown, the capitalist mode of production can accommodate a quite uneven articulation between the several distinct fractions of capital. Hence institutions concerned with the maintenance of the mode of production's overall cohesion and equilibrium have also developed unevenly (Castles, 1982). It is impossible now to imagine a state which functions in the interests of capital-in-general in anything other than the very broadest of senses; for example, the preservation of private-property relations. There is no such thing as capital-in-general because of the conflicting interests of the different fractions and because of the different historical and institutional circumstances under which capital formation and accumulation takes place. It is for these reasons that it has been argued that political processes acquire a degree of 'relative autonomy' so that the state can establish a general framework in which the particular fractions of capital function. This general framework is itself contested, because it almost always entails the sacrifice of some particular interests and fractions. Hence we may witness state actions which are not reproductive of the whole of capital although they are cohesive of a formation in which dominant classes continue to dominate through the unhindered process, yet changing structure, of capital accumulation (Poulantzas, 1975, pp. 78–81). From this perspective the key feature of the state was its reproductive character, its ability to be able to reproduce the conditions of production. In Althusser's work this led to a stress on the role of ideology, conflated into a concept of the ideological state apparatus, which performs required functions together with the more familiar repressive state apparatuses.

In these views the state was pre-defined, because of its reproduction/ideology function, as a capitalist state, because that is the character of the society being reproduced (Crouch, 1979). It could cease to be capitalist only if capitalism itself ceased to exist. The argument tends to imply, also, that there are no specific problems with which the state could not deal. Basic capitalist parameters always set the range of responses to any disequilibria and these responses would never be incompatible with the capitalist character of the economy. If the state functions always as the institutional source of capitalist cohesion in a capitalist society there is little point in attempting to gain concessions or reforms from it; they will always (in the long run) be in the interests of capital. This induces either a fatalistic acceptance of the state and its parliamentary forms or a utopian belief in the possibility of somehow radically 'smashing' it.

An associated consequence of this view was that it suggested especially for Marxist writers that the nature of the capitalist state is such that it has little capacity to be able to respond positively to working-class demands, through the forcing of radical reforms or the granting of concessions. Empirically, given the degree of mobilisation, contestation and struggle which has occurred around the appropriate limits of state intervention in liberal capitalist democracies by combatants in the class struggle (Esping-Andersen and Korpi, 1984) this view must be regarded with little credence. Some state policies do work to the advantage of workers; some work against the interests of capital. The actual complexion of government policy will depend on the ability of respective political contestants to mobilise resources. The normal course of economic development regularly and predictably presents fissures in the extent to which the state operates unambiguously in the interests of capitalists:

The state imposes on each capital various laws, rules, conditions, procedures and taxations which govern the operation of these separate units. And these result significantly from the force and organization of working-class and popular politics, from the determined resistance of the working-class and others to reproduce the conditions of their own reproduction. Such working-class resistance is never straightforward since it will entail alliances and coalitions with other classes, fractions and social forces. And it will always meet the constraints of action imposed by the existing degree and forms of capital accumulation, the relationship of national to international capital, the movements of money capital and the constraints of the balance of payments, etc. (Urry, 1981, p. 115)

The state apparatuses are thus the site of a constant battle between different organisations of labour and capital for control of the resources they have available to them. This is a struggle which is historically patterned. The power of state organisations as they enforce legal obligations or fulfil welfare functions for 'social problems' unresolved through the market has been a matter of massive political conflict in the major OECD countries, especially since 1974, when recession became evident. State organisations not only develop their own internal structures of bureaucratic control, but they must do so in the absence of the external discipline and 'rationality' of the market, subject to the often incommensurate irrational pressures of a plurality of organisations, classes and fractions in civil society.

If the inputs into state organisations are mediated by class struggle, this entails that the outputs – specific state interventions – will always be problematic for the capitalist class. The crucial intervening variable is the nature of the transformation processes – organisation/public administration – which attempt to mediate between class struggle, popular demands, executive dictate, pluralist pressure and specific state interventions.

The transformation processes are structured in a number of class-specific ways. These include both the structure of hegemony incorporated into the state organisations' taken-for-granted practices of administration and the structures affecting the range of relevant issues and interests with which the state has to deal.

THE STATE AND ORGANISATION

All states are composed of complex and often internally contradictory and inconsistent organisational apparatuses. It would be theoretically inappropriate to impose a single logic of rationality on to these institutions and practices. Moreover, state organisations are dissimilar to capitalist organisations in a number of ways which conservative governments, which seek to re-commodify, de-regulate or privatise state activities have not been slow to acknowledge. From this sense of difference it may be possible to construct an *organisational* perspective on the state. The fact of competition between corporate institutions leads to precise calculation within capitalist organisations and the internal adoption of certain modes of rationality. But it can be argued that there is no analogous objective social mechanism in the state sector by which state organisations can reduce costs and orient themselves towards such an ideal of rationality. It has been argued, for example, that in a tax-financed situation, where state organisation is governed by the principle of an allocative economy, there may be competition for resources which cannot be accumulated or reproduced. Competitive struggle for material benefits takes a form different from that which prevails in the private sphere; and individual material interests will be satisfied differently (Mandel, 1975, p. 579). In a purely allocative economy any saving on expenditure leads to a reduction in allocations. In terms of the dynamics of power and status within organisations, increased or large allocations can be potent resources of both a material and symbolic nature. Hence the contrast between private capital's need to control the costs of the managerial labour process, and the ambiguous and contradictory location of those state personnel charged with similar control, but who at the same time seek to increase their allocation. Mandel argues that the allocation principle, whereby expenditures are under a constant and automatic inflationary pressure, 'governs all public administration in a commodity-producing society'. Such arguments suppose that no internal auditing according to politically derived standards of accountability and efficiency is possible. They are generally relevant in circumstances where an executive faces a bureaucracy with strongly organised solutions to possible problems, including an executive wishing to develop the means to implement a sophisticated audit of expenditures and achievement of goals. They are far less relevant whenever state authorities have their own ability to raise and accumulate revenues on an entrepreneurial basis.

State organisations which are none the less governed by an allocative economy become 'formally' irrational in economic terms. All forms of cross-subsidisation are examples. An administrative example of the latter would be the existence of staff ceilings which, quantitatively, may be rational (in terms of a cost-reduction exercise) but qualitatively may be irrational inasmuch as they diminish the quality of a service whose rationale justifies their existence. Additionally, these organisations may be characterised by a tendency to a reactive avoidance of responsible planning in the face of competing and contradictory pressure and conflicts, not only from fractions of capital but also from labour, as well as other popular forces in civil society. To the extent that these possibilities are realised, charges of 'administrative overload' and endemic inefficiency that have surfaced since the 1970s achieve an ongoing political potency. The dictates of formal rationality may still, of course, produce a substantive irrationality (Higgins, 1985b).

In so far as state organisation is constructed in the absence of market discipline, or some alternative such as a public audit, terms such as effectiveness and efficiency lose their common-sense commensurability. The outcome of this rationality-deficit is that public administration comes to be characterised less by its rational goal-orientation and more by a political goal-orientation, which is already preconstituted in bourgeois terms. The recourse to non-market criteria also has objective organisational determinants. These have been well captured in a definition of organisation which has been proposed by Cohen *et al.* (1972). This definition refers only to organisation which characteristically displays problematic preferences, unclear technology (because it lacks any rational rules for monitoring, reflecting and re-formulating what it is doing) and fluid participants (who vary in the amount of time and effort they devote to the decision process). These three properties of organised anarchies are particularly conspicuous in public organisations.

The model of organised anarchy stands many assumptions on their head. Organisation has to occur without consistent, shared goals due to changing political interpretation of electoral mandates; so decision-making often proceeds under ambiguity. When a decision is made it is often without recourse to either explicit bargaining or markets: rather, it seems to relate more to the phenomenological attention of members to topics. Here, phenomenology is constituted through the active bringing-to-attention-of-the-administration by agents, agencies, lobbies, ministers, issues and classes 'outside' the formally constituted bureaucracy whose socially constructed subjectivities – of habit, thinking, feeling, being – may be more or less in, or of, the bureaucracy. Having accepted an absence of market criteria, either political negotiation assumes a key role, or organisation develops. As Cohen *et al.* argue, organisation becomes that set of extra-market procedures through which organizational participants arrive at an interpretation of what they are doing and what they have done while in the process of doing it. From this point of view, an organization is a collection of choices looking for problems, issues and feelings looking for decision situations in which they might be aired, solutions looking for issues to which they might be the answer, and decision-makers looking for work. (Cohen *et al.*, 1972, p. 4)

There are four elements of organisation in this process. First, organisation problems, as they are registered by the organisation; second, organisation solutions – answers looking for questions to attach themselves to; third, participants, who, as has already been pointed out, constitute an 'unrepresentative' and elite-centred bureaucracy, and, finally, choice situations where various kinds of organisation personnel, problems and solutions come together. Some of the 'selection rules' guiding these choice situations have been specified by Weick (1969, pp. 72–3). For instance, organisation members may typically select those choices which require least effort on their part; choices that have occurred most frequently in the past; that have been most successful and predictable in the past; that will produce the least disruption to the organisation; that will produce the most stable changes; that can be completed most rapidly; that are available and are not involved in commitments elsewhere; that will utilise the most rather than the least experienced personnel; that appear the most relevant given the form in which the problem is registered and which appear most rewarding. Even crisis situations can be interpreted in ways that preserve this inertia.

Such criteria serve to reinforce the conservative ethos of elite recruitment through providing an objective context of organisational conservatism: an organisational climate geared to the preservation of existing internal and external expectations concerning the limits of organisational action. (This points to the advantages Weber identified in charismatic leadership – it could disrupt routine in ways in which decisions produced according to rational criteria would not.) This is not peculiar to public administration, of course, but would be common to most large-scale organisations. What is peculiar to public administration as opposed to private organisation is that this conservatism is not subject to any external requirements other than those registered as political demands – usually mediated through the minister. However, as ministerial experience has shown, the politics of bureaucracy can frequently serve to counter ambiguity by subverting political ends with administrative means, or 'ploys' as Meacher (1980), Blackstone (1983) and a British television series have suggested.

One author who has been concerned to incorporate similar qualifications is Crouch (1979). The state may well have its primary functions oriented to preserving the continuity of capital accumulation: but, in addition, in order to preserve electoral legitimacy, governments are not readily able to ignore popular pressure even where it conflicts with what they define as economic interests. This pressure finds expression in demands for material prosperity – employment and stable prices, for example. Before the advent of Thatcherism in Britain, stability seemed to be the key: the politics of public administration was unambiguously conservative. Crouch unwittingly uncovers what may be a clue to the apparent failure of recent attempts to dismantle and de-regulate the panoply of the modern state:

> The state's personnel ordinarily have a strong interest in maintaining the stability of institutions which stand between the society and the collapse into civil war: the ease of their own jobs, the prestige of the institutions with which they are identified, ultimately perhaps their own physical safety and (in the case of elected politicians and those about them) their survival in office all depend on continuing social stability. It is that pursuit of stability which provides the clue to the ultimate motivation of state action. (1979, p. 40)

Once prosperity passes and is unable to provide the basis for stability, vested interest and institutional inertia take over. Archaic forms of state action remain, until overlaid by a new generation of rules, procedures, practices and collective behaviours. We have argued elsewhere that lack of new institutional developments in times of macro-economic disruption can reproduce iatrogenic solutions to new problems for extended periods (Clegg *et al.*, 1986).

A considerable advantage of this perspective is that it unhinges the actions of the state apparatuses from the conscious direction of some sector of the ruling classes and regards them rather more as the outcome of a conflict between distinct sets of agents – the capitalist class, the working class, other movements within civil society, and the administrators and managers of the state apparatus. The stress on the routine organisational practices of these state employees, the higher civil service, also focusses our attention not simply on the class-specific inputs to and outputs from the state, but the actual processes of transformation which occur within the state apparatus, quite independently of the consciousness of any particular group (Block 1977, pp. 7–8; Pollard, 1982).

The preceding characterisation of the state moves away from the antinomies of *either* a structuralist *or* an instrumentalist perspective, and incorporates some aspects of the organisational perspective. It begins to focus attention on the limits of the state's *structural selectivity* (Offe, 1975) in attending to some issues, enacting some laws, formulating some policies, regulating some areas, *but not others*. In this view, the relative autonomy of the state is recognised, as well as the limits placed on this by its operating environment, and its form as a complex organisation; indeed, it is precisely the latter that ensures that the state can never respond in an unmediated way to all representations.

THE ORGANISATION OF CAPITAL AND THE ORGANISATION OF THE STATE

Various aspects of the state have been analysed as conducive to the reproduction of capitalist interests. A key variable is often elucidated in terms of the need of the state for the maintenance of a high level of economic activity. More abstractly, it has been said that the state in capitalist society attempts to fulfil two basic but sometimes contradictory functions. These are 'accumulation' and 'legitimation'. On the one hand, the state, in complex and frequently organisationally contradictory ways, seeks to maintain or create the conditions in which profitable accumulation is possible; but on the other, it aspires to maintain hegemony. The state, in this argument, cannot afford to neglect the profitable activities of the key capitalist enterprises: to do so is to risk drying up the source of its own power – the surplus production capacity of the economic system and the taxes drawn from this surplus. Public support, in terms of the legitimacy ceded to the government and the state, may ordinarily be expected to decline sharply if the regime can be perceived as being unable to alleviate social disasters, such as unemployment, inflation or resource shortages. It is commonly argued that the state has to maintain 'legitimacy' through retaining the loyalty, apathy or acquiescence of economically exploited and socially oppressed groups and classes, while, at the same time, profiting from their further exploitation. However, 'those who accumulate capital are conscious of their interests as capitalists, but in general they are not conscious of what is necessary to reproduce the social order in changing circumstances' (Block, 1977, p. 10). The latter concern is a preoccupation which the managers of the state are structurally obliged to develop, because, as Crouch (1979) argued, their power rests on the basis of uninterrupted prosperity and political and economic order. The extent to which the state, through these managers, is able to respond to changing circumstances is not a function of individual, but of collective consciousness (Clegg *et al.*, 1983). Moreover, the capacity of state institutions to secure stability is subject to dramatic transformation itself, according to phases of capitalist expansion and recession. In addition, structural change in the economy generates quite altered 'functional' requirements from time to time, as well as time-lags in their implementation. Nor are these 'functions' unitaristically targeted. Large legitimacy deficits may continue to coincide with accumulation crises, if these are regional rather than national and if the government in office is not dependent on those regional constituencies for support. The state, after all, is an electorally fragmented entity on a regional basis under liberal democratic conditions.

Of equal importance, if less immediately apparent, is the legitimacy ceded not by the electorate as a whole, but capitalists in particular. The withdrawal of legitimacy, or the weakening of tacit support by capital does not have to wait upon the procedural conventions of parliamentary elections. It can be registered much more immediately and subtly. This will be through the mechanism of individual capital's private investment decisions. Through these, capital has a collective veto over state policies. A failure, or even hesitancy, to invest in any specific nation state, will be interpreted as a crisis of 'business confidence': the amalgam of factors which coalesce in the capitalist community's evaluation of the risks and potentials – financial, social and political – attaching to any particular investments. Considerations of class control and conflict, of political stability and disorder, of a friendly or hostile government, will all be important in the evaluation of any nation state as a site for investment within the world economy.

Business confidence, the psychological representation of the investment cycle, is the crucial variable. It is through such means that capital, collectively, in its investment decisions, is able to set a range of powerful limits on the possibilities of state action. However, in so far as the state is an arena of class struggle, the effectivity of working-class struggle as well as the actions of capital must be considered. This is demonstrated clearly in Marx's analysis of the length of the working day.

In addition to identifying struggle *within* the state, it is possible to identify those mechanisms *about* which class conflict will have to be structured to influence patterns of reproduction. This is to differentiate class conflict *within* the political form of the state from class conflict *about* this form. Class conflict within the state is that conflict which is able to manifest itself within the given organisational and procedural *rules of the game*, in the actually existing state structures. This conflict concerns

which political forms are most conducive to the articulation of the undistorted interest of various classes; supposedly each class tries to generalise and institutionalise those political forms which are most conducive to the self-enlightenment of the members of that class as to its 'true' interest and which, at the same time, minimize the adversary class's chance of articulating its interests. (Offe and Weisenthal, 1980, p. 95)

The national interest and capitalist interests can, it has been demonstrated, frequently be orchestrated in harmony. However, we have been at pains to argue that one cannot maintain that the state's output of legal enactments, the key resource available to the state in defining the 'rules of the game' in civil society and the economy generally, will necessarily be reproductive. Law is *the* intermediary between civil society, the economy and the state. Political and class struggles are manifested materially in the changing regulation and legal forms enacted by the state. The subjects engaged in these struggles are, of course, usually already constituted as legal subjects by the state. Thus, neither the state, nor its constitution of subjects, is neutral or independent of these struggles. Forms both of the state and of subjects are an object of class struggle. The logics of collective action are indeed different but they are not fixed or immune from ruptures to tradition implied by varying state institutional centres of policy-making.

The state is never wholly determined within the 'rules of the game'. In consequence, the central question concerning state interventions will be the extent to which their actual content is a result of ruling-class domination or contrary popular pressure. This may produce interventions which are not optimally reproductive: they may, for instance, be compatible whilst at the same time having contradictory effects (Clegg and Dunkerley, 1980, pp. 550–5). Under sufficient popular pressure they may even be non-reproductive: that is, they may be transformative of the underlying principles of organisation of the state and society. Struggle may materialise about the state. The state, in other words, may become an instrument for translating the interests of labour into redistributive and egalitarian practice. It is becoming increasingly common for post-war struggles over economic policy and welfare-state provision to be seen in this way (e.g. Korpi, 1983).

With this conception, the theory of the state achieves a position in which elements of not only the instrumental, structural and organisational but also structural selectivity approaches can be incorporated. A similar conception of the state informed Marx's *Capital*. The success of working-class struggle in shortening the working day was the decisive factor in the transition from what Marx termed the formal to the real subordination of labour and the consequent move from the absolute to the relative appropriation of surplus value contingent upon a new regime of productivity enhancement. This is indicative of the general point: class struggle is a decisive factor in the transformation of both the state and capitalism itself. The state is changed by taking on new functions and apparatuses as a result of the changed legal statutes, while capital has to reconsider its competitive possibilities in terms of the changed limits to its activity, prescribed by the state. It is for this reason that working-class struggles to protect itself from the depredations of the market society have been instrumental in facilitating both the further development of capitalism and the expansion of the state. Corporatist mechanisms, for instance, impose new demands on both state managers and business-group participants.

The translation of working-class pressure into state reforms and capitalist rationality is not an unproblematic and smoothly functioning process, for a number of reasons. Working-class demands are rarely articulated in holistic terms or granted in their original form. Anticipation of this can often lead to an inflation of demands in expectation of a negotiated settlement. Elements of repression can coexist with concessions. Considerable time-lags invariably occur between concessions being granted after working-class pressure and the development of state powers which are proposed to enable enhanced accumulation. Radical demands are ceded which cannot be translated into potential benefits for capital. Occupational health and safety legislation often falls into this category. Where there is pressure for reform, state managers in both the government and civil service have to balance a delicate equation. If reforms of a critical issue are blocked or refused, there may well be an escalation of class antagonisms if the reforms are not made. This can exacerbate any problems of business confidence, in such a way that a mildly reformist government may appear more stable to large capital interests than a more conservative one (Block, 1977).

Once again, it is important not to overstate the case. The perceived threat to business confidence has in many cases not been sufficient to prevent potentially radical reforms, particularly during periods of national mobilisation such as depression, war and post-war reconstruction. It is in such periods that the role of the state has quantitatively expanded for different reasons. In wartime, the importance of international business confidence declines in the face of the generally patriotic climate and the high levels of economic activity engendered by military production. The expanded spheres of legitimate policy activity developed in such periods can have quite long-lasting consequences for the balance of political power. But the conditions for the maintenance of altered organisational priorities are not usually understood by the parties who are their bearers. In serious depressions or post-war reconstruction the dynamics are different. Should state policy attempt to revive the economy, it is probable that business confidence will emerge as a key variable as the political balance shifts (Kalecki, 1943).

One important theoretical consideration is the gap between reform in law and in actual practice. Not all legal changes are enacted in the spirit which might have guided their drafting. Further, not all forms of reform achieved in these 'exceptional' periods succeeded in outlasting them, as Lowe's (1975) case study of 'The erosion of state intervention in Britain 1917–24' makes clear. Minimum wage legislation failed and the explicitly interventionist Ministry of Labour, which had been newly created in 1916, was thwarted by active Treasury opposition – the institutional form of the most narrowly orthodox, classical and free-market economics. Treasury was also the senior civil-service department, in whose managers was vested control over civil-service promotion into the highest echelons of the service. In the face of an ideological hegemony able to oppose any interventions in the free market and a threat to their own careers, the civil servants involved with the administration of the proposed areas of state intervention retreated. Not surprisingly, economic orthodoxy was re-instituted. There have been many instances of similar retreats from politically initiated reforms in Britain's recent economic history (Opie, 1972; Pollard, 1982).

The pressure towards orthodoxy need not necessarily be, and seldom is, as explicit as indicated above. Writers such as Edelman have noted how accepting a belief about a public issue is to define one's own identity. Hence, many state managers hold beliefs which affirm their personally neutral roles, beliefs which coexist with a belief in institutions they have supported. To accept the contradiction of a neutral ideology and a partial practice is to live out the mythologies of the roles attached to the positions these managers occupy 'while at the same time maintaining a measure of personal integrity by recognising facts inconsistent with the role' (Edelman, 1977, p. 151). Hence, the 'naturalisation' of state activities, that is, the presentation of government action as if there were no alternative is an effect of practices whose partiality, as self-interested exceptions, can be seen to affirm the eidolon of neutrality. A realistic party programme that seeks to articulate an interest in a complex economy and civil society, despite the alliances it may build in these spheres, will still need definite mechanisms for the generation and implementation of its programme.

Such mechanisms have recently been the focus of conflicting interpretation. In the British debates over the 'permanent' swing to the right apparently represented by the neo-liberalism of the Thatcher government, it has been claimed that 'a new common sense' has been created, one which justifies less rather than more intervention by the state. In this time of (post-1974) economic crisis, this common sense is said to link the rhetoric and prejudices of racism, anti-statism, national chauvinism and irrational moralism with a more specific sense of the failure or disruptiveness of social democracy, labourism, union power and welfarism. Stuart Hall has used the term 'authoritarian populism' (1980, 1981, 1984, 1985) to suggest that neo-liberalism is a distinctive form of conservative response to economic recession. Not only does it eschew the intervention of previous Labour and non-Labour governments but it also creates the ideological climate for a permanent downgrading of expectations, a permanent retreat from the welfare state. There has been a widespread cross-class endorsement of unfettered market mechanisms even though these are linked directly to policies which exacerbate deindustrialisation and manufacturing decline. An alternative view (Jessop *et al.*, 1984, 1985) is that the Thatcherist state has in fact been far less a break with the past than Hall supposes. Thatcherism is a conjuncturally specific phenomenon. It certainly is different in form and substance from other post-war Conservative governments but it offers sentiments that are not at all unlike the anti-interventionist rhetoric that prevailed in the 1930s. Then, as now, anti-collectivist argument was deployed quite ruthlessly to modify, repudiate and, as far as possible, to undermine policy measures which would have replaced market mechanisms with political controls over economic activity.

The state has not been able to assert successfully a unitary logic over policy-making deliberations. This persistence of contestation (albeit less evident in the UK than in the non-English-speaking world), combined with the demonstrable failure of the economics of monetarism to 'reflate' the British economy, provides fissures in the ideological façade of the new Right. Evidence exists in the fact of Britain's division into 'two nations' (an impoverished north and still affluent south), to support the argument that alternative politics cannot be willed away by even so relentless a state apparatus as Thatcher's (Jessop *et al.*, 1984).

Strategically, this critique of the authoritarian populism thesis is important. The monetarist response to post-war Keynesianism need not be seen as hegemonic but merely as an indication of the inadequacy of labour's own political and economic understandings. It has been argued in both empirical (Apple, 1983) and theoretical terms (Robinson, 1972) that the era of full employment has less to its credit than could have been the case precisely because the political struggle for the control of investment and economic democracy was consistently abrogated by labour parties, academic economists and the policy-making institutions of the post-war era. Without a clear understanding of the reasons for the boom and the limitations to institutional development that it allowed, labour movements and Labour governments were in no position to cope with the recession when it occurred. Inadequate policy responses followed; so did unemployment; and so, also, did the basis for electoral scepticism that gave the conservatives in Britain, the US and Australia, their historic victories.

For those who continue to proclaim the ideological dominance of the seemingly contradictory elements of the new Right (increasing authoritarianism and anti-statism) the lessons remain unlearned. A more appropriate response would be to set in train the institutional and political rebuilding that would be necessary for renewed capital accumulation, economic growth and industrial expansion in the core capitalist countries. This would require quite massive political interventions (such as were contemplated and jettisoned, in 1945) and attendant political (and class) realignments (Clegg *et al.*, 1986).

Although British proponents of an alternative economic strategy have been loathe to accept lessons from the non-Anglo-Saxon world concerning revamped relations between extra-parliamentary institutions and sound macroeconomic performance (Higgins, 1985a), the loss of manufacturing capacity in the UK is testimonial to the need for an alternative accumulation strategy. This requires a renewed attention to policy-making. The magnitude of the task shows that the state in Britain has in the past been too weak, too unwilling to intervene and too 'residual', rather than too strong, too interventionist, or too statist. Compared with Scandinavian models of economic and welfare development, British governments have been too slow to integrate labour movements into policy-making institutions and too unwilling to foster the organisational acumen that trade unions need to expand their political role. As

Jessop *et al.* conclude, 'a new productivist orientation to left economic policies' is needed:

> In this context corporatism should not be unequivocally rejected by the Left. A supply-oriented corporatism in which there is a genuine political exchange (not merely a policy of wage restraint in return for nothing) would provide an important basis for extending economic democracy and deepening political representation. Such corporatist relations should *prefigure* socialist forms of economic and political organization rather than reproduce the bureaucratic corporatism and elitist tripartism of earlier experiments. (Jessop *et al.*, 1985, p. 100)

Of the 'corporatisms' that do exist, or that are currently being constructed, current understanding is only partial. The ideal type definition provided a decade ago by Schmitter, for example, seems especially unhelpful as a guide to contemporary attempts to develop political alternatives to market-criteria macro-economic decisions. Schmitter has conceived corporatist arrangements in a way which seems to exclude purely tripartite arrangements between government, business and trade unions. His often-cited conceptual specification envisages the representation of a diverse range of 'interests' that are 'recognized or licensed (if not created) by the state' and which 'control' both leaders and demands (1974, p. 13). This type of corporatism seems neither to capture the essentials of emergent 'corporatist' forms, nor to specify sufficiently the range of decisions and demands likely to be considered by such forums (McEachern, 1985). For these reasons another term, 'political trade unionism', has been proffered to highlight the expanded role of trade unionism (away from industrial militancy and into public policy-making) that anti-recessionary strategies seem to imply (Higgins, 1985a).

Higgins's argument, following Korpi (1983), is that neither social democratic/Labour governments nor the political parties of labour can be relied upon to increase political control over investment. What is also required is that a transformed, solidaristic, trade-union movement, organized with a commitment to income equality and anti-market liberal priorities for the deployment of capital, is able to assert collectivist criteria in the sphere of public policy. It is this shift in the locus of political control of the economy that demonstrates the conflicts necessarily underpinning capital accumulation and alternative strategies for the re-establishment of accumulation.

> Ultimately, political unionism rests on a much wider definition of class conflict than corporatism offers, one that encompasses all manifestations of capitalist social power and economic control, and one that neither sees the state as an insuperable obstacle to working-class politics, nor the unions themselves as incapable of pursuing a higher level of political ambition. As opposed to corporatism's politics of abstention, political unionism offers the politics of contestation. (Higgins 1985a, p. 364)

In order to illuminate ways in which conservative, structural aspects of capitalist states may be confronted it is instructive to consider some implications of the Swedish case. Interest in Sweden derives not only from its well-elaborated model of political and economic development but also from its particular history of both blue-collar and white-collar involvement in public-policy formation.

At issue is an assertion of the possibility of political agency over structural determination.

THE WORKING CLASS, POLITICAL ORGANISATION AND STATE POLICY

Full-employment capitalism has been a feature of only a small number of countries for a short period of time. In a number of Western democracies during the late 1950s and early 1960s, nominally full rates of employment were achieved, but only in Sweden did these survive and take root through the 1970s and into the present (Apple, 1983). Hedborg and Meidner (1984) stress the role of labour union and Labour Party solidarity and mobilisation as well as the importance of generating policy options outside, and independently of, the state apparatus. Given the conservatism typically characterising structures of the state, this is precisely what is required if social change is to occur beyond that achieved through the authoritarian, populist mode of leadership, which appears to be the alternative liberal-democratic strategy.

In times of near full employment, problems for capitalist development and investment strategies derive from wage-drift inflation in both the highly concentrated, monopoly sector and in the more fragmented, competitive sector. During recessionary restructuring of economic activity, however, only the monopolised sector is able to pass on wage increases because of its control over pricing policy and the market, despite declining turnover. The 'normal' operation of a capitalist growth economy therefore contains potential impediments to the accumulation of capital. The reason for this is that labour discipline is undermined by high wages and high employment to the detriment of private profit. Additionally, in a fully employed mature economy, outlets for profitable and socially acceptable investment funds are progressively drying up. These impediments become actual during the ensuing recession as realignments, restructuring and renegotiations involving industries, the labour process, the role of the state and established relations between capital and labour all take place.

It is in the interests of working-class organisations, therefore, to mobilise for institutional arrangements and political conditions which facilitate efficient, high-growth, high-income economic strategies. It had been recognised by both Keynes and Kalecki that such a state of full employment cannot be sustained by capitalism without a somewhat comprehensive socialisation of investment (Keynes, 1936) or without the development of new social and political institutions which would reflect the increased power that the working class would thereby attain (Kalecki, 1943).

Swedish strategies for full employment entailed a macro-economic management in which the rights of private capital were not sacrosanct and in which the labour movement was democratically involved in the production of a relatively unskewed distribution of income among wage earners. A 'solidarity' wages policy or a genuine social contract, whereby all workers benefit from productivity increases in the strongest sector and where incomes policies are not used as tactics in a strategy of real wage reduction, became the basis from which subsequent demands for democratic control over the timing and direction of technological investments were launched (Meidner, 1978).

A solidarity wages policy does not emerge 'naturally' from a disinterested and benevolent state. Although policies initiated in the 1930s to influence the content, as well as the level, of economic activity in Sweden were partly successful, elsewhere such measures were not seriously contemplated. In the Swedish case, in the 1930s, contemporary arguments suggested the use of what one can recognise as Keynesianism, counter-cyclical public spending. It was argued that full employment should be generated by intervention, on a selective basis, in both private and public investment.

This was later supplemented by the solidarity wages policy which scrapped the market principle of a firm's capacity to pay a given wage in terms of its own profitability. Acquiescence in such a principle is in effect a subsidy by labour to inefficient managements and uncompetitive capital. Inefficient firms, in market terms, were to be rationalised, but under the aegis of a labour-directed active manpower policy. This would be vindicated as the state contained inflationary pressures by re-allocating high profits to investment sectors which could be developed under the redistributive justice of an efficient but administered resource allocation.

Politically, this forged an alliance between the labour movement and the social democrats in which the initiatives that had been developed by labour received widespread electoral support. Most important, the policy advanced was one which placed the burden of state intervention on to the conditions of capital formation rather than one which allowed wage costs to set the level of business confidence.

Policies such as those favoured by the Swedish Federation of Trades Unions were able to be formulated and implemented only through the development of policy options, planning, and strategic information organised at a central, national level. The capitalist state, like any other complex of organisational forms, as we have argued, suffers from rigidities, bureaucratic inertia and political caution. It cannot be expected to transform itself or undermine its implicit mission. The Swedish Rehn–Meidner model ensured that wages policy, distribution policy and investment policy would be integrated not as in a capitalist policy state but as responsible to labour. The Meidner plan and the Co-determination Act 1976, together, provided the pre-conditions for a socialist democratisation of organisational relations of production, at least in the sphere of legal ownership and actual possession. They demonstrate the necessity of economic and political democracy being followed in a united strategy.

The organisational arrangements through which these goals might be achieved elsewhere would need to transform the terms on which planning and investment decisions are traditionally based: by elimination of profitability as the criterion for investment; by replacing the market as the prime mechanism for resource allocation with overtly political mechanisms; and by de-commodifying an increasing proportion of social production.

For labour, the advantages of involvement in institutions which are structured to allow a more broadly democratic determination of the scale, content and trajectory of capital accumulation, derive from the political implications of the Kaleckian analysis of full-employment capitalism. Implicit in this is the recognition that insistence on permanent full employment and production for use is ultimately incompatible with capitalism's underlying social relations. The caveats that have been sounded to labour involvement derive from either the experience of labour's past incorporation into wages policy determination on unequal or unsustainable terms (Panitch, 1979), or else from a civil and pluralist constitution of labour as just one of a number of interest groups which are entitled to representation. This latter point is one which Offe (1981, 1983) cites in his claims that fragmented political conflict is increasingly unaccommodatable in the mechanisms of competitive party democracy. As the resulting tensions and limitations on the ability of the state to respond have become more apparent, a consequential 'wave of postpluralist realism' has created a perception of malfunctioning in the institutions of democratic representative government 'which are serious enough to explain the resort to corporatist political structures' (Offe, 1981, pp. 129, 146). Pluralist corporatism, by adjudicating multifarious civil demands, systematically presupposes consensus and therefore discriminates against labour organisations seeking to change the 'rules of the game' (1981, p. 153). Under such conditions, familiar bargaining over wages and unfamiliar demands for economic democracy at a macro-economic level can be met only by the displacement of pluralist assumptions or by sustained repression. What is required of new institutions is not a problem-solving conflict resolution but a regeneration of forums for a conflictual politics.

Explicitly political and non-repressive strategies which respond to 'post pluralist' conditions are premised on what Regini (1983) has called a 'class-oriented' rather than an associational basis of representation. Under these circumstances, unions seek to represent a much wider constituency than simply their own members, through having political status attributed to them. What this entails is a delegation of public functions to the unions and their possible incorporation within the state. Certain organisational effects of this process have been noted, particularly the resultant tendency for the unions' organisation to become more bureaucratised and for inter-union organisation to become more centralised than would be the case where a market, rather than a political, strategy has predominated.

These cautions, however, should not detract attention from the functional necessity of new institutional forums for macro-economic decision-making. Just as parliament has not been the site of these decisions in the past, the boardroom should not continue to be so in the future. The task is to bring labour, capital and the state together in ways which preclude the use of recession as a strategy for economic restructuring or workforce discipline. Neither should corporatist forms be used merely as forums for interest-group representation or as a surrogate parliament. New institutions may well embrace representation from regional and particular lobbying interests at the time when actual investments are made (Abrahamsson and Broström, 1980), but they should not be expected to incorporate the multifarious representations that are constantly being formed and reformed in civil society. Labour's involvement in full-employment planning cannot be regarded as analogous to other specific political demands. Some objections to corporatism therefore seem to err by insisting, as, for example, Hall has done, that 'corporatism excludes the great mass of the people . . . the range of democratic participation is not expanded' (1983, p. 197). Broadening the basis for political control of the economy involves the establishment of permanent and stable institutions whereby labour's participation is not an unequal or *ad hoc* matter.

If the 'massive inequality' which Macpherson regarded as always accompanying liberal freedoms and market allocation (1973, p. 180) is to be displaced by 'post-liberal' organisational developments, then the instability and unresponsiveness of tripartite structures that is foreshadowed and feared by Panitch, Schmitter, and Hall will need to be countered. Our argument is that this can be achieved by the whole-hearted participation of labour *qua* labour. Systems of pluralist, interest-group representation may indeed produce unstable corporatisms where the demands of constituent members are constrained (Schmitter, 1974, p. 13). A less diffuse corporatism, however, could develop institutional mechanisms which allow a democratically formulated yet economically regenerative allocation of enterprise surpluses to investment. Such an allocation would accord with the distributional concomitants of collectively controlled investment decisions and maximum levels of capital formation.

Organisation and strategy are crucial because the ability of classes to affect social, political and economic outcomes is always contingent (Korpi, 1985). It is this susceptibility to political influence which requires that policies aimed at regenerating capital accumulation according to *alternative* investment criteria will need to be based upon comprehensive political strategies. The potential of such strategies to be effective will depend less upon the formulation of associated manifestos and statements than upon the capacities of classes to mobilise resources and the forms of organisation and practice thereby developed.

REFERENCES

Abrahamsson, Bengt, and Anders Broström, 1980. *The Rights of Labor*. London, Sage Publications

Althusser, Louis, 1971. *Lenin and Philosophy and Other Essays*. London, New Left Books

Althusser, Louis, and E. Balibar, 1970. *Reading Capital*. London, New Left Books

Apple, Nixon, 1983. 'The historical foundations of class struggle in late capitalist liberal democracies', in S. Clegg, G. Dow and P. Boreham, eds., *The State, Class and the Recession*, pp. 72–128. London, Croom Helm

Blackstone, Tessa, 1983. 'No minister', *New Socialist*, 9: 42–5

Block, Fred, 1977. 'The ruling class does not rule: Notes on the marxist theory of the state', *Socialist Revolution*, May–June: 6–28

Castles, F. G., 1982. *The Impact of Parties: Politics and Policies in Democratic Capitalist States*. London, Sage Publications

Clegg, Stewart, Paul Boreham and Geoff Dow, 1986. *Class, Politics and the Economy*. London, Routledge and Kegan Paul

Clegg, Stewart, Geoff Dow and Paul Boreham, 1983. 'Politics and crisis: the state of the recession', in S. Clegg, G. Dow and P. Boreham, eds., *The State, Class and the Recession*, pp. 1–50. London, Croom Helm

Clegg, Stewart and David Dunkerley, 1980. *Organization, Class and Control*. London, Routledge and Kegan Paul

Cohen, Michael D., J. G. March and J. P. Olsen, 1972. 'A garbage can model of organizational choice', *Administrative Science Quarterly*, 17(1): 1–25

Crouch, Colin, 1979. 'The state, capital and liberal democracy', in C. Crouch, ed., *State and Economy in Contemporary Capitalism*, pp. 13–54. London, Croom Helm

Edelman, Murray, 1977. *Political Language: words that succeed and policies that fail*. London, Academic Press

Emmison, J. M., 1983. Lay Conceptions of the Economy: a theoretical and empirical analysis of ideology and economic life. PhD thesis, Brisbane, University of Queensland

Esping-Andersen, Göstar and Walter Korpi, 1984. 'Social policy as class politics in post war capitalism: Scandinavia, Austria and Germany', in J. H. Goldthorpe, ed., *Order and Conflict in Contemporary Capitalism: Studies in the Political Economy of Western European Nations*. Oxford, Clarendon Press

Hall, Stuart, 1980. 'Popular-democratic vs Authoritarian populism: two ways of taking democracy seriously', in A. Hunt, ed., *Marxism and Democracy*. London, Lawrence and Wishart

1981. 'Moving right', *Socialist Review*, no. 55, 11(1), January–February: 113–37

1983. 'Thatcherism, racism and the left', *Meanjin*, 42(2): 191–202

1984. 'The crisis of labourism', in J. Curran, ed., *The Future of the Left*. Oxford, Policy Press and New Socialist

1985. 'Authoritarian populism: a reply to Jessop *et al*', *New Left Review*, 151, May–June: 115–24

Hedborg, Anna and Rudolf Meidner, 1984. *Folkhemsmodellen*. Stockholm, Rabén and Sjögren

Higgins, Winton, 1985a. 'Political unionism and the corporatist thesis', *Economic and Industrial Democracy*, 6(3), August: 349–81

  1985b. Manufacturing decline and the sociological critique of enterprise calculation. Paper presented to Sociology Department, University of New England, Armidale, NSW, November

Jessop, Bob, 1977. 'Recent theories of the capitalist state', *Cambridge Journal of Economics*, 1: 353–73

  1978. 'Marx and Engels on the state', in S. Hibbin, ed., *Politics, Ideology and the State*, pp. 40–68. London, Lawrence and Wishart

Jessop, Bob, Kevin Bonnett, Simon Bromley and Tom Ling, 1984. 'Authoritarian populism, two nations and Thatcherism'. *New Left Review*, 147, September–October; 32–60

  1985. 'Thatcherism and the politics of hegemony: a reply to Stuart Hall', *New Left Review*, 153, September–October, 87–101

Kalecki, Michal, 1943. 'Political aspects of full employment', *The Political Quarterly*, 14(4): 322–31

Keynes, John Maynard, 1936. *The General Theory of Employment, Interest and Money*. London, Macmillan

Korpi, Walter, 1983. *The Democratic Class Struggle*. London, Routledge and Kegan Paul

  1985. 'Power resources approach vs action and conflict: on causal and intentional explanation in the study of power', *Sociological Theory: A Semi-annual Journal of the American Sociological Association*, 3/2: 31–45

Lowe, Robert, 1975. 'The erosion of state intervention in Britain 1917–24', *Economic History Review*, 31(2): 270–86

McEachern, Doug, 1985. 'National Economic Summit: business and the Hawke government', *Journal of Australian Political Economy*, 19, December: 5–13

Macpherson, C. B., 1973. *Democratic Theory: essays in retrieval*. Oxford, Oxford University Press

Mandel, Ernest, 1975. *Late Capitalism*. London, New Left Books

Marx, Karl, 1970. *Critique of Hegel's 'Philosophy of Right'*. J. O'Malley, ed., Cambridge, Cambridge University Press

  1975. 'A contribution to the critique of Hegel's *Philosophy of Right*', in *Karl Marx: Early Writings*. L. Colletti, ed., pp. 243–58. Harmondsworth, Penguin Books

Marx, Karl and Friedrich Engels, 1964. 'The manifesto of the communist party', in L. S. Feuer, ed., *Marx and Engels: Basic Writings on Politics and Philosophy*. London, Fontana Books, pp. 43–82

Meacher, Michael, 1980. 'How the mandarins rule', *New Statesman*, 5 December: 14–15

Meidner, Rudolph, 1978. *Employee Investment Funds: An Approach to Collective Capital Formation*. London, Allen and Unwin

Offe, Claus, 1975. 'The theory of the capitalist state, and the problem of policy formation', in L. N. Lindberg, R. Alford, C. Crouch and C. Offe, eds., *Stress and Contradiction in Modern Capitalism: Public Policy and the Theory of the State*. New York, D. C. Heath, 125–44

  1981. 'The attribution of public status to interest groups: observations on the West German case', in S. Berger, ed., *Organizing Interests in Western Europe: Pluralism, Corporatism and the Transformation of Politics*. Cambridge, Cambridge University Press, pp. 123–58

  1983. 'Competitive party democracy and the Keynesian welfare state: some reflections on its historical limits', in S. Clegg, G. Dow and P. Boreham, eds., *The State, Class and the Recession*. London, Croom Helm, pp. 51–71

Offe, Claus and H. Wiesenthal, 1980. 'Two logics of collective action: theoretical notes on social class and organizational form', in M. Zeitlin, ed., *Political Power and Social Theory: a Research Annual*, pp. 67–116. Greenwich, Conn., JAI

Opie, Roger, 1972. 'Economic planning and growth', in W. Beckerman, ed., *The Labour Government's Economic Record 1964–1970*. London, Duckworth

Panitch, Leo, 1979. 'The development of corporatism in liberal democracies', in P. C. Schmitter and G. Lembruch, eds., *Trends Towards Corporatist Intermediation*. London, Sage Publications, pp. 119–46

Poggi, Gianfranco, 1978. *The Development of the Modern State: A Sociological Introduction*. London, Hutchinson

Pollard, Sidney, 1982. *The Wasting of the British Economy: British Economic Policy 1945 to the Present*. London, Croom Helm

Poulantzas, Nicos, 1973. 'The problem of the capitalist state', in J. Urry and J. Wakeford, eds., *Power in Britain*, pp. 291–305. London, Heinemann

   1975. *Classes in Contemporary Capitalism*. London, New Left Books

Regini, Marino, 1983. 'The crisis of representation in class oriented unions: some reflections on the Italian case', in S. Clegg, G. Dow and P. Boreham, eds., *The State, Class and the Recession*. London, Croom Helm, pp. 239–56

Robinson, Joan, 1972. 'The second crisis of economic theory', *American Economic Review (Papers and Proceedings)*, 62(2): 1–10

Schmitter, Philippe C., 1979. 'Still the century of corporatism?', in P. C. Schmitter and G. Lembruch, eds., *Trends Towards Corporatist Intermediation*. London, Sage Publications

Therborn, Göran, 1977. 'The rule of capital and the rise of democracy', *New Left Review*, 103: 3–41

   1978. *What Does the Ruling Class Do When It Rules? State Apparatuses and State Power under Feudalism, Capitalism and Socialism*. London, New Left Books

Urry, John, 1981. *The Anatomy of Capitalist Societies: The Economy, Civil Society and the State*. London, Macmillan

Weick, Karl E., 1969. *The Social Psychology of Organizing*. Reading, Mass., Addison–Wesley

Wells, David, 1981. *Marxism and the Modern State: An Analysis of Fetishism in Capitalist Society*. Brighton, Harvester

Wilson, H. T., 1983. 'Technology and late capitalist society: reflections on the problem of rationality and social organization', in S. Clegg, G. Dow and P. Boreham, eds., *The State, Class and the Recession*, pp. 152–238. London, Croom Helm

14

Industrial democracy and the capitalist state

APRIL CARTER

Industrial democracy is now fashionable in many circles in the West, and there have been significant moves to extend existing forms of worker participation and to introduce new forms during the 1970s. Explanations of the popularity of industrial democracy are varied and the reasons for espousing it sometimes seem to be in direct conflict. It may, for example, be seen as a way of increasing productivity and profits. Or it may be seen as a way of overcoming the alienation of the assembly-line worker and promoting a socialist ideal.

This essay examines some of the issues raised by industrial democracy within Western capitalist societies: (i) whether industrial democracy should be viewed as a development of sophisticated capitalist organisation, or as a response to trade-union and social-democratic power; (ii) whether industrial democracy is workable in the case of multinationals; (iii) whether industrial democracy is a natural extension of political democracy, or a temporary vogue which will become increasingly irrelevant; (iv) how concepts of industrial democracy fit differing models of democracy; (v) what the main obstacles are to achieving board-level industrial democracy within existing companies; (vi) what the main obstacles are to achieving consistent state support for the principle of industrial democracy; and finally (vii) whether industrial democracy as a strategy raises the same difficulties as parliamentary socialism and what conclusions should be drawn.

DEFINING INDUSTRIAL DEMOCRACY

Before proceeding, it is necessary to distinguish between the various measures which fall within the general rubric of 'industrial democracy'; especially as use of a cover-all term can suggest somewhat misleadingly that identical methods are being advocated for diametrically opposed capitalist and socialist ends. One basic distinction often drawn is between those types of participation or representation that allow workers to be consulted, but preserve for management the final power of decision; and those institutional arrangements which ensure worker control (at least in principle) over strategic decisions and over management itself. This distinction suggests that *participation* can be comfortably accommodated in a sophisticated version of management and good labour relations, whilst *control* remains an uncompromisingly anti-capitalist tactic.

But a simple contrast between participation and control obscures important distinctions. It is, for example, important to note that worker participation can be introduced at three levels of the firm, corresponding to three levels of decision-making: *on the shop floor*, where the issues are allocation of jobs, the pace of work, and possibly the hours of work; *at the middle level*, where worker representatives on works councils can discuss conditions at work, welfare policies, wages, and possibly staffing and redundancies; and *at board level*, where strategic decisions about range of products, pricing policy, investment, location or closure of plants and company mergers are made. Group autonomy and control over the work process has been asserted with some success in the past by skilled craft workers, and so what is at issue is in part the extension of this privilege to the assembly-line worker. Either participation or control at shop-floor level may have important effects on the degree of work satisfaction or self-esteem of the workers involved. But they have no direct impact on the power structure of the firm at higher levels. Worker consultation at intermediate levels has become increasingly widespread – all nine EEC countries make some provision for consultative or works councils – but these councils tend to be regarded by trade unionists as a managerial device and to be challenged by strong shop-steward movements which aim to replace them with collective bargaining. Representation of workers at board level – even minority representation – raises more directly the possibility that industrial democracy might affect the distribution of power within enterprises, and trade unions tend to be divided in their assessment of its implications, as evidence submitted to the Committee of Inquiry on Industrial Democracy in Britain (the Bullock Committee) indicates.

Because worker representation on company boards has potentially radical implications, it may prove to be more significant in challenging inequalities in power than some forms of worker control. Small-scale producer co-operatives, for example, may exist in a capitalist economy without posing any threat to the system. On the other hand, worker representation on the board of a major company involves at least the potential for asserting worker interests and power. Nevertheless, the basic distinction between participation and control has considerable importance at board level.

The degree of worker representation which exists at present in Western Europe and Britain falls clearly into the category of participation. This is true even in West Germany where co-determination was introduced by the Western occupation powers soon after the Second World War. Although workers in the coal, iron, and steel industries won the right to 50 per cent representation on their supervisory boards in 1951, and 1976 legislation provides for employee representation on supervisory boards to be raised from one-third to a half in all companies with over 2,000 workers, the initiative has remained in practice with the smaller management board of directors (because of the two-tier board structure in German industry which restricts the legal powers of the supervisory board). The right of coal, iron, and steelworkers' representatives on the board to approve the appointment of the Labour Director of the inner management group – sometimes cited as the most effective form of worker representation in these industries – was not extended to other companies under the 1976 law. Even the Bullock Report, which was responsive to trade-union demands, pulled back from advocating 50 per cent trade-union representation on British (single-tier) boards of directors by allowing for a third group chosen jointly by shareholder and employee representatives.

INDUSTRIAL DEMOCRACY AND CAPITALISM

Legal provision for extensive worker participation at intermediate and board levels can be viewed with some plausibility as an extension of sophisticated management and a product of the organisational development of advanced capitalism. The interpretation assumes that worker participation on the shop floor can increase productivity, that middle-level consultation can smoothe out unnecessary friction and meet worker grievances, and that top-level representation can ease worker co-operation in introducing new technology and changing plant locations, thus generally promoting the efficiency of the firm. The fact that West Germany has enjoyed co-determination, that the majority of EEC countries have made some kind of provision for worker representation at board level, and that the EEC has published a Green Paper designed to pave the way for European-wide company law requiring such representation, all lend colour to the theory that worker participation benefits economic productivity.

If however one challenges the assumption that worker representation does promote economic efficiency it becomes doubtful whether it primarily serves the interest of owners and managers. The causal connection between West German economic success and co-determination is debatable. The Bullock Report implies that there is such a connection. But it does so in noticeably vague phraseology which suggests lack of clarity (or at least agreement) about the nature of this linkage, and it is possible to produce a range of alternative arguments to explain West German success (Chiplin *et al.*, 1977). The logic of the argument that worker participation leads to efficiency can also be challenged, since management could be delayed in carrying through decisions by the need to work through participatory bodies – an issue raised in the

Confederation of British Industry (CBI) evidence to the Bullock Committee – and is concerned about divulging confidential information and relinquishing its prerogative to make strategic decisions. If good industrial relations are necessary to high productivity, then good wages and conditions and job security, and provision for re-training to deal with new technology, may be more central than the right to be represented on boards of directors. It is interesting that research into two British experiments in worker participation initiated by socially concerned owners (the John Lewis Partnership and the Scott Bader Commonwealth) indicates that workers value good working conditions and job security more highly than their democratic opportunities, which many fail to utilise (Poole, 1978, p. 72 and Pateman, 1970, p. 82). Both these schemes also include an element of profit-sharing which, within a capitalist frame of reference, creates incentives for hard work and might be expected to prove more effective economically than participation in decision-making.

Even if particular managements might calculate that worker representation would be advantageous, it seems unlikely that directors would positively welcome a policy which made it mandatory and which enforced a percentage of worker directors. Indeed it was these two issues, together with the specifically trade-union representation recommended by the Bullock Report, that the CBI most bitterly contested. Worker representation, once conceded in principle, could open the door to eventual worker veto power or even dominance on boards. The West German law of 1976 increasing worker representation could be interpreted as evidence that once industrial democracy has been established as customary and given political legitimacy, it is a trend difficult to reverse.

Therefore it seems more plausible to suggest that moves towards worker representation at board level represent the growing economic and political strength of the working class, expressed through trade unions or socialist parties. The 1977 Swedish scheme for co-determination, which required employers by law to negotiate with unions on a wide range of issues affecting the workforce, and the 1973 Swedish experiment in worker representation at board level, can plausibly be seen as a reflection of the unusually high membership and effective central organisation of Swedish trade unions, and of the unique strength of the Swedish Social Democratic Party which had been in power almost uninterruptedly since 1932 (Gregory, 1978, pp. 7–9). In interpreting the West German programme of co-determination, it is well to remember that German capitalists had been discredited for their association with Nazism and that the Western occupation powers, who introduced a form of co-determination in 1947, saw the trade unions as a force for democracy. It is also notable that the threat of a strike by the miners and metalworkers won 50 per cent worker representation on supervisory boards in the iron, steel, and coal industries in 1951, whereas a decline in union militancy and effectiveness, and a swing to the right in the prevailing political mood, resulted in less favourable worker representation in other industries when a further law was passed in 1952 (Grosser, 1974, pp. 302–17). Support for trade-union representation on company boards was espoused in Britain in the 1970s by the Labour Party, in a context of effective union militancy against the previous Conservative government and union involvement at a national level in economic policy-making. Under the Thatcher government it has, however, disappeared from the political agenda.

THE MULTINATIONALS

The touchstone of a debate about the extent to which industrial democracy reflects developments in management and organisation in the most advanced capitalist sector must be the attitude of multinational companies. There are some grounds for thinking that multinationals will be responsive to the idea of participation. Big corporations are predisposed to project an image of corporate responsibility and social concern and therefore to promote a reputation for good labour relations. Although multinationals have the economic power to neutralise intransigent trade unions by switching their operations elsewhere, they may also be more willing than smaller and weaker firms to make concessions to labour in the interests of long-term co-operation and smooth technical change. ICI is a good example of a company which has adopted this policy in Britain, introducing a profit-sharing scheme and measures to increase shop-floor autonomy, and has been willing to co-operate with unions over introduction of new technology at their Gloucester nylon-spinning factory (Poole, 1978, p. 61). There are, however, much stronger grounds for doubting whether multinationals would willingly accept a significant worker representation on their boards, which might hinder their freedom of action both at home and abroad. In Britain, trade-union representatives are more likely to oppose policies creating large-scale redundancies and to raise questions about company involvement in defence contracts or about the health hazards of company products. Multinationals' investment and activities abroad are liable to arouse even greater political doubts among worker directors. The operations of ICI's subsidiary in South Africa have brought it under fire from anti-apartheid groups, and many multinationals (for example, Unilever and Lucas) were criticised by a House of Commons Select Committee in the 1970s for paying their black employees in South Africa poverty-level wages. Sanctions-busting by subsidiaries of Shell and BP, who were delivering oil to Rhodesia, could have been aired publicly much sooner if there had been worker directors aware of this breach of sanctions. Even if worker representatives on boards were insulated from knowledge of many of the company's activities (as seems quite likely), investigative journalists and campaign groups could supply them with information on major political issues and hope that worker directors could then make use of their position on the board.

Whether national governments can effectively constrain multinational companies is a central and problematic issue both in democratic and socialist terms, and is raised sharply by proposals to legislate on industrial democracy at board level. There are two separate issues involved. The first is whether worker representation can and should be imposed on home-based multinationals. The Bullock Report noted that neither the West German nor Swedish legislation exempted multinationals incorporated in their country (although the Dutch did make some exceptions). It also noted that if home-based multinationals were exempt, the result would be the exclusion of a sizeable proportion of the British workforce, and therefore recommended that industrial democracy legislation should apply to these companies. This is one of the issues on which the Minority Report signed by the three industrialists on the Bullock Committee (including former chairmen of ICI and Esso) queried the realism of the majority report and objected to representatives of British employees having the vote on investments outside the UK or on issues wholly concerning subsidiaries. The Minority Report was much more sharply opposed to the Majority Report on the second question of British subsidiaries of foreign-based multinationals, which Bullock also wanted to include (with some qualifications about the special role of the parent company) in legislation. The Minority group argued that a law to impose employee representation on subsidiaries would ignore the need for centralised decisions on capital expenditure, financial control and profit allocation. Such a move, it was suggested, would invite attempts to bypass the law through altering the legal status of companies by turning them into branches of the parent body. Further, it was proposed in the Minority Report that foreign investors would be deterred from committing themselves to British operations if their plans for subsidiaries could be frustrated (Bullock Report, 1977, pp. 184–5 and 192–3).

It is not unreasonable therefore to deduce that multinationals would use their economic power either to boycott investment in a country requiring significant worker representation on their boards, or to close down existing plants, or to nullify such legislation. So, in practice, pressure from multinationals may modify government policy, although concerted EEC legislation could strengthen individual governments. The conflicting arguments posed in the Majority and Minority Reports reflect the dilemma multinationals pose for exponents of industrial democracy: that considerations of realism (whether viewed from a capitalist or Marxist standpoint) suggest multinationals will not tolerate moves towards worker control; but the democratic arguments for worker participation in decision-making in the economic sphere suggest that it is self-contradictory to omit the most powerful sector of industry and the large number of workers employed in it. We must now turn to these democratic arguments.

TRENDS TOWARDS INDUSTRIAL DEMOCRACY?

One tempting hypothesis about the extension of industrial democracy is that it reflects a long-run trend towards greater democratic control in Western industrialised societies. This trend can be analysed, in Tocquevillian terms, as a consequence of the breakdown of the hierarchies of aristocratic society and the increasing assertion of an equal right to the exercise of judgment and power by all sectors of society, which necessarily leads to greater democracy. Therefore workers are throwing off former habits of deference, which tended to characterise the relation between workers and owners or managers in the past; women are resisting patriarchal laws and attitudes; and the young are attacking the social authority of the old. Although there may be oscillations in the movement towards equality and full democracy the trend is irreversible. This social revolution in the West is paralleled by and receives impetus from the political liberation of the former colonies.

The inevitability of a trend towards greater democracy can be questioned if the vogue for participation, and the women's and students' movements of the last two decades, are ascribed – like pressure for industrial democracy itself – to the affluence of Western capitalism, which briefly created expanding opportunities for employment and unusual economic independence and purchasing power for women and the young, as well as the adult male working class. An impression of the ephemeral nature of these movements is reinforced by the element of changing fashion in liberal intellectual circles, the variability of media coverage, and the built-in obsolescence of particular movements. The scepticism of some Marxists about the political importance of all these tendencies is likely to be reinforced by the impact of economic recession and by long-run technological trends, which may well weaken the economic power of the young, drive women back into the home, and focus attention on the basic conflict between organised labour and capital. In a period of affluence and high employment managements were impelled to woo labour. Unions could afford to widen their horizons. However, in a recession companies can cease to worry about any form of industrial democracy and rely on the old-fashioned discipline imposed by the reserve army of labour, while trade unions will turn back to basic issues like jobs and the level of real wages.

Ironically, it is also possible to construct an argument against the relevance of industrial democracy by reversing all the assumptions of the previous paragraph. First, it can be argued that industrial democracy is tied to an old-fashioned concept of a blue-collar working class in mechanised industry and that new technology and increasing automation is in the process of eroding the existence of this class. Industry will increasingly be staffed by skilled technical and administrative staff – a salaried professional stratum who enjoy various privileges and a considerable degree of autonomy and influence in their work by virtue of their skills, even if they remain ultimately dependent on those with economic power. If the real problem of the future is how the mass of the population who are unemployed are to be maintained, and to achieve a sense of status and purpose provided in the past by work, then industrial democracy appears increasingly irrelevant. Second, it can be argued that industrial democracy, like other socialist concepts, has been implicitly tied to a purely male image of the working class and ignores the problem of housewives isolated in their homes, who have been more dependent, lacking in self-respect and powerless than assembly-belt workers. Third, the tendency to extend the period of compulsory education and increase the range of higher education excludes many young adults from the sphere of industry. Finally, the growing number of old-age pensioners have by definition retired from work. All these considerations add up to a strong case for community-based forms of participatory politics: for on the one hand there are increasing opportunities for that leisure which the Greeks thought essential to political activity; and, on the other hand, community politics offers possibilities of new purpose, self-confidence and power to groups especially vulnerable to self-distrust and manipulation. But they can suggest that industrial democracy is the wrong focus for participatory democrats.

None of the preceding considerations, however, add up to a convincing case against the possibility, relevance and desirability of a form of industrial democracy which vests some degree of control in the hands of the employees. If short-term recession and long-term technology both mean that industry requires fewer but more highly skilled workers, they should remain in a strong position to press for a greater say in decisions, since the mass of unemployed will be unable to compete with them. If in addition the economy is being increasingly polarised into a high-technology sphere dominated by giant corporations, and an alternative economy of small-scale technology and craftsmanship, the latter could increasingly become the sphere of workers' co-operatives as well as of individual enterprise and the family firm. It might also pay governments in periods of high unemployment to provide funding for small-scale co-operative enterprises which can create a new jobs and services, and this has happened in Britain where under the auspices of the Co-operative Development Agency and of the Industrial Common Ownership Movement over 300 co-operatives were formed between 1977 and 1980. There are in addition grounds for doubting whether, in the long run, technical development will necessarily reduce jobs, since it may create others – especially in the administrative and service sectors.

There is, however, a more fundamental objection to assessing the relevance of industrial democracy solely in terms of economic and technical necessities and trends. A genuinely democratic society should be able to control the economy and technical development to meet its socially defined needs. It should not simply be governed by economic and technical inevitability. Creating democratic control over technology and democratising economic power are at the heart of the case for worker control of industry. As economic issues have become increasingly central to politics – though economic decisions are well insulated from direct parliamentary control or public accountability – there is every reason to try to subject major corporations to democratic checks from within. There are also persuasive arguments for creating forms of democratic participation and control at the workplace in terms of promoting the self-confidence and sense of efficacy of workers and increasing their ability to direct their own lives. Where the effect of work is to limit individual awareness and capacity through drudgery or mechanical routine, then there is a double reason for taking democracy to factories and offices: to multiply the opportunities for people to acquire political understanding, experience and effectiveness and to counteract the deadening impact of work itself. In addition their jobs still dominate many people's lives, determining how they spend the majority of their time and determining their income, status and possibilities in their private, social and political capacities; so industrial democracy is an attempt to give people more control over their own destiny.

MODELS OF DEMOCRACY

The democratic case for worker participation can be argued from a number of different theoretical standpoints which stress differing values and imply varying degrees of worker activity and control. Four models of democracy which can be adapted to industry – elitist democracy, liberal democracy as interpreted by John Stuart Mill, pluralist Tocquevillian democracy, and Rousseauist participatory democracy – are sketched out below.

Elitist democracy

Management-initiated forms of joint consultation at shop-floor and intermediate levels, which would enable managers to explain policies affecting the workforce and workers to express their concerns, but reserve final decisions to management, reflect an elitist approach to democracy. The pure elitist theory of democracy elaborated by Schumpeter, which stresses the importance of restricting political decisions to an experienced and knowledgeable governing group, limits the citizens' role to periodic election of two competing teams of leaders. It is, however, arguable that since elitist theory does require an electorate capable of intelligent choice, and responsible enough to exercise self-restraint and delegate responsibility to parliamentary representatives for national policy-making, it would be strengthened by allowing limited forms of participation at a local level where citizens have more direct knowledge required for decision-making and where they can acquire an awareness of the complexity of political issues. Consultation on issues which directly affect people's interests can also enable experts to make better policy decisions and ensure smoother implementation. This form of elite-controlled participation might well underpin rather than undermine the power of the elite.

Liberal democracy

Minority representation of workers on boards of directors still weighted (at least initially) towards shareholder representatives could correspond to a model of liberal democracy. There is an elitist strain in many formulations of the liberal-democratic approach, entailing some distrust of the ignorant workers and therefore a desire to safeguard the role of the enlightened and expert in decision-making. But compared with pure elitism it displays a much more generous desire to extend the benefits of political participation and delegate decisions, stressing the educative value of participation and political activity as one important means of self-development and exercising autonomy. Liberal-democratic theory also recognises (drawing on its utilitarian roots) that people require political power to protect their legitimate interests. Within industry this approach implies the need to supplement formal representation with shop-floor and intermediate level opportunities for participation, but stresses the role of individuals in the democratic process and would therefore avoid granting the trade unions a direct role in electing worker directors or in lower-level committees. The German system of co-determination, including their works councils elected by secret ballot of all employees, provides an institutional framework for this concept of industrial democracy.

Pluralist democracy

The pluralist model shares with liberal-democratic theory stress on the value of participation and decentralisation (Mill after all borrowed from De Tocqueville), but makes political activity more central to the development of confidence and initiative and to the maintenance of a free society, enabling citizens to resist the encroachments of arbitrary power and provide alternatives to centralised administration. Pluralism sees informed publics as the way to avoid the dangers of central manipulation of opinion, and the importance of group organisation as individuals can more easily be isolated and controlled. Pluralism implies, in an industrial context, worker autonomy on the shop floor, effective worker bargaining power at the middle level and strong worker representation on the board. It also implies free access to information within the company and a role for trade unions in the operation of industrial democracy, though it would not be compatible with trade unions monopolising the process of worker representation. Since pluralism implies antagonism to concentrations of economic power it could imply limits to company size and scope. It could also suggest curbs on major shareholders and measures to give shareholders real democratic rights in selection of directors and over company policy. Moves have been made in this direction by individuals and institutions who have used shareholder meetings to query company policies in South Africa and on other controversial issues.

Participatory democracy

A system of pure workers' control, especially in a small-scale firm capable of direct decision-making by the whole collective, rests primarily on a Rousseauist version of participatory democracy. This theory elevates political activity above all other forms of individual and social expression, sees participation as a duty as well as a right, looks to collective agreement as the key to combining individual autonomy with the necessity of achieving a common good, is hostile to group pluralism which is seen as divisive, and is uncompromisingly egalitarian. Producer co-operatives in the West could embody this view of participatory democracy, but it is a theory of democracy more in tune with a socialist society (the Marxist theory of democracy draws on this tradition) and is therefore less relevant to industrial democracy in a liberal capitalist state. A theory requiring direct democracy also runs into exactly the same problems of size in industry as it does in the state, and the possible solution – confederation resting on a base of direct democracy – is difficult to reconcile with existing reality in both contexts. (A possible compromise solution has been adopted in principle by the Yugoslavs and enshrined in the 1976 Law on Associated Labour, which recognises the reality of the increasing scale of Yugoslav enterprises, which may comprise plants in many different locations, but requires that small-scale industrial units enjoy direct democracy and some autonomy in economic decisions and activity. How this works in practice is more doubtful and is not fully clear (Wilson, 1979, 216–24).)

The pivotal model for analysing schemes for industrial democracy in our society is probably the liberal-democratic one, which corresponds most closely to parliamentary democracy in the political sphere, although its individualist bias would tend to be modified in the industrial context by the reality of trade-union power, just as it is modified in politics by the power of political parties. If this model were widely established it could, over time, evolve towards pluralist democracy, if the conflict between democratic ideals and the realities of economic and political power resulted in effective action to strengthen democratic processes.

OBSTACLES TO INDUSTRIAL DEMOCRACY INSIDE COMPANIES

This optimistic prospect must however be tempered by asking some basic questions about the possibility of achieving genuine industrial democracy inside companies. The first set of problems arises in connection with worker representatives on boards: will they have sufficient knowledge; will they be excluded from real decisions; and will they be able to check the permanent managers? There is a genuine initial problem of inexperience and therefore lack of expertise by worker directors, which could in principle be overcome by special training and accumulated experience. There is also the possibility of enabling them to draw on their own (trade-union) financial and legal experts. The relative ignorance of worker directors could however be artificially prolonged by manoeuvres designed to exclude them from access to important information and decisions, and the value of outside expert advice limited by invoking confidentiality of board materials. The problem of confidentiality was discussed in the Bullock Report which tended to the view that worker representatives would encourage a desirable trend towards more open government in industry, though granting the need for some secrecy. But the pressures on worker directors to act 'responsibly' might operate in the direction of making them accept a large degree of secretiveness.

There is certainly evidence that worker representatives have been excluded from decisions by the device of hiving-off crucial planning and drafting to sub-committees, which then present the board with a virtual *fait accompli*, and that information has been withheld from the board as a whole until the last minute. The Swedish Industrial Board found that both these methods had been used in Sweden and that there had been some tendency for use of sub-committees to increase after the 1973 Act requiring employee representation on boards. Bullock also quoted research suggesting similar manoeuvres had been used by West German boards (1977, p. 94). A Warwick University report on the two-year Post Office experiment of adding seven union nominees to the board found that 90 per cent of the material presented to the board offered no choice of options and that important issues were excluded from the agenda. Many managers had admitted that the style and content of board meetings had changed to exclude sensitive issues from debate, and in some cases union nominees did not know strategic issues were being decided outside the board. The Warwick report also pointed to the fundamental problem of ensuring board control where a group of people meeting once a month nominally control a large and technically complex organisation; any board is liable to manipulation by managers and technical experts (*New Statesman*, December 21/28, 1979). Exclusion of worker representatives may be easier when they are in a minority – Bullock drew this conclusion – but it is also arguable that worker directors, with real veto power, would prompt even greater measures to emasculate their influence.

A second basic question about industrial democracy is whether workers in practice want any of the possible forms of participation or representation and will exercise their democratic rights if given them. This is an issue familiar from debates about electoral apathy. Similar arguments can be used to show either that apathy is only human and democratic theory should take account of this fact, or that apathy is a reflection of powerlessness. There is evidence that workers do not necessarily use, or appear to value highly, democratic channels open to them where forms of industrial democracy have been introduced. Small-scale evidence from two British experiments in co-partnership was cited earlier. Much more extensive evidence can be gleaned from studies of worker self-management in Yugoslavia, which suggests that, despite a full panoply of institutions enshrining workers' control, in practice managers dominate firms. It also suggests some apathy and lack of interest among the workers, who showed a greater inclination by the late 1960s to look to stronger trade unions (Broekmeyer, 1970; Zukin, 1975, p. 184). On the other hand, lack of worker activism can be plausibly explained by the effective restrictions on workers exercising real influence, and their resistance to wasting time on empty rituals. Added considerations in the Yugoslav context are the inexperienced nature of the workforce when self-management was introduced and the fact that it was initiated from above. Brief revolutionary experiments in worker control suggest workers have espoused forms of industrial democracy with enthusiasm, although it is possible to question whether these examples provide a realistic model for more humdrum daily working life.

The debate about worker interest in industrial democracy is not, however, identical with the general debate about the value and viability of participatory politics. One of the reasons often cited for introducing industrial democracy is the alienating nature of work on the assembly line. There is in fact some interesting evidence from Yugoslavia that suggests assembly-line workers are more interested in the politics of the workers' assembly and workers' council than workers in craft or automated industries (Supek, 1971). If, however, skilled craftsmen and technicians enjoy more rewarding work, and have greater autonomy by virtue of their skills, then the obvious way to recompense those with repetitive mechanical jobs is to extend the kind of experiments made by Standard Motors at Coventry, and at Saab and Volvo plants in Sweden, which allow workers group control over the whole process of making a car, and hence greater flexibility in the range of jobs and autonomy in allocating work to group members. If all workers can enjoy a degree of satisfaction and freedom at work it is even arguable that there may be a positive conflict between spending more time on the job as opposed to giving up significant amounts of time to political activity within an enterprise. On the other hand if the assumptions of participatory and pluralist democratic theory are correct, group organisation and autonomy on the shop floor might be expected to enhance workers' ability and willingness to make political demands. (In practice this factor is probably much less significant where there is already an active shop-stewards' movement.)

The third major question to be raised about the value of industrial democracy as a means of extending opportunities for significant political participation is whether the size of companies undermines the possibility of genuine democracy. Quite apart from the problems posed by multinationals, there has been a striking tendency for companies to increase in size. It is not clear that this tendency is due to technical requirements or 'economies of scale'. A number of authors have suggested that increasing company size is due primarily to market strategy and considerations of power and prestige, and Barratt Brown comments that the fact that company size has increased much more dramatically than plant size 'only emphasizes the point that it may well be the nature of the capitalist market for goods and capital that makes for bigness beyond a certain size, rather than the returns to scale' (Coates and Topham, vol. III, 1975, p. 97). This conclusion, if correct, may strengthen a socialist case for workers' control but underlines the problems of introducing industrial democracy within a capitalist economy and the capitalist state.

GOVERNMENT ATTITUDES TO INDUSTRIAL DEMOCRACY

The political obstacles to achieving consistent government support for the principle of worker control or board-level worker representation are well illustrated by the vicissitudes of both these policies in Britain in the late 1970s. The Labour government decided to support three worker co-operatives, launched on the initiative of the workers after the owners had decided to close the enterprises down, by extending them government loans. The *Scottish Daily News* collapsed shortly after the co-operative had launched its new version of the paper. The Kirkby Manufacturing and Engineering Co-operative (KME) was disbanded in 1979, and the Meriden motorcycle co-operative was prepared in 1980 to sacrifice the co-operative in order to avoid total closure and entered into negotiations with various private companies. The co-operatives were vulnerable for economic reasons and in particular lacked financial resources, which made them dependent on government help. They also aroused ideological and political hostility, probably because of the active role of shop stewards in blocking attempts to close KME and Meriden, and because government loans were given under the auspices of the controversial

Tony Benn, who was Minister of Industry at the time. As a result, much press coverage was hostile, and civil servants and many government ministers were less than sympathetic. The Labour government refused, for example, to make a further loan of £6 million to KME in February 1979, although a firm of management consultants had pronounced the firm viable. The government was, however, prepared to give a private industrial company £4.5 million to take over the co-operative. The Permanent Secretary of the Department of Industry was reported to have opposed the co-operatives throughout, and Brian Sedgemore, who had been Benn's Parliamentary Private Secretary, told the House of Commons in January 1979 that civil servants and ministers at the Department had drawn up plans, 'behind the backs of the board, the workers and the managers' of the Meriden co-operative, to sell it to a Japanese company.

The fate of the Bullock Report, commissioned by the Labour government in 1975, is perhaps more significant as an indication of the political difficulties facing any attempt to achieve significant worker representation in industry. When the Report was published in January 1977 it met with strong opposition from the CBI, who declared that they had fundamental objections to three of the proposals: the legal imposition of union-nominated directors on company boards; parity of representation for union and shareholder directors; and the trade-union monopoly in choosing worker directors. When Mr Callaghan and Labour ministers met the CBI soon after the publication of the report, they agreed to consider laying the Bullock proposals aside in favour of discussing participation below board level. *The Times* of 16 February 1977, commented that this delaying tactic was due to the government's dilemma: 'It knows that, if it goes too strongly in the direction suggested by Bullock, it will face immense opposition from the employers probably resulting in non-cooperation on their industrial strategy.' The government was, however, also anxious to please the TUC, which had strongly supported union-appointed directors, and which could damage the 'social contract' on pay rises. The White Paper finally produced in May 1978 refused to 'impose a standard pattern of participation on industry by law' and called for extension of participation through voluntary agreement (*The Guardian*, 24 May 1978).

The response of a singularly unadventurous Labour government, in a difficult economic situation and lacking a majority in parliament, is not a definitive guide to the future of industrial democracy in Britain. But the available evidence does suggest that strong union and Labour-Party pressure will be required to overcome the resistance of industrialists and civil servants to any significant measures of worker representation and to override the tendency of Labour governments once in office to compromise on the party's declared policies. The evidence also supports the conclusion drawn earlier in this essay from West German and Swedish experience that the strength of trade unions and of social democracy will probably determine the extent of industrial democracy which is achieved. Whether unions and socialist parties operating within the capitalist state can move beyond worker representation to institutionalise worker control of industry is a question which leads us to the heart of the socialist debate about industrial democracy and into the classic debate about the limits of parliamentary socialism.

INDUSTRIAL PARLIAMENTARIANISM?

Within industry, one great danger from the standpoint of the trade unions is that worker directors will be co-opted and become virtually indistinguishable from shareholder representatives. There are interesting parallels between worker representation on boards and the policy of promoting worker rights through representation in parliament. So long as workers are confined to minority representation on boards it might be argued that they confront all the problems of parliamentarianism – pressures towards compromise and responsibility as defined by the dominant ethos, and constraint by the real power holders – without being able to achieve the prize potentially available to socialist parties of winning formal government power. But even if in due course minority representation is converted into a majority on the board, it is arguable on the parliamentary analogy that the diversity of the workforce who are the electorate, and the requirements of company profitability and productivity, will limit the scope for change in policy, and that the major owners of the company's capital or the policy of financial institutions will structure decisions.

From a socialist standpoint it may therefore appear more realistic, and more consistent with the goals of protecting workers' rights, to forget about board-level representation and concentrate on extending the rights and powers of trade unions to influence company policy. The General and Municipal Workers Union suggested in the wake of the Bullock Report that unions should be given alternative choices in pursuit of industrial democracy, one of which should be to invest them with joint power of regulation over major corporate decisions, to be determined by legislation setting out procedures for negotiations and to be enforced by government sanctions against uncooperative managements. This approach, which has been adopted in Sweden, strengthens the unions and avoids possible conflicts between them and worker representatives on boards. But, as Carole Pateman (1970) has argued, this form of extended collective bargaining still leaves management in a superior position with the ultimate power of lock-out or closure of a plant. There are also legal pitfalls in seeking to ensure that employers observe required bargaining procedures. But the most important political objection is that governments could not be relied on to apply sanctions to major companies who ignore collective bargaining procedures, so that such legislation would in practice probably be unenforceable.

Realism and the lessons of experience could therefore lead socialists in the West to turn their backs on the promises of industrial democracy and all political programmes of gradual reform. Taken to extremes, this strategy would also involve repudiating finally the parliamentary road to socialism. The alternative is to make maximum use of representative institutions, to extend the scope of democracy from the political to the economic sphere, and to invoke the devices of populist democracy to counter the pressures towards conforming with the *status quo*. The devices available are the same in industrial democracy as in political democracy: frequent re-election, accountability to electorates, opening up previously classified information, popular initiatives and referenda. The last resort available to democrats to counter economic and institutional power – civil disobedience and direct action – is much more readily available to trade unions, who are used to going slow and going on strike. If industrial democracy risks repeating the problems and inadequacies of parliamentarianism, and, as at present envisaged, falls well short of the socialist goal of worker control, it also promises the possibility of importing a more radical commitment to democracy into parliamentarianism.

REFERENCES

Broekmeyer, M. J., ed., 1970. *Yugoslav Workers' Self-Management*. Dordrecht, D. Reidel Publishing Co.

Bullock Report, 1977: Report of the Committee of Inquiry on Industrial Democracy. London, HMSO

Chiplin, Brian, John Coyne and Ljubo Sirc, 1977. *Can Workers Manage?* London, The Institute of Economic Affairs

Coates, Ken and Anthony Topham, 1975. *Industrial Democracy in Great Britain*, vols. I–IV. Nottingham, Spokesman Books

Eccles, Tony, 1981. *Under New Management*. London, Pan Books

Gregory, Denis ed., 1978. *Work Organisation: Swedish Experience and British Context*. London, Social Science Research Council

Grosser, Alfred, 1974. *Germany in Our Time*. Harmondsworth, Penguin Books

Pateman, Carole, 1970. *Participation and Democratic Theory*. Cambridge, Cambridge University Press

Poole, Michael, 1978. *Workers' Participation in Industry*. London, Routledge and Kegan Paul

Supek, R., 1971. 'Tehnološke promjene i samoupravna demokratija' (Technological change and self-managing democracy), *Preglad*, Sarajevo, June

Wilson, Duncan, 1979. *Tito's Yugoslavia*. Cambridge, Cambridge University Press

Zukin, Sharon, 1975. *Beyond Marx and Tito*. Cambridge, Cambridge University Press

ENDPIECE

15

A defence of the welfare state

GRAEME DUNCAN

My starting point is the bad press, academic and popular, of the modern welfare state, in the sense of a complex of institutions or the political apparatus: ideologically, if not in fact, it appears to be in bad shape. What I have to say touches upon a variety of literatures – the academic literature concerned with overgovernment, ungovernability or governmental overload; the neo-Marxist literature focussing upon the legitimation and the fiscal crises of the state; and especially, the more obviously polemical neo-liberal literature which aims to demolish the state's excessive claims, that is, to pursue social justice and to satisfy the people's needs. There is much pessimism or suspicion, stemming from different ideological perspectives, about the capacity of the governments of advanced societies to do much (of value). Whether or not there has been, amongst the populace, a revolution of falling expectations, a long-term drop in high-flown ambitions of personal advancement, is a more debatable assertion.[1]

Although a defence of the welfare state need not be confined to the beliefs or demands of electors, in the sense that many of them may be at times unhappy with good or unavoidable arrangements, it would make me pause for thought if it was the case that masses of people come to reject it explicitly. Has there been in fact a widespread withdrawal of affection for or attachment to the welfare state? Hugh Thomas, for example, refers to 'our generation's growing scepticism of state interference at home'. Others, including writers of the Left, have taken popular support for Mrs Thatcher to demonstrate a widespread resentment at the growth of the state. However, I doubt very much whether the three successive conservative victories in the UK can be seen as anything like a rejection of statism or of the welfare state or of central power, or as a choice for a free market.[2] Apathy, cynicism, disillusionment are not the same as rejecting 'the state', even though anti-statist rhetoric can be assumed to have some impact, especially amongst those who see themselves as contributors to rather than recipients of social security. The welfare state is too complex and diverse a set of institutions to be the object of widespread disaffection, and some parts, for example, the National Health Service, are much more popular than others, for example, public housing. Where there is apparent hostility to 'the state', it may be the result of the fact that people can't get through, can't get access to the services and the goods which the state, *in some form*, must provide or ensure. And where that is the case, the appropriate response is to invent the arrangements which best meet that need.

The party attacks upon too-active governments – by conservatives in Britain, republicans in America and liberals in Australia – make an ideological case for a small or a minimal state which will allow individuals and groups to do more things for themselves. Other values, for example, economic productivity and freedom, serve and are served by that self-reliance. Beyond a certain short point, it is argued, state action wastes, stultifies, robs, degrades, invades rights. Both academic theorising and political rhetoric express grave doubts about the interventionist and the welfare states and demand dramatic changes in the character and the role of governments. These changes, if they occur, must find recognition in political and social theory. This is not remote philosophical argument over the drawing of boundaries. It arises from the deep and real problems of the modern state, and it represents the conflicting interests of social groups: to reduce the role of government is to redefine the political to someone's advantage. It is, to a significant degree, despite the occasional air of distance from the actual world, a contest over power and who should have what.

The target of both attack and defence shifts and is often underspecified. Concretely, the state is many things. It is bureaucracy, nationalised industries, a public health service, phone tapping and police raids, military forces and road building, the secret service, tax collectors, the provision of personal social services. The state has many faces, benign and oppressive, flexible and cramped: to challenge it is not to challenge one clearly identifiable thing. Moreover, governments in modern capitalist societies do not have identical histories, structures or range. They vary, as do political cultures, so that the same argument does not have equal weight in all circumstances. The theoretical task is to recognise both the specificity of particular states and the existence of general or common problems in states of a certain kind. My special interest is in the case that can be made for the active, reforming, social-democratic or welfare state(s), facing severe difficulties in those societies where ideology ended in the 1960s but returned to haunt in the 1980s. The slogan form of the argument which I want to evaluate is 'Roll back the frontiers of the state' but, just as the larger critiques of the Left and Right overlap, so 'Roll back the frontiers of the state' has a Left as well as a Right variant. Defenders of 'the state' can build their case partly through exposure of the inconsistencies of its enemies, who readily talk of a reduced state while ignoring its common expansion in a military and perhaps also a moral sense. Ideology and reality fall apart. But the defensive case can also be built out through critical reflection upon and a reshaping of some neo-liberal arguments.

During the past century one clear trend has been the enormous growth, in most developed countries, of the weight, cost and range of the state. The expansion of the public sector, penetrating society in a far-reaching way, is revealed in the high proportion of national income of which the state disposes, the increasing proportion of public employees in the total workforce, and the variety of activities and enterprises in which the state is engaged. The expansion of government functions which occurred was in part the expression of a new balance of power within society, although it was not simply a product of the rise and representation of the masses. Middle-class intellectuals and reformers were active in the process of change and, more abstractly, problems facing the capitalist system necessitated intervention, in the interests of economic development as well as of social harmony. The emergence of a more intrusive state challenged the 'free-market' system and was justified in these terms, while leaving unsettled significant conflicts about the right balance between communal needs and individual rights, and between public and private activity. Indeed, given the contradictory nature of the system, no such balance can be struck.

At this point it is useful to distinguish the different states, or the different aspects of the state, which emerged in Britain and elsewhere. We can distinguish at least the planning and regulatory state, the owning state, and the welfare state, which are likely to be supported by different arguments and underlain by different interests. The welfare state is quite distinct from public ownership, or government direction of the economy, or government-sponsored structural change. For example, in the 1970s Britain was second amongst the West European states in the size of the public sector and sixth in the percentage taken by health and social-service expenditure of the gross domestic product. There is no general correlation between the size of the welfare state and the size of the public sector.

During the immediate post-war years in Britain (and Australia) the welfare state, as it is known commonly, was established. This new order meant essentially provision for the welfare of all citizens by means of government-operated, or at least government-financed, services. The goal was to ensure the survival, in tolerable circumstances, of all members of society, and hence there was special concern with provision for the unemployed, the old, the poor, and the otherwise disadvantaged or vulnerable. One familiar image is that of a 'net' or a 'floor' through which the weak and the feckless should not be allowed to fall. Minimum conditions or standards of health, economic security and civilised life are guaranteed. In Britain, the welfare state was the essence of a 'post-war settlement', or settlement of class claims, and consisted of a series of policy commitments, to health, housing, education and transport in particular. Accounts of the motivations behind these developments, and of how far they can go, vary. Obviously the free play of market forces has been modified, and it is possible to perceive in the new arrangements a demo-cratisation and humanisation of capitalism. Michael Harrington presents the welfare state as a transitional social phenomenon, 'perched midway between the *laissez-faire* past and the collectivist future' (Harrington, 1973, p. 454). Both goals and achievements need to be separated here. It is one thing to aim at providing basic resources for all people, to ensure that essential physio-logical, or even human, needs are satisfied, another to seek significant redistri-bution or equalisation, and different again to pursue the reduction or regulation of private powers, perhaps to protect the market against threatening disequilibria. Of course, these separate goals, which are often fudged analyti-cally, may be connected intimately, for example, greater public control may be necessary to ensure minimum provision for all, or the provision of such a minimum – given the level of the minimum and the size of the national cake – may have equalitarian implications. Many of the socialist champions of what seemed to be radical welfare provision were optimistic about how the liberal promise of a career open to talents could be made a reality. In *The Future of Socialism*, Crosland praised the active and responsive state which had replaced the passive state. The unfettered market was ended and the new and final arbiter of economic life was the political authority. Exercised by the right representatives, worlds could be transformed.

Yet often to Marxist critics, the welfare state has seemed a deceptive and perhaps dangerous compromise. It becomes a palliative, a means of pacifying the working class and subordinating it to the changing needs of capital, creating more efficient working instruments and an enervating social harmony falling far short of the full achievement of the claims of labour and of humankind. Even if capitalism can accommodate some reform, though, there is a strict upper limit imposed by the need for profits and investment in a stumbling and inefficient system.

In my view, there are dangers in the common Marxist method of working with millennial choices only, between a corrupt old world and a new moral one, with a consequent rejection of compromises and half-way houses. A belief in the inability of capitalism to change for the better, of the incapacity of governments in capitalist societies to alter arrangements significantly, relied upon a very far-reaching and demanding view of what constitutes a genuine change. Only systemic change counts: change within is dismissed as a façade. The image of a sharp break and a full social transformation gives a low weight to changes or reforms within capitalism (social democrats and labourites are essentially impotent) and is liable to misunderstand the actual political aspir-ations and interests of the subordinate class. This strain of criticism easily leads to a downgrading of the welfare state, a failure to recognise its achieve-ments, thereby weakening responses to the neo-liberal and conservative upsurge.

My own account of the state refuses to dismiss it outright as either a subordinate element of society or as inevitably and unremittingly biassed and deficient. I assume that the state can and should do certain things of value, though a conception of what these are should be 'realistic' and economical rather than grandiose.

Even granted this position, the record and future of the welfare state cannot be assessed in an unequivocally positive way. For while it is true to say that the expansion of government services did increase the opportunities, freedoms, choices and possibilities of many ordinary (and some extraordinary?) people, it does not appear to have had any significant redistributive effect.[3] A defence of its achievement or of its promise in such terms would be misleading. What did happen during the early decades was that the minimum level became higher, though this was done painlessly through a healthy rate of growth. Seven years after the appearance of *The Future of Socialism* Crosland was to emphasise, in *Socialism Now*, the problem of inflation in a slow-growth economy. Where were the resources for the welfare state now to come from? He stated rather than resolved the problem. It was no accident that neo-liberal theory came alive in the straitened circumstances of the late seventies. It is one response to a problem upon which many contemporary Marxists also focus, but they tend to call it a crisis. Can a genuine welfare state and a mixed economy coexist when times are hard? Must welfare provision diminish? One possible response from the left would be to develop a significantly redistributive and egalitarian socialism, though to do so would require a more realistic and incisive theory of class and state and a more radical practice than those of the gentle dreamers who thought that the welfare state could achieve wonders, leading quietly and easily to genuine equality.

Objections to the multiplying welfare state from a liberal or neo-liberal perspective have been continuous, though the recession has given them added pungency and appeal. Claiming moral and economic superiority for the minimal state, they clearly challenge the political consensus which grew up during the fifties and sixties in advanced and affluent societies. In the British case, the agreed fundamentals seemed to include a mixed economy with a large public sector, a creative and interventionist role for government, a considerable range of social services and an established position of the unions as a powerful estate. Elections were seen to be about minor variations rather than basic differences. That continuity and comfortable blandness were attacked head-on by Mrs Thatcher in the late seventies – dragging a number of erstwhile socialists with her – though the bolder words have not been translated easily or automatically into actual programmes.

The Thatcher approach to Britain's low-productivity, low-growth, low-wage economy was apparently simple and tough-minded: government should do less so that it costs less, and vacates much of the field to private and voluntary forces which will begin to make hay even when the sun isn't shining. There were many lessons in elementary economics and the hard facts of life, much talk of the need to tighten belts (though for some much more than others). The ideological centre of Thatcherism is a defence of individual and society against the state, with the aim of re-adjusting the balance in favour of individual and society, thereby returning to the practical realities demonstrated in the nineteenth century, 'when British policy rested on sound money and a modest regulatory role for government'. Only with a modest, abstaining state will respect for it be combined with 'respect for the large number of private associations which contribute so much to the stability and richness of a society' (Thatcher, 1978).

Clearly a particular view of British history is assumed. This view emphasises the strengths of *laissez-faire* in the nineteenth century, and finds the sources of social costs outside the free-market system.

For a long view, Hugh Thomas's *An Unfinished History of the World* is illuminating. Thomas declares his essential faith in the strength and value of Anglo-Saxon institutions, and refuses to apologise for the sources of progress. He forcefully rejects soppy left-wing histories of England's industrial transformation. Britain owed its past success to the rarity with which the government sought to supervise commerce and industry. Decline, he argues, came with the spread of state intervention, under the sway of radical and socialist ideas, following the French Revolution. The result, using Burke's phrase, was 'the omnipresent state and the solitary individual without resources'. Champions of the state had ignored the central role played by commerce and free enterprise in maintaining democracy, leading to wholesale state intervention in the workings of the market; overmighty institutions, especially the unions, arrogated to themselves corporate power and aspire to take over the state; the civil service expands incessantly and without control; entrepreneurs lose their nerve as they are 'exhausted by problems of labour, hampered by taxation, tempted by increasingly corrupt practices, or at least tax evasion' (Thomas, 1981, p. 553). Taxation exceeds its role. It has 'ceased to be simply a source of revenue and become, instead, an instrument of social justice, welfare and economic management: which is not its proper function' (Thomas, 1974, p. 586). Taxes need to be cut, bureaucracy reduced, state power weakened and decentralised. The goal of the conservatism which Thomas in fact supports is 'to free industry and society generally from the shackles which have grown up round it during an age of war, crisis, and ignorant "planning"' (Thomas, 1974, p. 560).

But the most weighty contemporary critic of the expanded and expanding state is Friedrich Hayek. His critique comprises both historical and more abstract analysis. *Capitalism and the Historians*, a small volume which he edited in 1954, sought to expose 'historical myths' which have helped shape opinion, and particularly a dominant socialist view of economic history. Hayek writes:

Certain beliefs, for instance, about the evolution and effects of trade-unions, the alleged progressive growth of monopoly, the deliberate destruction of commodity stock as the result of competition (an event which, in fact, whenever it happened, was always the result of monopoly and usually of government-organized monopoly), about the suppression of beneficial inventions, the causes and effects of 'imperialism', and the role of the armament industries or of 'capitalists' in general in causing war, have become part of the folk lore of our time. (Hayek, 1954, pp. 8–9)

Capitalism, the highly productive competitive order to which we owe our present-day civilisation, is seen by Hayek as having been unjustly discredited by myths and emotional histories which blame it for depressing the living standards of the weakest elements of society. On the contrary, he argues that capitalism, when it had full commercial freedom, was the source of the general upward trend of living standards and of expectations of continued improvements. The source of the anti-capitalist propaganda of the radical intelligentsia was the interested conservative press, striking out at the rising class of manufacturers.[4]

The object of Hayek's more general attack is a complex but connected body of ideas and practices, including social justice, intellectualist conceptions of human design, controls, monopoly, exclusive rights, do-gooders, central government, and domination by ideological minorities (who use pleasing but empty words). Hayek is not opposed to ideals (see 'Why I am not a Conservative', the postscript to *The Constitution of Liberty*, where he rejects the conservative's nostalgia and lack of clear principle and a scheme of progress) for he has his own, and his own idealised history. The tone is not urgent – the approach and the style are too grand for that – but Hayek's assumption has been that the destruction of spontaneous forces (freedom) by the organised forces of society is at hand.

He urges that 'in the ordering of our affairs we should make as much use as possible of the spontaneous forces of society, and resort as little as possible to coercion' (Hayek, 1946, p. 13). In familiar nineteenth-century terms, the state is associated with coercion, stultification and regulation, society with spontaneity, experimentation and freedom.

In order to explicate what may seem to be a straightforward preference, expressed in heavily loaded language, we need to look more closely at Hayek's conceptions of freedom, the market and human nature. The definition of freedom is a narrow one, roughly equivalent to Berlin's notion of negative liberty. Hayek rejects 'social' or totalitarian democracy in favour of liberal democracy. Freedom does not depend upon the range of choices open to people – these may be limited by impersonal, including natural, forces – but refers only to the relation of men to other men. Consequently the power of the state, in a free society, will be limited to 'instances where it is required to prevent coercion by private persons' (Hayek, 1960, p. 21). Of human nature we realise, first, that any individual cannot know very much. 'It is because every individual knows so little and, in particular, because we rarely know which of us knows best that we trust the independent and competitive efforts of many to induce the emergence of what we shall want when we see it' (Hayek, 1960, p. 29). But why should we want it when we see it? Next, people are (naturally) unequal in energy, talents and luck. And their varying individual initiative (what critics call 'untrammelled egotism', although Hayek stresses the necessity of ingrained moral beliefs and voluntary conformity to certain principles: it all depends what these are!) is vital to personal and to social progress. The condition of free evolution or spontaneous social growth is the spirit of individual initiative, which is awakened only by a regime of freedom. What, then, distinguishes a regime of freedom? It is that order which, accepting the insufficiencies of the human mind and the power of individual initiative, is characterised by 'an impersonal mechanism, not dependent on individual human judgments, which will certainly co-ordinate the individual efforts' (Hayek, 1960, p. 4).

So the market, which orders without commanding, comes into its own. The justification of a market, as opposed to a state, system is that only the market can co-ordinate human societies in freedom, with its impersonal allocations and rewards. In doing so, it calls forth a spirit of enterprise which presupposes inequality, but which spreads progress because discoveries filter down to the rest of society. Markets foster what Hayek calls echelon development: the few with resources, skill and/or luck develop things which are at first, and could only be, luxuries for a minority, but there is a pay-off to the larger society in that the good things spread. 'It is because scouts have found the goal that the road can be built for the less lucky and the less energetic . . . Many of the improvements would indeed never have become a possibility for all if they had not long before been available for some . . . Even the poorest today owe their relative well-being to the result of past inequalities' (Hayek, 1960, p. 44). A country deliberately levelling differences will lose its advantages, as Hayek thinks has happened to Britain. Greater equality (though the dimensions of this are not clear) will lead to a static if not stationary society, as the sad examples of Britain and the Scandinavian countries show, in comparison with the burgeoning, inequality-stimulated economies of West Germany, Belgium and Italy (Hayek, 1960, p. 49). Rampant envy may fuel the destructive pursuit of an end to significant inequality.

Clearly, then, market allocations are not justified by Hayek in terms of social justice. Market processes are impersonal, independent of any over-riding will or desire, and the rewards to individuals, arising from circumstances which no one knows in their entirety, meet no criteria of merit. The benefits and burdens allocated by the market could be deemed just or unjust only if they were the result of deliberate allocation to particular persons. In a free market they cannot be considered meaningfully in this way. The value of services is discovered in the market place when people put their price upon them. Justice, then, applies to the relations between individuals, to individual conduct and the process of competition, not to results or to the characteristics of social wholes. Social or distributive justice misapplies the notion of justice to social actions, concerning the treatment of individuals and groups.

Hayek consequently berates the notion of social justice as 'punitive', 'inappropriate', 'vacuous', 'indefinite', 'a seduction'; 'a will-o'-the wisp', 'a category of nonsense', a 'quasi-religious superstition', 'an open sesame'. People, inspired by special interests, demand social justice and demand it increasingly: it is not merely socialists who are infected. Moral reformers may preach it, but its appeal arises from much more sordid sentiments than we imagine.[5] The goal of social justice is both weak philosophically and dangerous practically. In the first case, there is no agreed and relevant standard of social justice. Whereas minimum public assistance (or minimum unemployment benefit) can be defined firmly and objectively (as the food and shelter necessary to existence – though this is also a conventional standard), that is not the case with social justice. The weakness of the welfare state is thus, in one respect, a conceptual weakness, in that it ignores the firm line between community acceptance of the duty to prevent destitution and provide a minimum level of welfare, and state assumption of the power to determine the 'just' position of everybody and to allocate to each what it thinks he deserves (Hayek, 1960, p. 289). But in leaping over that line in pursuit of the mirage of social justice, powers are required which would destroy the 'spontaneous order of free men'. To seek equality of material position (in my view, hardly the end of most socialist or welfare statists, anyhow) would require a government armed with totalitarian powers, and necessarily committed to the destruction of the market and of personal freedom. '"Social justice" can be given a meaning only in a directed or "command" economy (such as an army) in which the individuals are ordered what to do; and any particular conception of "social justice" could be realised only in such a centrally directed system' (Hayek, 1960, p. 69). The choice seems clear. The naturalistic outcomes of the market are in their very nature unprincipled, while the imposition of irrelevant and empty conceptions of social justice upon them leads inevitably to tribalism, rampant collectivism, fiercely coercive government, and the destruction of both market and freedom.

The market is justified thus, in very far-reaching terms. Fierce competition within a framework of law promotes both the greatest and the most general prosperity, as long as it remains pure. Such a system has a self-corrective capacity, an ability to cleanse or purge itself, hence Hayek's recommendation of bigger and better bankruptcies for Britain. It is a liberal version of Marxist crisis theory, according to which the free market shakes itself out and destroys inefficient industries. Secondly, a free-enterprise society is a condition, and a guarantee, of personal and political freedom. Hayek condemned the progressive abandonment of 'that freedom in economic affairs without which personal and political freedom has never existed in the past' (Hayek, 1946, p. 10). The connection is not merely contingent or historical: economic freedom and economic pluralism are necessary to political freedom and political pluralism.

The other side of the defence of this claim is that statism (socialism, collectivism) is the enemy of freedom, narrowly defined. State systems are less productive because their instruments are blunt and the motivations upon which they call are weak (i.e. public motives – although the underlying envy and malice may be powerful for destruction, of course). Government intervention is ineffective and wasteful at the very least. It fails notoriously to direct investment to productive ends, 'for reasons inherent in non-competitive bureaucratic organizations' (Hayek, 1976, p. 99). It fosters illusions regarding equality, and insistent high expectations which promote inflation and social dislocation. It softens people by doing things for them that they would do better themselves.[6] For example, a state monopoly of insurance may make clients exclusively dependent upon government and unable to help themselves through private pension schemes (Hayek, 1960, p. 297), and a medical monopoly can provide, equally for all, at best 'the bad average standard of service' (Hayek, 1960, p. 299).

But the state destroys freedom even more thoroughly. It is inevitably oppressive because it works against and must therefore override human nature. Its goals are agreement and stability, and its instruments are specialists and experts who don't understand or command the whole, although they imagine that they do. The logic of intervention and authority is that it multiplies, feeding on obstacles consisting of people who are diverse and free. Hence the slippery slope which leads to damnation. In Hayek's overstated case, Fascism and Nazism become almost the necessary outcomes of the socialist (planning) trends of the preceding period. Neither the theory nor the practice of socialism provoke hope for freedom's prospect. Milton Friedman, commenting on socialist theory, claims: 'None of the people who have been in favour of socialism and also in favour of freedom have made even a respectable attempt at developing the institutional arrangements that would permit freedom under socialism' (Friedman, 1962, p. 19). But even if this charge is true – and I don't think that it is[7] – it would not follow that a free-market system either promoted or guaranteed freedom, unless that is defined in an exceedingly narrow and deformed way.

These critiques have a fairly clear centre, but jump between different visions, programmes and historical cases: they appear not to be critiques of any programme or any Western society in particular. They are weak for a number of reasons apart from their generality, but before noting these, it will be useful to consider their practical implications.

What recommendations follow from these critical analyses of the state? Obviously its role is to be limited sharply, but is that role defined tightly enough, with criteria which are sufficiently specific? The central claim is that the state should be limited to the maintenance of the free-market system, that is, to preserving the legal framework for free and equal competition. It is to preserve the world of contracts and free-contracting individuals, and not itself to pursue substantive ends, such as social justice. Friedman, while insisting that the specific functions of government can never be laid down forever, because circumstances change, presents the major functions of government as

> to protect our freedom both from the enemies outside our gates and from our fellow-citizens; to preserve law and order, to enforce private contracts, to foster competitive markets. Beyond this major function, government *may enable us at times* to accomplish jointly what we would find it more difficult or expensive to accomplish severally. However, any such use of government is fraught with danger. (Friedman, 1962, p. 2)

The terms are evasive and the limits unclear. Moreover, national defence or internal security may be used to justify as much intervention as may social welfare. Free marketeers may reject intervention in the name of social justice but support it in the name of military need or even social unity, remembering that Bismarck bought domestic peace partly through a rudimentary welfare state. But the contemporary welfare state is presented as obviously excessive.

In Britain, while 'dismantling the welfare state' may exaggerate what is being done, or even attempted (unlike the United States), the dominant ideology of the state holds that much more voluntary and private activity is needed. The notion of 'going beyond the welfare state' appears to mean carrying out necessary tasks by agencies other than state ones. The declared goal of 'privatisation' means the sale of whole or parts of nationalised concerns (especially the profitable ones) and the provision of particular services, for example, rubbish collection, or hospital laundry services, through private contractors. Along these lines, other desirable changes include the sale of council houses, more private health insurance, student loans, more charges for social services, and greater community involvement in financing and managing local schools. The emphasis is both on cutting costs *and* on a greater use of private and voluntary agencies. Minimum provision itself is not, presumably, under direct threat.

A major consequence of the emphasis upon private and voluntary activity is that the family is called upon to resume its ancient but neglected tasks. As the systematic assault on local government and on the National Health Service reveals clearly, the whole notion of cheaper and more voluntarily provided social services presupposes the resurrection of the family. Families, that is, wives and mothers, have a proper or natural role, that of staying at home and looking after children, the man of the house, and the old and ill. Women, it seems, are not suited to be full inhabitants of the market-place, not full possessors of the rights asserted so fiercely against the state on behalf of some. The thrust of the argument moves against one of the most significant post-war changes, which established the right of women with children to choose whether they wished to stay at home or take paid employment. It normally inverts the historical record as well, assuming that the welfare state has undermined valuable relationships or arrangements which would otherwise have been there. In fact the welfare state emerged because of the inadequacy and the coercive character of much of the traditional arrangements, though by reducing reliance on them it may have weakened them further.

And yet the bark has been more decisive than the bite. From that fact we can learn something. The British government has been unable to reduce the Public Sector Borrowing Requirement – actually public expenditure has grown in real terms under Thatcher. Necessary sustenance and support are provided to 'private' industry, indirectly through the provision of infrastructure (research, education, transportation and so on) and directly, through taxation arrangements, grants and subsidies. Some big state pensioners – British Leyland, British Steel, British shipbuilders – have been bailed out through what is euphemistically called 'constructive intervention'. Government influence has been exerted on wage and price decisions. An apparently committed free-enterprise government clearly intervenes in economic life to sustain what can only absurdly be called a free-market system. The doctrinal or ideological character of the notion of rolling back the frontiers of the state is clear. Politics is never a matter of simply following declared ends.

The contradictions may be embedded, not only in the relations between ideology and practice, reinforcing views of the necessary pragmatism of democratic politicians: they may lie within neo-liberal theories of the state themselves. For free-market politicians tend to want both a strong and a weak state, as exemplified in Mrs Thatcher's critique of Labour in the confidence debate of 1979. The Labour government was assaulted both for doing too much – in regard to its range of activity, when it did things that people should be doing for themselves – and for being too weak, in relation to alleged rivals to its authority, especially the unions. So efforts are made to strengthen the state as regards internal order and external security, while pursuing free and voluntary activity (within limits) in the economic realm. Government is to retreat in some respects, leaving a subsidised free market, while being strengthened where authority and security, not to mention the welfare of big industry, are concerned. The clamour for the free market can coexist with a clamour for hand-outs and for the imposition of a traditional moral order.

It must be admitted that neo-liberal theories cannot be judged directly against the realities of contemporary England or contemporary Anywhere. England is no laboratory of Hayekian or even Friedmanite ideas, as both have been quick to point out. However, the ahistorical character of the free-market treatment of the economy is replicated in its own positive doctrine. The pure model of the free economy can only be given historical support – as in Mrs Thatcher's invocation of mid-nineteenth-century British government and economy – at some cost to accuracy. This may occur through selective reference to periods of remarkable prosperity – certainly as compared with the present – or by ignoring governmental inputs. Where there was relative economic freedom and prosperity, the explanatory factors will be contestable as a rule, for example, a particular national capitalism, or free economy, may just have been very lucky, in terms of the things to which it had access, relative advantage and so forth. Moreover, the growth of government does not seem to be an adequate explanation for the economic problems facing contemporary capitalist states. The recession has hit countries with public sectors which are very different in size, with governments whose functions vary significantly, and with different taxation levels, for example, Australia is low on both public expenditure and taxation levels. Wilenski concluded, after examining taxes, size of government and rate of growth, that there is no correlation 'between the size of the public sector and rates of growth and standards of living' and again, 'there is no rank order correlation between economic performance, the degree of income inequality and the extent of governmental redistribution' (Wilenski, 1983, pp. 13 and 15).

Finally, there is a tendency for 'free' market systems to become less free as time goes on, not necessarily because of governmental intervention (which, anyhow, we may choose to justify) but because, given the normal operation of different capacities, energy and luck, the common result is growth of monopoly and the ultimate destruction of the competitiveness of the system. In the circumstances, to counterpose the basic principles or pure model of the free market to the normally messy reality of the mixed economy is as appropriate as it is to counterpose pure communism to actual liberal democracies. The comparison of model and reality is dramatic but false.

To date, my defence of the state has consisted in a broad account of anti-statist or free-market doctrines and then an indication of their deficiencies. While there are serious problems facing modern capitalist states – problems of legitimacy, a lack of civic virtue or civic attachment, disaffection, unsatisfied expectations, unemployment and so on – I agree with William Connolly that the difficulty is partly one of displacement, in that the (welfare) state is easily held accountable or blamed for issues which arise elsewhere. Given a widespread shortage of civic virtue, connected with the 'widely held belief that the state does not, and perhaps cannot, speak effectively to the grievances of diverse constituencies', Connolly presses on to claim that 'the welfare state is set up to be the primary target of a disaffection really rooted in the civilization of productivity itself' (Connolly, 1981, p. 140). While the nature of popular disaffection needs much probing, the notion of displacement, the suggestion that a crisis of capitalism may become perceived as a crisis of the state, is an inventive one. However, if the problem is the existence of basic conflicts between an ideally democratic polity (a sphere of citizenship, equality, participation) and an economy which is the site of structural inequality, class domination and excessive demands on state resources, more than straightforward political adjustments will be required to overcome it. Certainly the welfare state has not succeeded in these terms, and one good result of examining the problems identified by Connolly and many others, and the response of governments to them, may be the invention and development of new forms of state activity, more deserving of the reflective allegiance and supportive action of people.

In arguing for a more positive conception of the state than that of Hayek or Friedman, I will begin with a bald, familiar and general claim. The welfare state of the late twentieth century contributes far more to the freedom and the economic security of its citizens than did the state of the late nineteenth century. Intervention to secure tolerable standards of living, health and educational facilities for ordinary people, to protect consumers and limit pollution, has given weak and disadvantaged groups more opportunities, opened up new options, while sometimes challenging the powers enjoyed by privileged groups. State intervention, where the market proved inadequate or merciless, has increased the life-chances of the masses, though whether enough and in exactly the right way is another matter. The claims that government action is justified to ensure that everyone has their human and social needs – what is taken as normal for civilised beings in the 1980s – satisfied, to control the power of large private bodies (and government in its turn requires to be checked and balanced), to reduce the political significance of inequality, to pursue ends which market forces or self-interested groups would often ignore or override, for example, environmental protection, must have their character and assumptions clarified. But the general contribution made by welfare institutions to the betterment of ordinary lives should be underlined, and it should also be acknowledged that an effective welfare state strengthens rather than burdens the economy.

This broad claim is compatible with a recognition of the limitations of existing welfare states. It is understandable that in Britain the popular image of

Labour's statism is not very positive. Survey data cited by Dick Leonard revealed that the Conservative Party was seen more commonly as the party of freedom, with Labour being regarded as the party of restriction and control. 'Because of its continuing emphasis on social responsibility and on the need for public authorities to ameliorate or counteract the pressures of the market place, a democratic socialist party is always liable to be branded as a party of bureaucrats' (Leonard and Lipsey, 1981, p. 56). It is easy to point to the frequent incompetence, distance and inaccessibility of the state, so that we cannot remain content with one typical (Labour) response: more means better.

One positive result of the utopian programmes and the fundamentalist rhetoric of Reagan and Thatcher, Friedman and Hayek, could be the impact upon complacent left-liberals, socialists and reformers, forcing them to reflect more deeply on the role and the possibilities of governments, and to closely scrutinise public authority to ensure that it is precise, flexible and economical. The issue of the limits of government would be taken seriously again. We need to go beyond airy generality regarding possible futures, e.g. Dahrendorf's comment that tomorrow's politics will be free 'to the extent that it maintains a reasonable level of economic development while concentrating on such issues as human activity and decentralisation' (Dahrendorf, 1981, p. 291). In rejecting the paternalist state associated with Fabianism, what alternative models are available? Actual experimentation is scarce though rhetoric and theory are not, ranging as they do through traditional anarchism with its small co-operative or mutual-aid associations, Illich's diatribes against massive, remote systems of health, transport, education and so forth, and recent continental socialism, with its rediscovery of the potentialities of civil society. These writings may be as virulent about the state as is contemporary neo-liberalism, but they rest upon different values – or values differently interpreted – and different social theories. These values include individuality, freedom and choice, but also equality, community and participation, and it is demanded that people have real powers rather than merely formal rights. Hence the misappropriation of the rhetoric of freedom and choice by the Right is challenged, while the notion of freedom and its conditions is deepened.

Argument over human nature and social conditions is clearly central. The claim that government should act in various ways to help lift the dead hand of circumstance assumes that many people do not have the will, the motivation, the responsibility, the knowledge or the luck to make a go of life. It assumes, in the present and in the likely future, the great weight of hostile conditions, highlighted in the fate of those trapped in the culture of poverty. Some scramble up, admittedly, and we may be delighted, appalled or simply amazed at their progress (our response will depend largely on what they do, and how they present themselves afterwards). But for most disadvantaged people the case is different. People do not develop through some kind of spontaneous emergence of the faculties, out of the blue as it were, but are heavily dependent upon circumstances, which may be very restrictive. In saying this I am not dissolving people into social conditions, or claiming that environment is everything. But I am denying that opportunity is simply the existence of a number of doors that might be opened.

One response to these moralising words would be to reject them both as patronising and as assuming a body of omniscient experts regulating the whole of society to a supposed common benefit. But this does not follow. In any desirable society it must be accepted that people are diverse, recalcitrant and certain to fall short of ideal plans. Government, however, can provide encouraging facilities and services which in no way turn their subjects into automata, but which help bring out more of their capacities. It is the opposite of this project that a host of malingerers, parasites or slaves should creep under the comforting umbrella of the state. The goal is emphatically that, as far as possible, conditions should be established that encourage people to do more things for themselves. This requires an increase both of opportunities and of the capacity to recognise and take advantage of them, both an increase of the field of choice and a strengthening of agency, which are intimately linked. We may be able to distinguish between deserving and undeserving poor or disadvantaged, but my argument ignores the highly complex activity of ascribing responsibility or blame. Its appeal is to humanity rather than to justice. Generalised neo-liberal charges tend to focus on 'bludgers', people apparently happy to live subsidised lives. But while such people undoubtedly exist, there is plenty of evidence of widespread desire amongst welfare recipients to avoid dependence, to do things for themselves, for example, Australians forced on charity during the Great Depression (Macintyre, 1985, ch. 4).

The denial that a lot of people can plausibly be said to exercise free will in a social context – alternatively, the claim that many people are incompetent, disadvantaged, wasted, demoralised and damaged, and are therefore incapable of entering social life as free agents and full participants – is only the first stage of the argument. Beginning with people as they are, there is good reason to think seriously about rolling back the frontiers of the state. Focussing more narrowly, there is no reason why the socialist as much as the neo-liberal should not present the ideal of social security as 'a springboard not a sofa'. This means that institutions, arrangements and practices which cannot assume that all can be self-reliant – some people need care and control, either long-term or for the time being – must allow as much independence as possible, promoting and prefiguring a future of greater autonomy and choice. State provision, in its various forms, should be used to reduce dependence: the longer goal of welfare institutions should be to encourage and maintain independence, whether amongst the old, the unemployed, the young, the mentally ill or whoever.

One of the crucial tasks for socialists, given legitimate doubts about traditional state-provided services, is to devise a welfare system in which consumer choice and client participation play a much greater part than is common now. Civil society may become, in the new image, a bubbling sphere of democracy, popular activity, education, drawing on immediate interest and concern. Examples which come to mind include housing co-operatives, women's refuges, and independent health, educational and law centres. But civil society, as the discussion of the market suggested, breeds its own inequality and coercion. So-called voluntary or private arrangements may involve restraint, chance, dependency, despotism even. Thus, for example, taking up a familiar contemporary argument, there is no ground for associating dependency or lack of self-reliance with the use of direct state provision but not with family provision. We cannot assume that self-reliance comes with putting the family at the centre of welfare, both because of the responsibilities which that imposes upon the appropriate female (returning her to traditional drudgery, perhaps) and because family relationships may be coercive if not destructive (see Laing and Esterson, 1972). The family may be mythical or idealised, in that it may not exist generally or it may not pick up the pieces, see, for example, the difficulties of the young unemployed at home. Voluntary, private and family arrangements may involve discretionary power that can be very nasty. The family may be the best centre of affective ties that we have, and perhaps it should be used more, via state subsidy, but the more remote state provision or help, universal and as of clear legal right, can be less stigmatising, and more encouraging of dignity and self-reliance.

It is clearly difficult to indicate unambiguously and precisely the social arrangements which are most conducive to the development of people's capacities, especially if it is assumed that they should be enabled, as far as possible, to pursue their own paths to pleasure, self-development, good works or whatever. It is neither necessary nor possible for all good things to be done by government. Libertarian denunciations of interventionist government do find empirical support. But there is no general reason why we should expect public authorities to be more or less efficient than private: it is neither correct nor essential to moral purity to claim that one is always better than the other. In some cases it is appropriate for government to provide the necessary resources, or to define mandatory rules or conditions, rather than being the agent itself. The state may support voluntary or private enterprise by trained state personnel, or may monitor such enterprises, or perform other regulatory or co-ordinating functions to maintain standards. Where a particular service can be provided efficiently or economically and without cost to other important and relevant values through private or non-state enterprises, it is perfectly reasonable to do it that way. But privatisation itself may become an ideological commitment – perhaps even better if dearer – and other values may clash, for example, the policy of consumer choice in buying council houses against the goal of maintaining an adequate housing stock.

Defenders of a full system of welfare services should go beyond the contemporary welfare state, though not in either a Marxist or a neo-liberal direction. Marxists and neo-liberals share a distaste for the allegedly pacifying effects of the welfare state, but differ as to appropriate initiative of the liberated people. I have no disagreements with either that the effects of welfare state activities and programmes can be debilitating, or deficient in other ways. However, I do not share the confidence of either about the alternative outcomes. Neither the neo-liberal combination of advancement through greed with charity for the losers, nor the Marxist denunciation of half-way houses in terms of an imagined perfection, take adequate account of the facilitating or enabling role which a responsive and responsible welfare state may play. If this is to be done, unattractive and not necessarily efficient large institutions will have to be replaced by small, more flexible and more client-centred ones, which amongst other things may satisfy affective needs more readily. The pleas from Left and Right for more decentralisation, more genuine choice, and fuller democratisation at lower levels have a lot of contemporary appeal, and can be used to prompt positively both social imagination and social experimentation. The developing intensity of the neo-liberal assault on the social services suggests that this cannot wait upon the lengthy processes of armchair theorising, valuable though that may be: the need is for constructive action, rigorous thought, and struggle at all levels of the social and political system.

NOTES

1. James Alt, in *The Politics of Economic Decline* (Cambridge, 1979), documents reduced expectations regarding the capacity of governments e.g. in respect of rising prices, in 1970 60 per cent of his sample thought that government could do a lot, whereas in 1974 only a quarter thought this. This seems a surprisingly sudden change. He sees the story of the mid seventies in Britain as in large measure a story of 'a politics of declining expectations . . . not a politics of protest, but a politics of quiet disillusion, a politics in which lack of involvement or indifference to organised party politics was the most important feature'. The people, he claims, 'no longer expect government to provide the goods' (pp. 269–70).

2. Part of the problem of interpretation concerns the so-called electoral mandate: it is extremely unusual for mandates to give governments the right to do anything in particular.

3. If anything, it seems to have gone the other way. In Julian Le Grand's view, public expenditure on the social services 'has not achieved equality in any of its interpretations. Public expenditure on health care, education, housing and transport systematically favours the better off, and thereby contributes to inequality of final income', *The Strategy of Equality* (London, 1982), p. 137. He finds the same thing for the other measures of equality/inequality.

4. More often, however, the gospel of 'social justice' aims at much more sordid sentiments: the dislike of people who are better off than oneself, or simply envy . . . that animosity towards great wealth which represents it as a 'scandal' that some should enjoy riches while others have basic needs unsatisfied, and camouflages under the name of justice what has nothing to

do with justice. At least all those who wish to despoil the rich, not because they expect that some more deserving might enjoy that wealth, but because they regard the very existence of the rich as an outrage, not only cannot claim any moral justification for their demands, but indulge in a wholly irrational passion and in fact harm those to whose rapacious instincts they appeal. (Hayek, 1976, p. 98)

5. Cf. Michael Fogarty: 'to treat redistribution – in other words, an assault by one class on the income of another – as an essential ingredient in social security is to raise a serious and unnecessary opposition to its development' (Fogarty, 1961, p. 135). What makes income sacrosanct and settled?

6. As one writer from the right puts it, we see the emergence of mass society and mass man, 'whose attitude towards the society that gave him life will be parasitical, concerned with taking rather than giving, and anchored in no conception of his country's past' (Moss, 1975, p. 44). This clearly links with the earlier, anti-democratic mass-society theory of Ortega and others.

7. As one exception with whom Friedman might be expected to be familiar, I was tempted to cite G. D. H. Cole. But then I read (Thomas, 1981, p. 574) that 'one child of "Guild Socialism" was Fascism'! Others who could be mentioned contra but post-Friedman are such Eastern European Marxists as Vajda, *The State and Socialism*, and Bahro, *The Alternative*.

REFERENCES

Connolly, W., 1981. *Appearance and Reality in Politics*. Cambridge, Cambridge University Press

Dahrendorf, R., 1981. 'The politics of economic decline', review article, *Political Studies*, 29(2)

Fogarty, M., 1961. 'Social welfare', in A. Seldon, ed., *Agenda for a Free Society*. London, Hutchinson

Friedman, M., 1962. *Capitalism and Freedom*. Chicago, University of Chicago Press

Harrington, M., 1973. 'The welfare state and its neo-conservative critics', *Dissent*, Autumn

Hayek, F., 1946. *The Road to Serfdom*. London, Routledge and Kegan Paul

    ed., 1954. *Capitalism and the Historians*. Chicago, University of Chicago Press

    1960. *The Constitution of Liberty*. London, Routledge and Kegan Paul

    1976. *The Mirage of Social Justice*, vol. II of *Law, Legislation and Liberty*. London, Routledge and Kegan Paul

Laing, R. and R. Esterson, 1972. *Sanity, Madness and the Family*. Harmondsworth, Penguin Books

Leonard, R. and D. Lipsey, eds., 1981. *The Socialist Agenda: Crosland's Legacy*. London, Jonathan Cape

Macintyre, S., 1985. *Winners and Losers*. Sydney, Allen and Unwin

Moss, R., 1975. *The Collapse of Democracy*. London, Maurice Temple Smith Limited

Thatcher, M., 1978. 'The Ideals of an Open Society', speech in London, 8 May 1978

Thomas, H., 1981. *An Unfinished History of the World*. Trowbridge and Esher, Nationwide Book Service

Wilenski, P., 1983. 'Small Government and Social Equity', *Politics*. (Australia), 18, no. 1, May

INDEX

Abercrombie, N., 5
Abrahamsson, B., 273
Abyssinia, 36
academic(s), 51, 298
Adorno, T., 156
Afghanistan, 49
Africa, 73
alienation, 87–90, 116–17, 255, 289
Alt, J., 314
Althusser, L., 254, 257
Alvey programme, 224, 226
anarchism, anarchy, 36ff., 99–100, 107
Anderson, P., 120
Anti-Ballistic Missile Treaty, 1972, 46
anti-parliamentarism, 71–4
anti-statism, 159, 162–4, 177, 267–8, 297ff.
apathy, 289, 297
Apple, N., 268, 270
Arendt, H., 65–6
Aristotle, 80
Asiatic mode of production, 93–5
Attlee government, 218
Australia, 3, 268, 299, 309, 312
autocracy, 63, 68
autonomy, *see* state

Bagehot, W., 74, 76, 80
Bahrdt, H. P., 131
Bahro, R., 315
Baker, Kenneth, 223–4
Bakhunin, M., 99–100
balance of power, 37
Balibar, E., 257
Barker, E., 15, 18
Barratt Brown, M., 290
base/superstructure, 137, 157
Bauer, B., 88–9
Beer, S., 76, 235, 236
behaviouralism, 40
Bell, D., 139
Belloc, H., 162

Benn, Tony, 131, 182–3, 220–3, 290–1
Benson, I., 224
Bentham, J., 17, 18, 21, 109, 162
Berki, R., 39, 53
Berlin, I., 303
Bernstein, E., 167
Beym, Robert, 129
billiard-ball model (International Relations),
    33, 34, 41, 50, 53
Bismarck, O., 125, 307
Block, F., 262, 263, 266
'bludgers', 312
Bodin, J., 15
Bolshevism, 168–9, 172, 176
Bonaparte, Louis, 91–3
Bonapartism, 91–3, 95, 114–115
Boreham, P., 184–5
Bosanquet, B., 15, 163
Bottomore, T., 59
bourgeois (ie), 9, 59, 86ff., 110ff., 124ff.,
    136ff., 224ff.
    petty, 96
    society, 21ff., 86ff., 105
bow-and-arrow theory, 21
Britain (Great Britain, United Kingdom), 13,
    72, 108, 124, 162ff., 181–5, 187ff.,
    218ff., 249, 266–8, 278, 297ff.
Broekmeyer, M., 289
Brostrom, A., 273
Bull, H., 36–7, 48–9
Bullock Report, 185, 278, 279, 280, 282,
    288, 291
    Minority Report, 282
Bunyard, P., 220
Burnham, D., 227
bureaucracy, 1, 11, 23, 58, 59, 60, 91–3, 95,
    96ff., 114–15, 119, 123–32, 159ff., 184,
    221ff., 255–74 *passim*, 298, 306, 311
Burke, E., 302

Callaghan, James, 291